CLOCKWORK MUSIC

by the same author

COLLECTING MUSICAL BOXES
PLAYER PIANO

Clockwork Music

AN ILLUSTRATED HISTORY OF
MECHANICAL MUSICAL INSTRUMENTS
FROM THE MUSICAL BOX TO THE PIANOLA
FROM AUTOMATON LADY VIRGINAL
PLAYERS TO ORCHESTRION

ARTHUR W. J. G. ORD-HUME

Illustrated with contemporary material

CROWN PUBLISHERS, INC.
NEW YORK

ISBN 0 517 500000
Library of Congress Catalog Card Number: 72-83407
First published in the United States of America 1973

PRINTED IN GREAT BRITAIN
in 10 point Monophoto Plantin
BY WILLIAM CLOWES & SONS, LIMITED, LONDON, BECCLES AND COLCHESTER

CONTENTS

A Persian philosopher, being asked by what method he had acquired so much knowledge, answered, ' By not being prevented by shame from asking questions when I was ignorant.'

ACKNOWLEDGEMENTS

Gathering material is never something which one may hope to do effectively alone. If one is to attain any measure of success, then one is dependent to a large extent on the help and co-operation of others. This book is no exception. The majority of material contained herein has appeared over the past eight years or so in the Journal of the Musical Box Society of Great Britain, *The Music Box*, which I had the privilege of founding, and editing for almost nine years. Indeed, the original concept of this book was as a yearbook-type collage of some of the more interesting material *The Music Box* has contained over that period. The gathering together of suitable material, plus a deal of other material which I have and which I hoped to include, would, it soon became obvious, result in the sort of publication quite beyond the production facilities of the Society.

It then occurred to me that by weaving this material into a more extended format and coupling it with a historical text, the work might have a wider appeal. This is what I have now done but, by virtue of the manner in which it all began, the major number of acknowledgements must justly go to members of the Musical Box Society of Great Britain and its United States sister organisation, the Music Box Society International. I have a fear of omitting anybody through oversight but, should this misfortune occur, know that it is not wilful but because I am fallible. It is entirely through the support and fellowship created by these two dedicated and, I am happy to say, closely integrated groups that much of the priceless material contained in this book has been unearthed.

My thanks, then, go to my friend, the late John E. T. Clark, author of *Musical Boxes*, who started so many of us off on our quest for musical boxes. Expressed in no particular order, equal thanks to Lieut.-Col. Jackson Fritz, Hughes and Frances Ryder, Howard and Helen Fitch, Douglas Berryman (director of the West Cornwall Museum of Mechanical Music near Penzance), Dr Cyril de Vere Green, F.D.S., R.C.S.(Eng.), D.D.S.(Tor)—founder and first secretary of the Musical Box Society of Great Britain—Mrs C. H. Currie, Frank Greenacre, Alan Smith (City of Liverpool Museum), R. Coulson, J. C. Day (manager of Thibouville-Lamy Ltd, London), Frank W. Holland (founder and keeper of the British Piano Museum), the late Philip Coole (keeper of the Ilbert Collection, British Museum), the late Ronald Bayford, Alan K. Clark, Ernie Bayly (editor of *The Talking Machine Review*), Alan Ridsdill, Lyndesay G. Langwill (author of *Church and Chamber Barrel Organs*), Professor Alfred Chapuis (author of *Automata, Histoire de la Boîte à Musique*, etc.), Mrs Ruth Bornand, Q. David Bowers (author of *Put Another Nickel In*, and American mechanical music historian/researcher), G. J. Goodacre, Jack Tempest, A. J. L. Wright, C. W. Cramp, Ron Benton, Richard Jefferies, W. J. Bassil of Messrs Goddards Ltd, Bruce Angrave, Gerry Planus, Victor Chiappa, Keith Harding, Jim Hirsch, Tom Potter, Mrs Anita Brown, Dr Helmut Zeraschi (author of *Drehorgel*), Montagu Watson, Roger Hough, the late Dr Benoit Roose, Rex Montgomery, the late Francis C. Buckley, Norman Evans, R. Bowyer, Ralph Hyde, F.L.A. (assistant keeper, Prints and Pictures, Guildhall Library, London), Serol Verulsaquin, Professor Macario Santiago Kastner, Dr Robert Mackenzie-Griffiths. Jack MacLean of Harvey Johns Photographers, Camden Town, photographed some of the original material with his usual expertise. Thanks also go to Graham Webb who is that rare combination of an enthusiast and dealer. Grateful thanks are, of course, due to the many publications from which I have extracted material, particularly *Musical Opinion* and *The Illustrated London News* and not forgetting *Meccano Magazine*.

No list of acknowledgements would be complete without expressing my gratitude to the London Museum, the Victoria & Albert Museum, the British Museum and the Guildhall Library. Specifically, I thank Donovan Dawe, F.R.Hist.Soc., A.L.A., Principal Keeper, Guildhall Library for his guidance through the extensive archives of London. Also special thanks to Michael Wilson (author of *The English Chamber Organ*) of the Victoria & Albert Museum. Among the other overseas reference sources, my thanks also to the Franklin Institute, Stamford University and the Smithsonian Institute in the United States, the Conservatoire des Arts et Métiers in Paris, the Kunstgewerbemuseum in Berlin and the Lenin Library, Moscow.

Last but not least, this work would not have been possible had it not been for the enthusiastic co-operation of Trevor-Hobbs Ltd of Garrick Street, London, who undertook the copying onto film negative of much of the often fragile original material loaned to me.

In my first book in this series, *Collecting Musical Boxes and How to Repair Them*, I wrote on this page 'Individually, we all know something. . . . Together, we may know everything.' That this is a truism should now be self-evident. However, one must discourage the belief that a person may become either professor or expert just by assimilating the works of others. I am happy to confess that I am still able to learn something new almost every day in my searches and researches—even if that learning be only the truth in how ignorant I was yesterday.

'Wisdom requires three things: knowledge to discern; judgment to weigh; and resolution to determine.'

London, 1971   *Arthur W. J. G. Ord-Hume*

PREFACE

During the twenty or so years in which I have been working with and collecting mechanical musical instruments, I have amassed a great deal of information and history, a fair proportion of which has been published during the past eight years in the Journal of the Musical Box Society of Great Britain, *The Music Box*. Many of the early issues of that limited-circulation quarterly publication are now long out of print and back numbers are as scarce as the proverbial gold dust. Some of the material herein is from those editions and all of it, I venture to suggest, is deserving of a wider audience.

This book could be described as a scrapbook—a collection of interesting, amusing, trifling and dated ephemera. It could also be described as the first illuminated history of the musical box, indeed, of mechanical music as a whole. Whatever you, the reader, choose to call it depends on just how much you want to gain from it. For some, a collection of old advertisements of long-defunct companies from aged publications is valueless; for others it is a priceless asset and an aid and inspiration to further study. For me, my archives have proved a source of almost endless information and interest.

On its own and with no explanation as to what the items are all about, this collection and its usefulness would be seriously impaired and for this reason, I have subdivided it into sections and provided each with an introductory text. Every item also bears a suitable descriptive caption.

What are you going to find in here? For a start, there is a complete catalogue of Polyphon musical boxes, published in the early 1900s. There is a catalogue of barrel organs, original descriptions of organettes, a facsimile of a very rare treatise written by Vaucanson on his incredible automaton duck, a description of a visit to a street barrel piano factory in the 1900s, a reprint of the classic and very scarce Jacot musical box repair manual, an interview with the inventor of the disc musical box in 1885, a description of a concert given by an automaton violinist, a catalogue of Aeolian Orchestrelle player organs of seventy years ago, a rare catalogue of carousel organs made in Waldkirch by Ruth & Söhne, and so on. Oddities and the unusual abound—such as the American Steam Man and Tipu Sahib's macabre 'Man-eating-Tiger-organ'. Then there is the Steel Tarantula Spider and the Anthropoglossos. . . .

My search for material for my archives has ranged far and wide and has been years in compiling. Friends have sent me material from all over the world. One word of warning, though. A great deal of this material is very old, poorly printed on poor quality paper and in some cases has not taken kindly to the intervening years. The reproduction of this material has been undertaken under specially controlled conditions using the most modern equipment available. The results in many cases are actually better than the originals. However, in some instances the quality remains far from perfect and you must bear in mind that, unlike this Preface which is being written and printed in the second half of the twentieth century, the vast majority of what you are about to see first saw the light of day between 60 and 230 years ago.

Before we begin, though, spare a moment and ponder on the writings of philosopher, statesman and essayist Francis Bacon who was born in London in 1561 and died in 1626. In his philosophic romance *New Atlantis* published two years before his death he used strangely prophetic words: Wee have also Sound-houses, wher wee practise and demonstrate all Sounds, and their Generation. Wee have Harmonies which you have not, of Quarter-Sounds, and lesser Slides of Sounds. Diverse Instruments of Musick likewise to you unknowne, some sweeter than any you have; Together with Bells and Rings that are dainty and sweet. Wee represent Small Sounds as Great and Deepe; Likeweise Great Sounds; Extenuate and Sharpe; We make diverse Tremblings and Warblings of Sounds, which in their Originall are Entire. Wee represent and imitate all Articulate Sounds and Letters, and the Voices and Notes of Beasts and Birds. Wee have certaine Helps, which sett to the Eare doe further the Hearing greatly. Wee have also diverse Strange and Artificial Eccho's, Reflecting the Voice many times, and as it were Tossing it: And some that give back the Voice Lowder then it come, some Shriller, and some Deeper; Yea some rendring the Voice, Differing in the Letters or Articulate Sound, from that they receyve, Wee have also meanes to convey Sounds in Trunks and Pipes, in strange Lines, and Distances . . .

INTRODUCTION

Why a book on clockwork music? And what *is* clockwork music? I will answer the second of my two self-imposed questions first because it is the easier. Clockwork music is mechanically produced music. However, a perusal of subsequent pages will reveal that some of the instruments are not, in fact, wound up, but are hand-turned, worked by electricity, operated by kinetic energy or simply by hot air. Here I think the justification for this apparent diversion from my title lies in the fact that my definition of clockwork music is that which was common enough a hundred and more years ago—namely that anything operated by a mechanism containing some form of regulator or escapement to monitor the power applied is taken as clockwork whether there be a spring driving it, or the mechanism be like a player piano driven by foot-power with the escapement in the shape of a regulatory air valve, or whether the regulation of power depends on the sensitivity of the person turning the handle.

Now back to the first question. During the past few years, there has been an enormous growth in the interest of ordinary people as well as collectors, musicologists and museums in mechanical music and its instruments. When, in 1967, my book *Collecting Musical Boxes and How to Repair Them* was published, it was only the third major reference work ever to have been written on the subject in the whole history of mechanical music. Since that time, a second book of mine, *Player Piano—The History of the Mechanical Piano and How to Repair It,* has looked specifically at the self-acting piano. Both of these books have been concerned with looking back on the instruments of mechanical music from a recent point in time. However talented an author may be, no man alive may relive the burgeoning years of these instruments of mechanical music. No man can accurately relate the true story or re-create the atmosphere into which these often beautiful and incredibly complicated devices were born. The task is, indeed, impossible, no matter how hard we may yearn for the past and for H. G. Wells' Time Machine.

In offering this book, I have attempted to record the past through the medium of contemporary material suitably embellished with illustrations and have cemented the fragments of ephemera into an explanatory text. There is no bibliography as such—detailed bibliographies and other references are to be found in the titles mentioned above.

It is only comparatively recently that mechanical musical instruments and automata are beginning to receive their just approbation. I am reminded of a terse comment contained at the end of a brief and sometimes inaccurate article on the related subject of automata published in the *Penny Cyclopaedia* put out in 1835 by The Society for the Diffusion of Useful Knowledge. This pragmatises: 'In looking at the preceding instances, our readers will regret that so much power of invention has been wasted upon trifles. What is Vaucanson compared with Arkwright in the estimation of posterity?'

Thus, even in that far-off year, contemporary Man was cultivating an eye for the practical rather than the wasteful and the artistic. There were still people who made furniture and designed buildings which were delightfully ornamented, fussily decorated and carved for no other purpose than to embellish. What good indeed was Vaucanson's automatic duck in furthering the growth of the nation's industry and wealth! Today, of course, the sharp warning in the words of the long-dead professor of the above-mentioned society has been heeded to the full. Here, in the glory of the closing decades of the twentieth century, we no longer build things that are beautiful or make things just for the satisfaction of practising real craftsmanship. We compute with grey boxes where once we thought with grey matter and while we are regularised into cyphers and symbols which can be read by an automatic deity, our everyday things are progressively being denuded of the unnecessary and the fussy bits. Just look at our cities and their component boxes—and the people who live, eat, sleep and reproduce three hundred feet up in the air without ever knowing the fragrance of a butterfly-bedizened back garden through an open window. If today there are those who believe Earth to be another planet's Hell, it has been going that way since at least 1835. This book, then, is a look back at the bad old days—a memorial to wasted power of invention and misguided thinking. And a salutary reminder of the fate of Lot's wife.

CHAPTER 1

Mechanical Music in Antiquity

THE performance of music by mechanical means is something which has taxed the inventive mind of Man since earliest times. The oldest mechanical musical sound known to Man is probably that of the organ and it may come as a surprise to many to record that the invention of the organ predated the birth of Christ by something like three hundred years. The earliest stringed instruments are not much younger and in the *Deipnonophistae* of Athenaios (who lived in AD 220) he quotes Aristocles as referring to stringed and wind instruments. St Augustine, who died in the year AD 430, also wrote of various instruments of music which could have been automatic or otherwise.

It was these primitive instruments which Man thought to mechanise in order that sounds could be produced at will without actually playing upon the instruments. The problems to be overcome were manifestly complex to our inventive predecessors. First, some idea of the cause and production of musical sounds had to be gained, after which a suitable mechanism had to be evolved. One of the earliest of all automatic instruments was the Aeolian Harp which depended for its musical sounds on a current of air passing through its tuned strings. These were still being made in the early part of the last century.

The first recorded attempt at describing the construction of an instrument which could play by itself is to be found in the manuscripts of the Banū Mūsā, written in or about AD 890.

Today we are so accustomed to great changes and new inventions materialising not just within our lifetimes but within the space of but a few years that we may fail to identify that this is all the product of a highly-developed technology sired in a developed civilisation. This civilisation has taken since the beginning of time to develop and, for many thousands of years through the progress of Mankind, the points on the graph of achievement are immensely far apart and even then they are in themselves but tiny advances. One needs only to look at the Stone Age, the Iron Age and the Bronze Age to appreciate this long, drawn-out process of development. It was not until around the time of the Industrial Revolution that the curve of our hypothetical development graph began to increase its upward thrust, gaining impetus with the coming of the railways to the point where, to extend our analogy, the curve today is an almost vertical straight line.

This explains why from the Banū Mūsā until the early sixteenth century we find next to nothing in the way of recorded development in mechanical music or its history. But it was the imaginative designs of Robert Fludd, alias de Fluctibus (born 1574; died 1637) which he published in his work *De Naturae Simia* (Oppenheim, 1618), which inspired a wider appreciation of the possibilities of mechanical musical instruments. Fludd was probably more of an artistic visionary than a practical inventor and, exquisite though his designs appear, their practicability is highly suspect. Fludd's work was largely copied and variously expanded by two further experimental philosophers, Caspar Schott (born 1608; died 1666) in his work *Technica Curiosa* (Nurnberg, 1664) and Athanasius Kircher (born 1601; died 1680) in his book *Musurgia Universalis* published in Rome in 1650.

No doubt fired by imagination of this type, practical organ builders (mainly, it must be said, in Europe) began to turn their attention to the mechanical organ and by the mid-eighteenth century, Marie Dominique Joseph Engramelle (born 1727; died 1781) had contributed his masterly *La Tonotechnie ou l' Art de Noter les Cylindres* (Paris, 1775), and Dom Francois Bedos de Celles (born 1706; died 1779) had published his monumental reference work *L'Art de Facteur d'Orgues* (Paris, 1778). Both these works dealt at length with the construction of mechanical or self-acting organs and both formed the foundation of the subsequent rapid development of the instruments of mechanical music.

Mechanical organs had been popular in the sixteenth century in Europe and the most famous of these instruments was that at the Villa d'Este at Tivoli near Rome. Powered by water which was used to compress air for the musical pipes, this is supposed to have been built in 1549 and it was depicted by Kircher and then copied by Schott. Its original appearance must still remain doubtful since Kircher himself copied his sketch from a much earlier drawing attributed to the Neapolitan physician, Giovanni Battista della Porta (born about 1538; died 1615), who published a work called *Magia Naturalis*.

These water-powered organs were immensely fashionable and popular in their time. Among the most famous was the instrument in the grounds of the house of Cardinal Pietro Aldobrandini near Frascati. These organs functioned by having water spill continuously on to a water-wheel 'with great force' as related by Montaigne (1580–1581) in his *Journal de Voyage*. As this wheel turned, connecting rods from a crank pumped air using bellows which drove a pinned barrel assembly through gearing. Only one such water organ survives today and that is the one in the famous mechanical theatre at Hellbrunn, five miles from Salzburg.

It is at Salzburg itself that the oldest mechanical musical instrument in the world to remain in playing condition is situated. Admittedly it has had many restorations through the centuries but the organ in the Hohen-Salzburg dates from 1502. This is the famous *Hornwerke* or *Stier*, so named after its characteristic sounding of the chord F A C at the end of each performance. The two barrels for this organ play, among other tunes, music by Leopold Mozart, Wolfgang Amadeus Mozart, Paul Hofhaimer, Josef Haydn and Johann Ernst Eberlin.

The technique of mechanical music was now understood and the mechanics of making it basically appreciated. The seventeenth and eighteenth centuries saw the manufacture of some remarkable works of art which incorporated music. The centre of the art at this time (for it could hardly be termed anything as vulgar as 'industry') was Augsburg, or Augspurg as it was frequently called. The masters of this age were Schlottheim, Langenbucher, the father and son Bidermann, Max Genser, C. E. Kleemeyer and others. It is a sad reflection on the changing state of the world that a number of the instruments which these craftsmen conceived, after surviving for around two hundred years, were destroyed during the 1939–45 war. Unique has become a much-used and generally misused word today, but these pieces were each quite unique and represented the zenith of the skills of watchmaker, silversmith, goldbeater, artist and mechanician. Some were lost in the wanton destruction of Dresden, others when the order was given for the systematic razing of Berlin.

The type of skill and competence needed to make these early musical automata was, as already implied, very closely allied to that of the clock and watchmaker and for this reason almost all musicwork★ was the province of the horologist.

An in-depth study of early musicwork is out of place in this present work. Aspects of the development from primitive mechanical organ and carillon up to the present day are covered in three separate studies by the present author, *Collecting Musical Boxes*, *Player Piano* and *Barrel Organ*, the last-mentioned to be published next year and the first two already in print.

---

* The Germans use the word *musikwerk* to define mechanical musical instruments. It is easy to anglicise this to 'musicwork' and in this form it is more acceptable than the 'automatophonic instruments' of Dr Buchner and the clumsy triad 'mechanical musical instruments'.

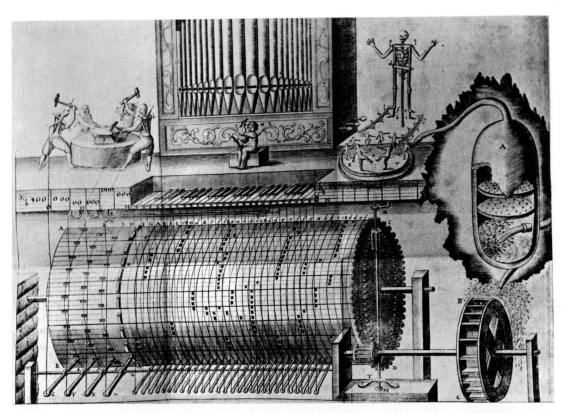

Kircher's design for a water-powered organ with automaton figures was based on the instrument in the gardens of the Villa d'Este at Tivoli which is said to date from 1549. His fanciful interpretation shows air being compressed by water in the cylinder (*right*), the water then spilling on to the water-wheel to turn the pinned barrel. On the left, automaton blacksmiths beat on an anvil, a cupid 'conducts' above the finger keyboard of the organ and right of centre is an articulated figure operated by racks from a turntable carrying dancers. The flow of water was certainly expected to do a lot as was the fixed volume of air, for the compressor apparently included no air inlet.

CHAPTER 2

Automaton Displays and Museums of Ingenuity

O F ALL the automata ever made and of all the clever mechanicians who were involved in their design and construction, the works of a select group of men stand out. These are the Frenchman, James de Vaucanson (born 1709; died 1782); the Swiss father and son Pierre Jaquet-Droz (born 1721; died 1790) and Henri Louis Jaquet-Droz (born 1752; died 1791). A further man, Henri Maillardet, who was born in 1745 and who died sometime after 1800, deserves inclusion in this clique.

Vaucanson went to Paris in 1735 at the age of twenty-six and spent some while experimenting with the reproduction of artificial life before abandoning everything else in favour of creating automata 'that could excite public curiosity'. He devised three pieces, each being of extreme precision and merit. These were the flute-player (who actually played a real flute controlled by lips and fingers), the tabor- and tambourine-player, and the artificial duck. The first and last of these were presented before the Académie des Sciences in Paris in 1738 and the other one in 1741. Of the three, it was the duck which secured for itself and its creator the greatest approbation. Quoting from Vaucanson's prospectus, here was 'An artificial duck made of gilded copper who drinks, eats, quacks, splashes about on water, and digests his food like a living duck'. Chapuis and Droz in their book *Automata*, provide a full and detailed history of this remarkable piece of ingenuity which will not be repeated here. The idea of such an automaton was not entirely new since, according to the French missionary and traveller Jean Baptiste Labat in his *Récit de Voyages*, the Compte Julien de Gennes (born 1652; died 1704) had built among other machines nearly fifty years earlier a peacock that could walk and digest its food.

Preserved in the British Museum is a translation of Vaucanson's own account of these three pieces which were on show at the Long Room at the Opera House in the Haymarket, London, during 1742. This rare and valuable document is reproduced here. The fate of the duck, long thought to have disappeared, has been traced by Alfred Chapuis. He has discovered that it enjoyed a period of ownership by Bontems, the Parisian singing-bird manufacturer, during the last century, but the trail finally peters out at Dresden between the wars, the final clue being some tantalizing photographs found in 1921 of the tattered remains of the mechanism.

A second duck having similar attributes was developed from this one by a German named Rechsteiner who had restored Vaucanson's duck. This, too, is now lost.

Automaton writers and keyboard players were made by a number of craftsmen, but none achieved the fame of the three made by the Jaquet-Droz father and son and extant today in Switzerland. A fourth writer, made by Jaquet-Droz and Maillardet, was discovered in Philadelphia where, following its unfortunate accidental incineration when the home of its owner took fire, it was rebuilt by the Franklin Institute where it survives today. Maillardet gained his fame with his Musical Lady, also built in conjunction with Jaquet-Droz, which he showed in London at Wigley's Great Promenade Room, Spring Garden, early in the last century. This talented clockwork lady could play sixteen tunes and the music was played as by a human performer by the depression of the piano keys by her fingers. As well as playing the instrument, she moved her head and her breast heaved in a lifelike impression of breathing.

The entertainments of the early part of the last century were many and varied, yet by today's general standards they were possibly either in bad taste or just plain dull. In bad taste because the unhappy freak specimens of *homo sapiens* (such as the child born without hands or arms who demonstrated artistry with her toes and continually performed her toilet by dint of dexterity before the admiring and paying public, or the child born with two perfect heads who was exhibited at Bartholomews Fair) were exploited. And dull because so much entertainment still demanded that one ability which today entertainment hardly ever calls for—imagination. There were endless conjurors like the miraculous Mr Hoare who, judging by his notices, was possessed of remarkable talents. Then there was Mr Harry Phillips who toured the country showing a grotesque bottled mermaid during the 1880s; the automaton artists such as Prosopographus exhibited by a Mr Herve at 161 Strand, London between 1826 and 1835, and the Corinthian Maid shown in 1830 at 109 Strand; and the monsters of one doubtful species or another which seemed to be discovered, preserved and exhibited with alarming regularity over the years. Of the automaton artists, David (later Sir David) Brewster passed fair comment in his *Edinburgh Encyclopaedia* of 1830 when he described how these so-called automatons or androids could either conceal a living person or be operated by simple mechanical rods from some distance away. This is undoubtedly how those examples which wrote down words called out from the audience were operated. Fraud? Well, certainly no more of a deception than any magic or sleight-of-hand show. Even Von Kempelen's fantastic automaton chess-player continued to play to a marvelled audience long after it had been established beyond all reasonable doubt that there was, somehow, somebody concealed within the seemingly inhospitable cabinet of meaningless cogs beneath the chess-board.

At the St James's Hall in London's Piccadilly was exhibited for a time in the 1830s a show called 'The Anthropoglossos or Mechanical Vocalist' which sang 'The Dark Girl Dressed in Blue', 'Polly Perkins' and other popular songs. This all-singing automaton head was the work of Giacopo Saguish of Constantinople. The talking heads or statues of antiquity were either made of wood or stone and a tube passed from the mouth of the head to a room below or behind where a flesh-and-blood person would speak into the other end, his voice apparently emerging from the mouth of the statue. More subtle illusions were created with pieces such as 'The Invisible Girl' where a voice would seem to emerge from a globe suspended in a frame. In truth, the clever refraction of sound via an india-rubber tube conveyed a real voice into the sphere. But Mr Saguish's Mechanical Vocalist was a theatrical deception. First seen in Paris in the early nineteenth century, the show consisted of a drab-coloured, poorly-illuminated room wherein an astonished audience could peer across a rail to where, apparently on a three-legged stand, there rested a shallow bowl containing an animated, loquacious human head. What the dim lighting concealed was that the 'stand' consisted of a pair of mirrors which in reflecting the sides of the little stage gave the impression of an open space beneath the head. Behind the mirrors, of course, there sat a person. One cannot help feeling that had the modern tape-recorder been available, people like Mr Saguish could have justly created a sensation without mirrors!

Another and equally spectacular 'android' was that exhibited at the London Hippodrome in 1905. Called Enigmarelle, this seven-foot high figure possessed incredible abilities. It would walk on to the stage, write its name in somewhat backward-sloping manuscript upon a blackboard, and then ride a bicycle in a circle. Its head was of wax, its feet of steel and its legs of wood and iron. The motive power comprised no less than seven motors—three being spring, and four electric which drew their power from wet-cell batteries concealed in the trunk. Unbuttoning its waistcoat revealed a mass of wheelwork and wires, levers and cranks. Unfortunately, within all this trumpery there beat no mechanical heart, but that of a real live man.

The United States produced its own race of robots, the famed Steam Man chugging his way along in a cloud of coal-induced smoke, and the Electric Man, built in North Tonawanda, New York, in the 1890s, purposefully dragged its cart of electric batteries at speed along the streets to the delight of young and old alike. Sadly, details of their means of directional control, and of starting and stopping, do not survive. One recalls the invention of Hachberger, the Boston engineer who was concerned that horses were being frightened by the introduction of steam trams on Mr Train's passenger tramway between New York and Harlem in 1832. He believed he could overcome the problem—by disguising the locomotive to look like a giant horse . . .

Later, much later, came the race of robots named Sabor and made by the Swiss engineer, Auguste Huber, and Electro made by the Westinghouse Electric Company for the New York World's Fair in 1939. But I am away from my subject, and a long way ahead of the story. Back, then, to the eighteenth century.

The biggest revolution in entertainment came with the fantastic popularity of the panorama and all the other 'oramas' which followed. All stemmed from the remarkable little Eidophysikon devised by Philip de Loutherbourg, R.A. (born 1740; died 1812) which enjoyed an unjustifiably brief popularity in London during the 1780s and 90s.* Panoramas such as the one in Leicester Square, the Diorama and, later, the Colosseum in Regents Park, as well as devices such as Harry H. Hamilton's Panstereorama and both the Udorama and the Cosmorama by M. Dalberg in Leicester Square were all attempts to titillate the public by taking them out of their own diminutive surroundings and appearing to elevate them above a chosen vista. Cinemascope was to do just this 160 years later. Certainly the most involved and complex exhibition appears to have been the Colosseum wherein Thomas Hornor (not Horner as so many writers have mistakenly transcribed) exhibited the old ball and cross from the top of St Paul's Cathedral and re-created the illusion of a cathedral-top viewpoint for the vast circular vista of Edmond Thomas Parris's painting of *London by Day*. This painting occupied the artist from 1824 until 1829 and due to the unexpected exit to America of Hornor's backer, the building was hurriedly opened to the public before the picture was finished. It must have shattered a measure of the illusion for visitors high up in the dome of the Colosseum and supposedly looking down from the top of St Paul's to see the diminutive figure of the artist (who later made his name in restoring Sir James Thornhill's paintings in St Paul's Cathedral) apparently suspended in the sky over some distant London suburb painting in tiny buildings.

Before the Colosseum was built, the Diorama was opened only a few hundred yards away in Regents Park. In June 1835, the French artist Charles Marie Bouton showed his diorama of *The Interior of the Church of Santa Croce, Florence*. Helmut and Alison Gernsheim, writing in their book *Daguerre* (Secker & Warburg, London, 1956) state that this was a close imitation of

---

* In *The Times* for 13 April 1793, there is a small advertisement on the front page which reads:
  'EIDOPHUSIKON at the Great Room, late Cox's Museum, Spring Garden. Mon. DE LOUTHERBOURG'S exhibition. . . . The room to be illuminated with wax.'

Daguerre's *Midnight Mass* even to the Grand Machine Organ which played the Kyrie from Haydn's Mass No. 1 during the midnight service. From surviving programmes, we know that this organ was loaned to the Diorama by Messrs Flight & Robson of 101 St Martin's Lane, makers of the famed Apollonicon.

The Apollonicon organ was built as a concert instrument in the 'great rooms' which formed part of the works of these famed organ builders. The instrument, opened in 1817, was five years in the making and was equipped with five keyboards arranged lengthways across the front of the organ and facing the audience so that up to five organists could play the instrument at the same time. The introduction of a pedal organ to the central console—at that time comparatively unknown in England—inspired the manufacturers to advertise the organ as possessing 'the extraordinary properties of a Finger Organ constructed for six Performers to play on at the same time'. These words were misconstrued even by contemporary writers as implying the existence of the necessary appurtenances to enable six players to sit down and play side by side. This was, of course, not so.

Aside from its manual capabilities, it was equipped with sets of pinned barrels, there being three to each set, by means of which lengthy orchestral pieces could be performed mechanically. Initially, the organ was driven by a steam engine but this was later superseded by man-power via a massive crank wheel. Although engineering drawings survive of the complicated and very ingenious mechanism, it is remarkable that no illustration of the complete organ is known to exist other than an artist's impression used as the frontispiece to Thomas Busby's *Concert Room Anecdotes* (London, 1825) and reprinted in the Organ Club Handbook (reprinted again here). This is so obviously inaccurate as to be quite worthless. If only the science and the art of photography had been widespread during the existence of instruments such as these! For the record, the world's first photograph was taken by the French physicist, Joseph Nicéphore Niépce in Gras during 1826 and almost another quarter of a century was to pass before photography became anything like a practical proposition.

At least two Apollonicon organs (more correctly, organs which bore that name) existed. The first was that described above and which remained at 101 St Martin's Lane until the late 1840s whereupon it was sold to the organ builder Hill who rebuilt it, considerably enlarged it, added a sixth console and installed it in the Royal Music Hall. It was finally lost around 1880 and in 1881 various parts of it were advertised for sale. The second organ was built by Bevington to accompany the panorama of *The Destruction of Lisbon,* but this organ was very short-lived, doubtless due to the financial uncertainties which plagued the life and times of the Colosseum into which it was built in the 1840s. The available details of both these instruments are recorded in *Barrel Organ* by the present author.

Music played an important part in most of the entertainments to be found in our cities. Signor Gagliardi for a short while during the autumn and winter of 1836–7 ran a museum of almost two hundred automaton figures, some of them musical, in Windmill Street off the Haymarket in London. According to the *Oxford Companion to Music*, in the 1880s the Maskelynes were exhibiting in London at the Egyptian Hall in Piccadilly (formerly Bullocks Museum) a mechanical cornet player and a mechanical euphonium player. Jasper Maskelyne claimed that the sounds which they produced were actually made by the instruments and certainly by all accounts these automata were accredited as sounding very lifelike.

No reference to museums of automata in bygone London would be complete without mention of that operated between 1772 and 1775 by James Cox. Cox was a noted mechanician, silversmith and watchmaker who worked at 103 Shoe Lane, Fleet Street. Seeing the possibilities of cashing in on the new openings for trade created between England and India, he constructed a number of elaborate automata combining the subtleties of ornamentation with those of mechanical intricacy. His enterprise was based on the ultimate sale of these pieces to Indian rajahs and princes. However, famine in the East, wars and the rumours of more wars put paid to his plans and he was left with his stock of mechanical marvels and no customers, since a profitable market was non-existent in Europe. Resolving to turn misfortune into fortuity, Cox leased the Great Room in Spring Garden (later to be known under various names in association with Wigley) and set up his goods as a museum, the doors opening in 1772.

The circumstances of the showing of these pieces were indeed curious. Cox obtained an Act of Parliament which received Royal assent on 21 June 1773, which enabled him to dispose of his collection by way of a lottery. The whole collection was valued at £197,000 and the lottery consisted of 120,000 tickets for the total of fifty-six pieces exhibited. After some delay due to reticence on the part of Cox, the drawing of the prizes began at the Guildhall on 1 May 1775 and soon the collection was dispersed. The inventory of the museum, complete with details of the lottery, is preserved in the library of the Guildhall in London. In 1779, a further sale was held of '. . . part of the stock of James Cox, bankrupt.' Cox died in 1788.

The famed silver swan which could move its fully-articulated neck in every direction, bears a striking resemblance in some of its constructional features to the work of Vaucanson whose duck (referred to earlier) was one of the most celebrated of all automata ever made. At the dispersal of Cox's collection, this passed with some other pieces into the possession of Thomas Weeks (sometimes spelled Weekes) of Coventry Street, Leicester Square. He leased numbers 3 and 4 Tichborne Street from Sir Henry Tichborne, along with 56 Great Windmill Street, and opened a show called 'Weeks's Mechanical Museum' sometime after 1800. The Tichborne Street address later became the first London Pavilion music hall and in 1858 one of the attractions for the visitor to London was Dr Kahn's Anatomical Museum at this address. Incidentally, sometime between Cox and Weeks, there existed Davies' Grand Museum about which very little is known except that the swan was shown and that the proprietor advertised his museum as 'originally Cox's'.

The earliest reference to Weeks' museum is 1802 and the collection certainly included many of Cox's items as well as the 'Tarantula Spider of Steel' which was shown for many years. This could walk across a table and comprised no less than 115 pieces, the entire motivating mechanism being contained within the body.

Weeks' museum was finally sold during 1834 (the first sale was held on 14 July the second on 15 and 16 September) and on the death of his son, Charles Weeks, on 23 March 1864, the sale of his effects (held on 26 May that year) revealed the remains of a number of the automata and various pieces of mechanism, all broken, badly rusted and dirty. All were sold for trifling sums. The swan was not there but it is probable that this was bought from Weeks' museum by a New Bond Street jeweller and watchmaker, Harry Emanuel, who is known to have bought a lot of the items at the sale. It was he who exhibited the swan at the Paris Universal Exhibition of 1867. In about 1871, it was bought for £200 by John Bowes and is now in the picture gallery at Bowes Museum, Barnard Castle, Yorkshire. Recently it has been restored to perfect condition.

The swan has thus fared better than the majority of its fellow exhibits in Cox's Museum, few of which can now be traced with certainty.* Many appear to have been lost due to Charles

---

* Cox's celebrated perpetual motion clock, first described in the commonplace book of the Scottish astronomer, James Ferguson, in 1769 as 'the most ingenious piece of mechanism I ever saw in my life', now stands in the Victoria and Albert Museum. Its motion, barometrically controlled, has been deprived of its 150 lb. of quicksilver at some time in the past.

Weeks' disinterest in 1864 and even more are known to have found their way abroad, specifically to China. At least one article became the property of a Liverpool-born traveller and showman named William Bullock who toured the country with a museum of curiosities gathered on his world-wide travels. In *A Companion to Bullock's Museum, containing a Description of upwards of Three Hundred Curiosities* (Sheffield, 1799), there is an entry: 'A superb Piece of Mechanism, originally a part of Cox's Museum, composed of gold and Jewelry, and containing a variety of curious movements and figures. In the bottom is a Cascade of Artificial Water with constant motion. This piece was sold by Mr Cox for £500.'

Bullock finally moved South to establish Bullock's London Museum at 170 Piccadilly, said to have been the only truly Egyptian building erected in London. This was designed and built for Bullock in 1812 by G. F. Robinson at a cost of £16,000. The collection was devoted mainly to natural history and finally Bullock became disinterested in being a showman, deciding to auction off his museum. This task he performed in 1819 with such all-round facility that he discovered that he possessed hidden talents as an auctioneer. He then offered manufacturers showroom space in the building and held periodic auctions, offering nationwide companies the opportunities of an 'instant' London saleroom for their wares. It was at this point that he changed the name of the building to the Egyptian Hall (a permanent exhibition was staged representing the Egyptian explorations of the traveller Giovanni Battista Belzoni) and the place became a venue for meetings, exhibitions and public entertainments until the era of Maskelyne's magic shows (later continued at the St George's Hall, Langham Place) and the Hall's ultimate demise beneath the breaker's axe in 1904. Among the many devices to be seen here in the hey-day of the Hall was the Eureka, better known as the Hexameter Machine. Shown in 1845, this machine turned out hexameter poetry in Latin at the rate of one line a minute, day in, day out—including Sundays. It also included a musical mechanism which played 'Fly Not Yet' and 'God Save the Queen'. The machine remains one of the great unsolved mysteries. Little or nothing was known of the inventor, except that he came from Bridgwater in Somerset and that he had spent thirteen years perfecting the machine. Ultimately it was announced that the machine was a swindle and it was removed and apparently lost, its remarkable facility for generating verses, whether by hoax or by machinery, being left unexplained. Also seen at the Egyptian Hall in the following year was Professor Faber's Euphonia (see Chapter 8), and the Rock Harmonicon which was a human-played xylophone made out of tuned stalactites.

A man of almost comparable ingenuity to Cox was John Joseph Merlin who was the principal mechanic at that museum for some time between 1773 and 1775. Merlin was born in September 1735, at St Peter's in the town of Huy on the river Meuse between Namur and Liège. His early activities are unrecorded but between the ages of nineteen and twenty-five he resided in Paris, after which he came to London, ultimately coming to work for Cox and finally settling in Little Queen Anne Street, Marylebone. He rapidly gained fame as a maker of mathematical instruments, watches, clocks and mechanical inventions of various kinds. After some years in Marylebone he moved to 11 Princes Street, Hanover Square, where in about 1783 he opened his museum. This collection was indeed varied and all the pieces came from Merlin's own hand. They included a 'perpetual motion resembling a curious clock' (was this based on, or copied from, the one Cox showed?) and the 'Quartetto Music-Cabinet'. The musical automata also included a barrel harpsichord which played seven tunes.

Merlin died in May 1803, and was buried at Paddington. A year after his death, in May 1804, his Princes Street museum was advertised to be sold by auction in one lot. However, it remained open for some years longer until finally closing about midsummer of 1808 and, as so often the case in such occurrences, no trace of any of its remarkable exhibits remains identifiable today.

In our survey of mechanical music and automata seen in London during the early years of the nineteenth century, we keep coming across the name Wigley in connection with Spring Garden, Charing Cross. Who was this Wigley? The Great Room in Spring Garden, according to *Notes and Queries* (8th series, volume 9) was the venue for the annual picture exhibitions of the Society of Artists of Great Britain between the years 1761 and 1772. In February 1764 it was the location of the first of a number of concerts directed by Johann Christian Bach and Karl Friedrich Abel. The young Mozart also made his first London appearance here. In 1772, Cox opened his museum at these premises. The room was famed for both its decorations and its warm-air central-heating system. Following that short-lived enterprise, the Great Room seems to have been used for a variety of exhibitions. In 1786, John and Charles Wigley, who were music publishers and instrument sellers, established themselves at 15 Coventry Street, Haymarket. In 1802, Charles Wigley was a partner in Wigley & Bishop at 6 Spring Garden, Charing Cross. His talents extended to that of jeweller which work he also undertook at this address. By 1806, Wigley was in business at 6 Spring Garden on his own and it is from this point that the names 'Wigleys Auction Rooms', 'Wigley's Great Promenade Room' and suchlike emanate. He began, however, by calling the place 'The Repository of Fashion' but then appears to have moved, leaving his name (and financial interest?) behind, for the next address we have for him is 11 Princes Street, Hanover Square, for the years 1806-7. This is the self-same address where Merlin ran his museum, which apparently did not close until mid-1808. Wigley, being a jeweller, may thus have acquired some interest in that collection after the death of its founder. In 1811, Wigley's address is shown in the Rates Books as being 204 Strand and by 1812 he was at 151 Strand. The Great Room was demolished in about 1825. So much for Wigley.

It has already been implied how widespread was the public interest in automata and in automatic music. The mechanics of so many of these appliances (such as Mr A. Bazzoni's Speaking Doll exhibited at 128 High Holborn in the 1830s) remain open to conjecture. But what of the human mimicry of the mechanical! In June 1834, the public was entreated to visit a unique exhibition by a notice which stated: 'THE MUSICAL PHENOMENA. 97b, Quadrant, Regent Street. Mr Richmond will repeat his most EXTRAORDINARY PERFORMANCE EVERY DAY at Two, Three and Four o'clock at which he will give POPULAR AIRS in the exact style of a MUSICAL SNUFFBOX. Mr R. is unassisted by any Instrument whatsoever!—the sounds coming from the Throat, Treble and Bass together, in so surprising a manner as totally to baffle any attempt at description. Admission One Shilling.' It is unrecorded whether or not verisimilitude was heightened by the presence of a large cardboard cut-out key protruding between Mr R's shoulder-blades. . . .

Vaucanson's automata were renowned far and wide, particularly his duck which ate and digested its food in a thoroughly lifelike manner. The inventor's own description of three of his famed pieces was published in Paris, an English translation appearing in 1742. From a surviving copy of this rare text contained in the British Museum, this appears in facsimile on the following pages.

AN
ACCOUNT
OF THE
MECHANISM
OF AN
AUTOMATON,
OR

IMAGE playing on the *German-Flute*:
As it was prefented in a *Memoire*, to the Gentlemen of the ROYAL-ACADEMY of SCIENCES at *PARIS*.

By M. VAUCANSON, *Inventor and Maker of the faid* MACHINE.

TOGETHER WITH

A DESCRIPTION of an artificial DUCK, eating, drinking, macerating the Food, and voiding Excrements, pluming her Wings, picking her Feathers, and performing feveral Operations in Imitation of a living Duck: Contrived by the fame Perfon.

AS ALSO

That of another Image, no lefs wonderful than the firft, playing on the Tabor and Pipe; as he has given an Account of them fince the *Memoire* was written.

Tranflated out of the French *Original, by* J. T. DESAGULIERS, L.L.D. F.R.S. *Chaplain to his Royal Highnefs the* PRINCE *of* Wales.

LONDON: Printed by T. PARKER, and fold by Mr. STEPHEN VARILLON at the *Long Room*, at the *Opera Houfe* in the *Hay-market*, where thefe Mechanical Figures are to be feen at 1, 2, 5, and 7, *o' Clock* in the Afternoon. 1742.

H. Gravelot, delin.

Vivares Sculp.

(4)

AN

ACCOUNT

OF THE

MECHANISM of an IMAGE

Playing on the *GERMAN FLUTE*, &c.

Presented to the Gentlemen of the *Royal Academy* of Sciences,

By Mr. *VAUCANSON*, the Inventor of it.

GENTLEMEN,

LESS sensible of the Applause of the Publick, than desirous of the Happiness of deserving yours, I come to discover to you, that it is only in following your Steps that I have been able to go on with some Success in the Track I have pursued, for the Execution of my Undertaking. You will know your Lessons in my Work. It is only raised on the solid Principles of Mechanicks, which I have taken from you.

To You I owe the Reflections I have made on the Sound of Instruments, on Mechanicks, and on the different Motion of the Parts wherewith Machines work. My Thoughts on the *German-Flute* will make the first Part of this *Memoire*: And in the Second, I shall do my self the Honour to give a Detail of the Pieces contain'd in my Work, their several Motions, and their Effect.

FIRST

A 2

FIRST PART.

My first Care has been to examine the Mouth of Wind-Instruments, to know well how to get Sound out of them, what Parts contribute to produce it, and how it may be modified.

You know, Gentlemen, that the Mouth of a *German Flute* differs from that of the other Wind-Instruments, such as the common Flute, the Flageolet, and the Organ-Pipe; because in these last the Wind introduced at a narrow Hole, but which is determined, strikes the Parts of the Body of the Instrument which are immediately under it, as the Bezel; and by the Quickness of its Return, and its Re-action upon the small Parts round about it, it suffers a violent Collision: Thus communicating its Vibrations to all the Parts of the Wood of the Flute, which in their Turn communicate them to the external Air round about them, it produces in us the Sensation of Sound.

But in the *German-Flute* the Mouth is undetermined, because in that Instrument the Wind passes through a greater or smaller Issue, made by the greater or less Opening of the Lips, as they approach towards, or recede from each other; as they come nearer to, or are further from the Hole of the Flute; or as they advance more or less over the said Hole.

All these Differences, which I reduce to four in the Mouth of the *German-Flute*, make it, in playing upon it, capable of a very great Number of Perfections, which are wanting in other Wind-Instruments, whose Mouth is determin'd; which I shall shew in explaining those Motions.

The Sound being first produced by the Vibration of the Air, and the small Parts of the Body of the Flute, is

(5)

is only determined by the Quicknefs or Slownefs of thofe Vibrations. If in an equal Time they are to be continued in a greater Number of the Parts of the Body ftruck, they will lofe more of their Motion, and confequently of their Swiftnefs; and thus, becoming flower in the fame Time, they produce a lefs lively Sound; and this makes the deep or low Tones.

This happens when all the Holes of the Flute are ftop'd. The Vibrations, which begin exactly at the Hole of the Mouth, muft be communicated to all the Parts of the Wood at the fame Time; therefore they are fuddenly weaken'd, becaufe their Force is divided among a great Number of Particles; which will make the Flute give the lowest Sound.

If you open the firft Hole next the Bottom of the Flute, the Vibrations find an Iffue fooner, which interrupts their Continuation in the reft of the Parts of the Body of the Flute: They have fewer Particles to ftrike, (the Pipe being fhortned by opening the faid Hole) thus, lofing a little lefs of their Force, becaufe there are now fewer Particles among which they muft be divided, they will have a little more Swiftnefs; and being quicker in the fame Time, they will produce a lefs deep Sound, and that will be a Tone higher. The other Tones will rife gradually, as the upper Holes are unftopp'd.

When you come to unftop the Hole which is neareft to the Mouth, that Hole dividing the inward Space of the Flute into two equal Parts, the Vibrations will find an Iffue in the Middle of the Way that they are to run, to continue to the End of the Pipe; therefore they will go out with as much more Force and Velocity, having only half the Particles, among which they muft divide themfelves; and confequently will produce a Sound as high

(6)

high again, which will be the Octave. But as a Part of thofe Vibrations is always communicated to the other half of the Body of the Flute, the Wind muft be forc'd a little, to produce in thofe Vibrations Accelerations, which by the Increafe of their Motion will fupply the Want of thofe that are loft in the other half of the Flute; then you will have a full Octave. That Note is alfo produc'd by ftopping all the Holes of the Flute, as in that of the firft Octave: But then you muft double the Force of the Wind, to produce double Vibrations in the whole Body of the Flute, which amounts to the fame Thing.

This is what is practifed in the Tones of the fecond Octave, where the Pofition of the Fingers and Opening of the Holes is the fame as in the Firft. You muft blow with a double Force to produce double the Number of Vibrations in the fame Time; which makes the fecond Octave: Becaufe the more or lefs acute Sound confifts in the greater or lefs Number of Vibrations in the fame Time.

Again, the Wind muft be given with a triple Force to produce the third Octave; but Vibrations, fo fuddenly redoubled, not finding fufficient Iffue in the firft Hole to hinder their going on in the reft of the Body of the Flute, becaufe of their extreme Swiftnefs, we muft be forced to open feveral Holes in the lower Part of the Flute; thus the Pipe being more open, the Vibrations will have a greater Iffue and a full and open Sound will be form'd, without being oblig'd to give the Wind quite a triple Force.

By this changing of Openings, different from what is required in natural Sounds, an Iffue may be given fooner or later, and greater or lefs, to produce Semi-Tones; which muft alfo be done in the laft high Sounds, where a quicker and greater Iffue muft be given, that the Vibrations

(7)

Vibrations may not lose their Velocity in communicating with too many Parts of the Body of the Flute. What remains is to shew how the Wind is modified, and what are the Parts in a living Person which contribute to give it more or less Force.

The Pressure of Pectoral Muscles upon the Lungs drives the Air out of the Vehicles that contain it: When this come up to the Mouth thro' the *Trachea Arteria*, (or Wind-pipe) it goes out of it by the Opening which the Lips form as they are applied to the Hole of the Flute. The greater or less Force of the Wind depends, first, upon the greater or less Pressure of the Muscles of the Breast, which drive it out of its Receptacle; secondly, upon the greater or less Opening of the Lips at its going out: So that when you would blow weakly, the Muscles then must act weakly, and the Lips making a large Opening, the Wind is driven slowly; and consequently its Return producing Vibrations equally flow, and still farther slacken'd by their Communication with all the Parts of the Wood of the Flute, low Sounds will be form'd.

But when you wou'd rise to the Octave, that is, produce Sounds as high again, the Muscles must act with a little more Force; and the Lips, coming nearer together, must a little diminish their Opening; then the Wind being more strongly compress'd, and having a smaller Issue, will double its Swiftness, and produce double Vibrations, and thereby give Notes as high again, that is, the Octave. As you rise gradually to the high Sounds, the Muscles will act with more Force, and the Opening of the Lips will be proportionably contracted, that the Wind, driven in a more lively Manner, and forced to go out at the same Time by a smaller Issue, may considerably increase its Swiftness, and consequently produce accelerated Vibrations, which make acute Sounds.

But

(8)

But the *German-Flute* (as I have already said) having this Difference from other Wind-Instruments, that its Mouth is undetermined, the Advantages that arise from it, are that the Wind may be modulated by the greater or less Opening of the Lips, and by their different Position upon the Hole of the Flute, and by the Performer's being able to turn the Flute inwards or outwards. By this Means the Sounds may be swell'd and diminish'd, soften'd, and strengthen'd, produce Echoes, and give Grace and Expression to the Tunes that are play'd; which Advantages are not to be found in those Instruments whose Mouth is determin'd: which I shall shew in explaining the Mechanism of the different Operations perform'd on the *German-Flute*.

Sound consisting in the Vibrations of the Air produced by its Entrance into the Flute, and its Return upon that which succeeds it; if, by a particular Position of the Lips, it enters into the whole Bigness of the Hole of the Flute, that is, goes thro' the longest Chord of the Hole, or the true Diameter of it, (which is done by turning the Flute outwards) then it strikes a greater Number of the Particles of the Wood, and at its Return finding an Issue equally large, it communicates with a greater Quantity of external Air; and this produces the louder Sounds.

But when the Flute is turn'd inwards, the Lips cover more than half the Hole, the Wind going in thro' a smaller Opening, and being able to return only thro' the same, in order to communicate with the external Air, it can strike only a less Quantity of it, which makes the Sound soft. These two Differences may have several Degrees, which depend upon placing the Lips over a greater or less Chord of the Hole of the Flute, by turning it more inwards or outwards.

Therefore

(9)

Therefore when there is Occasion to swell a Note, first you turn the Flute inwards, that the Lips coming over the Edge of the Hole may suffer but a small Quantity of Wind to go in or out, which then is driven weakly to produce a weak Sound; then insensibly turning the Flute outwards, the Lips allow of a greater Passage and Return to the Wind, which at that Time is driven with greater Force, that it may be communicated to a greater Quantity of Air, and there y increase the Sound; or diminish it anew, by insensibly turning the Flute inwards, as in the first Operation.

All these Variations of the Mouth may be perform'd in any one Sound whatsoever, whether it be an high or a low one; because the Wind, tho' driven with different Degrees of Velocity during the Note that your wou'd swell to soften, must always be so regulated as to produce the Vibrations which determine that Note: In the Beginning, when the Sound will be weak, because it will strike a less Quantity of external Air, yet it will have Vibrations equal to those that are produc'd in the Middle of the Note where the Sound encreases in Force, because it will be communicated to a greater Quantity of Air; the Vibrations not being stronger or weaker on Account of their Velocity, but on Account of the Quantity of the Parts that they act upon, and which they put in Motion.

Wou'd you produce a soft Sound to represent an Echo? Place the Lips over the Hole quite to its Edge, by turning the Flute much inwards: then the Sound being able to be communicated but to a small Quantity of external Air, thro' so small an Hole, makes us hear a Sound that seems to be afar off, by its striking our Organs weakly.

These are Conveniences which cannot be found in Instruments whose Mouth is determined and invariable.

†

B

What

(10)

What remains to explain is that stroke of the Tongue, which is absolutely necessary for playing on all Wind-Instruments.

The tonguing an Instrument is nothing else than a short Interruption of the Wind, by the Interposition of the End of the Tongue in the Passage of the Lips.

These, GENTLEMEN, have been my Thoughts upon the Sound of Wind-Instruments, and the Manner of modifying it. Upon these Physical Causes I have endeavour'd to found my Enquiries; by imitating the same Mechanism in an *Automaton*, which I endeavour'd to enable to produce the same Effect in making it play on the German Flute. The Parts which compound it, their Situation, their Connection, and their Effects, will be the Subject of the second Part of this *Memoire*, as I first proposed.

SECOND PART.

The Figure is about six Foot and an half high, sitting upon a Piece of a Rock, placed on a square Pedestal, four Foot and an half high, and three Foot and an half wide.

In the forepart of the Pedestal (the Pannel being open'd) on the right Hand there is a Movement, which by Means of several Wheels mov'd by a Weight, carries round underneath a steel Axel or Arbor, two Foot and a half long, with six Cranks in its Length at equal Distances, but looking different Ways. To each Crank are fasten'd Strings which terminate at the End of the upper Boards of six Pair of Bellows, two Foot and an half long, and six Inches wide each, placed at the Bottom of the Pedestal, where their lower Boards are made fast, so that as the Arbor turns, the six Pair of Bellows rise and fall successively one after another.

In

In the hind Part of the Pedeſtal, above each Bellows, there is a double Pulley, whoſe Diameters are unequal, namely, one of three Inches and the other of an Inch and an half; which is done to give the Bellows a greater Riſe, becauſe the Strings joyn'd to them go round the great Diameter of the Pulley, and thoſe that are faſten'd to the Arbor which draws them, wind round the ſmall Diameter.

On the great Diameter of three of theſe Pullies on the right Hand, there are alſo wound three Strings, which, by Means of ſeveral little Pullies, terminate at the upper Boards of three Pair of Bellows placed in the upper Part of the Pedeſtal, before and at the Top.

Each String, as it ſtretches, when it begins to draw the Board of the Bellows, to which it is fix'd, moves a Lever placed above, between the Axis and the double Pullies in the middle Part of the loweſt Space of the Pedeſtal. That Lever, by Means of different leading Pieces terminates at the Valve of the lower Board of each Bellows, and keeps it raiſed, that the Air may go thro' without any Reſiſtance, whilſt the upper Board, as it riſes, encreaſes the Cavity of the Bellows. By that Means, beſides gaining Force, we avoid the Noiſe which that Valve commonly makes, as the Air cauſes it to tremble when it comes into the Bellows . Thus the nine Bellows are moved without any Shake, or Noiſe, and with but a ſmall Force.

Theſe nine Bellows communicate their Wind, in three different and ſeparate Pipes. Each Pipe receives that of three Pair of Bellows: The three which are in the lower Part of the Pedeſtal on the right Hand forwards communicate their Wind to a Pipe which runs up along the upright Piece of the Pedeſtal on the ſame Side; and theſe three Bellows are loaded with a Weight of four Pounds each: The three which are on the left Hand in the ſame Row,

Row, give their Wind thro' a Pipe like the former, which riſes along the upright Piece on the ſame Side; and thoſe below are only loaded with two Pounds each: The three Pair of Bellows, which are in the upper Part of the Pedeſtal, give their Wind thro' a Pipe which runs horizontally under them, and are loaded only with the Weight of their upper Boards.

Theſe three Pipes, by different Elbows, end in three ſmall Receptacles in the Breaſt of the Figure. There they re-unite into one, which goes up thro' the Throat, or Wind-Pipe, and widening makes a Cavity in the Mouth terminated by two Lips which bear upon the Hole of the Flute: Theſe Lips give the Wind a greater or leſs Iſſue, as they are more or leſs open; for the Performance of which, as well as that of coming forward or being drawn back, there is a particular Piece of Mechaniſm.

Within the forementioned Cavity there is a little moveable Tongue, which by its play can open or ſhut the Paſſage of the Wind that goes thro' the Lips of the Figure.

By this Mechaniſm has the Wind been conducted to the Flute; and by the following Contrivances it has been modified.

In the anterior Face of the Pedeſtal on the Left, there is another Movement, which by is Wheel-work, turns a Cylinder two Foot and an half long, and ſixty four Inches in Circumference: This Cylinder or Barrel is divided into fifteen equal Parts, of an Inch and an half each.

In the poſterior Face of the Pedeſtal in the upper Part of it, there is a Key-Frame, drawing or bearing on the Barrel, made of fifteen very moveable Levers, whoſe Ends on the Inſide have a little Nib or lifting Piece of Steel, which anſwers to each Diviſion of the Barrel. At the other of theſe Levers are faſten'd Wires and Chains of Steel, which lead to the different Receptacles of Wind, to the Fingers, to the Lips, and to the Tongue of the Figure. Thoſe

B 2

(13)

Thofe which anfwer to the different Receptacles of Wind, are three in Number, and their Chains rife perpendicularly behind the Back of the Figure, quite up to the Breaft, where they end, being each fix'd to the Valve of one of the Receptacles: And this Valve being open, fuffers the Wind to pafs into the Pipe of Communication, which rifes, as I have already faid, thro' the Wind-pipe into the Mouth.

The Levers which anfwer to the Fingers, are feven in Number, and their Chains alfo rife perpendicularly quite up to the Shoulders; and there they make an Angle or Bend, to go thro' the upper Part of the Arm to the Elbow, where they bend again to run along the Arm as far as the Wrift, where each of them ends in a Joynt fix'd to a Tenon made by the End of the Lever contain'd in the Hand, imitating the Bone which the Anatomifts call *Metacarpos*, which, in the fame Manner, makes a Joynt with the Bone of the firft *Phalanx*: So that the Chain being drawn, the Finger may rife.

Four of thefe Chains are inferted in the right Arm to move the four Fingers of that Hand; and three in the left Arm for three Fingers, there being only three Holes which anfwer to that Hand.

The end of each Finger is arm'd with a Skin or Leather, to imitate the Softnefs of the natural Finger, that the Holes may be exactly ftopt.

The Levers of the Key-Frame, which anfwer to the Motion of the Mouth, are four in Number: The Steel Wires which are faften'd to them make Leaders to go to the Middle of a Ratchet within; and there are faften'd to Chains, which rife perpendicularly parallel to the Back-Bone in the Body of the Figure, whence paffing thro' the Neck, they come into the Mouth, where they are faften'd to thofe Pieces, which being fix'd

(14)

fix'd to the Lips within, give them four different Motions: The one opens them to give theWind a greater Iffue; the next contracts the Paffage in bringing them nearer together; the third draws them back; and the fourth makes them advance over the Edge of the Hole.

There is but one Lever more upon the Key-Frame, to which is likewife faften'd a Chain which rifes like the reft, and ends in the Tongue, which is in the Cavity of the Mouth, behind the Lips, to ftop the Hole, occafionally, as I faid before.

Thefe fifteen Levers anfwer to the fifteen Divifions of the Barrel, by their Ends which have the Steel Elbows or lifting Pieces, at an Inch and an half Diftance from each other: When the Barrel turns, the Bars of Brafs fix'd upon its divided Lines meet with the lifting Pieces, and keep them raifed a longer or a fhorter Time, according as thofe Bars are longer or fhorter: And as the Ends of all thofe lifting Pieces, make one right Line, parallel to the Axis of the Barrel, cutting all the Lines of Divifion at right Angles; every Time that a Bar is fix'd at each Line, and that all the Ends of thofe Bars make amongft them alfo a right Line, and parallel to that which is form'd by the lifting Pieces of the Levers, each End of a Bar (as the Barrel turns) will touch and raife at the fame Time the End of a Lever; and the other Ends of the Bars likewife forming a right Line parallel to the firft, will, by the Equality of the Length of the Bars, each let fall its Lever at the fame Time. One may eafily fee by this, how all the Levers may act, and at the fame Time concur to the fame Operation, if it be neceffary.

When there is only Occafion for fome of the Levers to act, you place Bars only at thofe Divifions which anfwer to thofe Levers which you wou'd have to move: You

(15)

You may even determine the Time, by placing them nearer to or farther from the Line form'd by the lifting Pieces; and their Action may end sooner or later, according to the different Length of the Bars.

The End of the Axis of the Barrel on the right Hand is terminated by an endless Screw with single Threads, distant from one another a * Line and an half, containing twelve Threads, which make an Inch and an half in Length, equal to the Divisions of the Barrel.

Above this Screw a Piece of Brass is fix'd to the Pedestal Frame, which holds a Pivot of Steel of about one Line Diameter, that falls in between the Threads of the Screw, and serves instead of a Nut to it; so that the Barrel in turning is obliged to follow the same Direction as the Threads of the Screw, being guided by the Steel Pivot which is fix'd: Thus as the Barrel turns round, each Point of it will describe a Spiral Line, and consequently make a progressive Motion from Left to Right.

By this Means each Division of the Barrel, determined at first under each End of a Lever, will change its Point at every Revolution, because it will recede from it a *Line* and an half, which is the same Distance as the Threads of the Screw.

Therefore the End of the Levers fasten'd to the Key-Frame remaining unmoveable, and those Points of the Barrel, to which they answered at first, moving away each Moment from the Perpendicular, by forming a spiral Line, (which by the progressive Motion of the Barrel, is always directed to the same Point, that is to the End of each Lever) it follows that the End of each Lever meets every Moment new Points upon the Barrs of the Barrel; which are never repeated, because they form Spirals between them, which make twelve Turns upon the

* A Line is the twelfth Part of an Inch.

(16)

the Barrel, before the first Point of the Division can come under another Lever than that under which it was first determin'd.

It is in this Space of an Inch and an half that all the Bars are placed, which Bars themselves also form spiral Lines, that the Lever (under which each of them must pass during the twelve Turns of the Barrel) may act.

As one Line changes in Respect of its Lever, all the other Lines change in Respect of theirs; thus each Lever has twelve Lines of Bars of sixty four Inches in Length, which all go under it, and which all together make a Line of seven Hundred and sixty-eight Inches long, Upon this Line are fix'd all the Bars sufficient for the Action of the Lever during the whole Play.

What remains is to shew, how these different Motions have contributed to produce the Effect which I proposed in this *Automaton*, comparing them with those of a living Person.

To make it produce Sound form the Flute, and form the first Note, which is *D* below, I begin first to dispose the Mouth; for which End I fix upon the Barrel a Bar under the Lever, which answers to those Parts of the Mouth that serve to increase the Opening of the Lips. Secondly, I fix a Bar under that Lever which serves to draw back those Lips. Thirdly, I fix a Bar under that Lever which opens the Valve of that Receptacle of Wind, which is supplied by the small Bellows that are not loaded. Lastly, I fix a Bar under the Lever which moves the Tongue, to give a Stroke with the Tongue; so that these Bars in the same Time touching the four Levers, which serve to produce the foresaid Operations, the Flute will found *D* below.

By the Action of the Lever, which increases the Opening of the Lips, the Action of a living Man is imitated, who increases that Opening for the low Sounds.

By

(17)

By the Lever which draws back the Lips, I imitate the Action of a Man who removes them farther from the Hole of the Flute, by turning it outwards.

By the Lever which gives Wind from the unloaded Bellows, I imitate the weak Wind which a Man gives, when he drives it out of the Receptacle of his Lungs, by only a light Compression by the Muscles of his Breast.

By the Lever which moves the Tongue, in unstopping the Hole thro' which the Lips let the Wind pass, I imitate the Motion of a Man's Tongue, when he pulls it back from the Hole to give Passage to the Wind to articulate such a Note.

It will then follow, from those four different Operations, that by giving a weak Wind, and making it pass thro' a large Issue in the whole Bigness of the Hole of the Flute, its Return will produce slow Vibrations, which must be continu'd in all the Parts of the Body of the Flute, because all the Holes will be shut, and, according to the Principle settled in my first Part, the Flute will give a low Sound: and this is confirm'd by Experience.

If I wou'd make the Flute found the Note above, namely *E*, to the four first Operations for *D*, I add a fifth; I fix a Bar under the Lever, which raises the third Finger of the Right Hand to unstop the sixth Hole of the Flute; and I make the Lips to come a little nearer to the Hole of the Flute, by fixing or making a little lower the Bar of the Barrel which held up the Lever for the first Note, namely for *D*. Thus, giving an Issue to the Vibrations sooner, by unstopping the first Hole from the End, as I said above, the Flute must found a Note above; which is also confirm'd by Experience.

All these Operations will be continued pretty nearly the same in the Notes of the first Octave, where the same Wind is sufficient for forming them all. It is the diffe-

C

(18)

rent Opening of the Holes, by raising the Fingers, which characterises them : All that is requir'd is to fix on the Barrel Bars under the Levers which must raise the Fingers to form such a Note.

In order to have the Notes of the second Octave, we must change the Situation of the Mouth, that is, we must place a Bar under that Lever which serves to push the Lips beyond the Diameter of the Hole of the Flute, and thereby imitate the Action of a living Man, who in that Case turns the Flute a little inwards.

Secondly, we must fix a Bar under that Lever, which bringing the Lips towards one another diminishes their Opening; as a Man does to give a less Issue to the Wind.

Thirdly, a Bar must be fix'd under the Lever which opens the Valve of that Receptacle that contains the Wind coming from those Bellows which are loaded with two Pounds; because the Wind being then driven with more Force, acts in the same Manner as that with which a living Man blows by a stronger Action of the Pectoral Muscles. Besides, Bars must be plac'd so as to run under the Levers necessary to raise the Fingers requir'd.

From all these Operations it will follow, that a Wind driven with more Force, and going thro' a smaller Passage, will double its Swiftness, and consequently produce double the Number of Vibrations; and these make the Octave.

As you rise up to the higher Notes of this second Octave, the Lips must still be brought closer, that the Wind in the same Time may encrease its Velocity.

In the Notes of the third Octave, the same Levers that go to the Mouth act as in those of the second, with this Difference, that the Bars are a little higher: Which makes the Lips advance quite over the Edge of the Hole of the Flute, so as to leave but a very small Hole. You must only add a Bar under that Lever which

(19)

which opens the Valve of the Receptacle which has its Wind from the most loaded Bellows, that is those that are press'd down with four Pounds. Consequently the Wind, blown with a stronger Compression, and going thro' a Passage still smaller, will increase its Velocity in a triple Ratio; whereby you will have the triple Octave.

In all these different Octaves some Notes are harder to produce than others; and then they must be managed by bringing the Lips over a greater or a less Chord of the Hole of the Flute, and by giving a stronger or a weaker Wind, which is the same that a Man does to sound the same Notes, being oblig'd to manage his Wind, and to turn the Flute inwards or outwards, more or less.

It is easy to conceive that all the Bars fix'd upon the Barrel must be longer or shorter, according to the different Situation necessary for the Fingers: which I shall not particularize here, least I should exceed the Limits of a short *Memoire*, such as I proposed to give.

I wou'd only have it observed, that in swelling of Notes, I have been oblig'd, during the same Note, insensibly to substitute a strong Wind to a weak, and a weaker to a stronger, and at the same Time to vary the Motion of the Lips; that is, to put them into the proper Situation for each Wind.

For a soft Sound, that is to imitate an Echo, I have been oblig'd to advance the Lips over the Hole of the Flute, and send a Wind sufficient for forming such a Tone; but whose Return, by such a small Issue as its Entrance into the Flute, can only strike a small Quantity of external Air; which, as I have said, produces an Echo.

The Quickness and Slowness of different Airs have been measur'd upon the Barrel, by Means of a Lever; one End of which being arm'd with a Steel Point serv'd to mark the Barrel, as the Lever was struck upon. At the other

C 2

(20)

other End of the Lever was a Spring, which immediately raised the Point up again.

The Movement was set a going, which turn'd the Barrel with a Velocity proportionable for the several Tunes.

At the same Time a Person play'd on the Flute the Tune whose Time was to be measured; whilst another Person beat Time upon the End of the Lever, whose Point mark'd the Barrel, and the Distances between the Points prick'd on were the true Measure for the Tunes to be mark'd. Then the Intervals were sub-divided into as many Parts as the Measure had Times or Bars.

The Fear of tiring you, GENTLEMEN, has made me pass over a great many little Circumstances, which tho' easy to suppose are not so soon executed: the Necessity of which appears by a View of the Machine, as I found it in the Practice.

GENTLEMEN, after having drawn from your *Memoires* the Principles which have guided me, it wou'd be no small Satisfaction to me, if I could flatter myself to see you acknowledge, that I have happily applied those Principles in the Execution of my Work. In the Approbation that you will deign to give it, I shall find the most glorious Reward of my Labour, and shall have greater Encouragement to pursue Hopes yet more flattering, which make my utmost Ambition.

An ABSTRACT of the Register of the ROYAL-ACADEMY of SCIENCES.

April 30, 1738. N.S.

THE Academy having heard Mr. VAUCANSON's Memoire read, containing the Description of a wooden Statue, copied from the Marble Faune of Coyfevaux, that plays on the German-Flute; on which it performs twelve different Tunes, with an Exactness which has deserv'd the Admiration of the Publick, and of which great Part of the Academy has been Witness; they have judg'd this Machine to be extremely new and simple Contrivances, as well for giving the Fingers of that Figure the necessary Motions, as for modifying the Wind which goes into the Flute by encreasing or diminishing its Velocity,

Velocity, according to the different Notes; by varying the Position of the Lips, and moving a Valve which performs the Office of the Tongue; and lastly, by imitating by Art all that is necessary for a Man to perform in such a Case. Besides, Mr. VAUCANSON's Memoire is written with all the Perspicuity and Exactness that the Subject is capable of; which shews the Author's Skill and great Knowledge in the different Parts of Mechanicks. In Witness whereof I have sign'd the present Certificate. Paris, May 3, 1738. N. S.

FONTENELLE, Perpetual Secretary of the ROYAL-ACADEMY of SCIENCES.

The Approbation of the Royal Censor.

I Have, by Order of my Lord Chancellor, read a Manuscript entitl'd, The Mechanism of an Automaton playing on the Flute, presented to the Gentlemen of the Royal-Academy of Sciences, by Mr. VAUCANSON, Author of this Machine. Mr. VAUCANSON explains in his Memoire those physical Principles that he has employed for the Invention and Execution of his Automaton, which is one of the most wonderful Productions of Art: It imitates a true Player on the Flute so perfectly, that the Publick continues to see and bear it with Admiration. Therefore we believe that the Impression of Mr. VAUCANSON's Memoire will be very useful to satisfy fully the Curiosity of the Publick. Paris, June 12, 1738.

H. PITOT

Mr. VAUCANSON's Letter to the ABBE DE FONTAINE.

MY second Machine, or Automaton, is a Duck, in which I represent the Mechanism of the Intestines which are employed in the Operations of Eating, Drinking, and Digestion: Wherein the Working of all the Parts necessary for those Actions is exactly imitated. The Duck stretches out its Neck to take Corn out of your Hand, it swallows it, digests it, and discharges it digested by the usual Passage. You see all the Actions of a Duck that swallows greedily, and doubles the Swiftness in the Motion of its Neck and Throat or Gullet to drive the Food into its Stomach, copied from Nature: The Food is digested as in real Animals, by Dissolution, not Trituration, as some natural Philosophers will have it. But this I shall treat of, and shew, upon another Occasion.

The Matter digested in the Stomach is conducted by Pipes, (as

in an Animal by the Guts) quite to the Anus, where there is a Sphincter that lets it out.

I don't pretend to give this as a perfect Digestion, capable of producing Blood and nutritive Particles for the Support of the Animal. I hope no body will be so unkind as to upbraid me with pretending to any such Thing. I only pretend to imitate the Mechanism of that Action in three Things, viz. First, to swallow the Corn; secondly, to macerate or dissolve it; thirdly, to make it come out sensibly changed from what it was.

Nevertheless, it was no easy Matter to find Means for those three Actions, and those Means may perhaps deserve some Attention from those that may expect more. They will see what Contrivances have been made use of to make this artificial Duck take up the Corn, and suck it up quite to its Stomach; and there in a little Space to make a Chymical Elaboratory to decompound or separate the Integrant Parts of the Food, and then drive it away at Pleasure thro' Circumvolutions of Pipes, which discharge it at the other End of the Body of the Duck.

I don't believe the Anatomists can find any thing wanting in the Construction of its Wings. Not only every Bone has been imitated, but all the Apophyses or Eminences of each Bone. They are regularly observ'd as well as the different Joints: The bending the Cavities, and the three Bones of the Wing are very distinct. The first, which is the Humerus, has its Motion of Rotation every Way with the Bone that performs the Office of the Omoplat, Scapula, or Shoulder-Blade: The second Bone, which is the Cubitus of the Wings, has its Motion with the Humerus by a Joint which the Anatomists call Ginglymus; the third, which is the Radius, turns in a Cavity of the Humerus, and is fasten'd by its other Ends to the little End of the Wing, just as in the Animal. The Inspection of the Machine will better shew that Nature has been justly imitated, than a longer Detail, which wou'd only be an anatomical Description of a Wing. To shew that the Contrivances for moving these Wings are nothing like what is made use of in those wonderful Pieces of Art of the Cock mov'd by the Clock at Lyons, and that at Strasburgh, the whole Mechanism of our artificial Duck is exposed to View; my Design being rather to demonstrate the Manner of the Actions, than to shew a Machine. Perhaps some Ladies, or some People, who only like the Outside of Animals, had rather have

(23)

have seen the whole cover'd; that is, the Duck with Feathers. But besides, that I have been desir'd to make every Thing visible; I would not be thought to impose upon the Spectators by any conceal'd or juggling Contrivance.

I believe that Persons of Skill and Attention, will see how difficult it has been to make so many different moving Parts in this small Automaton; as for Example, to make it rise upon its Legs, and throw its Neck to the Right and Left. They will find the different Changes of the Fulchrum's or Centers of Motion: they will also see that what sometimes is a Center of Motion for a moveable Part, another Time becomes moveable on that Part, which Part then becomes fix'd. In a Word, they will be sensible of a prodigious Number of Mechanical Combinations.

This Machine, when once wound up, performs all its different Operations without being touch'd any more.

I forgot to tell you, that the Duck drinks, plays in the Water with his Bill, and makes a guggling Noise like a real living Duck. In short, I have endeavour'd to make it imitate all the Actions of the living Animal, which I have consider'd very attentively.

My third Machine, or Automaton, is the Figure playing on the Tabor and Pipe, which stands upright on its Pedestal, dress'd like a dancing Shepherd. This plays twenty Tunes, Minuets, Rigadoons, and Country-dances.

One would at first imagine that the Difficulty in making of this has been less than the German-Flute. But, to praise one more than the other; I would have it observ'd, that here an Instrument is play'd upon, which is very cross-grain'd and false in itself; that I have been forc'd to articulate Sound by Means of a Pipe of three Holes only, where all the Tones must be perform'd by a greater or less Force of the Wind, and half stopping of Holes to pinch the Notes: That I have been oblig'd to give the different Winds, with a Swiftness which the Ear can hardly follow; and that every Note, even Semi-Quavers, must be tongued, without which the Sound of this Instrument is not at all agreeable. In this the Figure out-does all our Performers on the Tabor-Pipe, who cannot move their Tongue fast enough to go thro' a whole Bar of Semi-Quavers, and strike them all. On the contrary, they far above half of them; but my Piper plays a whole Tune, and tongues every Note. What a Combination of Winds have I been oblig'd to make

for

(24)

for that Purpose? In carrying on my Work, I have made Discoveries of Things which could never have been so much as guess'd at. Could it have been thought, that this little Pipe shou'd, of all the Wind-Instruments, be one of the most fatiguing to the Lungs? For in the playing upon it, the Performer must often strain the Muscles of his Breast with a Force equivalent to a Weight of 56 Pounds. For I am oblig'd to use that Force of Wind, that is, a Wind driven by that Force or Weight, to sound the upper B, which is the highest Tone to which this Instrument reaches: Whereas one Ounce only is sufficient to sound the first Note, or produce the lowest Tone, which is an E. Hence will appear, how many different Blasts of Wind I must have had to run thro' the whole Compass of the Tabor-Pipe.

Moreover, as the different Positions of the Fingers are so few, some won'd be apt to think that no more different Winds won'd be necessary than the Number of Notes on the Instrument; but the Fact is otherwise: that Wind, for Example, which is able to produce a D following a C, will never produce it, if the same D is to be founded next to the E just above it; and the same is to be understood of all the other Notes. So that upon Computation it will appear that I must have twice as many different Winds, as there are Tones, besides the Semi-Tones, for each of which a particular Wind is absolutely necessary. I own freely, that I am surpriz'd myself to see and bear my Automaton play and perform so many and so differently varied Combinations: And I have been more than once ready to despair of succeeding; but Courage and Patience overcame every Thing.

Yet this is not all: This Pipe employs but one Hand; the Figure holds a Stick in the other, with which he strikes on the Tabor single and double Strokes, Rollings varied for all the Tunes, and keeping Time with what is play'd with the Pipe in the other Hand. This Motion is none of the easiest in the Machine; for sometimes we must strike harder, sometimes quicker, and the Stroke must always be clean and smart, to make the Tabor sound right. The Mechanism for this consists in an Infinite Combination of Levers, and different Springs, all moved with Exactness to keep true to the Tune: But these won'd be too tedious to give a particular Account of. In a Word, this Figure in its Contrivance is something like that which plays on the German-Flute; but differs from it in many of the Means of its Operations.

F I N I S.

The TRANSLATOR to the READER.

THOSE who have neither seen, nor heard a true Account of M. VAUCANSON's Machines, may wonder that I should take any Pains to promote the Advantage of Persons who are exposing any thing to publick View : As it would be very mean to cry up trifling Performances, and commend what amuses the great and small Vulgar, by Confederacy, such as the pretended Mathematical Figures, &c. But on the other hand, it is laudable to encourage those who are truly ingenious, by doing Justice to the most curious Peices of Art that perhaps have ever been perform'd; which I cannot do better than by translating into English this Memoire of Mr. VAUCANSON, that in a few Words gives a better and more intelligible Theory of Wind-Musick than can be met with in large Volumes. And here the Reader will also find a clear Explication of every Part of his Contrivances, which requires no small Skill to do with such Perspicuity, without Figures.

In giving this Paper an English Dress. I am still acting in my Province, which has been for many Years to explain the Works of Art, as well as the Phænomena of Nature.

J. T. DESAGULIERS.

P. S. Whilst this Memoire was printing, I received the Description of the Duck and that of the Figure playing on the Tabor and Pipe; which Mr. VAUCANSON describes in a Letter to a Friend. Therefore to do him Justice in every Respect, and for the Satisfaction of the Curious, I have subjoined the Translation of his Letter.

Makers of automata of all types were numerous in the eighteenth and nineteenth centuries. They frequently turned their prowess to financial gain by establishing 'cabinets' or museums, or by taking their pieces on tour. The museum of James Cox was the first and probably the finest of these museums to be seen in London. Modesty seldom prevailed and their advertisements were invariably ingratiatingly self-laudatory. On the facing page is a contemporary engraving of Cox which he published. This fine display of the engraver's art is matched by the beautiful trade announcement on the next page published by James Green, a maker of fine musical clocks, who flourished between 1722 and 1804. This piece, from the Guildhall Library, dates from about 1770 and its multi-lingual wording demonstrates Green's recognition of lucrative markets outside the British Isles.

James Cox inv.t   Engrav'd by John Keyse Sherwin, Pupil of M.r Bartolozzi, for a Frontispiece to the Descriptive Inventory of
M.r Cox's Museum.

Publish'd according to Act of Parl.t Jan.y 7. 1774.

James Green

At the Spring Clock in Cullum Street Fenchurch Street

L O N D O N

Makes and Sells all Sorts of Repeating, Plain *and* Musical Clocks,
Likewise All Sorts of Repeating Plain and Horizontal Watches,
The greatest Choice of Clock and Watchmakers Tools.

JACQUES GREEN

A L'Enseigne de L'Horologe dans Cullum Street Fenchurch street
a Londres, Fait et vend toutes Sortes d'Horologes a Repetition,
de Musique et Communes comme aussi Toutes Sortes
de Montres a Repetition Horizontales et Communes et une
grande Variete d'Outils pour Les Horologeurs.

DIEGO GREEN

A la Ensena del Relox de Meza en Cullum-street, Fenchurch-street,
En Londres, Haze y vende Todos generos de Reloxes de Meza
de Sala y de Faltriquera, Musicales, Horizontales y de Repeticion
Tambien La mas perfecta y escogida Cantidad de Instrumentos
para Reloxeros.

Jacob Green

Woonende in the Spring Clock in Cullum Street Fenchurch Street
tot LONDON Maakt en Verkoopt alle Sorten van
Repeteer, Musicalse en Ordinaire Klocken, Als ook alle Soorten van
Repeteer Horizontale in Ordinaire Oorlogies, Neffens de
groot Ste Keur van Klocken en Oorlogie Makers Instrumenten.

Webb scrip.   Thorowgood sculp.

40

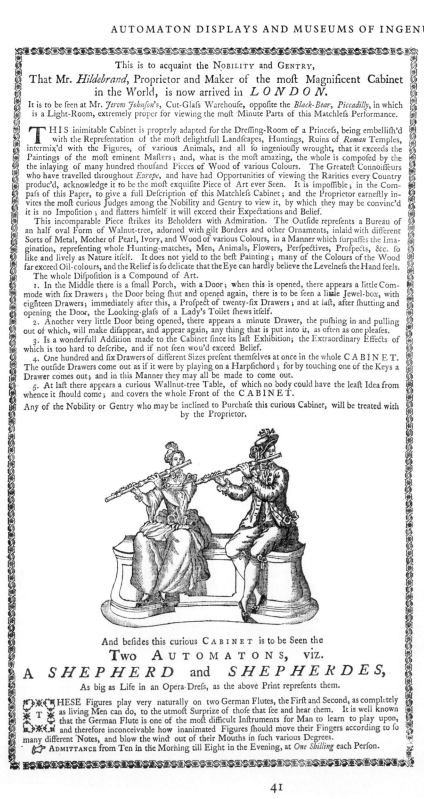

This is to acquaint the NOBILITY and GENTRY,

That Mr. *Hildebrand*, Proprietor and Maker of the moſt Magnificent Cabinet in the World, is now arrived in *L O N D O N*.

It is to be ſeen at Mr. *Jerom Johnſon's*, Cut-Glaſs Warehouſe, oppoſite the *Black-Bear*, *Piccadilly*, in which is a Light-Room, extremely proper for viewing the moſt Minute Parts of this Matchleſs Performance.

THIS inimitable Cabinet is properly adapted for the Dreſſing-Room of a Princeſs, being embelliſh'd with the Repreſentation of the moſt delightfull Landſcapes, Huntings, Ruins of *Roman* Temples, intermix'd with the Figures, of various Animals, and all ſo ingeniouſly wrought, that it exceeds the Paintings of the moſt eminent Maſters; and, what is the moſt amazing, the whole is compoſed by the the inlaying of many hundred thouſand Pieces of Wood of various Colours. The Greateſt Connoiſſeurs who have travelled throughout *Europe*, and have had Opportunities of viewing the Rarities every Country produc'd, acknowledge it to be the moſt exquiſite Piece of Art ever Seen. It is impoſſible; in the Compaſs of this Paper, to give a full Deſcription of this Matchleſs Cabinet; and the Proprietor earneſtly invites the moſt curious Judges among the Nobility and Gentry to view it, by which they may be convinc'd it is no Impoſition; and flatters himſelf it will exceed their Expectations and Belief.

This incomparable Piece ſtrikes its Beholders with Admiration. The Outſide repreſents a Bureau of an half oval Form of Walnut-tree, adorned with gilt Borders and other Ornaments, inlaid with different Sorts of Metal, Mother of Pearl, Ivory, and Wood of various Colours, in a Manner which ſurpaſſes the Imagination, repreſenting whole Hunting-matches, Men, Animals, Flowers, Perſpectives, Proſpects, &c. ſo like and lively as Nature itſelf. It does not yield to the beſt Painting; many of the Colours of the Wood far exceed Oil-colours, and the Relief is ſo delicate that the Eye can hardly believe the Levelneſs the Hand feels. The whole Diſpoſition is a Compound of Art.

1. In the Middle there is a ſmall Porch, with a Door; when this is opened, there appears a little Commode with ſix Drawers; the Door being ſhut and opened again, there is to be ſeen a little Jewel-box, with eighteen Drawers; immediately after this, a Proſpect of twenty-ſix Drawers; and at laſt, after ſhutting and opening the Door, the Looking-glaſs of a Lady's Toilet ſhews itſelf.

2. Another very little Door being opened, there appears a minute Drawer, the puſhing in and pulling out of which, will make diſappear, and appear again, any thing that is put into it, as often as one pleaſes.

3. Is a wonderfull Addition made to the Cabinet ſince its laſt Exhibition; the Extraordinary Effects of which is too hard to deſcribe, and if not ſeen wou'd exceed Belief.

4. One hundred and ſix Drawers of different Sizes preſent themſelves at once in the whole C A B I N E T. The outſide Drawers come out as if it were by playing on a Harpſichord; for by touching one of the Keys a Drawer comes out; and in this Manner they may all be made to come out.

5. At laſt there appears a curious Walnut-tree Table, of which no body could have the leaſt Idea from whence it ſhould come; and covers the whole Front of the C A B I N E T.

Any of the Nobility or Gentry who may be inclined to Purchaſe this curious Cabinet, will be treated with by the Proprietor.

And beſides this curious C A B I N E T is to be Seen the

Two A U T O M A T O N S, viz.

A *S H E P H E R D* and *S H E P H E R D E S*,

As big as Life in an Opera-Dreſs, as the above Print repreſents them.

THESE Figures play very naturally on two German Flutes, the Firſt and Second, as completely as living Men can do, to the utmoſt Surprize of thoſe that ſee and hear them. It is well known that the German Flute is one of the moſt difficult Inſtruments for Man to learn to play upon, and therefore inconceivable how inanimated Figures ſhould move their Fingers according to ſo many different Notes, and blow the wind out of their Mouths in ſuch various Degrees.

☞ ADMITTANCE from Ten in the Morning till Eight in the Evening, at *One Shilling* each Perſon.

The love of novelty and nicety which distinguished the period is shown by this circular advertising Mr Hildebrand's ingenious cabinet. We are more interested in the automata which accompanied its showing. The Shepherd certainly resembles Vaucanson's flute-player shown on page 26, although the dress is different. Other craftsmen, though, made flute-players and the anonymous author of the poem *Zodiacus Vitae* tells of such a piece made early in the sixteenth century by a potter and which he saw in Rome. The notice reproduced here is late eighteenth century.

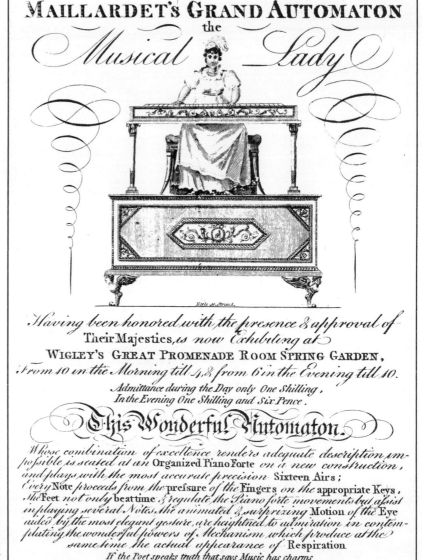

MAILLARDET's GRAND AUTOMATON
the
Musical Lady

Having been honored with the presence & approval of
Their Majesties, is now Exhibiting at
WIGLEY's GREAT PROMENADE ROOM SPRING GARDEN,
From 10 in the Morning till 4, & from 6 in the Evening till 10.

Admittance during the Day only One Shilling,
In the Evening One Shilling and Six Pence.

This Wonderful Automaton.

Whose combination of excellence renders adequate description im-
possible is seated at an Organized Piano Forte on a new construction,
and plays with the most accurate precision Sixteen Airs;
Every Note proceeds from the pressure of the Fingers on the appropriate Keys,
The Feet not only beat time & regulate the Piano forte movements but assist
in playing several Notes, the animated & surprizing Motion of the Eye
aided by the most elegant gesture, are heightned to admiration in contem-
plating the wonderful powers of Mechanism which produce at the
same time the actual appearance of Respiration

If the Poet speaks truth that says Music has charms
Who can view this Fair Object without Loves alarms
Yet beware ye fond Youths vain the transports ye feel
Those Smiles but deceive you, her Hearts made of steel
For tho pure as a Vestal her price may be found,
And who will may have her for Five Thousand Pounds.

In the Evening the Rooms will be brilliantly illuminated & as Shakespere
describes it ——— Lined with Looking Glass,
That you may see your shadow as you pass.
And the whole enriched by Transparencies executed by an Artist of the first ability
who's accuracy of Outline & delicacy of touch have renderd him in this stile
of Painting unrivalled, particularly in an accurate delineation of
THE VESTAL BURIED ALIVE.

Henri Maillardet's Musical Lady was seen in London in the 1820s and, unlike other and subsequent automaton virginal players, the fingers of the automaton's hand actually depressed the keys of the instrument which itself was not mechanical. This was one of the most successful and deservedly popular of contemporary automata. Joseph Gurk's Panharmonicon, the poster for which is seen on the facing page, was first seen in Germany in 1810 and came to London in November 1811. London was considered one of the most profitable places in Europe for exhibitions of this type.

42

ROYAL GREAT ROOMS,

Spring Gardens, Charing Cross.

PANHARMONICON
Exhibition of Music,

BY MECHANICAL POWER,

EQUALLY GRAND AS A FULL ORCHESTRA BAND,

Performing the most select Pieces of Military Music,

COMPOSED

By MOZART, HAYDN, KROMMER, ROMBERG, &c. &c.

INVENTED BY

from

J. J. GURK,

Vienna.

THIS	GREAT DRUM
Panharmonicon	*Trumpets,*
CONSISTS OF	BELLS,
210	OBOES,
INSTRUMENTS,	BASSOONS,
VIZ.	Triangles,
French Horns,	*Common Drum*
Kettle Drums,	AND
CLARINETS,	German Flutes.
Cymbals,	

Commences playing precisely at 1 o'Clock until 4, and from 7 to 10 in the Evening,

ADMITTANCE ONE SHILLING AND SIXPENCE.

N. B. The whole of the Music is performed in each Hour, concluding with God Save the King, or Rule Britannia.
Private Parties may command Admission from 4 to 6, paying 3s. each Person.

A coloured Engraving of the Panharmonicon may be had at the Rooms, price 6d.

TOPPING, PRINTER, Blackfriars, London.

WEEKS'S
ROYAL MECHANICAL
EXHIBITION,
3, TICHBORNE STREET,
Piccadilly, London.

This ingenious and entertaining Exhibition, which continuing to engage the attention of the scientific and curious, is respectfully submitted to the notice of the Public as one of those pleasing entertainments which creates wonder and surprise at the extraordinary perfection of mechanism, contained within spaces so confined and minute.

The Exhibition consists of a variety of highly finish'd CLOCKS, in the form of Temples, CABINETS, CARRIAGES, &c. &c., the greater part of which is decorated with splendid JEWELLERY, and has been expressly designed as presents to China, Turkey, &c.

A faint description of some of the principal pieces is under, (but it must be observed, it should be seen to be justly estimated.)

1. Represents a small figure of a Lady seated upon rock work, before her are ten bells, which she strikes to several pleasing Airs, beating time with her foot, while two smaller figures are seen dancing to the music.

2. A most expensive Clock decorated with Jewellery. Under a canopy is seen a figure which strikes the hours, this is a signal for a number of smaller ones to be put in motion.

3. A beautiful pair of Clocks in the form of Temples, in which is introduced a variety of moving figures, from the base to the summit, which terminates with a Butterfly hovering to the music of bells. These Temples are highly decorated with Jewellery.

4. A case containing a romantic view of a water-mill and bridge, over which a number of figures are seen passing and repassing; the water is represented falling from the rocks, and gradually passing through the bridge, &c.

5. A pleasing representation of a Pelican, in the act of feeding its young with blood. It appears to peck the breast, while the blood flows into the mouths of the young.

6. A pair of splendid Cabinet Clocks made in or'molu, in the pedistal is a lively scene representing a masquerade, at either end a variety of figures, and at the top a beautiful bouquet of flowers composed of rich Jewellery; the Lotus forming the centre, which expands and contracts during the time the figures are in motion.

7. A splendid Clock, the case in or'molu highly chased after the eastern style; at the upper part are three figures which strike the hours and quarters, this sets a number of others in motion, to very pleasing bell music.

8. A beautiful miniature representation in Silver of a Ship in full sail round a globe of artificial water, which moves in a different direction.

9. A handsome or'molu Bird-cage containing a Canary, which not only moves its beak, wings and tail, but also hops from perch to perch, the same as life, singing its notes

as it passes, to the surprise of the spectators. The under part of the cage shews an excellent clock.

10. An excellent self-playing Organ, the front opens and discovers a garden with a number of figures in various directions; in the centre is a beautiful fountain, a carriage is seen passing round it, this together with the figures, water, &c., are all seen moving at the same moment.

11. Is a most splendid Star, the rays being made of highly burnished or'molu and spiral glass; the glass is put in motion, and has the appearance of rising from the centre, and terminating at the outer points, over these is a most superb Jewelled Crown. (This star was exhibited in front of the House on His Majesty's birth night, and was the theme of general admiration.)

12. A most beautiful small Bird-cage, in pure Gold; the base is delightfully pencilled in enamel, and the ground in mazarine blue, the upper part is formed of beautiful Gold filigree and enamel. Within the cage is a small bird, with all the animation of life, that sings in the most enchanting style; this little article is finished in the most superior manner.

13. The Temple of Fountains, a most superb piece of mechanism standing nine feet high, composed of beautiful or'molu; adorned with rich Jewellery, enamel and glass-work, presenting at one view water rising and falling in every direction.

14. A pair of splendid Clocks adorned with Jewellery, of a most expensive kind, round these a number of figures &c., are seen moving, while the centre displays a pair of small beautiful enamel Cabinets, containing many useful requisites.

15. A very superbly decorated Clock, in the style of Louis XIV. the case covered with Crimson Velvet, the mountings of rich chased or'molu,interspersed with Jewellery; upon the striking of the Hours by one of the figures, a number of others are immediately put in motion to soft music.

In addition to the above, a number of smaller pieces of mechanism (all equally ingenious,) are exhibited, which want of space will not allow to be particularised, to these will occasionally be added many new pieces.

Open from Twelve to Five.—Admittance, Two Shillings each person.

WEEKS'S continue to manufacture WEIGHING MACHINES, INVALID BEDSTEADS, COUCHES, and CHAIRS of every description, after the manner of MERLIN, with great improvements.

The following notice was taken of the Exhibition on its Opening in July last, by the Literary Gazette.

WEEKS'S MECHANICAL EXHIBITION.

The admirers of ingenious and minute mechanism, will be much pleased with this splendid little Exhibition; which principally consists of a collection of valuable and superbly ornamented Clocks, the striking of the hours of which, is followed by the Singing of Birds, the Dancing of Peasantry, the passage of Boats, the falling of Cascades, the revolving of Wind-Mills, the fluttering of Butterflies, the expanding and closing of Flowers, and a number of other amusing Varieties. LITERARY GAZETTE.

Between 1802 and its sale in 1834, Thomas Weeks's museum assumed some of the reputation of Cox's which preceded it. It included a number of Cox's items. Here one could see lifesize canaries which sang and flitted from perch to perch; seventeen enamelled solid gold boxes concealing singing birds; gold, diamond-studded clockwork mice; a cage containing a small bird—'the perfection of its art'—which warbled the exact notes of the nightingale, and numerous examples of mechanical music-work. On the next page, along with a further notice of Weeks's Museum dating from 1805, is the announcement of an early nineteenth century exhibition of *androides* and other automata.

MICROCOSMS.

EXHIBITION

OF

MECHANICAL WONDERS,

Which the Proprietor (a Native of Germany) has the honor to inform the Nobility, Gentry, and Public, he intends exhibiting

This and every Evening, (except Sunday) till further Notice,

At No. 90, KING-STREET, RAMSGATE.

This extraordinary Piece of Workmanship was originally destined for the East Indies, and was constructed by several eminent Mechanics;—it is of a Pyramidal form, 6 feet in height & four feet square at the base, resting upon a Rock. On one side is observed TWO SERPENTS pursuing each other with as much Agility as if alive—higher up appears an ELEPHANT, twisting his Trunk, in the act of defending himself against a LION; he is guided by TWO NEGROES, armed in the Indian manner; on his Back is a Tower surmounted by a Magnificent Canopy, and under which is seated THE GREAT MOGUL, observing the surrounding objects,—the Crescents on his Armour, produce by their contrast, a most splendid effect.

On the second side of the Pyramid, is represented a most beautiful LANDSCAPE, with a Bridge covered by various MOVING FIGURES.—Further up, A TULIP and PASSION FLOWER opening and closing their Leaves, very much deserve the attention of the Connoisseurs.

On the third side is seen a STAR, with five spiral points of brilliant lustre, on each side of which is a SERPENT in the form of Archimedes's Screw.

On the fourth side is a View of THE PALACE and GARDENS of THE MOGUL, with Persons walking therein.—A LILY and SUN FLOWER, formed by the nicest Mechanism, in the Centre of which is a NOSEGAY, very beautifully and exquisitely finished.

The Mechanism of this Piece is so complicated, and the Workmanship so highly finished, that it is difficult to comprehend at the first glance, all the objects which present themselves at once to the Spectator. The whole of it is of Gilt Bronze. The Flowers—the Dresses of the Figures—and the Decorations in general, are ornamented with Gems, in the richest and most elegant manner.

Another highly remarkable Piece of Mechanism, not less worthy of attention, is

The FLUTE PLAYERS.

These are Two Figures of natural size, playing on the Flute, Solos, Duetts, and several Airs, not by means of Pipes, but by mere effect of Mechanism, of which one may be convinced by several proofs.——The Figures themselves produce the Sounds by blowing in the Flutes and fingering the Notes.—A little Boy sitting between these Flute Players, accompanies them with a Tamborine, beats Time, moves his head, and salutes the Company several Times.

To the above-mentioned Two Pieces, has been added a

Mechanical Landscape,

Representing a View near Constantinople, on the Coast of the Black Sea, where the Grand Seignor possesses a Summer Palace, and at which place he has annual water parties. Gondolas and Boats of different Nations are observed in several directions, with the sailors rowing with the greatest precision.——A number of Swans are seen swimming about, which by their various movements have the appearance of Life. The painting of this Landscape is brilliant and exquisite, and the various movements of the Figures in strict imitation of nature, are all performed by

CLOCK WORK.

The Exhibition Room will be open every Evening from 7 till 10 o'Clock.

Admittance—First Seats 1s.—Second Seats 6d.—Children Half-price.

N. B.——Private Parties wishing to see the Exhibition out of the regular Hours, will please to make the Proprietor acquainted with the same one Day previous.

[Burgess, Printer, High-Street, Ramsgate.

PROPOSALS

FOR RAISING BY SUBSCRIPTION, OF 2s. 6d. EACH,

(And for which the Subscriber will have a Ticket of Admission,)

A SUM OF MONEY

FOR COMPLETING A

PARADOXICAL AUTOMATON,

TWO FEET AND A HALF HIGH

Which Figure is now in Hand, and will be elegantly executed by Mr. FLAXMAN, Carver and Modeller, No. 29, *Old Compton Street, Soho.*

The Exhibition is to take Place in about five Weeks; timely Notice of which will be given.

THE AUTOMATON, which will be placed on a pedestal, and stand in the middle of a room, will act without the aid of *mechanical powers* or *confederacy*; and display the most astonishing effects of the attracting and repelling powers. It can never be out of order; neither heat, cold, moist, nor dry, can affect its regularity, and will be capable of performing various feats at will; such as *Drawing a Sword, Firing a Pistol, Ringing a Bell,* &c.; and will also perform one of the most surprising Tricks with Cards in the world.

All Automata hitherto exhibited begin to act as soon as they are set, or wound up; but the present acts on totally different principles; and when set, nothing whatever moves but at the period fixed, whether for minutes, hours, weeks, months, or longer periods.

In an adjoining room, a smaller AUTOMATON will also be exhibited, representing a Boy, having a tube, ten inches long, in his mouth, and at the upper end of which will be fixed a very fine needle, whereon two or three glass globes will keep continually turning round, as bubbles, without any interruption whatever, and without requiring more than once setting.

Subscriptions will be received by the following Gentlemen, who will furnish the Subscribers with Tickets of Admission, viz.—Mr. FAULDER, Bookseller to his Majesty, *New Bond-street*; Mr. DEBRETT, Bookseller, *Piccadilly*; Mr. CHAPPLE, Bookseller, *Pall Mall*; Mr. ROWE, Stationer, No. 3, *Fleet-street*; Mr. LOXAM, Sword Cutler, No. 88, *Cornhill*; Mr. FLAXMAN, Carver and Modeller, No. 29, *Old Compton-street, Soho*; Mr. SIMON, Hatter, No. 14, *Vere-street*; and Mr. GRESNALL, *Old Compton-street.*

The Price of Admission to Non-subscribers, will be FIVE SHILLINGS.

If any Gentleman should be desirous of seeing the original Automaton perform, previous to the regular exhibition, he may be accommodated, by sending a line, the day before, mentioning the hour, and paying 10s. 6d. to Mr. A. G. No. 48, Evesham Buildings, SOMMERS TOWN.

A. NEIL, Printer, Chalton Street, Sommers Town.

A poster advertising an out-of-town exhibition (*left*) appears to refer to the same flute-players as those mentioned on page 41. The automaton with the opening and closing passion flowers may well have been one of Cox's since he excelled in the making of ingenious, jewelled automaton flowers. Above is surely one of those many ruses to raise money. Usually the pleas were in connection with finance to complete a perpetual motion machine, or to make gold from pewter. It dates from about 1820.

Mechanical singing birds, also known contemporarily as 'piping bullfinches', amazed and amused the wide-eyed Georgian Londoners. This flyer dates from about 1825 and it is interesting to note the reference to steam as 'that dangerous power'. Improper understanding brought about a great many steam boiler explosions. Below is a notice dating from about 1810 concerning an exhibition which had but a short following at the Great Room, Spring Garden, Charing Cross. Observe the use of colourful non-words, a feature which characterised the times and remained throughout the growth of mechanical music. From 'Panathene' we may ponder over the 'Autoharmonicon' ...

Now Exhibiting

At No. 5,
BURLINGTON ARCADE, PICCADILLY,
A MOST SURPRISING

Mechanical
Singing Bird,

The Black and Blue Creeper, of South America,

IN A MAGNIFICENT CAGE,

Which sings the natural notes in so perfect a manner, as to strike the beholder with admiration and astonishment. He also pipes a pleasing air in excellent style, and while performing, hops from Perch to Perch. The Throat expands and contracts as he warbles his native notes; the Beak and Tail move, the Wings flutter, and he has in fact all the appearance of a living Bird.

A CURIOUS AND ENTERTAINING

Automaton Conjuror,

Which produces a variety of changes in Cups and Balls accompanied with significant and amusing Gestures.

A MECHANICAL BOAT,

Which impels itself at a very swift rate in a large Trough of Water, being the Model of one designed for the Accommodation of from Ten to Twenty persons, to go at an equal rate with STEAM VESSELS, without the use of that dangerous Power.

Admittance 1s. Children 6d.—Open from Ten in the Morning till Nine at Night.

C. BAYNES, Printer, 9, Cook's Court, Carey Street.

EXHIBITION OF THE PANATHENE,
OR,
Magnificent Musical Temple,
GREAT ROOM, SPRING GARDEN.

The NOBILITY, GENTRY, and the PUBLIC in general, are respectfully informed, that the most beautiful Combination of the FINE ARTS ever submitted to their Inspection, called THE PANATHENE, is now open for Exhibition in the above Room. A TEMPLE of such complicated and magnificent Workmanship, and which affords such Gratification to the Visitors, can be but very imperfectly described through the Medium of a Hand-bill, the Circulation of this brief Account is therefore intended merely to convey to the Reader some Idea of its Beauties. This SPLENDID STRUCTURE stands 23 feet in height, and is 16 feet square at the Base; its exterior Appearance presents to the Eye a most enchanting Combination of PAINTING, SCULPTURE, ARCHITECTURE, CARVING, &c. &c. The MUSIC in the Interior consists of various self-acting INSTRUMENTS, among which is the much-admired AUTOHARMONICON, or self-acting Piano-Forte, and a MUSICAL CLOCK, all of which are alternately in continual Play, performing the most select Pieces, favorite Airs, and Quadrilles. Independent of its Novelty, it possesses every possible Variety, and is different, in every Respect, to any Thing that has ever been exhibited in this Kingdom. The various Departments of this TEMPLE have been executed by the great Masters, among whom are—T. STOTHARD, Esq. R. A.; H. HOWARD, Esq. R. A.; C. TOWN, Esq.; Signors OUDINOT and VIZA; Messrs. LONGMAN, HERRON, ROGERS, GARBANATI, JACKSON, HESSE, ADAMS, RICKETTS, WHITE, and many Others of the first Talent.

☞ *A Synopsis of this TEMPLE is given to each Person on Admission.*

OPEN FROM TEN TILL DUSK.—ADMITTANCE, ONE SHILLING

Printed by W. GLINDON, 51, Rupert Street, Haymarket

Curious and Surprising Mechanism.

A

Tarantula Spider,

MADE OF STEEL,

That comes independently out of a Box, and runs backward and forward on the Table;
stretches out and draws in its Paws, as if at Will; moves its Horns, Claws, and
opens them with Ease.

THIS singular Automaton, that has no other Power of Action than the Mechanism
contained in its Body, must fix the Attention of the Curious. The Thing might
have been thought impossible, on Account of its Smallness and Difficulty, being
composed of 115 Pieces!

TO BE SEEN, AT ONE SHILLING EACH PERSON, AT

Weeks's Museum, Titchborne Street, Piccadilly,

Where Subscriptions are received for the ensuing MUSEUM, similar to that once
unrivalled and brilliant Assemblage of Mechanism, Jewellery, &c. exhibited by Mr.
JAMES COX, in Spring Gardens, 1773.

A Specimen of the Museum—Two magnificent CLOCKS, engaged for the
EMPEROR of CHINA, at *Nine Thousand Pounds*, in the Form of TEMPLES,
supported by Sixteen Elephants, and embellished with upwards of Seventeen Hundred
Pieces of Jewellery, in the first Stile of Elegance. To be seen, at 2s. 6d each.

N. B. Candelabras made and repaired, in a superior Stile.

☞ Weighing Machines, and Chairs of every description for Invalids..

Handy, Printer, 50, Brewer Street, Golden Square.

NEW-YORK: Printed by *John Peter Zenger* where Advertisements are taken in.

To be SEEN,

At Mr. *Pacheco*'s Ware-House, in *Marketfield-Street*, commonly
known by the Name of *Petticoat-Lane*, opposite the Cross Guns,
near the Fort.

A CURIOUS MUSICAL MACHINE, arriv'd from *England*, the
third Day of *May* last, which peforms several strange and di-
verting Motions to the Admiration of the Spectators, *viz.* The
Doors fly open of their own accord, and there appears six Ringers in white Shirts all busy pulling the Bell-Ropes, and playing several Tunes, Chimes, and Changes: They first appear with black
Caps and black Beards at one Corner there is a Barber's Shop and a Barbers
Pole hung out, and at the Shop Door stands the Barber's Boy, who, at
the Word of Command, gives three Knocks at his Masters Door, out comes
the Barber with his Rasor and Bason to shave the Ringers, then the
Doors shut themselves whilst the Barber is Shaving them, then the Doors o-
pen themselves the second Time, and the Ringers appear all clean shaved and
clean Caps put on; afterwards they ring a long Peal of Changes, and then
fall the Bells to Admiration, after that the Barber walks into his Shop again,
his Boy standing ready to open the Door for his Master and then shuts it after him; last of all the great Doors shut themselves again. All being performed entirely by Clock-Work, in imitation of St. Brides Bells in *London*.
There will be a small Entertainment of Slight of Hand, before the Clock-
Work is seen.

*The Proprietor of it will wait on any Gentlemen or Ladies;
at their own Houses*

THE *same will be shewn every Day in the Week, Sundays excepted at 4 o'Clock
in the Afternoon, and at 7 in the Evening. The Price for Grown Persons
1 s. and for Children 9 pence.*

Not only singing birds but other specimens
of the watchmakers' skill in automata also
captured the imagination of the public.
Weeks's Museum showed for a time the
Tarantula Spider comprising 115 pieces.
This was all the more remarkable for being
completely self-motivating. Just to prove
that exhibitions of remarkable automata were
not the prerogative of London alone, as far
back as 18 July 1743, *The New York Weekly
Journal* carried the announcement reproduced left. It also serves to remind us that
until the 1780s, America's currency was, like
ours, pounds, shillings and pence.

More exhibitions of automata (*top*) advertised in 1829. But in February 1834 Londoners had the chance to marvel at the so-called Exeter Clock. It was later shown at the Great Exhibition, 1851 (*the catalogue illustration faces*). Recently historians have cast some doubt over who completed the clock.

THE EXETER CLOCK.

This should be visited by all admirers of ingenuity. There are thirteen distinct movements on it; and it is said, by those who have an opportunity of knowing, to be superior to the celebrated clock at Strasburgh. The world owes this wonderful production of ingenuity, perseverance, and mechanical skill, to Jacob Lovelace, born in the city of Exeter, 15th March, 1656, who, to the disgrace of the age, ended his days in great poverty in that city, 1st of April, 1716, aged sixty years; having been thirty-four years in completing it. It is enclosed in an elegant cabinet, ten feet high and five feet wide, ornamented with oriental figures and finely executed paintings, bordered by richly-carved fretwork.

PUBLIC AMUSEMENTS.

THE EXETER CLOCK.

WE visited this ingenious piece of mechanism lately, and can report, that it is well worth half an hour's inspection for the curious. Nothing can afford a more melancholy and striking lesson to the lovers of Fame, than the history of the inventor of this piece of human ingenuity. The poor man who constructed this clock in 1656, *Jacob Lovelace*, was a native of the city of Exeter, and spent the best part of his life and fortune in realizing this vision of his fancy. Having completed it, which cost him the labour of thirty-four years, he ended his days, probably broken-hearted, in the workhouse of that city, unpitied, unhonoured, unknown; and the fame for which he had toiled, after 168 years, sheds its cold halo round his almost forgotten grave! Such is the fate of Genius! It too often lives unacknowledged, and dies unlamented; leaving to posterity, (as in this instance) the honour of finding out its deserts, and blowing the bubble of Fame over its unconscious ashes. There are thirteen different movements in this beautiful cabinet, which is ten feet high, and five wide, ornamented with oriental figures, and finely executed paintings, and a moving panorama, descriptive of day and night, proving that many scenic representations of later days, for which our modern artists claim the invention, were known and in use in the 17th century, even by a country mechanic. Were we to look more closely into the wonders of our own day, we should find, that poets, painters, and musicians, as well as mechanics, are more indebted to the genius of the age that has gone before us, than they would willingly have it believed.

The celebrated clock of Strasburgh had only nine movements, and is now out of repair. The present exhibition, therefore, is the only thing of the kind extant, that we are aware of. Till the last month, we are informed, it was never removed fifteen miles from the place where it was made, but has lately been purchased by some discerning individual for the purpose of exhibiting in London.

When the German philosopher Albertus Magnus (born 1193; died 1280) contrived a speaking head, his worthy pupil, Thomas Aquinas, the Italian theologian, allegedly smashed it to pieces. As with other so-called speaking statues, a voice was made to issue from the mouth of the figure, in this case by means of a tube. The Anthropoglossos on the next page was but a variant of this seen in London in the 1830s. Far cleverer was the Invisible Girl seen even earlier, the detail of which is shown in the two sketches below. The voice of the woman was conveyed by a tube and trumpets into the central globe. Questions asked by spectators were answered by a faint and apparently juvenile voice which emanated from all four trumpets. The sketches are from *Cyclopædic Science* by John Henry Pepper, remembered by us today for his invention of the stage illusion known as 'Pepper's Ghost'. The myth of the speaking statue was used by Mozart in *Don Giovanni*.

The Talking Head of Albertus Magnus.

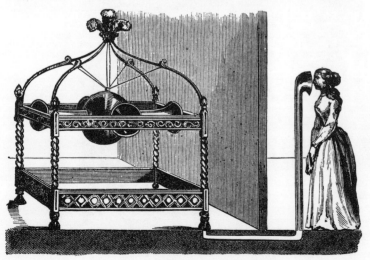

The Invisible Girl.

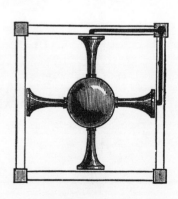

The Globe and Trumpets.

ST. JAMES'S HALL,
PICCADILLY.

THE ANTHROPOGLOSSOS,
OR,

MECHANICAL VOCALIST,

WONDER OF THE WORLD.

NOW OPEN DAILY from 11 till 10 o'clock.

The Programme will be varied daily, and will include :

- " THE DARK GIRL DRESSED IN BLUE."
- " POLLY PERKINS."
- " ANNIE LYLE."
- " A GIPSY'S LIFE IS A JOYOUS LIFE."
- " GOD BLESS THE PRINCE OF WALES."
- " GOD SAVE THE QUEEN."

The Words of each Song will be distinctly articulated.

NEVER, it is believed, since the very first sound of the human voice emanated from the earliest created of mankind, causing the oral mystery of sounded syllables to float upon the balmy airs of Paradise, until now, has aught been perfected which could approximate in any real degree to the Divinely bestowed " music of speech." Many and varied have been the efforts made, from time to time, to accomplish this apparently impossible purpose, but all have proved alike worse than futile. It has been reserved for Mr. GIACOPO SAGUISH, of Constantinople, to become the wonderful and fortunate Inventor of an Automaton Head, which (miraculous to relate) he has so contrived, by means of the nicest and most exquisitely constructed mechanism, that it can rival Nature herself in its vocal and elocutionary powers. To say that this astonishing Phenomenon is unique is to express the very least of the wonders which it exhibits, and to the witnessing of which the generous, talent-appreciating public of Great Britain is now most respectfully invited. While so doing, it is humbly yet confidently hoped, however high the expectations respecting this real prodigy may be raised, that in no single instance shall any person with whose patronage the Exhibitor may be favoured, meet a disappointment, but rather that each and all shall be compelled to acknowledge the " half has not been told them."

Admission, ONE SHILLING.

Tickets at Mr. AUSTIN'S Office, St. James's Hall, 28, Piccadilly, W.

PRINTED BY J. MILES AND CO., WARDOUR STREET, OXFORD STREET,—W.

On SATURDAY, May 12th, 1832,

The following Selection of Music

Will be performed

BY MR. PURKIS,

ON THE

APOLLONICON,

A Grand Musical Instrument,

Invented and Constructed by

Messrs. FLIGHT AND ROBSON, ORGAN-BUILDERS,*

101, St. MARTIN's-LANE;

Under the immediate Patronage of His Majesty.

Commencing at 2 o'Clock—ADMITTANCE 1s.

The **Mechanical Powers** of the Instrument will commence the Performance with
Mozart's OVERTURE to FIGARO, and conclude with
Weber's Celebrated **Overture to Der FRIESCHUTZ.**

PART I.

SYMPHONY...Haydn.
AIR—'Dovo sono,'...Figaro,........................Mozart.
DIVERTIMENTO—from Preciosa,......................Purkis.
SONG—'On yonder rock reclining,'..................Auber.
GRAND MARCH—(MS).....................................Winter.

PART II.

OVERTURE—Le Seigneur du Village....................Boildieu.
POLACCA—'The horn of Chase,'...................T. Phillips.
GLEE—'When the wind blows,'.......................Bishop.
BALLAD—'The banks of Allan Water,'...............
FINALE—, Huntsmen's Chorus'—Der Frieschutz.........Weber.

NB. **Mr. Purkis' Performances** will be continued **every Saturday**
DURING THE SEASON, commencing at Two o'clock.

The MECHANICAL POWERS of the APOLLONICON are exhibited DAILY, from 1 till 4,
PERFORMING

Mozart's Overture to **Figaro,** & *Weber's celebrated Overture to* **Der Frieschutz;**
In the execution of which, it has been honored with the approbation of the most eminent Mechanical and Musical Men of the Age, and is allowed to possess a grandeur and variety of effect, with a precision and delicacy of expression, superior to any other Instrument in Europe.—The Music arranged for and set on the Cylinders by the late Mr. JAMES FLIGHT, Jun.

* **Organs suitable for Churches, Chapels and Music Rooms,** are completed of various prices and descriptions.

The most famous of all the makers of mechanical organs in London was Flight & Robson. Benjamin Flight was originally in business at Exeter Change, a rather odd bazaar which stood in the Strand. After Flight left, his premises became Pidcock's Menagerie, and a giant elephant trumpeted where once he had built clockwork organs. In partnership with Joseph Robson, he built the Apollonicon concert organ which could be played by five organists at once, all seated in a row across its front, or by sets of pinned barrels, three to each piece of music. More frequently, though, in place of five maestros, the blind organist Purkis presented concerts of popular music, each one being opened and ended by a mechanical overture (*above*). No general view of the Apollonicon is known to survive, only the contemporary artist's impression (*right*)

The pace of life 130 years ago was slower than now, and the destruction of Lisbon by earthquake, tidal wave and fire more than 85 years earlier (*depicted in the engraving above*) still held an audience spellbound when it was presented as a cyclorama at the Colosseum in Regents Park (*below*). For this, organ builders Bevington & Sons built what today we would call a theatre organ. They called it 'the Apollonicon' but were forced to drop the name after justly loud complaints from Flight & Robson who had coined it for their own organ.

Among the many fake automata in history, Von Kempelen's chess-player is surely the best known. Its literature is copious, experts and cranks alike theorised, pragmatised, dogmatised—but all agreed it must be a deceit. The device ultimately went to the United States and was exhibited in Philadelphia at the Chinese Museum at Ninth and Chestnut Streets, and destroyed in a fire there on 5 July 1854. *The Illustrated London News* related the history in its issue for 20 December 1845.

THE AUTOMATON CHESS-PLAYER REDIVIVUS.

By an extract of a letter from a Correspondent in New York, we learn that, after years of oblivion and neglect, this marvellous piece of trickery, which so long excited the admiration of the scientific world at Vienna, Berlin, Paris, and London, has been dragged from its dusty obscurity, once more to delight and astonish the sight-seeing multitudes of the other hemisphere. Our communicant, indeed, speaks of the figure now exhibiting as of another wonder, the invention of a pianoforte maker of New York; but we have cogent reasons for believing that the long-celebrated Automaton of Kempelin, and the Chess-playing Turk of the Broadway, are one and the same. Age may have dimmed the lustre of his eye, and weakened the thin, small voice which of old astounded the gaping visitors with its feebly enunciated " check ;" but there, in his ancient turbaned glory, with beard and calumet, and flowing robes—there, in unmistakeable imperturbability, sits the Wizard who, for half a century, put at nought the penetration of the wisest heads in Europe. Since the revelations of M. Mouret, the celebrated Chess-player, whose skill directed the movements of the Automaton for years, a good deal has been written explanatory of the means by which this remarkable deception was carried on; but even now, except among people immediately interested in the game of Chess, very little is known upon the subject. Most persons, to be sure, have heard of " The Automaton Chess Player," and entertain a vague notion that it was in some measure conducted by human agency—a sort of " Jack-in-the-Box :" but how this was effected—the wonderful ingenuity shown in the concealment of the player—the exquisitely delusive semblance of massive wheels and springs, and intricate mechanism, with which every nook and cranny of both chest and figure were apparently filled—and, above all, the originality of conception displayed in the device by which the imprisoned agent became acquainted with his opponent's moves during the progress of a game—are as much a mystery to the world at large, as ever—and we shall therefore take advantage of the present opportunity to say a few words on the subject.

The Automaton Chess Player was invented in the year 1769, by Wolfgang de Kempelin, a native of Hungary, Aulic Councillor to the Royal Chamber of the domains of the Emperor of Germany, and long distinguished for his skill in Mechanics. His object in constructing it appears to have been merely to afford a passing amusement to the Empress Maria Theresa and the Court; and there is much reason to believe that the exaggerated enthusiasm with which it was received, and the pompous announcements of its marvellous powers, afforded but little gratification to the inventor himself, who frequently spoke of it as an ingenious trifle, the chief merit of which consisted in the happy choice of means employed to hide the deception. In 1783, the Chess Automaton was publicly exhibited in Paris, and excited the surprise and admiration of all who saw it : from thence it was removed to London, where at the time Chess was extensively practised and patronised by the higher classes. It was subsequently taken by special invitation of the Emperor, to the Court of Frederick the Great, at Berlin; this Prince was devotedly attached to Chess, and in a moment of liberality he proffered an enormous sum for the purchase of the Automaton and its secret. The offer was accepted, and in a private interview with De Kempelin, he was furnished with a key to the mystery which had baffled the whole seientific world. In a short time, however, Frederick threw aside the novelty so dearly bought, and for many years it lay forgotten and neglected amidst the lumber of his Palace.

M. de Kempelin died in 1804, but in two years after, when Napoleon occupied Berlin, we find the Chess Automaton in the field again, under a new master. On one occasion of its exhibition at this period, Napoleon himself is said to have entered the lists. After some half-dozen moves he purposely made a false move, the figure inclined his head, replaced the piece, and made a sign for Napoleon to play again. Presently, he again played falsely; this time the Automaton removed the offending piece from the board, and played his own move. Napoleon was delighted, and to put the patience of his taciturn opponent to a severer test, he once more played incorrectly, upon which the Automaton raised his arm, and, sweeping the pieces from the board, declined to continue the game.

After a second tour of the leading cities in Europe, where it was received with unabated enthusiasm, in 1819 it was again established in London. Of its subsequent history but little is known. For some years it was exhibited in Canada and the United States, and was finally understood to have returned to New York, where it has remained ever since.

Of the appearance, and manner of exhibiting this remarkable figure, the reader will obtain a pretty intelligible idea from the cut prefixed, and the following brief description :—

Upon entering the apartment where it was exhibited, the Automaton, attired in handsome Turkish costume, was seen seated behind a chess-board, affixed to a chest, about three feet high, two feet deep, and four feet long. Both the figure and the wooden chair on which he sat were attached to the chest, and this being upon castors, the whole was moved with facility about the chamber. The exhibitor commenced operations, by showing the interior of the chest, which was divided by a partition into two unequal parts, both apparently so occupied by machinery, that the concealment of a human being appeared impossible. After opening the doors in front and behind, pulling out, at the same time, a long shallow drawer, at the bottom of the chest, containing a set of chess men, a cushion, and some counters, two lesser doors were also opened; and then, in order to make the exposure of the inside complete, lights were shown at the back openings, enabling the spectators to see right through the interior. The machine was then turned round, and

lights were again exhibited at the different openings, in such a way that every corner seemed visible. At the same time, the Automaton's robe was turned over his head, so as to display the internal structure, which was seen to be full of wheels, cylinders, and other clock-work; and, in this exposed state, the whole apparatus was wheeled round, for the inspection of the visitors. After allowing sufficient time for examination, the exhibitor closed all the doors, removed the machine behind a balustrade, and invited any one who chose to play a game of chess.

As soon as an antagonist appeared, the eyes of the figure were apparently directed to the board, and, after some moments of seeming meditation, it began the battle. First, leisurely raising its arm from the cushion on which it rested, the hand was directed towards the piece to be played; the fingers then opened, took hold of the piece, and deposited it on the proper square; while, during the operation, a noise of wheel work was heard, which ceased only when the Automaton's arm had returned to rest again on the cushion. Many attempts, like that just related of Napoleon, to disconcert it, by playing falsely, were made for fun by visitors, but always without success; for, upon the least infringement of the established rules of the game, the Automaton, after tapping upon the chest, with an air of offended dignity, would replace the erring piece, and then proceed to take advantage of the illegal move, by playing one of his own men.

Upon the termination of every game, the doors were again unclosed, and the whole machine subjected to a second inspection by the persons present.

It is certainly difficult, in the face of this gratuitous display of the whole internal structure of the machine, to conceive the possibility of a concealed confederate, and yet, such is the simple and unscientific solution of this celebrated mystery. The chess-player who directed the movements of the Automaton was really hidden in the interior; and all that mass of finely-executed clock-work, wheels, and springs, and cylinders, so ostentatiously exhibited to the admiring world, was merely a sham, substantial enough in appearance to fill up every portion of both chest and figure ; but so con-trived that it would collapse or expand to suit the exigencies of the hidden agent's various positions while the inside was shown. Thus, during the exhibition of one portion of the machinery, he was enabled to take refuge in another, sometimes in the body of the automaton, and at others in a por-tion of the chest. These changes were of course in obedience to precon-certed arrangement, and a few repetitions were sufficient to accustom him to the routine. While conducting a game, he sat at the bottom of the chest, with a small pegged chess-board and men on his lap, and a lighted taper affixed : within reach were a handle by which he could guide the arm of the Automaton, an elastic spring for moving its fingers, and a cord in com munication with bellows for producing the sound of "Check." The most ingenious and interesting part of the contrivance remains to be told. Most scientific men concurred in attributing the phenomena of these perform-ances to human agency ; but even admitting the concealment of a player in the chest, the means by which he could be informed of the moves made on the Automaton's chess board, baffled all conjecture. Some supposed that he looked through the beard or waistcoat of the figure ; others, that an in-timation of every move was conveyed to him by the exhibitor ; but upon reflection insuperable objections to both these theories were found, and the problem remained unsolved till M. Mouret himself furnished an account of all the mysteries connected with the Automaton. From him we learn that the concealed player was seated immediately under the chess board of the Automaton, and that the reverse of this chess board, which formed part of the ceiling of his narrow cell, was an exact representation of the chess-board above, but to the side presented to the imprisoned player *at every one of the sixty-four squares was suspended, by the finest silk, a tiny metallic ball.* Now, as the chess men with which the Automaton played above had each of them a magnet inside, the moment any one of them was placed upon a square it attracted the little ball attached to the corresponding square below and fixed it to the board, so that, by the time the exhibitor had arranged all the men on the board, thirty-two (the number of the pieces) of the balls beneath would be drawn up close to the under chess-board, while the other thirty-two would remain suspended. To illustrate this portion of the subject we will imagine the pieces duly arranged, and the game about to be opened by the Auto-maton. Looking up at the chess board on his little ceiling he sees by the thirty-two balls drawn up that the men are properly placed on the board be-fore the public, so, duly turning the handle which directs the arm of the figure, and putting in motion the springs by which its fingers act, he causes it to take up the piece intended to be played, and, watching the board on his ceiling at the same time, he observes, as the Automaton's fingers take up the piece, the corresponding ball to fall, as before described, and when this piece is placed on the destined square, he sees also the ball below it drawn up. Having completed his first move, and carefully repeated it on the small board in his lap, he sits anxiously awaiting the move of his opponent. Pre-sently he sees one little ball fall and another rise ; he makes the move thus indicated on his own board, and in this manner proceeds with the game to its conclusion.

This brief description of the once celebrated "AUTOMATON Chess Player" may not be unacceptable to the general reader, and for the amusement of Chess amateurs we append two games recently played by the Automaton in New York.

THE AUTOMATON CHESS PLAYER.

GAME No. 1.

Played by the "Automaton," at a private exhibition of it at New York, against Mr. Stanley:—

WHITE (AUTOM.)	BLACK (MR. S.)	WHITE (AUTOM.)	BLACK (MR. S.)
1. K P two	K P two	21. Kt takes Q	B to K 5th
2. K B P two	P takes P	22. R to B 2nd	Kt to Q 2nd
3. K Kt to B 3rd	K Kt P two	23. B to K B 4th	R to K B sq
4. K B to Q B 4th	Q P one	24. B to Kt 5th (ch)	K to B 2nd
5. Q P two	K B to Kt 2nd	25. Q R to K B sq	R to K Kt sq
6. Q B P one	Q B P one	26. B to R 4th	Q R to K B sq
7. Q to Kt 3rd	Q to K 2nd	27. B. to Kt 3rd	R takes Kt
8. Kt takes P	Q takes Kt	28. R takes R	R to K B sq
9. B takes P (ch)	K to Q sq	29. K to Kt 2nd	R takes R
10. B takes Kt	Q takes K Kt P	30. R takes R	Kt to K B 3rd
11. R to K B sq	Q takes K P (ch)	31. K to B 2nd	B takes R
12. K to B 2nd	K B to B 3rd	32. K to B 3rd	K to Q 2nd
13. Q to K B 7th	B to K R 5th (ch)	33. B to R 4th	K to K 3rd
14. K to Kt sq	P to K B 6th	34. B takes Kt	K takes B
15. R takes P	Q to K 8th (ch)	35. K to B 4th	Q P one
16. K to K B sq	B to K B 7th (ch)	36. K R P two	K R P two
17. Q takes B	R takes B (ch)	37. Q R P two	Q R P two
18. K to R sq	Q to K 5th (ch)	38. Q Kt P one	Q Kt P two
19. Q to B 3rd	B to K B 4th	39. K to Kt 3rd	K to B 4th
20. Kt to Q 2nd	Q takes Q	40. K to B 3rd	

Drawn Game.

GAME No. 2.

Played by the Automaton at New York, against Mr. Z——, of the New York Chess Club.

WHITE (AUTOM.)	BLACK (Mr. Z.)	WHITE (AUTOM.)	BLACK (Mr. Z.)
1. K P two	K P two	19. Q B P one	B to K B 2d
2. K Kt to B 3d	K Kt to B 3d	20. B takes P	Q to B 2d
3. Kt takes P	Q P one	21. K R P one	K Kt P two
4. K Kt to B 3d	Kt takes P	22. R P takes P	P takes P
5. Q P one	K Kt to B 3d	23. Kt to K 4th	P takes P
6. B to K 2d	B to K 2d	24. B takes P	B takes B
7. Castles	Castles	25. Q takes B	Q takes Q
8. Q Kt to B 3d	Q B P one	26. R takes Q	Kt to R 4th
9. K R P one	K R P one	27. B takes Kt (ch)	K takes B
10. K Kt to R 2nd	K Kt to R 2d	28. B takes B (ch)	R takes R
11. K B P two	K B P two	29. Kt takes Kt	Q R to K B sq.
12. B to K B 3d	Kt to Q 2d	30. R to K sq.	R to B 4th
13. Kt to K 2d	Q Kt to K B 3d	31. R to K 7th (ch)	K to K 3d
14. Kt to K Kt 3d	Q P one	32. K Kt to K 5th (ch)	K takes Kt
15. B to K R 5th	Q to B 2d	33. K Kt P two (ch)	K to Kt 4th
16. B to K Kt 6th	B to Q 3d	34. P takes R	R takes P
17. Q to B 3d	B to K 3d	35. Q P one	
18. B to Q 2d	Q to her 2d		Black resigns.

A STEAM MAN

A good many years ago what was supposed to be a steam man was exhibited all over the country, but finally the "steam man" presumably died, as his remains were seen quite recently in one of the downtown New York junk stores. The steam man which we illustrate was invented by Prof. George Moore, who exhibited him very widely in the United States.

In our illustration we show the section and general view of the steam man. In the body is the boiler, containing a very large heating surface which is supplied with a gasoline fire. Below the boiler is situated the engine. While this steam engine is not at all large, it runs at a very high speed and is of high power, the combination of boiler and engine giving about one-half horse-power. From the engine the exhaust pipe leads to the nose of the figure, whence the steam escapes when the machine is in motion. Through the head the smoke flue is carried, and the products of combustion escape from the top of the helmet. The steam gauge is placed by the side of the neck. The skirts of the armor open like doors, so as to give free access to the engine. The main body of the figure is made of heavy tin. By reducing gear the engine is made to drive the walking mechanism of the figure at reasonable speed.

In our sectional view we show the combination of levers by which the figure is made to walk. The engine imparts a swinging to the whole length of the leg from the hip; a second swinging motion, from the knee downward, is accomplished by a similar system of levers and connections; and, finally, a true ankle motion is given to the foot by the rod running down through the lower leg. The heels of the figure are armed with calks, or spurs, which catch on the surface on which it is walking and give it its power. As exhibited, the steam man is connected to the end of a horizontal bar about waist high, which is fastened to a vertical standard in the center of the track. Thus supported, the man walks round in a circle at quite a rapid rate of progress.

For the last eight years the inventor has been at work on a larger steam man which he hopes to have in operation sometime. The new one is designed for use on the open streets, and is to draw a wagon containing a band. In the upper figure we indicate the method of attachment to the wagon which has been adopted. By the long spring at the side of the figure an elastic connection is secured, so that the figure shall always have its weight supported by the ground. The present man, which is about six feet high, when in full operation, cannot, it is said, be held back by two men pulling against it. The larger man, built for heavier work, is expected to pull as many as ten musicians in his wagon. Our cuts show the general appearance of the figure, which is attired in armor like a knight of old, and which appears to be thoroughly operative. The action is quite natural, and the hip, knee, and ankle motion of the human leg have been very faithfully imitated. The figure moves at a brisk walk and can cover about four or five miles an hour. ∎∎∎

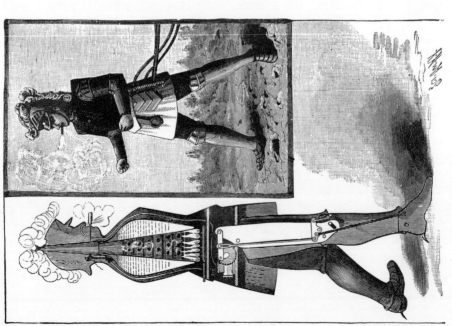

THE STEAM MAN.

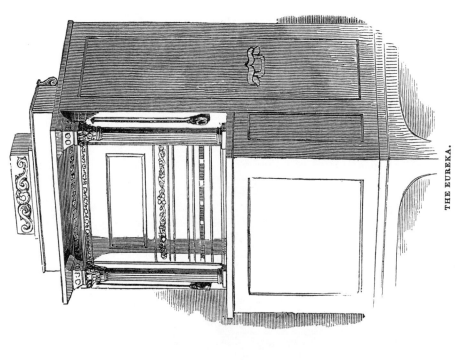

THE EUREKA.

THE EUREKA.

Such is the name of a Machine for Composing Hexameter Latin Verses, which is now exhibited at the Egyptian Hall, in Piccadilly. It was designed and constructed at Bridgwater, in Somersetshire; was begun in 1830, and completed in 1843; and it has lately been brought to the metropolis, to contribute to the "sights of the season."

The exterior of the machine resembles, in form, a small bureau book-case; in the frontispiece of which, through an aperture, the verses appear in succession as they are composed.

The machine is described by the inventor as neither more nor less than a practical illustration of the law of evolution. The process of composition is not by words already formed, but from *separate letters*. This fact is obvious; although some spectators may, probably, have mistaken the *effect* for the *cause*—the *result* for the *principle*, which is that of Kaleidoscopic evolution; and, as an illustration of this principle it is that the machine is interesting—a principle affording a far greater scope of extension than has hitherto been attempted. The machine contains *letters* in alphabetical arrangement. Out of these, through the medium of *numbers*, rendered tangible by being expressed by indentures on wheel-work, the instrument selects such as are requisite to form the verse conceived; the *components* of words suited to form hexameters being alone previously calculated, the harmonious combination of which will be found to be practically interminable.

The rate of composition is about one verse per minute, or sixty in an hour.

"Each verse remains stationary and visible a sufficient time for a copy of it to be taken; after which the machine gives an audible notice that the Line is about to be decomposed. Each Letter of the verse is then slowly and separately removed into its former alphabetical arrangement; on which the machine stops, until another verse be required. Or, by withdrawing the stop, it may be made to go on continually, producing in one day and night, or twenty-four hours, about 1440 Latin verses; or, in a whole week (Sundays included), about 10,000.

"During the composition of each line, a cylinder in the interior of the machine performs the National Anthem.

"As soon as the verse is complete, a short pause of silence ensues.

"On the announcement that the line is about to be broken up, the cylinder performs the air of "Fly not yet," until every letter is returned into its proper place in the alphabet.

"There is on the frontispiece of the machine, above the line of verse, a tablet, bearing the following inscription:—

"Full many a gem, of purest ray serene,
The dark, unfathom'd caves of ocean bear,
And many a flower is born to blush unseen,
And waste its fragrance on the desert air."

Full many a thought, of character sublime,
Conceived in darkness, here shall be unrolled,
The mystery of number and of time
Is here displayed in characters of gold.

Transcribe each line composed by this machine,
'Record the fleeting thoughts as they arise;'
A line, once lost, may ne'er again be seen,
'A thought, once flown, perhaps for ever flies,'"

The *primum mobile*, or first moving power of the machine, is a leaden weight of about twenty pounds, with an auxiliary weight of ten pounds, applied to another part of the movement: these are occasionally wound up, and the velocity is regulated in the usual manner, by a worm and fly.

"The entire machine contains about 86 wheels, giving motion to cylinders, cranks, spirals, pullies, levers, springs, ratchets, quadrants, tractors, snails, worm and fly, heart-wheels, eccentric-wheels, and star-wheels—all of which are in essential and effective motion, with various degrees of velocity, each performing its part in proper time and place. And in the front of the interior is a large Kaleidoscope, which regularly constructs a splendid geometric figure. This action is performed at the commencement of the operation, and at the precise time when the line of verse is conceived, previous to its mechanical composition."

From Albert A. Hopkins' *Magic, Stage Illusions & Scientific Diversions*, published in New York in 1901, comes the story of the Steam Man. It is the only reference known. Another, and more tantalising lost treasure is the Eureka, described above. *The Illustrated London News* published this on 19 July 1845. Nothing further is known and the fate of the Hexameter Machine is unrecorded. It may yet survive, somewhere, to reveal the solution to its mystery. *The Meccano Magazine* of June 1939 brings us up to date on *androides* and robots overleaf.

A Robot that Walks, Talks and Smokes

Aluminium Giant with Electric Brain

AFTER two years of life as a sheaf of blueprints and scattered pieces of metal in the laboratory of the Westinghouse Electric Company at Mansfield, Ohio, "Elektro" is ready to go places and do things. He is built up of more than 900 hand-made parts, and these were bolted or welded into place, his motors were tuned up, and his electrical brain set in a whir of excitement to enable him to become a scientific actor at the 1939 New York World's Fair.

Elektro is the youngest of a famous line of mechanical men that have been born in the Westinghouse laboratories. He is less than two years old, but already has a vocabulary of some 77 words and is a real prodigy, for he can walk, talk, count up to 10 on his hands, and smoke cigarettes by the dozen, yet never tires or gets hungry. He stands seven feet in his aluminium feet and has a chest expansion of 82 in. His chest indeed is always expanded because, like the rest of his body, it is made of aluminium over a steel frame. His feet are 18 in. long and half as broad.

This mighty automaton takes food from the nearest light socket, for he is an electric robot. He is never brain-weary because his brain lobes are 48 electrical relays. These devices do all the thinking for him; and he merely obeys their promptings, which are delivered through his nervous system of motors, levers, gears and chains. His spinal column is made of wire, of which enough is wound round his coils to encircle the world at the Equator. All told, he has a bag of 26 tricks. He not only walks forward, but can go backward just as readily, and he can bow his head as prettily as a debutante or turn it 45 deg. in either direction. If in the mood, he will bring either hand up to his face in a patriotic salute, and if properly coached he will raise his hands and count on his fingers, bending them one at a time in approved finger-counting style.

Elektro's favourite colours are red and green. As a matter of fact, they are the only colours he sees, and when they are flashed with a light before his eyes he speaks out "red" or "green" as the case may be. He is at its best when it comes to smoking, however, for he not only puffs and inhales, but also blows the smoke out in great billows from both nostrils.

Elektro has to be "bossed" by human commands. When these are spoken softly into a microphone he jumps to obey, although there is no visible connection between him and the microphone. What happens is that the spoken words set up vibrations that are converted into an electric impulse, which lifts a shutter in front of an electric lamp and sends a flash of light across the room to a photo-electric cell, or "electric eye," in the control unit that serves as Elektro's brain. The cell acts as a sensory nerve. It receives the light command, translating it into a feeble electric current that is amplified and sent on to the bank of relays, which close and open electric circuits to start Elektro's motors turning.

Talking to Elektro is like dialing an automatic telephone, using light impulses instead of numbers to cause the relays to act. It makes no difference what words are used to give the command so long as the proper number of light impulses are produced. One word or impulse places a series of relays in position to act. Two words close the electric circuit, and release current to the motors employed in any particular movement of the robot. Three words activate relays to stop Elektro, and four words bring all the relays back to their normal position of rest.

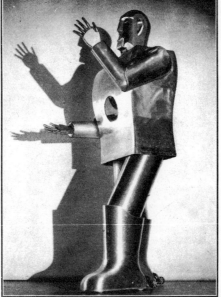

Elektro, the Westinghouse Moto-Man, who walks, talks, smokes and distinguishes colours. This giant robot is 7 ft. high, and performs for the benefit of visitors to the New York World's Fair. Photograph by courtesy of The Westinghouse Electric Company, New York.

Signal lights on the control panel show which movement of the robot is next in sequence. By speaking single words or a series of words properly spaced, the operator can cause the relays to skip over any number of these "points of motion," and when the light flashes over the one desired a two-word command will start the proper relay.

Just as an electric eye converts light waves into electric currents to put life into the robot, two other electric eyes enable it to recognise colours. A filter in front of one tube lets only red light through to the cell, and similarly a filter in front of the other tube permits only green light to reach the tube. When the proper lights are flashed in Elektro's eyes, one or the other of these electric eyes energises a relay to start the movement of a turntable on which is a record that produces the word "red" or "green."

Elektro's walking is accomplished by means of four rubber rollers under each foot, and these are driven by chains and shafts connected to a motor in the middle of the automaton. Another small motor works the bellows for Elektro's smoking. Nine motors are required to operate the fingers, arms, head and turntables for talking. Like some radio programmes, Elektro does his talking by means of transcriptions. His speech lasts about a minute and uses only 75 words, and a solenoid makes his aluminium lips move in rhythm to his speech-making.

But if robots could really talk, Elektro might do a little boasting on his own, for he may be slow, but he is as strong as a giant. If the energy of all of his 11 motors could be applied to a single task, he would exert, not one man-power, but a horse-power, for he would be capable of lifting a 550-lb. weight at the rate of a foot in a second.

Elektro is a dullard by comparison with any man, however, and he can never hope to compete with human intelligence and muscular control. There are 292 different muscles in the human body, capable in combination of producing unestimated thousands of different movements beyond the 500 most elementary motions. Elektro weighs 260 lb., and does 26 tricks, so that he requires about 10 lb. for every motion. Theoretically he would have to weigh about 5,000 lb., in order to accomplish the most rudimentary human movements.

Even in his present stature Elektro's "brain" weighs approximately 60 lb. and occupies more than 4 cu. ft. of space outside his body. The "brain" or control unit includes 48 electric relays and signal lights in addition to the controlling photo-electric cell. According to J. M. Barnett, the inventor of the Westinghouse "Moto-man," the "brain" alone would have to contain 1,026 electric relays in order to "think" for a robot capable of duplicating the 500 elementary human motions. It would then weigh nearly half a ton, and occupy about 108 cu. ft. of space!

Automatons have indeed come a long way since the first speculations on the possibility of making mechanical men. Elektro's direct forbear is Willie Vocalite, a robot developed a few years ago in the Westinghouse research laboratories. Willie is voice-operated, and can stand up and sit down, but can't walk. Their common ancestor was named Televox, but he responded only to sounds transmitted by telephone wires and went through life without an electric eye. These are actors on the stage of electrical living, and the scientific principles they dramatise are already quietly at work in industry.

CHAPTER 3 ·

The Early Musical Box

THE familiar cylinder musical box is a direct descendant of the forms of mechanical musical instrument which were common in the sixteenth and seventeenth centuries. The flute-playing clock (this is a mis-nomer since the clock contained no *flute* as such but flute-toned organ pipes) with its small, compact but nevertheless adequate mechanical organ, the clockwork spinets made by Bidermann and others, and the carillons of various sizes from cathedral-sized marvels such as that at Bruges and Ghent, down to the carillon clocks popular for 250 years—all these had certain common features.

These commonalities comprised the music in the form of what would today be termed a 'programme' and a sounding device (either pipework or bells) for spreading forth the music. Between the two parts was a mechanism which could take signals from the programme and transmit them in proper sequence to the sounding device. The programme, a direct precursor of that which today operates a computer, consisted of a barrel arranged with projections conforming to the notes to be sounded, their relationship one to another, and their duration. The transmission mechanism was in the form of a keyframe positioned so that the barrel projections would raise a small lever as they passed beneath it, the lever operating pull-downs (to bells) or stickers (to windchest/pipes) to produce musical sounds.

Clock and watchmakers were conscious of the advantages of miniaturisation in order to produce a small object capable of making music. The problem was that the smaller the unit components, the higher the pitch of the sound produced until the point was reached where a tiny bell or organ pipe produced a sound which had, to all practical intents, an indeterminate pitch and was virtually useless. The gong, in the form of a coiled strip of steel, was only slightly better but had the disadvantage that it was fairly large and even so little as an octave of gongs still took up considerable space. On top of all this, the resonance of the gong detracted from its musical merits since no effective and compact means could be found of damping the vibrating metal without altering its vibrational mode, certainly not within the confines of the watchcase or small clock.

A Swiss watchmaker, Antoine Favre, is credited with the invention, in 1796, of 'the means of establishing carillons without hammers'. A sliver of steel, shaped, polished, tempered and then screwed into position so that the projections on a rotating cylinder could pluck at its free extremity, was proved to be capable of emitting a pure musical sound at an acceptable pitch and volume for its size. From these small beginnings, the cylinder musical box developed and, almost a hundred years later, the disc-playing musical box.

Setting the music on to the brass cylinder for a musical box was done in the same way that music was pinned for a musical clock. The difference was that whereas the pins for the cylinder of a musical clock might be numbered at no more than a hundred or so, those in something as advanced as, for example, an overture-playing musical box might have upwards of ten thousand tiny pins set in its surface.

A celebrated Edinburgh clockmaker named Thomas Reid (born 1746; died 1831) described in his *Treatise on Clock and Watchmaking,* published in 1826, a machine for setting music on to the barrels of musical clocks played by bells. He also claimed that his invention could be used for setting music upon barrels for organs. This article and its illustrations are reproduced here.

Machines for pinning musical box cylinders were necessarily much larger and more complex. Today it is not known for sure how these machines operated other than that each note would be represented by a small prick or dent in the surface of the metal which was then drilled through by hand. At least one of these machines was in use in London by Joseph Fackler at his workroom behind Edward Jerome's coffee rooms at 112 Clerkenwell Road in 1892, also sometime at 6 St John's Square. He moved in 1899 to adjoining 41 Great Sutton Street where his business survived until 1956.

Distributing musical boxes in London during the middle of the last century was the prerogative of a handful of importers and jewellers. Best known among these were the firms of Thomas Cox Savory & Co of 47 Cornhill, who first advertised musical boxes in 1845, and Wales & McCulloch who had premises at 32 Ludgate Street in the 1850s and at 22 Ludgate Hill and 56 Cheapside by the 1880s. The former company later became A. B. Savory & Sons and by 1867 the business was amalgamated as The Goldsmiths' Alliance Ltd at 11 and 12 Cornhill. In later years, the main distributors for boxes became Nicole Frères. Periodic catalogues of instruments were published by these importers and the wide choice of music available makes interesting reading. Of particular interest to the musical historian are musical box interpretations of works long since forgotten and in some cases lost. Many of the operatic and overture-playing boxes which were made in the early years of the musical box when quality was at its best perform long-lost music. One such box, belonging to Bruce Angrave, plays the overture to Gaetano Donizetti's opera, *Il Belisario.* Written in 1836, this is one of between sixty and seventy operas he wrote, less than half a dozen of which are ever performed today. Composers whose names were household words and who vied with today's accepted masters in popularity and who are now unknown have their works preserved in many a musical box.

A significant detail often overlooked today when listening to an old musical box is that these were all tuned to the 'unequal temperament' or meantone system. This feature is particularly noticeable in some boxes, especially those of Lecoultre, Ducommun Girod and F. Nicole who made use of modulation into what in the meantone system were referred to as 'the bad keys'. The effects specifically make their presence most obvious in the treble register. This is a point to bear in mind during overhaul work and any thoughts of tuning to the accompaniment of a piano should be put out of mind. It is believed in many circles that Bach, implying Johann Sebastian, was the first to advocate equal temperament and a number of people offer as evidence the '48' preludes and fugues. Of course J. S. Bach was sensible to the shortcomings of the meantone system and, as is well-documented, he perfected a 'smoothed-out' system for his own clavichord and harpsichord. It was thus for the 'well-tempered' clavier, and not the 'equal-tempered' clavier that Bach wrote the '48'. It fell to Bach's son, Carl Philipp Emanuel, to advocate equal temperament as such. This is not to denigrate the influence of 'Old Bach', for his teachings played a valuable part in the development of the keyboard instrument and the fact that he always tuned his own instruments to suit his liking did not go unnoticed.

Having dispatched not only the 'Great Bach', but also the horny subject of temperament

MUSICAL BOXES.— An extensive assort-
ment of fine-toned BOXES, of superior quality, by the celebrated makers, Messrs, Nicole Bro'hers, G'neva, playing upwards of
600 airs, overtu'es, &c, selected from the works of Mozart, Weber,
Rossini, Bellini, Donizetti, &c; together with the most eminent
English Composers. A catalogue of the music, with lists of prices, is
now published, and may be had gratis, on application to T COX
SAVORY and Co, Watchmakers, &c, 47, Cornhill, seven doors from
Gracechurch-street.

MUSICAL-BOX REPOSITORY, 32, Lud-
gate-street (opposite Everington's), London.— WALES and
M'CULLOCH are direct Importers of Nicole Frère's celebrated
MUSICAL-BOXES, playing, with unrivalled brilliancy of tone, the
best Popular, Operatic, and Sacred Music. Large sizes, four airs, £4;
six, £6 6s.; eight, £8; twelve airs, £12 12s. Snuff-boxes, two tunes,
14s. 6d. and 18s.; three, 30s.; four tunes, 40s. Catalogue of tunes, &c.,
gratis, and post-free, on application.

MUSICAL BOX DÉPOTS, 22, Ludgate-
hill, and 56, Cheapside. — Most extensive variety in
London. Popular, operatic, and sacred music. Large sizes,
ordinary make, four airs, £2 2s.; six, £2 12s.; and eight airs,
£3 3s.; ditto, by Nicole Frères, £1 per air; superb instruments,
from £4 to £260. Choicest music and newest accompaniments.—
Catalogues of tunes and prices gratis on application to WALES
and McCULLOCH, as above.

To begin with, musical boxes were sold only by high-class jewellers, silversmiths and watchmakers. Two of the earliest to specialise advertise here in notices dated 1851, 1855 and 1881.

within the space of just one paragraph, we must return to the cylinder musical box. Competition from the disc musical box and, later, the early phonographs, dictated that quality should suffer to the point where the techniques of mass production coupled with poorly set-up and drastically abbreviated tunes rendered the majority of cylinder musical boxes of no intrinsic value, certainly not to the musicologist today. The point was reached where the instruments were actually given away as a free gift incentive to buy other goods such as magic lanterns.

Many boxes bore the tunesheets and other marks of the British importers, often mistakenly identified as manufacturers. It is, for example, only in recent times that it has been established that Thomas Dawkins, always accredited as making musical boxes, was in truth no more than an importer. Movements were obtained from Ami Rivenc, dismantled, the familiar Dawkins trademark stamped on to the governor cock, fitted with a Dawkins tune-sheet, re-assembled, fitted into a London-made case and sold under the Dawkins name. This firm also supplied boxes to the National Fine Arts Association of Farringdon Road with the label 'The National Music Box'. The Dawkins business was started at Frankfurt-am-Main in 1781. Upon the death of its founder, the company was bought by Thomas Dawkins who married the daughter of the founder. Dawkins moved the business (that of music string manufacturer) to 17 Charterhouse Street, London and added the making and importing of musical instruments. These were mostly military band instruments. Thomas Dawkins died in January 1879, and his wife, Rosetta Weisbart Dawkins, died on 21 April 1899, in her eightieth year. The family home was Lyndhurst House, Rosslyn Hill, Hampstead. Upon the death of Thomas Dawkins, the business was carried on by his son, Thomas Dawkins junior, who became sole proprietor. The business ceased about 1914.

A few doors from Dawkins's shop, overlooking Smithfield Market, were the London showrooms of Jerome Thibouville-Lamy of Paris. A major dealer, Thibouville-Lamy bought out most of the Mirecourt musical instrument manufacturers prior to 1867 and contracted for musical boxes from a number of makers, so it would appear. Among these was the house of L'Épée. Before opening in London Thibouville-Lamy's agent here was Woog.

A certain myth or worship has been built up over the years concerning those musical boxes manufactured by Nicole Frères and, indeed, many a mediocre box has been revered for no other reason than that it bears the stamp of this maker. True it is that they became world-famous creators of high-quality boxes, but so did several other contemporary makers, and yet still more firms, whose products did not receive so organised a distribution as those of Nicole Frères, deserve just comparison. The majority of makers up to the 1860–70 period turned out high-quality boxes, some of which are certainly of decidedly better quality, both as regards finish and performance, than those of Nicole.

The musical box trade took a long time to develop and was nowhere near as sophisticated in its methods as that of the disc-playing musical box in the years to come. Things were quieter and the pace was much slower and it was into this atmosphere that the products of Switzerland were imported to be dispensed by bewhiskered agents from spacious showrooms with a decorum to match the product. These were, after all, expensive items and the market lay, certainly in the early days, with the well-to-do and the nobility. Prior to about 1840, the major part of the trade comprised musical movements mounted in clocks, and musical snuff-boxes. The musical box on its own, although dating from around 1810, was not to gain a sizeable share of the market until between twenty and thirty years later. And so the snuffbox, the necessaire and the musical *objets d'art* represented the major stock-in-trade of the jewellers and watchmakers who sold musical automata. The *Musical World* of 1837 recounted the sad adventure of a gentleman, no doubt exuding pious abstemiousness, who happened to be in church one Sunday. In his pocket was a musical snuff-box which played 'Drops of Brandy' and 'The Glasses Sparkle on the

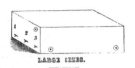

INSTRUCTIONS RESPECTING MUSICAL BOXES.

TO WIND UP, TURN THE KEY TO THE RIGHT.

Two Tunes.—Small Size. Left-hand stud, when pushed to the right, starts the music, and when put back again, the music stops at the end of the tune.

Right-hand stud changes the tune, and is moved either right or left, as the case may be, but not until the music has been stopped at the end of the tune.

Three or Four Tunes.—Small. Stud in front when pushed to right, starts music, when put back again, stops music at the end of the tune.

Stud at side, when pushed back (*i.e.* to the left) causes the tunes to play in succession when moved towards the front, the tune is repeated.

LARGE SIZES.— *Vide drawing above.*

No. 1.—This Stop, when pulled to the right, causes each air to change in succession ; and if pushed back causes the air to be repeated without changing.

No. 2.—Being pulled to the right, sets the music playing ; and when pushed back stops it at the end of the air.

No. 3.—Being pulled to the front, stops the music instantly. It is intended for the workman's use, and it is advisable not to use it, as if the music is stopped by it, and left long in that way, it is liable to sustain injury by so doing.

Three Pamphlets are published by A. B. Savory & Sons, as guides to their Establishment, in Cornhill. The first refers to Silver Plate, Electro and Sheffield Plate ; it is illustrated by wood engravings, and contains the weights and prices of the various articles required in family use. The second is on the construction of Clocks and Watches, and contains engravings of Jewellery, with prices. The third contains lists of Airs and prices of Musical Boxes of Swiss Manufacture ; all these may be had on application, or will be sent by post gratis ; and although an immediate purchase may not be contemplated, Messrs. S. will be much gratified by a visit to their Show Rooms, and they trust their goods will repay inspection as works of Art.

A. B. SAVORY & SONS, Goldsmiths & Watchmakers,
OPPOSITE THE BANK OF ENGLAND,
Nos. 11 & 12, CORNHILL, LONDON.

CLOCK AND MUSICAL BOX DEPÔT,
54, CORNHILL.

Musical box instruction sheet published *c.* 1850. The firm of A. B. Savory & Sons, formerly T. Cox Savory, was established in 1751 as Jonas Cockerton and in 1820 was known as Joseph Savory & Co. In 1867 it became The Goldsmiths' Alliance at 11 & 12 Cornhill.

Board'. Accidentally, he touched the start mechanism. Since little pieces of this type were never equipped with the 'instant stop' control provided on larger musical boxes produced until the 1870s, one may imagine the consternation and embarrassment as the snuff-box played out its inappropriate repertoire.

By the late 1880s and 1890s, quality had fallen off markedly and the musical box was cheap enough for almost everybody to buy. The 'family musical box' was usually one which played sacred airs and it would stand silent all week until Sunday when *paterfamilias* would command silence from the attendant family while the mechanism was called upon to perform some suitable hymn. These instruments are frequently found today to have survived the intervening years in almost perfect condition. The box playing popular songs would probably be played every evening after dinner and, in consequence, took a lot of use and wear and tear.

Prices varied from several hundred pounds down to a few shillings. For interchangeable movements, spare cylinders were available also by what is today considered to be a nominal sum. Against this should be remembered that a top salary was in the order of £500 per annum and that many clerks in the 1880s received an annual remuneration of between £100 and £150.* Twenty pounds for one of Messrs Wales & McCulloch's best-quality Swiss-made Nicole Frères musical boxes could represent around two months' salary for some. Musical boxes, one might infer, have never exactly been cheap. Except, that is, for those (mentioned on page 193) that were given away with magic lanterns!

* The wages in the piano- and organ-building trade, as an example, were an average of 8d per hour in 1895. This equalled 36s per week of fifty-four hours—an annual sum of around £93. Organ pipe voicers could earn half as much again.

DIRECTIONS FOR OILING A MUSICAL BOX.

1. To apply oil to the mechanism of a Musical Box, the only part necessary to be unscrewed is the little piece of brass on the top of cover of fly, and that only partially, so as to enable the piece of brass to be turned round a little way. But, as the jewel is loose, care must be taken not to turn the brass piece too far, lest the stone should fall out. After applying one drop of good salad oil to the hole, replace the brass piece with the jewel directly over the hole and screw it tightly down. While doing this with the right hand, *it is necessary to use the left by holding the fly between the forefinger and thumb*, and slightly bearing downwards, so as to prevent the pressure of the wheels throwing the fly up.

2. Convey, by means of a small iron skewer, two or three drops of oil to the worm pinion beneath the fly, which works in connection with the train of small wheels.

3. Two drops may also be advantageously applied to the pivot at each extreme end of the axle of cylinder.

4. It sometimes happens that, for want of oil on the steel rod which passes through the centre of cylinder, a little confusion in the music may arise from one tune running into another; noticeable more particularly when the barrel rebounds after the last air on the list has been played out. To obviate this, two or three drops of oil must be put on the steel rod close to the brass ends of cylinder, and while the cylinder is at the end of the first tune (after Stop No. 2 has been pushed towards the back), move the cylinder with the forefinger from right to left, several times, until the obstruction has been removed.

5. It is specially desirable that in oiling the mechanism nothing should be attempted until the mainspring has been exhausted, and run completely down, for want of winding.

WALES & McCULLOCH,

IMPORTERS OF MUSICAL BOXES,

22, LUDGATE HILL, LONDON.

Wales & McCulloch issued the instructions (*left*) with every box sold. The label above was displayed on the tune-sheet. Initially, the names of the tunes played were written on the box, sometimes on the bottom, but later on small decorative labels (*lower left*). Musical photograph albums first appeared in the 1880s with tunes and instructions combined (*below*). *Bottom right:* maker's trade card *c.* 1880. On the facing page is an early tune sheet by David Lecoultre of Brassus.

ADVICE TO PURCHASERS.

1. The mechanism of the musical part being necessarily delicate, although simple enough, it should be treated with gentleness. Children should not handle it.
2. The works are wound up by turning the key from left to right, as in a watch or clock. The key-hole will be found at the back of the Album. Guard against over-winding.
3. To set the music going, open the clasp full; to stop it, merely close the clasp and in a second or two at most the music will cease. By opening the clasp slightly the Album may be opened without the music playing.
4. The two tunes played are:—

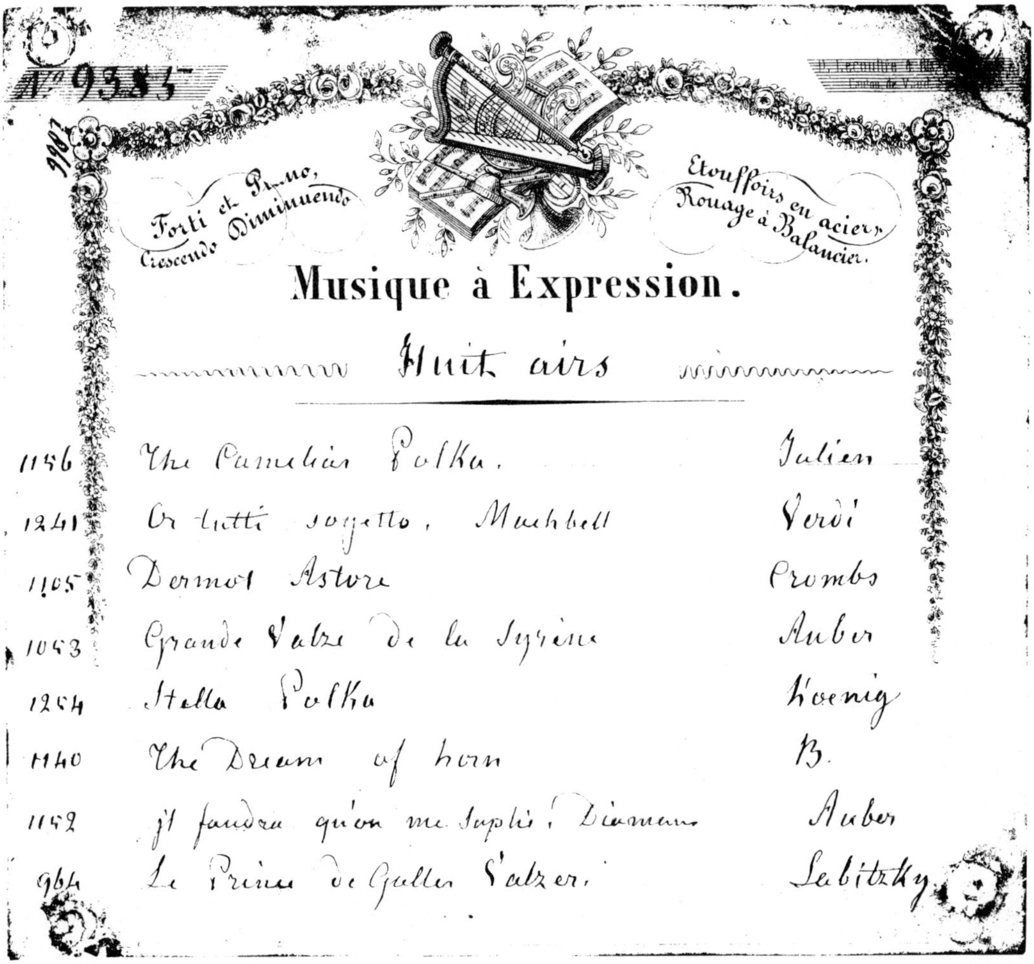

Nº 9385

9987

J. Lecoultre & Cie
Canton de Vaud.

Forti et Piano,
Crescendo Diminuendo

Etouffoirs en acier,
Rouage à Balancier.

Musique à Expression.

Huit airs

1156	The Camelia Polka.	Julien
1241	Or tutti soggetto, Macbeth	Verdi
1105	Dermot Astore	Crombs
1053	Grande Valse de la Syrène	Auber
1254	Stella Polka	Koenig
1140	The Dream of home	B.
1152	Il faudra qu'on me supplie! Diamans	Auber
964	Le Prince de Galles Valzer.	Labitzky

Tune sheets became a more functional and, later, decorative feature of the musical box in the middle of the last century. Often the make of an instrument can be determined by the name on the tune sheet or by its style and design. Top left (*facing page*) is an unidentified specimen dating from about 1880. The initials C & A might be those of an agent—it was not unusual for importers to have their own tune-sheets. Lower left is the tune sheet from a Nicole Frères 'revolver' box having six cylinders. Above is an unusual design used for a while by B. A. Bremond. Middle right is an example of a maker's tune sheet specially printed for the agent. A more flamboyant style was used by Thibouville-Lamy for boxes which they sold. Researches in America have suggested that many boxes sold by this firm were in fact made by L'Épée of St. Suzanne in France.

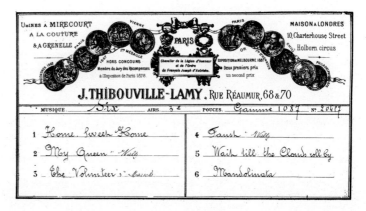

EXTRA GRAND MUSICAL BOXES.

ROSEWOOD INLAID CASES.

MANUFACTURED BY NICOLE FRÈRES.

FOUR OVERTURES. 33 by 16 by 10 inches.

£20.

(Price in former Catalogue, £31 10s.)

2000.	3131.
Overture to—	Overture to—
Semiramis—*Rossini*	Puritani—*Bellini*
Freyschutz—*Weber*	Norma ,,
Flute Enchantee—*Mozart*	Noces de Figaro—*Mozart*,
Guillaume Tell—*Rossini*	La Gazza Ladra—*Rossini*

2117.

Overture to Barber of Seville ...	..	*Rossini*
,,	Flute Enchantee ...	...	*Mozart*
,,	Faust	*Gounod*
,,	Une Nuit a' Grenade ...	*Kreutzer*

Pianoforte Accompaniment, £24 each.

(Price in former Catalogue, £38.)

Same size as above.

1362.	3157.
Overture to—	Overture to—
Guillaume Tell—*Rossini*	Pres aux Clercs—*Herold*
Don Giovanni—*Mozart*	Cheval de Bronze—*Auber*
Sonnambula—*Bellini*	Stradella—*Flotow*
Pres aux Clercs—*Herold*	Fille du Regiment—*Doni-* [zetti

3135.	1842.
Overture to—	Overture to—
Guillaume Tell—*Rossini*	Barber of Seville—*Rossini*
Gazza Ladra ,,	Semiramide ,,
Tancredi ,,	Guillaume Tell ,,
Fra Diavalo ,,	Flute Enchantee—*Mozart*

FOUR GRAND SELECTIONS.

No. 18179. £9.

(In former Catalogue, £16 16s.)

25 by 12 by 9½ inches.

Overture to Nebuchadnezzar—*Verdi*
,,   Othello   *Rossini*
,,   La Gazza Ladra   ,,
Kronungslieder Waltz—*Strauss*

OVERTURES,

With Piano Accompaniment.

Rosewood Inlaid Case, 24 by 10½ by 7½ inches.

No. 1712. £12.

(Price in former Catalogue, £21.)

L'Italienne a Alger—*Rossini*
Fra Diavolo—*Auber*
Robert le Diable—*Meyerbeer*
Der Freyschütz—*Weber*

EXTRA GRAND MUSICAL BOX.

Size, 30½ by 13½ by 11 inches.

BY NICOLE FRÈRES.

£23.

(Price in former Catalogue, £36.)

2128.

Home, sweet Home, with variations (1st Part)...	...	...	*Thalberg*
Ditto ditto (2nd Part)			,,
Carnival of Venice, with variations (1st Part)	...	...	*Schuloff*
Ditto ditto (2nd Part.)			,,
The Last Rose of Summer, with variations (1st Part)	...	...	*Thalberg*
Ditto ditto (2nd Part)		..	,,
Lily Dale, with variations ... (1st Part)	...	...	,,
Ditto ditto (2nd Part)	...	...	,,

The early catalogues of musical boxes were published by the agents. Above are two pages at random from such a list dating from around 1888. Notice the price of the 'variation' boxes on the right-hand example. The scarcity of this type today suggests that comparatively few were made. On the facing page, at the bottom, is the front cover of one of Nicole Frères' catalogues of about 1890. Centre is the front cover of a later one and its back cover (*top*) is devoted to illustrations of musical box sundries. An important publication for the trade musical box repairer was C. H. Jacot's repair manual, first published in January 1883. Jacot was one of the leading figures in the American musical box world of the period. The third edition of his scarce booklet is reproduced in facsimile on subsequent pages.

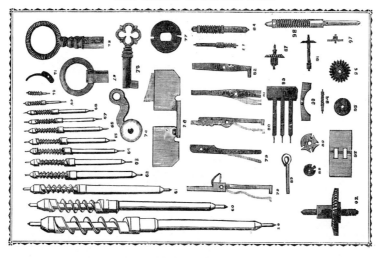

HOW TO REPAIR

MUSICAL · BOXES.

PRACTICAL INSTRUCTIONS

— TO —

WATCHMAKERS

— WITH —

COMPLETE ILLUSTRATED CATALOGUE OF
MATERIAL.

THIRD EDITION.

PUBLISHED BY
JACOT & SON,
No. 298 BROADWAY,
NEW YORK.

EDWARD STERN & CO., PRS., PHILADELPHIA.

NOTICE.

IN order to save useless correspondence, we will state here that no comb or cylinder can be duplicated, even by the manufacturer, unless the whole box is sent to the factory, which generally would cost more than a new one. But a comb can be made as good as new by us, especially if the box is one of our make. The price of such work is one dollar for each tooth.

If the pins of a cylinder are much damaged, we can replace them, but for CHEAP boxes this is hardly worth while, as the cost of such repairs would almost equal the value of the box.

INTRODUCTION.

THE rapid sale of the first and second editions of this little work, and the many complimentary letters received from watchmakers, have convinced us that it has filled a long felt want, since nothing so complete and practical had ever been published.

The first two editions being now exhausted, we publish a third, carefully revised and enlarged, having been led by inquiries from our readers to enter more fully into details, and to explain with greater clearness such points as still seemed difficult to understand. It also contains a much more complete list of material (at reduced prices) for repairing musical boxes.

We hope that this little book will continue to be of great assistance to the many watchmakers and others in the trade who repair musical boxes, and are convinced that all who consult it will find it invaluable.

C. H. JACOT.

New York, January 1st, 1890.

✤ THE ✤ MUSICAL ✤ BOX ✤

AND HOW TO REPAIR IT.

BY C. H. JACOT

THERE is hardly a watchmaker at the present time who is not called upon, occasionally, to repair a musical box, and there are so many of these instruments in this country, that a competent workman, who is able to repair them properly, will find his skill well remunerated, many of them being quite valuable and belonging to persons who are able and willing to pay liberal prices for good work; yet there are comparatively very few workmen, even among the best watchmakers, who can make these repairs in a creditable manner. We have seen many a musical box thrown aside as worthless that could have been put in order at very little time and expense if it were intrusted to one acquainted with this branch of work, while it often requires much time of one who is not acquainted with the theory of their construction, no matter how skillful he may be in other branches.

The reason is that while the mechanism is very similar to that of a clock, the musical part requires special knowledge, which can be obtained only in the factories where they are manufactured, or from workmen who have been engaged in them, and fully understand all the details and processes of manufacture. In the following article we shall endeavor to give all the directions as clearly as possible in writing, confining our instructions to the difficulties likely to be encountered by the workman in his repairs of musical boxes, taking for granted that he is a watchmaker, and therefore knows all about wheels, pinions, depthings, clickwork, etc., etc. Our instructions, moreover, are limited to what can be successfully accomplished by any intelligent workman, and we would advise him to send to us, or to some specialist (to be found in most large cities), such repairs as present greater difficulties than those explained below.

In order that our instructions may cover every disorder likely to be found in a musical box, we will suppose one that requires a thorough overhauling, and proceed in regular order, as we have practiced it for many years; so that when a musical box is brought to the watchmaker he will be better able to see what is to be done and the best means to adopt, no matter what the difficulty may be.

Examining the Box.

Before the repairer attempts anything let him first examine whether the box has "run."

A musical box is said to "run" when the cylinder is accidentally disconnected from the fly-wheel (which regulates its speed) while the mainspring is still wound. Hundreds of boxes are ruined by this accident every year, either by some part breaking or getting loose or more frequently by careless removal of the fly-wheel before letting down the mainspring. The controlling force (or governor) being thus removed, the cylinder suddenly whirls with lightning rapidity, bending and breaking the pins and also the teeth of the comb. See Illustration, page 22.

To prevent this accident care must be taken to ascertain that the mainspring is *entirely down* before removing the fly-wheel or any part of the mechanism, for the slightest "run" is certain to cause great damage by spoiling the hairsprings (or dampers) and bending the pins out of their proper position.

[We have just patented an attachment (see page 23) that is being introduced in all our boxes, which will render such accidents absolutely impossible, by automatically checking the cylinder when its speed is unduly increased.]

If it has "run" on one tune only and this be much damaged, it will be better to suppress it altogether, as will be explained further on, for it will not pay to replace all the broken pins; but if it has "run" on all the tunes the box is probably not worth repairing, and it would not be advisable to try as it will never give entire satisfaction either to you or your customer.

In making your estimate of the cost of repairs it is very important to examine carefully the condition of the cylinder pins, for if in bad condition much time will be spent on this part of the work. All the pins must be straight and bent a little *forward*, but never to one side or backward.

As it sometimes happens that a box has previously been taken apart by incompetent persons and put together carelessly, it is necessary, before winding or starting it, to ascertain that nothing is broken and that all screws are tight in place. Unless this precaution is taken, the box might "run" in your hands.

If the box is in running order listen how it plays; if it has a dull sound, strike a few light blows on different parts of the cylinder (where there are no pins), and if it sounds hollow, the cement, of which it is half full, does not adhere to the metal (the box having been exposed to an undue degree of heat). Sometimes it has melted so much that the cylinder cannot move on its shaft; more frequently the cement has melted only on one side, or on one end of the cylinder; this can be easily ascertained. The proper way to remedy this defect is by re-cementing, which will be explained further on.

Replacing Pins in the Cylinder.

If the pins have been broken only in few places they can be replaced, but this must be done with great care, as follows:

The broken pins must first be driven into the cylinder to make room for the new one. To do this we use a punch shaped as illustrated in Fig. 1, which is only to *start* it. Then use one a little thinner (see Fig. 2), which will drive it in deep enough *without enlarging the hole.* Now insert a pin a *trifle* thicker than the former, and drive it in with a punch having a hole corresponding to the length of the other pins and just large enough to hold it (see Fig. 3). By this means, when the punch has reached the surface of the cylinder, all the pins will be of equal length, which is very important. However, before driving the pin entirely, file the end *flat* so that it will fairly catch the teeth of the comb when the box is playing.

We can furnish steel pin-wire, tempered and half cut, of the proper length, ready for use (see price list of material).

Taking the Works Apart.

The next thing to be done is to take the movement out of the box, by removing the four screws on the outside (mark these so as to return them to their proper places); then place the movement on the bench, taking care that no tools lie under it to bend the pins of the cylinder.

Now remove the comb (the box having stopped at the end of a tune, so as to have no pins in contact with the comb), using a good large screwdriver. In Fig. 4 we give the shape of one we use, which has no chance of slipping and breaking the comb. It is made from an old file.

FIG. 4.

If the comb is rusted, scrape off the rust, but if this is on the teeth, be careful not to alter the pitch in doing so.

Broken Comb—How to Replace the Teeth.

If one or more teeth are broken, they can be replaced and be as good as new if it is done properly. When several are broken side by side, it is sometimes very difficult to tune them accurately, as it often

9

occurs that the scale is not marked under the comb, and we may not know how many notes are to be tuned on the same pitch, since the teeth of the musical box are not tuned in regular succession like a piano or organ. In such a case the tone is to be guessed, and your success will greatly depend on your musical talent.

How to Replace a Point.

If only the point of a tooth is broken, it is not necessary to replace the whole tooth, but only its point, as shown in Fig. 5. Raise

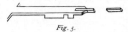

Fig. 5.

the broken tooth by introducing a wire under it and resting it on the others; then with a blowpipe take the temper out of the end of the tooth, just enough so that you can make a small notch with a narrow file; next fit into it a piece of tempered steel, and solder it in place with a small soldering iron; the point must then be finished in the manner explained further on. If the tooth is loaded with lead at the end, care should be taken not to unsolder it.

How to Replace a Tooth.

If only one tooth is broken, take a piece of steel and make one of the same shape as the broken or adjacent ones, with the point a little longer and wider; but a heel must be made as indicated in Fig. 6. Then temper the new tooth, drawing it to a dark blue, in order that

it can vibrate and at the same time be filed; then scrape clean its heel, so that the solder may flow. In the steel block

Fig. 6.

of the comb make a notch with a file of the same width as the tooth, as shown in Fig. 7. Put it in place firmly enough to remain in position while it is being soldered. Then

10

take a heavy soldering iron, such as is used by tinners, and solder it with soft solder and soldering fluid, care being taken that the solder runs all around it. Wash the comb in water, then in alcohol, to remove all traces of acid, and scrape off all superfluous solder. If the job is done properly the new tooth will sound as well as the others, and hardly show the mending.

In scraping, as well as in tuning, great care must be exercised not to file the other teeth, for very little filing, or even rubbing, with emery paper will lower the pitch, and, consequently, put them out of tune.

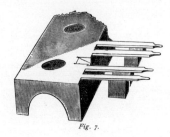

Fig. 7.

N. B.—When several teeth are broken side by side it will be necessary to procure from a material dealer a piece made in the factory for that purpose, having the same number of teeth and matching it in every way.

The tooth must then be finished and tuned by filing underneath. Finish the point of the tooth by filing it to its proper width to correspond with the other points, and at the same time to bring it exactly midway between the two adjacent points. To make the point of the exact *length*, hold the comb perpendicularly with the teeth resting on a piece of plate glass. This will readily show how much the point is to be reduced in order to bring it to the proper length. Be very careful not to make it too short.

11

Now bring the point of the tooth exactly to **the same** *level*. If it has to be lowered or moved to the right or left, it can be done in the following manner:

To shift it to the right or left, place the tooth so that it will rest evenly on a flat and tempered anvil (see Fig. 8), and strike on the left to move it to the right, with the sharp end of the hammer (two or three strokes will suffice), and *vice versa;* the tooth must be struck on the under side. To raise or lower a tooth, the anvil must be tempered and cut like the edge of a file (see Fig. 9); hold the tooth evenly on the anvil, strike a few blows with a small, flat, *soft* hammer, and the tooth will bend upward. Great care must be taken when doing this, since a tooth is easily broken with the hammer.

The comb now being repaired, replace it on the bed plate, and the line of dots made on every cylinder will enable you to see whether the new points are in their proper positions. To be fully convinced make the box play a few tunes, and if the pins pass in the centre of the points they are true; if not, correct as directed above.

Fig. 8.

Fig. 9.

Tuning New Teeth.

The next thing to be done is to tune the new tooth or teeth. Take a piece of brass a little thicker than the width of the tooth, fasten it in the vise, and make a notch lengthwise on the edge, as long as the tooth; then rest the tooth in it, with the under side up, and press the comb down, so as to make the tooth rise enough to be filed without danger of filing the others.

Use a square file, made for that purpose, about a quarter of an inch wide and six inches long, and sold by us. File the tooth near the point to raise the pitch, and near the heel to lower it. With regard to the teeth loaded with lead, it is only necessary to add to or cut from it.

12

If the tooth needs a hairspring, put it on before tuning, or the weight of the pin will alter the pitch.

If no teeth are broken, see if any of the points are worn; if so take an oil stone as long as possible and perfectly flat, and pass it two or three times over all the points, then examine whether they have all been touched, and repeat the operation, if necessary. A piece of plate glass with powdered oil stone will be still better.

If the box is old or has "run," the points are generally rounded, and the teeth are liable to slip aside from the pins, making a bad sound. The point must be flat underneath to give a clear, good tone.

Hairsprings.

We now come to the part most troublesome to watchmakers; that is, repairing the hairsprings or dampers, and for this reason we shall enter into some details. As they are of the first importance to insure the proper performance of the box and are easily damaged, the repairer must understand their use thoroughly and how to shape them, otherwise the box will give certain disagreeable, whistling sounds, which greatly impair the effect of the music.

This squeaking sound is produced by the sudden stopping of the vibrations of the steel tooth, caused by several pins coming in close succession under the same tooth; and the object of the hairspring is to stop these vibrations gradually, before the point of the tooth rests on the pin. Consequently, for the lower notes, which are loaded with lead, the hairspring must be stiffer than for the higher; but in repairing, it is easy to find the proper strength as generally only a few are missing, and it can be ascertained from the one next to it. The steel for hairsprings is sold by the foot, and numbered according to strength from No. 1 to 8, No. 1 being the stiffest.

Replacing Hairsprings.

Examine each hairspring, and break off all those that are worn or have a sharp bend (these having been caught between the tooth and pin); then place your comb upside down on a smooth piece of board about the width and length of the comb. Remove the pins

13

which held in place the hairspring, with a pair of small flat pliers, or by pushing them out from the back, and lay them on the bench *in the same order in which you take them out* so as to know where they belong, for if changed they may alter the pitch of the teeth. Then take your hairspring wire, introduce it in the hole, push the pin in firmly and cut the steel one-eighth of an inch longer than the point, and so on, for each one. When this is done straighten one of the original hairsprings to ascertain its exact length. To do this we use a gauge made of sheet brass bent at a right angle and of a graduated thickness on the edge (see Fig. 10). Place the gauge under the comb, as it lies inverted with the angle resting against the points of the

Fig. 10.

teeth, and the straightened hairspring projecting over the edge of the gauge. Move the gauge to either side until the projection of the hairspring corresponds with the thickness of the gauge, and note the exact place on the gauge. Having thus obtained the measure, cut the other hairsprings the same length, by resting the cutting pliers against the edge of the gauge. Use a sharp pair of pliers for this operation. It is important to have the hairsprings all of the same length, or they will be irregular in shape.

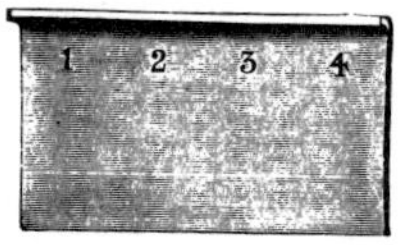

14

Shaping the Hairspring.

Fig. 11.

To give the shape and curve to the hairspring we use a pair of tweezers made for that purpose (see Fig. 11). Hold the comb upside down, horizontally, in your left hand; then, with the tweezers pressing lightly the hairspring, describe a curve with them, allowing the hairspring to slide slowly through. Repeat this operation two or three times, until it is of the same shape as those which have not been disturbed, or as Fig. 12. The hairspring must come nearly to the end of the point, but without touching it; the curve should be even and without any sharp bend, so that it will recede before the pin and press upon the point of the tooth, stopping gradually its vibrations (see Fig. 12). Any jeweller or watchmaker having musical boxes to repair ought to practice this operation until successful, since it is the greatest difficulty in repairing these instruments, and a good workman can always command high prices for this kind of work.

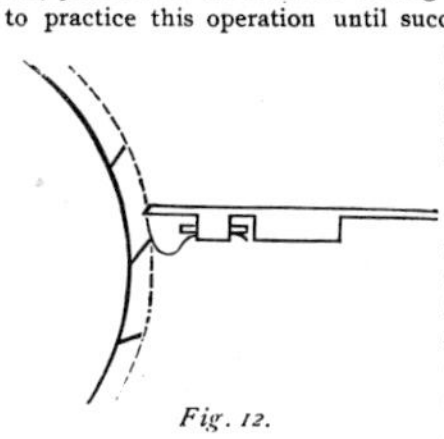

Besides those provided with a hairspring the comb has a number of teeth furnished with sections of barbs from ordinary hen feathers, which answer the same purpose as the hairspring for stiffer teeth. To replace them, follow the same directions as for small musical boxes.

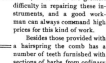

Fig. 12.

15

Squeaking in Small Musical Boxes.

In small musical boxes the most common defect is the squeaking of the comb. This occurs as in large instruments, when the dampers under the points are worn or have dropped off. Instead of hairsprings, however, barbs from ordinary hen feathers are used as dampers, but do not last as long, and must therefore be replaced more frequently.

Lay the comb inverted on a small wooden block, and with a knife or screw-driver scrape carefully the old dampers and shellac. The dampers should be cut from the wing feather of a hen, with a sharp pair of scissors; Fig. 13 shows the only serviceabe part of the feathers. Since barbs differ in width, they must be selected so as to correspond exactly to the width of the points.

The composition used for gluing the dampers is a thick solution of shellac in alcohol, with the addition of a little fine sealing-wax, to prevent snapping in the cold.

Hold the strip of barbs that have been cut, between the thumb and index finger of the left hand, and with a pair of tweezers separate one barb after the other, dip the *wide end* in the shellac and lay the flat side on the point, leaving the end projecting beyond the tooth. When all the dampers have been so placed and before the shellac is dry, see that each one is straight and covers the point. Then set it aside to dry, which will take about twelve hours. When dry, they are cut *even* with the points, using a pair of scissors.

In replacing the comb, follow the same directions as for large boxes (page 19).

PART TO BE USED.

Fig 13.

16

Repairing the Fly-Wheel Train.

We are now ready to examine the fly-wheel and train, and make the necessary repairs. If the box will run let it run down *entirely*, and to make sure that the mainspring is completely uncoiled, lift the click on the barrel bridge. If it will not run, let down the main spring as you would that of a clock, by holding the lever and raising the click. We repeat it again here: *Never unscrew the fly-wheel or any part of the mechanism without ascertaining if the mainspring is entirely uncoiled*; and, particularly, *when the comb is in place.* When you are thus sure that there is no danger, remove the fly-wheel. Now see if the cap jewel is worn by the point of the fly-wheel staff, which is often the case; if so, put in a new one, or, if you have none, shift the plate so that it will work on another spot, *but be sure to repolish the end of the fly-wheel staff*, which must be rounded, or the cap jewel will soon be worn again and cause the box to stop or go irregularly. See if the pivot holes, and especially the upper ones, are not too large; if so, bush them, or they will cause the fly-wheel to rattle when in the box. See also that the fly-wheel check is not too loose, nor so stiff as to check the fly-wheel too suddenly.

Then see if the small wheel next to the fly-wheel is in good condition; if the teeth are worn or have been injured, replace it at once, for in trying to repair it you will only lose your time. In placing the new wheel, rivet it well so that there will be no danger of its getting loose, for this may cause the ruin of the box. See also that the other wheel is well riveted. Then have all parts well cleaned as you would a French clock; put them together. Oil all the pivot holes and the fly-wheel staff where in contact with the wheel. Now try if they will turn freely; if not, adjust the depthing of the fly-wheel by turning the screw at the back of the bridge, then lay it aside until later.

Mainspring Barrel.

Next, examine the mainspring barrel. See that the click work on the lever bridge is in good order, and that the hole in the bridge is not too large. In removing the stopwork make a mark in the arbor so as to be able to replace the male stopwork in the same position. If the mainspring is stuck on account of bad oil, it must be taken out and cleaned. Oil the mainspring before replacing it in the barrel;

17

put the arbor with the barrel containing the mainspring on a lathe and polish it clean, and polish all the parts and put them together. Use good clock oil for the spring as well as everywhere. The click screws must be screwed in firmly and have a little oil on them, or they will work loose and may cause an accident. The lever must work a little stiff. A piece of drum-skin is to be placed between the lever and washer to lessen the friction, and all parts should be oiled. Leave the female stopwork to be placed later on, as we shall show.

The Cylinder.

RE-CEMENTING THE CYLINDER.

In order to secure the pins as well as to give body to the cylinder, which is of thin metal, it is partially filled with cement. This cement must adhere closely to the circumference, for if from heat or any other cause it should become detached, the box in playing will give a dull metallic sound, which can be remedied in the following manner :

Take all apart, including the start wheel. Then oil well the *cylinder-shaft* and *pin* with common oil, to prevent the cement from adhering to them when melted, and put it on a lathe large enough for that purpose ; see that it is well secured but turns freely, with the points oiled. Now take a shallow but wide tin-pan, put some alcohol in it and light it, keeping it under the cylinder, revolving the cylinder slowly with the hand and moving the pan from right to left in order to heat it uniformly. When you see the cement come out of the pin-hole at the right end of the cylinder, remove the pan and make the cylinder to revolve as rapidly as possible in order to drive the cement against the sides of the cylinder. As it gradually cools, revolve slower until it is cold enough to be taken in the hand (for a large cylinder, this requires about half an hour). Take it quickly from the lathe, pull out the shaft and remove the cement from around the pin-hole while it is soft, still turning it in the hand ; now let it cool entirely (half a day at least). The whole operation must be performed very carefully, as the least mishap may cause a disaster. If over-heated, the left end of the cylinder might be forced out, and the cement escape. If cooled too suddenly the cement will not adhere well to the metal. When perfectly cold the cylinder is to be polished,

18

and the best way to do this is to place it on a lathe, the same way as for re-cementing. Take a mixture of powdered scouring brick, or tripoli and alcohol, and spread it all over the cylinder ; then, with a wide, stiff brush pressing on the cylinder, make it revolve very rapidly, and in a few minutes it will be as bright as new. Polish until the alcohol is entirely evaporated and the cylinder perfectly bright and clean. Then take a sheet of thick paper, the width of the cylinder, and wrap it around, so that in handling, the warmth of the hand will not be felt. It is useless to say that in handling the cylinder the greatest care must be taken not to bend or break the pins.

Suppressing a Tune.

When only one tune has been ruined by a "*run*," it is best to suppress it altogether, which may be done as follows : While that air is playing make a mark on the side of the star wheel at the spot where the cylinder stud rests ; then take it apart and file the portion marked to the height of the preceding tune, which it will repeat. When the damaged tune is either the first or the last, you can substitute any of the others instead, by filing or soldering a piece of brass of the proper height. Or, by making that tooth of the star wheel longer, the tune will be skipped altogether. See that the end of the stud is properly rounded and polished, so as to slide easily over the incline of the star wheel.

Putting the Works Together.

When everything is nicely polished and cleaned you may commence putting together. The cylinder shaft must be well cleaned, and the cement carefully removed from it. Screw on the star wheel with a drop of oil under it ; then pass an oiled rag over the polished part of the shaft with just enough oil to moisten it, but never put any oil there, for in contact with the cement it will thicken so as to prevent its sliding readily. Clean the holes of the cylinder, making sure that no cement is left in or near them. Put it in place with the spiral spring and pinion, the latter with the number on the same side as the one stamped on the shaft ; try if the cylinder slides easily on the shaft. Screw on the bridges and see if the shaft is perfectly free without the

19

least end-shake, for if there were any it would be impossible to make the box play properly. In this case give a light tap with a hammer on the side of one of the bridges, and try again the play. If too stiff, strike on the end of the shaft with a piece of brass so as not to injure the point. Now put on the barrel, screw it firmly and see that the clicks work properly. Then screw on the fly-wheel train, and wind the spring a little to see if the fly-wheel turns freely. Put the stop piece in its place on the train-bridge, and see that when the pin falls in the notch of the cylinder wheel the other end stops the fly-wheel instantly.

This done, wind the spring fully, and let it run down a quarter of a turn, enough to place the female stopwork in its proper place, so that, in winding, the strain will be on the stopwork and not on the mainspring. If the male stopwork is not placed properly, turn it towards another side of arbor. Now put in its place the steel piece that causes the air to change ; let the box run, and see if the cylinder shifts easily and the star wheel has moved just enough for the stud to rest on the flat space ; if it goes too far it will make the pins catch on the edge of the points of the comb, or sometimes two tunes will play at a time, making a horrible discord and spoiling the hair-springs.

To Put the Comb in Place.

We are now ready to replace the comb, which has been previously set in order. Clean the upper surface with a little oil, and give it the finishing touches by rubbing in the direction of the teeth with the palm of the hand. Now put on the comb (the box being stopped at the end of a tune), and fasten it with only three or four of the screws, as it will probably be necessary to take it off several times. Let it run slowly, checking the fly-wheel with your finger, and look if the pins pass directly under the centre of the points ; if not, turn the cylinder stud in or out. If it is of a kind that cannot be turned, shift the comb with a good-sized hammer, striking on a large nail or piece of soft iron resting against one of the screw holes. See also that the teeth of the same chord fall at the same instant at both ends of the comb. The end falling late is too near ; shift it back. Be careful not to place the comb too close to the cylinder, for the hairsprings will get spoiled, the sound of the box will be harsh, and should the steel be hard-tempered some of the teeth might break. If too far, on the

20

other hand, the box will not sound loud enough, and, the hairsprings not working, the box will squeak.

Now, see how the hairsprings work. If they have been shaped as directed, they will not require much alteration. But if any of the hairsprings have not been properly shaped it will be now detected. Remember that they must come as near as possible to the end of the point without touching it. See also that no pins are bent to the right or left, else they will catch the points in the wrong tune and make a disagreeable noise ; they must be straightened. Do not mind a few broken pins, they will not be noticed ; but if bent, and catching the wrong point, they cannot fail to attract attention.

If the pins should pass in the centre of the points on all tunes but one, the star wheel has been injured ; punch it on the side so as to raise the spot where the cylinder stud rests.

If you have a musical box with two or more combs, care must be taken that all the notes of the same chord fall at the same instant on all the combs. To ascertain this, hold the fly-wheel with the finger, and let it play very slowly, and you will be better able to see if they do so ; but always fix one at a time, never attempt to set two combs at once. In this way also, it is much easier to detect any defect, either from hairsprings or bent pins. When the combs are in proper position and the hairsprings all fixed, put in all the screws and fasten them very firmly, or the box will not sound well. Remember that in musical boxes every screw must be driven as firmly as possible.

Now put the movement back in the case and the four screws that secure it, but without screwing them in entirely ; slip in the metal wedges opposite the screws, and drive in the screws hard. If any of the wedges are loose put in thicker ones, for the bed plate must press firmly against the box, or it will lose much of its tone. See that the start and change pieces are not too loose on the sideboard, then put it in place as well as the one on the left side.

Now listen while it plays, and if there is any rattling or disagreeable noise it is caused by something loose about the box, that vibrates when a corresponding note of the comb plays—either the washers of the case screws, the lock or any metallic appendage, or something lying loose in the bottom of the case. The lock should be well clogged with wax or grease to prevent rattling.

If the musical box has bells, see that the hammers stand neither too near nor too far.

21

Finally, take a piece of wide broken mainspring about ten inches long, and oil it well on the convex side. Then, while the box is playing, pass it over the steel pins of the cylinder, in order to prevent wear and a screeching noise. Care should be taken, however, that the oil does not spread over the surface of the cylinder.

Recapitulation.

For better understanding, let us recapitulate the order in which the work is to be done :

(1) Examine the box to see whether it is worth repairing ; see that it has not "*run*."

(2) See if the cylinder needs re-cementing ; this is frequently necessary in this climate.

(3) Repair the comb, in case any teeth are broken.

(4) Examine the hairsprings, and replace them where necessary.

(5) Repair mechanism, from fly-wheel to barrel, and clean it.

(6) Put together in the following order : Cylinder, mainspring barrel, fly-wheel train, finally the comb.

There is a great variety in the sizes and styles of musical boxes, but the above instructions will apply to nearly all of them, and will enable any intelligent watchmaker to repair them satisfactorily.

22

All Musical Boxes not provided with our Safety Check are liable to this accident.

23

NO MORE RUINED MUSICAL BOXES

WITH JACOT'S

PATENT ✠ SAFETY ✠ CHECK.

JACOT'S PATENT SAFETY CHECK.

Musical boxes are operated by one or several powerful springs, the speed being controlled and regulated by a series of wheels and pinions terminating in a fly-wheel. Now if the fly-wheel be broken or removed, or any of the wheels get loose from the pinion when the spring is wound, the cylinder will revolve with lightning rapidity, causing the partial or complete ruin of the instrument, by bending and breaking the pins on the cylinder as well as the teeth of the comb, as illustrated on page 22.

24

In order to prevent this destructive "*run*," (which, as dealers well know, is constantly occurring), we have invented and patented an attachment, illustrated on preceding page, which for simplicity of construction and perfection of action can never be equalled.

Secured rigidly to one end of the shaft of the cylinder is a ratchet wheel A, formed as clearly shown in the engraving. Pivoted so as to engage with the teeth of this wheel is a pawl B, having a weighted outer end ; the upper part of the inner end of the pawl is formed to fit the recesses of the teeth, and the lower part is so formed that each tooth, as it moves by, will raise the outer or weighted end. This movement brings the upper inner end of the pawl into one of the recesses, but before the tooth touches it, the lower part is freed from its tooth, allowing the weighted end to drop and thereby remove the upper part away from the wheel, as indicated by the dotted lines. This motion is, of course, made possible only by the slow movement of the cylinder. But if, from any cause, the cylinder should move rapidly, the pawl would be brought into engagement with one of the teeth of the wheel, and the motion of the cylinder would be instantly arrested. The device, as will be understood, is positive and absolutely reliable in its actions, and can be placed upon any instrument without necessitating a change in the arrangement of the parts.

Another important feature of this attachment, which will be appreciated by watchmakers, is that it can be used for checking the cylinder while the fly-wheel is removed for cleaning or repairing, thus saving the trouble of letting down the spring.

☞ To release the check after the fly-wheel is replaced, turn the latter a few times *backward* and the check will fall off itself. ☜

N. B.—All our boxes are provided with this indispensable attachment which we hold exclusively.

25

MATERIAL FOR LARGE MUSICAL BOXES.

BEFORE ORDERING MATERIAL, READ CAREFULLY THE DIRECTIONS ON INSIDE BACK COVER.

NET CASH PRICES.

No.	Article		Each.	Dozen.
1	Mainspring, 3/4-in. wide, 1 9/16-in. diam.,		$0.30	
2	" 7/8-in. " 1 7/8-in. "		.50	
3	" 1 1/8-in. " 2 1/4-in. "		.80	
4	" 1 3/16-in. " 2 1/4-in. "		1.00	
5	" 1 15/16-in. " 2 7/8-in. "		1.25	
6	" 1-in. " 1 7/8-in. "	for boxes with bells.	.70	
7	" 1 3/8-in. " 2 3/8-in. "	"	1.25	
8	" 1 5/16-in. " 2 5/8-in. "	"	1.25	
9	" 1 1/2-in. " 3 1/16-in. "	"	2.50	
10	" 1 5/16-in. " 2 5/8-in. "	Interchangeable cyl. boxes.	1.25	
11	" 1 3/4-in. " 3 1/2-in. "	"	3.50	
12	Male Stopwork for 6-inch cylinder box and under,		.15	$1.20
13	" " 13-inch " "		.20	1.60
14	" " 17-inch "		.30	2.40
15	" " extra large boxes,		.40	3.20
16	Female " 6-inch cylinder box and under,		.15	1.20
17	" " 13-inch " "		.20	1.60
18	" " 17-inch " "		.30	2.40
19	" " extra large boxes,		.40	3.20
20	Ratchet Wheel, 5/8-inch diameter,		.10	.80
21	" 3/4 " "		.15	1.20
22	" 7/8 " "		.20	1.60
23	" 1 " "		.25	2.00
24	" 1 1/8 " "		.30	2.40
25	" 1 1/4 " "		.40	3.20
26	" 1 7/16 " "		.50	4.00
27	Click, for 6-inch cylinder box and under,		.10	.80
28	" 13-inch " "		.15	1.20
29	" 17-inch " and over,		.20	1.60

26

MATERIAL FOR LARGE MUSICAL BOXES—Continued.

No.	Article	Each	Dozen.
30	Cylinder Pinion, 17/32-inch diameter,	$0.20	$1.60
31	" 21/32-inch "	.30	2.40
32	" 23/32-inch "	.40	3.20
33	" 15/16-inch "	.50	4.00
34	" 1 1/16-inch "	.70	5.60
35	" 1 3/8-inch "	.80	6.40
36	First Wheel, with pinion,	.50	4.00
37	" " extra large,	.75	6.00
38	" without pinion,	.25	2.00
39	" " extra large,	.40	3.20
40	Second Wheel, with pinion,	.40	3.20
41	" " extra large,	.75	6.00
42	" without pinion,	.20	1.60
43	" " extra large,	.35	2.80
44	Endless Screw, for 4 3/8-in. cylinder box, 1 11/32-in. long,	.25	2.00
45	" 4 7/8 to 6-in. " 1 15/32-in. long,	.30	2.40
46	" 8 1/8 to 13-in. " 1 21/32-in. long,	.35	2.80
47	" 13-in. cyl. interch. box, 2 9/32-in. long,	.50	4.00
48	" 17 3/8-in. cyl. interch. box, 2 9/16-in. long,	.75	6.00

Measure Endless Screw, from shoulder of lower pivot to end of the upper pivot.

No.	Article	Each	Dozen.
49	Endless Screw Fan,	.25	2.00
50	Click Spring, small,	.05	.40
51	" large,	.10	.60
52	Click Screw,	.05	.30
53	Stopwork Screw,	.05	.30
54	Comb Screw,	.05	.30
55	Cylinder Bridge Screw,	.05	.30
56	Barrel Bridge Screw,	.05	.30
57	Fly-wheel Train Screw,	.05	.30
58	Fly-wheel Bridge Screw,	.05	.30
59	Click Spring and Cap Jewel Plate Screw,	.03	.20
60	Casing Screw, small (to fasten movement in case),	.10	.80
61	Casing Screw, large (to fasten movement in case),	.15	1.20
62	Hairspring Wire, per foot,	.05	
63	Cap Jewel,	.10	.75
64	Piece for mending Broken Combs, per tooth,	.10	.80

27

MATERIAL FOR LARGE MUSICAL BOXES—Continued.

No.	Article	Each.	Dozen.
65	Pins for Cylinder, per 200,	$0.05	
66	Lock for Large Boxes, small,	.25	$2.00
67	Lock for Large Boxes, large,	.35	
68	Key for Lock,	.10	
69	Steel Washers for Comb,		.15
70	Star Wheel to Change Tunes in Large Box,	.35	3.20
71	Fly-wheel Check,	.05	.30
72	Bracket to hold open the Lids of Large Boxes,	.40	3.20
73	Hasp, small,	.10	.80
74	Hasp, large,	.15	1.20

Nos. 73 and 74 are intended to remedy the shrinkage of the lids of large and small boxes by moving forward the stud.

28

MATERIAL FOR SMALL MUSICAL BOXES.

No.	Article	Each.	Dozen.
100	Mainspring for 1-Tune Box,	$0.10	$0.80
101	Mainspring for 2, 3 and 4-Tune Box,	.15	1.20
102	Mainspring for 6 and 8-Tune Box,	.20	1.80
103	Barrel Arbor and Wheel, complete,	.30	2.40
104	Barrel Arbor,	.10	.80
105	Barrel Wheel,	.10	.80
106	Click Spring,	.05	.30
107	Click Spring, flat,	.05	.30
108	Click,	.05	.30
109	Male Stopwork,	.05	.30
110	Female Stopwork,	.05	.30
111	Cylinder Wheel,	.10	.80
112	Cylinder Pinion,	.05	.35
113	First Wheel, with Pinion,	.15	1.20
114	Second Wheel, with Pinion,	.15	1.20
115	Third Wheel, with Long Pinion,	.15	1.20
116	Third Wheel, without Pinion,	.05	[illegible]
117	Endless Screw, complete,	.15	1.20
118	Steel Cap Disk,		.15
119	Comb Screw,	.05	.30
120	Barrel Screws,		.15
121	Casing Screws,		.15
122	Fly-wheel Bridge Screws,		.15
123	Sundry Screws, assorted,		.15
124	Winding Key,	.05	[illegible]
125	Endless Screw for Crank Boxes,	.15	1.20
126	Crank for Small Boxes,	.05	.30
127	Files for Tuning Mended Combs,	.35	2.80
128	Files for Notching Combs,	.25	2.00
129	Files for Notching Teeth of Combs,	.15	1.20
130	Tweezers for Shaping Hairsprings,	.50	4.00
131	Gauge for Measuring Hairsprings,	.25	2.00

29
Material for Large Musical Boxes.

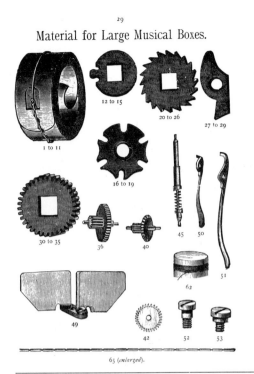

1 to 11
12 to 15
20 to 26
27 to 29
16 to 19
30 to 35
36
40
45
50
51
62
49
42
52
53
65 (*enlarged*).

30

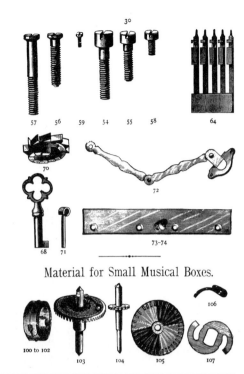

57   56   59   54   55   58   64
70
72
68   71   73-74

Material for Small Musical Boxes.

106
100 to 102
103   104   105   107

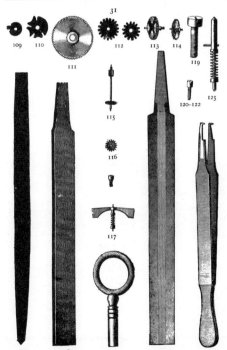

31

109   110   112   113   114
111
119
115
120-122
125
116
117
127   128   124   120   130

32

MATERIAL FOR SMALL MUSICAL BOXES.
NEW STYLE.

No.		Each.	Dozen.
132	Barrel Bridge,	$0.10	
133	Winding Key to Screw on Arbor.	.10	$0.60
134	Endless Screw, with Fan,	.20	2.00
135	Click Spring,	.05	.30
136	Endless Screw, with Wheel,	.25	2.50
137	Endless Screw, Cap Plate,	.05	.30

MATERIAL FOR SMALL MUSICAL BOXES.
NEW STYLE.

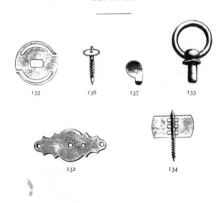

135   136   137   133
132   134

PAILLARD'S MUSICAL BOXES.

STYLES No 601 & 602.

Instructions for changing the Cylinders.

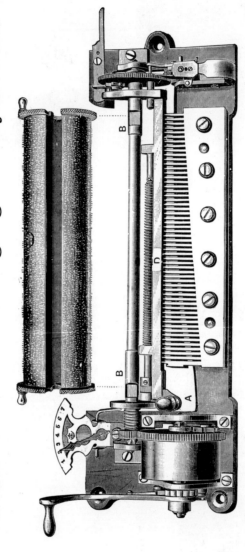

To take out the Cylinder, push the knob A to the left, at the same time pressing downward until it catches; then withdraw the Cylinder.

To insert another Cylinder, slide it in and over the slots B B, pressing it toward the comb, and lift knob A, which will push the Cylinder in place. The box will not start unless these instructions are properly followed.

It is important that no attempt should be made either to take out or insert a Cylinder before the tune is finished, when the bar D rests in front of the comb.

Paillard produced the unusual type of interchangeable cylinder movement shown at the left. It was patented by A. Junod & Co. of Ste Croix in 1890. The cylinders had full-length slots in them and were dropped saddle fashion over the arbor which remained fixed in the mechanism. Mention has been made of Jerome Thibouville-Lamy, the famous French maker and distributor of musical instruments. Here from their 1905 catalogue are pages relating to mechanical instruments sold from their London showrooms.

ESTABLISHED 1790.

Manufacturers of Musical Instruments
OF EVERY DESCRIPTION, AND OF
HARMONIC STRINGS.

JEROME THIBOUVILLE=LAMY & Co.,
10, Charterhouse Street,
Factories at Grenelle, Mirecourt, and La Couture.
LONDON, E.C.

Hors Concours Member of the Jury Universal Paris
Exhibitions, 1878, 1889, 1900.

Telegraphic Address: "TIBOUVIL, LONDON."

This Catalogue cancels all previous publications.
— 1905. —

VIEW OF OUR PARIS SHOWROOMS

PIANISTA THIBOUVILLE.

View of the Pianista placed before the Piano.

This apparatus can be adapted to any piano either of English or foreign make.

By means of the Pianista one can play the piano with expression, without any knowledge of music whatever.

View of the Pianista ready to be played.

LATEST IMPROVEMENTS.

Pianista Patented S. G. D. G.

JEROME THIBOUVILLE-LAMY'S patent **Pianista** with double pneumatic action has numerous advantages over the old system.

Besides the simplicity of the mechanism, which is a guarantee for durability, the double bellows give a greater power of touch and more precision in the fingering. The expression is also rendered more effective and the resistance of the handle is greatly diminished.

The direct action of the small bellows on the valve of the large ones reduces by more than ¾ the pressure of the notes of the Pianista; which permitting the use of merely paper, diminishes considerably the price of the music.

The result is therefore :—1st, Economy; 2nd, Strength and Durability; 3rd, Execution—clear and expressive.

The **Pianista** far excels any other invention giving the facility to play the piano without the knowledge of music.

Very elegant in appearance, and rather small in size, the Pianista can be adapted to all pianos. The only fixing required being the adjustment to the key-board of the Instrument (*see illustration*) after having regulated its height by means of screws fitted for that purpose.

Pianistas—*Continued.*

When adapted, it can very easily be taken off, in order to allow the playing of the piano in the ordinary manner.

Perforated cardboard is used with the pianista, the perforations represent exactly the notes of the piece of music which is to be performed. This cardboard is placed on the left side of the apparatus, each tune being bound as in a book, and drawn along by the turning of the handle and refolded into a book again, after having met the mechanism, destined to put into motion the keys which are to play the tune.

This arrangement of the music is simple and makes it easy for transport, especially for sending abroad.

The mechanism of the apparatus is made for shipment to distant countries; it is perfectly strong and durable.

But it is mainly due to the fact of its executing the different variations of forte and piano — a success which is not easily obtained, even by a clever artist—that gives an exceptional and quite artistic value to our invention : to obtain this, it is sufficient to press upon a lever placed on the left side of the apparatus; all the graduations can be passed through from the softest pianissimo to the strongest forte. Therefore we assure our customers that it is most curious to observe how surprising the music is performed when produced through the pianista, and how identical it is to that played on the key-board by the fingers of an artist : in short, the delusion is so complete, that it is very difficult on hearing, to judge whether the music is automatically produced, or is the genuine playing of a clever artist.

Superiority of the Jerome Thibouville-Lamy Pianista over the old or new inventions of apparatus to play the Piano mechanically.

If comparison is made between the various mechanical apparatus adaptable to the piano, numerous advantages will be found in favour of the THIBOUVILLE pianista.

Whatever the size or shape of the piano, one minute suffices to place the pianista in its position before the piano, or to remove it.

The THIBOUVILLE pianista is a mechanical construction which plays on the piano without any preparation ; the keys of the pianista touch the keys of the piano in the same capacity as an artist's fingers.

The THIBOUVILLE pianista being portable is useful for all combinations.

Mr. THIBOUVILLE'S invention (patented 1882) of the double pneumatic bellows adds to the pianista the inappreciable advantage of simplifying the mechanism, making it strong, and reducing by more than half the price of the music.

Since this invention we have sent some hundreds of pianistas to all parts of the globe, which have all arrived in perfect condition. It is indispensable in all houses where receptions or dances are held.

One can be assured that this instrument is easily understood.

We always have ready a number of these instruments and a large assortment of music : operas, romances, valses, polkas, mazurkas, etc.

Patent Improvement for instantaneously placing the Pianista before the Piano.

With this system no unnecessary trouble need now be taken with the revolving feet which serve to place the apparatus evenly on the floor. By means of a handle, applied to the top and under the small swing board on the right, the pianista is raised and the keys are promptly brought up to the proper height in a horizontal position, and in that position only the pianista works regularly and the trills and shades of the piano and forte are executed with facility.

The addition of this improvement increases the price of Pianistas ... ... £2.

To apply it to Pianistas already made the cost would be ... ... £4.

For Prices of Pianistas, see following Pages.

JEROME THIBOUVILLE-LAMY & Co., 10, CHARTERHOUSE STREET, LONDON, E.C.

JEROME THIBOUVILLE-LAMY & Co., 10, CHARTERHOUSE STREET, LONDON, E.C.

PIANISTA THIBOUVILLE—Continued.

This mechanical apparatus can be adapted to any piano, either of English or Foreign manufacture.

The pianista is easily adapted to all pianos, the only fixing required being the adjustment to the keyboard of the piano after the height has been regulated by means of the screw feet fitted for that purpose.

Numbers.		£ s. d.
948	Pianista, large size, new model, 54 notes, with double pneumatic action, fine rosewood or walnut case, with lid ... each	56 0 0
948B	" large size, extra fine case ...	60 0 0
949	" " imitation rosewood polished case, without lid	48 0 0
949B	" " dull varnish, without lid	46 0 0
	Extra for the new apparatus to fix instantaneously the Pianista before the piano, if applied while making the instrument	2 0 0
	Extra for apparatus applied to instruments already made	4 0 0
950	Books of perforated paper for the Pianista, tunes selected from catalogue ... per foot	0 0 8
	The same, but tunes not mentioned in catalogue ... "	0 2 8

PHONOGRAPHS.

"The Virtuose."

Style A.

Numbers.			£ s. d.
A	Phonograph, oak case, nickel horn, recorder and reproducer, crank handle ...	each	1 8 0
V	" "The Virtuose," all parts well nickel-plated, large brass horn, walnut case, recorder and special reproducer ...	"	3 10 0
	When the bell is removed the mechanism can be turned over and enclosed in the box with handle on top to carry by.		
	Pathé's moulded "B" records ...	per doz.	1 2 0

TUTORS.

		£ s. d.
Accordion, Concertina, Violin, Flute, or Mandolin ...	per doz., 13 as 12	0 7 0
Mandolin Tutor, by Fletcher (2/6) ...		1 10 0
" by Ellis (2/-) ...		1 10 0
Guitar Tutor," by Ellis (2/-) ...		1 10 0
Violin, in 24 lessons, by Weaver (1/-) ...		0 15 0
Zither Tutor, by Ellis (1/6) ...	each	0 2 2
American Organ Tutor (1/-) ...		0 1 3
Turner's Universal Banjo Tutor (1/-) ...	per doz., 13 as 12	0 15 0
five string (1/-) ...	"	0 15 0
A.G. Concertina Tutor. by Roylance (1/-) ...		0 15 0
English Concertina Tutor. by Roylance (1/-) ...		0 15 0
Violoncello Tutor. by Lindley (1/-) ...		0 15 0
Cornet " by Sheard (6d.) ...		0 7 0
Clarionet " by Westrop (1/-) ...		0 15 0
Nicholson's Flute School (2/6) ...	each	0 3 4

Musical Boxes—Continued.

SQUARE MUSICAL BOXES, with Handle, Superior Quality.

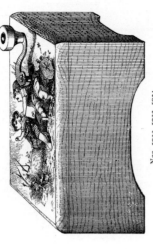

Nos. 5032, 5033, 5034.

Design showing actual size.

Our round and square musical boxes are unrivalled for quality. The prices vary according to the number of tongues.

MUSICAL BOXES, with Handle, 1 Air.

Numbers		£	s.	d.
5030	Square Musical Box, varnished wood, with chromo, 1 air, 12 tongues, per doz.	1	2	0
5031	" " " 1 " 18 " "	1	6	0
5032	" " " 1 " 28 " "	1	17	0
5033	" " " 1 " 36 " "	2	0	0
5034	" " " 1 " 48 " "	2	16	0

MUSICAL BOXES, with Handle, 2 Airs.

Numbers		£	s.	d.
5040	Square Musical Box, varnished wood, with chromo, 2 airs, 18 tongues, per doz.	1	15	0
5041	" " " 2 " 28 " "	2	4	0
5042	" " " 2 " 40 " "	3	10	0

MUSICAL BOXES, with Handle, 3 Airs.

Numbers		£	s.	d.
5045	Square Musical Box, varnished wood, with chromo, 3 airs, 28 tongues, per doz.	2	18	0
5046	" " " 3 " 36 " "	3	8	0
5047	" " " 3 " 50 " "	5	0	0

MUSICAL BOXES, with Handle, 4 Airs.

Numbers		£	s.	d.
5050	Square Musical Box, varnished wood, with chromo, 4 airs, 28 tongues, per doz.	3	12	0
5051	" " " 4 " 36 " "	4	0	0

MUSICAL BOXES.

ROUND MUSICAL BOXES, with Handle, Superior Quality.

Nos. 5006, 5007, 5008.

Nos. 5000, 5001.

Designs showing actual size.

Our round and square musical boxes with handle are unrivalled for quality. The prices vary according to the number of tongues.

MUSICAL BOXES, with Handle, 1 Air.

Numbers		£	s.	d.
5000	Round Musical Boxes, nickelled, with chromo, 1 air, 8 tongues, per doz.	0	17	6
5001	" " " 1 " 12 " "	0	19	6
5005	" " " 1 " 18 " "	1	4	0
5006	" " " 1 " 18 " "	1	6	0
5007	larger ... " nickelled, with chromo, 1 air, 28 tongues "	1	15	0
5008	" " " 1 " 36 " "	1	18	0

MUSICAL BOXES, with Handle, 2 Airs.

Numbers		£	s.	d.
5021	Round Musical Boxes, nickelled, with chromo, 2 airs, 18 tongues, per doz.	1	13	0
5011	" " " 2 " 28 " "	1	19	6
5022	larger ... " " " 2 " 28 " "	2	6	0
5028	nickelled, with chromo, 2 airs, 40 tongues "	3	4	0

MUSICAL BOXES, with Handle, 3 Airs.

Numbers		£	s.	d.
5025	Round Musical Boxes, nickelled, with chromo, 3 airs, 28 tongues, per doz.	2	18	0
5026	" " " 3 " 36 " "	3	8	0

Musical Boxes—Continued.

SMALL SPRING MUSICAL BOXES.

Winding with fixed key under box.

Numbers.			£ s. d.
5070	**Spring Musical Box,** white wood case, with chromo, 1 air, 19 tongues	each	0 8 0
5072	,, ,, ,, white wood case, with chromo, 2 airs, 28 tongues	,,	0 11 0
5073	,, ,, ,, white wood case, with chromo, 2 airs, 36 tongues, first quality	,,	0 12 0
5075	,, ,, ,, white wood case, with chromo, 3 airs, 36 tongues, first quality	,,	0 16 0
5077	,, ,, ,, white wood case, with chromo, 4 airs, 36 tongues, first quality	,,	0 18 0
5080	,, ,, ,, rich case, 2 airs, 41 tongues, first quality		0 16 0
5081	,, ,, ,, ,, 3 ,, 41 ,, ,,	,,	1 0 0
5082	,, ,, ,, ,, 4 ,, 41 ,, ,,	,,	1 4 0

MUSICAL BOXES, known as "Cartels."

(Good ordinary quality). Reduced size "Mignonette."

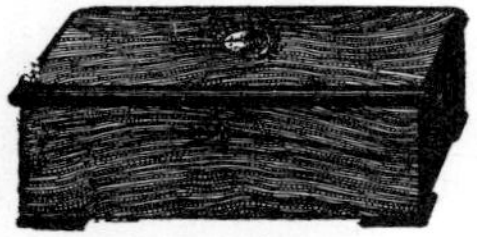

Nos. 5087 and 5089.

Length about 12 inches, width about 7 inches.

5087	**Musical Box,** "Mignonette," 4 airs, large barrel, 3¼ inches	each	1 14 0
5089	,, ,, ,, 6 ,, ,, 3¼ ,,	,,	1 16 0

No. 5092.

5091	**Musical Box,** nice case, 6 airs, 4¾ inches	each	2 2 0
5092	,, ,, ,, 6 ,, 4¾ ,, large barrel ...	,,	2 6 0

In "Cartel" musical boxes, the size in inches given after the number of airs, indicates the length of the barrel. The length of the barrel constitutes the real value of the musical box, as the comb, which is always the same size as the barrel, has a number of tongues proportioned to its length.

The box may be of small, medium, or large size without increasing much the price of the instrument, however it is preferable that the movement be set in a conveniently large box, but without exaggeration.

Musical Boxes—Continued.

MUSICAL BOXES, Good Quality.

Large box inlaid with Marqueterie.

Glass cover and lock.

Large barrel.

Powerful tone.

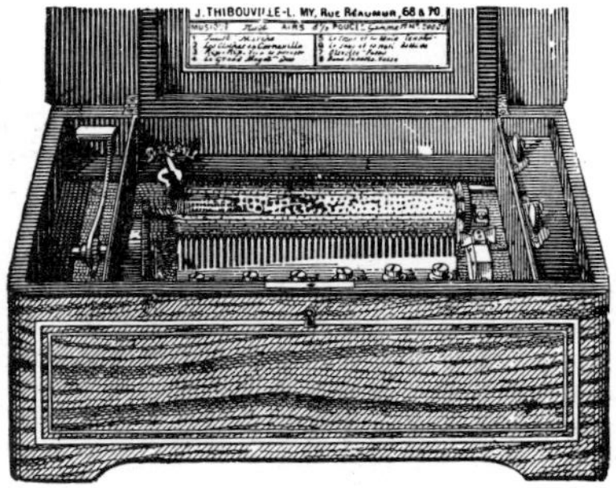

All our movements are nickel-plated and are fitted with tune indicator.

Numbers.			£ s. d.
5098	**Musical Box,** with glass cover and lock, 6 airs, 6 inches, inlaid case	each	3 0 0
	Same, with zither accompaniment	,,	3 6 0
5099	**Musical Box,** with glass cover and lock, 8 airs, 6 inches, inlaid case	,,	3 4 0
	Same, with zither accompaniment	,,	3 10 0
5100	**Musical Box,** with glass cover and lock, 8 airs, 8¼ inches, inlaid case	,,	3 15 0
	Same, with zither accompaniment	,,	4 5 0
5101	**Musical Box,** with glass cover and lock, 10 airs, 8¼ inches, inlaid case	,,	3 18 0
	Same, with zither accompaniment	,,	4 8 0
5102	**Musical Box,** with glass cover and lock, 12 airs, 10¾ inches, inlaid case	,,	5 10 0
	Same, with zither accompaniment	,,	6 6 0

MUSICAL BOXES "CLASSIQUES" First Quality.

We specially recommend the musical boxes styled "classiques." The barrels are of a regular length and possess a sufficient number of teeth to prevent jarring when a note repeats quickly, which is difficult to stop in the small instruments possessing only a limited number of teeth.

5114	**Musical Box "Classique" first quality,** fine inlaid rosewood case, with lock, 8 airs, 9 inches	each	4 12 0
	Same, with zither	,,	5 2 0
5115	**Musical Box "Classique" first quality,** fine inlaid rosewood case, with lock, 8 airs, 10¾ inches	,,	5 0 0
	Same, with zither	,,	5 12 0
5116	**Musical Box "Classique" first quality,** fine inlaid rosewood case, with lock, 10 airs, 10¾ inches	,,	6 0 0
	Same, with zither	,,	6 12 0
5117	**Musical Box "Classique" first quality,** fine inlaid rosewood case, with lock, 12 airs, 12¾ inches	,,	6 10 0
	Same, with zither	,,	7 10 0

Musical Boxes—Continued.

MUSICAL BOXES with Visible Bells.

Powerful Tone, Rich Case, Base Stand and Handles.

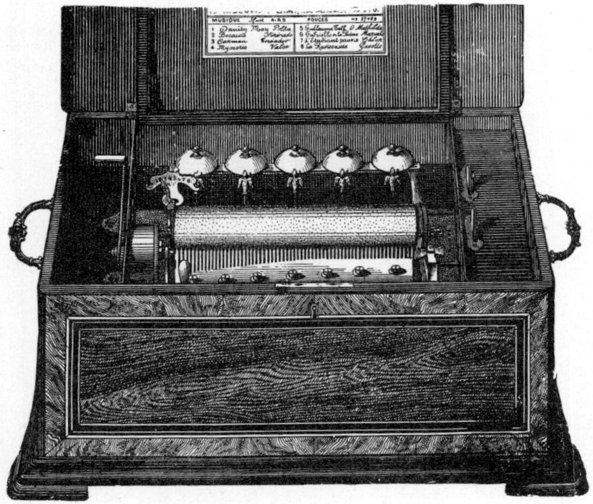

Numbers.			£ s. d.
5122	**Musical Box,** with bells visible, 6 airs, 4¾ inches	each	4 8 0
5126	,, ,, ,, 8 ,, 6 ,, ...	,,	5 0 0
5130	,, ,, ,, 10 ,, 10¾ ,, ...	,,	8 10 0
5133	,, ,, ,, 12 ,, 12¾ ,, ...	,,	11 0 0
	Extra for zither accompaniment :		
	To musical boxes 4¾ins. to 6ins.	,,	0 10 0
	,, 10¾ins. to 12¾ins.	,,	0 12 0

MUSICAL BOXES with Drum and Bells visible.

Numbers.			£ s. d.
5140	**Musical Box,** with drum and bells visible, 6 airs, 8¼ inches ...	each	5 10 0
5141	,, ,, ,, ,, 8 ,, 9 ,, ...	,,	6 6 0
5142	,, ,, ,, ,, 8 ,, 10¾ ,, ...	,,	8 0 0
5143	,, ,, ,, ,, 8 ,, 12¾ ,, 1st quality	,,	9 10 0
5145	,, ,, ,, ,, 10 ,, 10¾ ,, ...	,,	10 10 0
5146	,, ,, ,, ,, 10 ,, 12¾ ,, 1st quality	,,	12 0 0
5148	,, ,, ,, ,, 12 ,, 14¾ ,, ...	,,	12 18 0
5149	,, ,, ,, ,, 12 ,, 21¼ ,, 1st quality	,,	24 0 0

Musical Boxes—Continued.

MUSICAL BOXES, First Quality.

Rich Case, "Cabinet" Style.

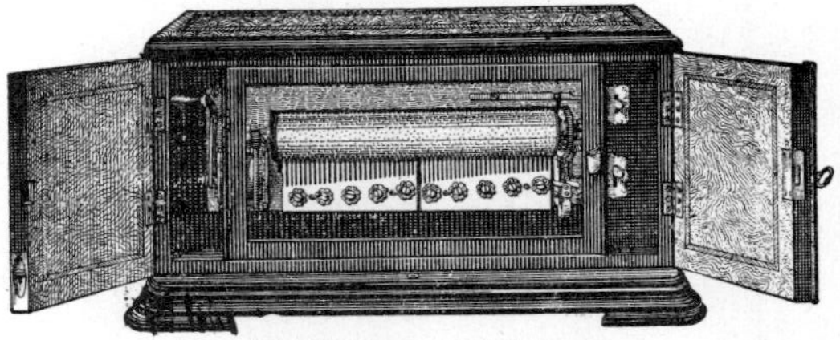

Length 21ins. Width 8ins.

Numbers.			£ s. d.
5161	**Musical Box,** cabinet style, **Forte Piano,** 2 combs, 8 airs, 10¾ins.	each	11 10 0
5163	,, ,, ,, **Mandolin Zither,** 6 airs, 10¾ins. ...	,,	12 10 0
5164	,, ,, ,, ,, ,, 8 airs, 10¾ins. ...	,,	13 10 0

MUSICAL BOXES WITH ACCOMPANIMENT, Extra Quality.

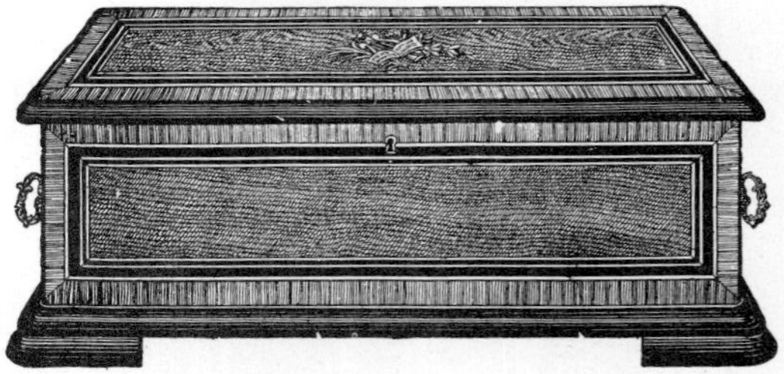

Numbers.			£ s. d.
5170	**Musical Box, Expressive Zither,** rich case, 6 airs, 8ins. ...	each	5 5 0
5171	,, ,, ,, ,, ,, 8 ,, 10¾ ,, ...	,,	6 12 0
5172	,, ,, ,, ,, ,, 10 ,, 12¾ ,, ...	,,	7 5 0
5173	,, ,, ,, ,, ,, 12 ,, 14¾ ,, ...	,,	8 8 0
5175	,, ,, **Guitar Accompaniment,** rich case, 6 airs, 8ins.	,,	10 0 0
5176	,, ,, ,, ,, ,, 8 ,, 10¾ ,,	,,	12 0 0
5178	,, ,, ,, ,, ,, 12 ,, 14¾ ,,	,,	17 5 0
5182	,, ,, **Zither Mandolin, Piccolo,** rich case, 6 airs, 12¾ins. ...	,,	12 12 0
5183	,, ,, ,, ,, rich case, 8 airs, 17ins. ...	,,	17 5 0
5189	,, ,, **Sublime Harmony, Forte Piano, Zither,** 2 combs, 6 airs, 12¾ins.	,,	13 0 0
5193	,, ,, **Sublime Harmony, Forte Piano, Concert Piccolo,** 3 combs, 6 airs, 12¾ins.	,,	14 0 0
5206	,, ,, with double spring box, sublime harmony, forte piano, 8 airs, 17ins.	,,	18 10 0

MUSICAL NOVELTIES.

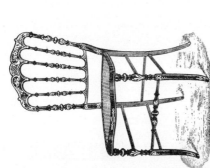

LIQUEUR FRAMES with Music.

Nos. 5170, 5171, 5172.

Numbers			£	s.	d.
5170	Liqueur Frame, complete, 4 decanters, 16 glasses, with music, 2 airs, 28 teeth	each	2	16	0
5171	" complete, 4 decanters, 16 glasses, with music, 3 airs, 30 teeth...	"	3	0	0
5172	" complete, 4 decanters, 16 glasses, with music, 4 airs, 36 teeth	"	3	10	0

CHAIRS with Music.

Numbers			£	s.	d.
5206	Chair, black wood gilded, cane seat, with music, 2 airs	each	1	14	0
5207	" " 3 "	"	1	18	0
5216	" gilt, rich woodwork " 2 "	"	4	0	0
5217	" " " 3 "	"	4	5	0

PLATES with Music.

Numbers			£	s.	d.
5191	Plate, large size, for dessert, 2 airs	each	1	3	0
5192	" "	"	1	7	0

89

Musical Novelties—Continued.

MUSICAL ALBUMS.

Numbers			£	s.	d.
5219	Musical Album, large size, red or black leather, music, 2 airs	each	0	17	0
5220	" stamped leather, all shades, 2 airs	"	0	18	0
5221	" morocco, gilt fastenings, 2 airs	"	1	3	0
5222	" plush, all shades, name plate, 2 airs	"	1	1	0
5228	" smooth plush, 2 airs	"	1	4	0
5224	" very rich, aluminium plate, large clasp, with music, 3 airs	"	2	0	0

DECANTERS, with Music.

Numbers			£	s.	d.
5160	Decanter, cut crystal, with music, 1 air	each	1	0	0
5161	" 2 airs	"	1	4	0

REVOLVING CIGAR CASES, with Music.

Numbers			£	s.	d.
5200B	Revolving Cigar Case, imitation rosewood, 6 large doors, 2 airs	each	1	2	0
5201B	" imitation rosewood, 6 large doors, 3 airs	"	1	4	0
5202B	" imitation rosewood, 6 large doors, 4 airs	"	1	6	0
5203B	" Chinese decorations, 6 large doors, 2 airs	"	1	4	0
5204B	" Chinese decorations, 6 large doors, 3 airs	"	1	8	0

SINGING BIRDS.

Numbers			£	s.	d.
5257	Singing Birds under globe, 3 chirping birds, with foliage, two of which hop from branch to branch, also two ducks and one swan swimming on a lake	each	10	10	0

BOITES A MUSIQUE (*Suite*)

MUSIQUES A CYLINDRES DE RECHANGE
QUALITÉ SUPÉRIEURE

BOITE SUR TABLE. — MEUBLE TRÈS RICHE

Numéros		PRIX NETS
5213	**Musique cithare**, boite riche sur table, qualité supérieure, 3 cylindres nickelés, 24 airs, cadran indicateur . . . . *la pièce*.	682
	Chaque cylindre de 8 airs en plus augmente de	133
5214	**Musique sublime harmonie piccolo**, boite riche sur table, qualité supérieure, deux claviers, 4 cylindres nickelés, 24 airs, cadran indicateur . . . . *la pièce*.	931
	Chaque cylindre de 6 airs en plus augmente de	200
5215	**Musique cithare** avec tambour, timbres, castagnettes, boite riche sur table, 3 cylindres nickelés, 24 airs, cadran indicateur . . . . *la pièce*.	832
	Chaque cylindre de 8 airs en plus augmente de	200
5216	**Musique orchestre, voix célestes**, tambour, timbres castagnettes, boite riche sur table, 15 pouces, 5 cylindres nickelés, 40 airs, cadran indicateur . . . . *la pièce*.	2.395
	Chaque cylindre de 8 airs en plus augmente de	240

Il suffit de donner le numéro de fabrique des boites à musique ci-dessus pour avoir des cylindres supplémentaires avec airs choisis au gré de l'acheteur.

The English catalogue was generally a translation of the original French one, but some of the instruments were omitted or not illustrated. Here are a few different pages from Thibouville-Lamy's Paris catalogue of around the same period.

DE JÉROME THIBOUVILLE-LAMY ET Cⁱᵉ, *rue Réaumur*, 68, 68ᵇⁱˢ ET 70 — PARIS

OBJETS A MUSIQUE

Numéros		Prix nets
5159	**Carafe** cristal taillé avec musique, 1 air, 19 lames . . . . . . *la pièce.*	12
5160	— 1 — 28 —	13
5161	— 2 airs, 28 —	14
5164	**Verre** cristal gravé, avec musique, 1 air, 28 lames. . . . *la pièce.*	14
5165	— 2 airs, 28 —	17
5167	**Bock** cristal taillé, avec musique, 1 air, 28 lames. . . . *la pièce.*	14
5168	— 2 airs, 28 lames —	17
5175	**Assiette** porcelaine, filet or, avec musique, 1 air, 28 lames . . . . . *la pièce.*	9
5176	— 2 airs, 28 lames.	11
5178	**Assiette** porcelaine, bande à fleurs, avec musique, 1 air.	11
5179	— 2 airs	13 50
5182	**Assiette** porcelaine, fleurs et oiseau, avec musique, 1 air.	13 50
5188	— 2 airs.	16
5184	— peinture artistique	20
5190	**Compotier** porcelaine, à fleurs, avec musique, 1 air . . . . . *la pièce.*	17 50
5191	— 2 airs	20
5194	**Dessous de plat,** garniture vieux chêne, avec musique, 1 air, 19 lames *la pièce*	9
5195	— 1 — 28	10
5196	— 2 airs, 28	13
5197	**Dessous de plat,** gar. vieux chêne, plaque émaillée et musique, 1 air, 28 lames.	13
5198	— 2 airs, 28 lames.	15

Le timbre augmente les dessons de plat de . . . . 3 fr.

13

INSTRUMENTS DE MUSIQUE ET CORDES HARMONIQUES

NOUVELLE MUSIQUE

MUSIQUE AVEC CYLINDRES DE RECHANGE JEU CONTINU

Le système de jeu continu permet de jouer entièrement, sans arrêt ni coupures, des airs d'opéra, des grandes valses, etc., nécessitant plusieurs tours de cylindre.

Numéros		Prix nets
5120	**Musique cithare** 3 cylindres, jeu continu représentant 18 airs, 12 pouces, 21 lignes, meuble riche sur table, double batillets, changement d'air à volonté, cadran indicateur, modérateur. . *la pièce*	1.465 »

Chaque cylindre jouant 6 airs augmente de . . . . 120 »
Chaque cylindre jeu continu d'une valeur de 6 airs augmente de . . 186 »

MUSIQUE HARMONIPHONES
A FLUTES OU VOIX CÉLESTES

		Prix nets
5130	**Musique harmoniphone,** voix célestes, 1 airs, 5 pouces 1,2 . . . . *la pièce.*	213
5131	— 6 — 10 —	306
5132	— 8 — 13 —	386
5133	— 10 — 15 —	466
5134	— 12 — 15 —	170

MUSIQUES HARMONIPHONES ORCHESTRE

		Prix nets
5150	**Musique harmoniphone,** tambour et timbres en vue, boîte riche, 6 airs, 13 pouces . . . . *la pièce.*	179
5151	**Musique harmoniphone,** tambour et timbres en vue, boîte riche, 8 airs, 13 pouces . . . . *la pièce.*	542
5152	**Musique harmoniphone,** tambour, timbres et castagnettes en vue, boîte riche, 8 airs, 15 pouces . . . . *la pièce.*	572
5153	**Musique harmoniphone,** tambour, timbres et castagnettes en vue, boîte riche, 10 airs, 18 pouces . . . . *la pièce.*	752
5154	**Musique harmoniphone,** tambour, timbres et castagnettes en vue, boîte riche, 12 airs, 18 pouces . . . . *la pièce.*	765

Les musiques harmoniphones sont avec cadran indicateur.
Le changement d'air à volonté augmente de . . . . . . 27 »

MUSIQUES HARMONIPHONES ORCHESTRE
QUALITÉ EXTRA — BOÎTE RICHE

		Prix nets
5155	**Musique harmoniphone,** qualité extra, voix célestes, tambour, timbres et castagnettes en vue, boîte riche, 8 airs, 16 pouces . . . *la pièce.*	1.115
5156	**Musique harmoniphone,** qualité extra, voix célestes, tambour, timbres et castagnettes en vue, boîte riche, 10 airs, 18 pouces . . . *la pièce.*	1.515

Les boîtes des musiques harmoniphones varient entre 48 à 55 centimètres de longueur sur 29 à 37 centimètres de largeur.

OBJETS A MUSIQUE (Suite)

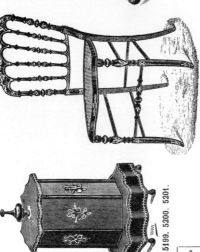

5203. 5204.

5205. 5206.

5199. 5200. 5201.

Numéros		PRIX NETS
	Porte-Cigares imitation palissandre ou bois noir, 6 grandes portes, musique 1 air, 19 lames. la pièce.	
5199		11 »
5200	— — — 6 — — 1 — 28 —	13 »
5201	— — — 6 — — 2 — 28 —	15 »
5202	décors chinois, 6 grandes portes, musique 2 airs, 28 lames	21 »
5203	rond modèle très riche, musique 2 airs, 28 lames	29 »
5204	— — — 3 — 28 —	34 »
5205	**Chaise** bois noir dorée, camée avec musique, 1 air, 28 lames . . . . . la pièce.	17 »
5206	— — — 2 — 28 —	18 »
5208	— dorée, meuble riche, garnie velours ou satin, 2 airs, 28 lames.	35 »

ALBUMS

Numéros		PRIX NETS
5219	**Album** grand format cuir noir ou rouge, musique 2 airs, 28 lames. . la pièce.	16 »
5220	maroquin frappé, toutes nuances, musique 2 airs, 28 lames.	20 »
5221	modèle riche, sujet fermoir doré, musique 2 airs, 28 lames.	27 »
5222	peluche toutes nuances, écusson, musique 2 airs, 28 lames.	19 »
5223	— unie, sujet aluminium, musique 2 airs, 28 lames.	26 »
5224	**Album** très grand format, modèle riche, écusson aluminium, impression dorée autour, grand fermoir, musique 3 airs, 36 lames	43 »
5214	**Chevalet** nickel pour album.	13 »
5210	**Chalet** sculpté, petit modèle, musique 1 air, 28 lames	14 »
5212	— grand 2 airs, 28 lames.	19 »

OBJETS A MUSIQUE (Suite)

CAVES A LIQUEURS

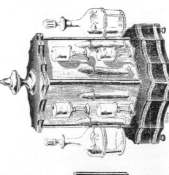

Nᵒˢ 5173, 5174

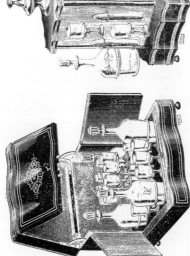

Nᵒˢ 5170, 5171, 5172

Numéros		PRIX NETS
5170	**Cave à liqueurs**, 4 carafons, 16 verres, avec musique 2 airs, 28 lames. la pièce	38 50
5171	— 4 — 16 — — 3 — 36 —	42 50
5172	— 4 — 16 — — 4 — 36 —	48 »
5173	**Cave à liqueurs** tournante, 2 carafons, 8 verres, musique 2 airs, 28 lames.	41 50
5174	— 3 — 28 —	45 50
5225	**Nécessaire à ouvrage**, coffret ébène, filets cuivre, musique 2 airs, 28 lames . . . . . la pièce.	33 50
5226	coffret chêne, filets cuivre, musique 3 airs.	36 »
5225ᵀ	28 lames.	29 50
5226ᵀ	6 — 3 — 28 —	32 »
5227	**Presse papier** à musique, effet de neige, 1 air, 28 lames . . . . . la pièce.	43 50
5228	— 2 — 28 —	46 »

The Picture Magazine.

MECHANICAL SINGING BIRDS.

The first automatic birds are quite old, and a remarkable specimen of them exists at the Conservatoire des Arts et Metiers. We represent this herewith (Fig. 1). It dates back to the last century. The birds are inclosed in a cage, and the mechanism is contained in the base of the latter. The construction of such birds has now reached great perfection.

FIG. 1.—MECHANICAL SINGING BIRDS OF THE EIGHTEENTH CENTURY.

FIG. 2.—MECHANICAL SINGING BIRD OF MODERN CONSTRUCTION.

In the first place, let us speak of the external appearance of these little automatons. At first sight, the bird is absolutely like the natural one, whose plumage it borrows, whether it represents a simple nightingale or is adorned with the brilliant feathers of a bird of paradise. Neither in the pose nor the form could the art of the taxidermist do better. The attitude of each species is carefully studied and leaves nothing to be desired, even by the most fastidious ornithologist. Certain of these birds are inclosed in a simple cage or are placed upon a branch forming a perch, while others, placed upon a tree, flutter from one branch to another, without it being possible to see the little rod, mounted upon a pivot and hidden in the leaves, that carries it back and forth. Again, others may be placed upon a stand (Fig. 2), or, owing to the small size of their pedestal, in a basket of flowers. There are others (and these are humming birds) that are concealed in a snuff-box (Fig. 3), and which, when the cover of the latter is raised, suddenly appear and begin to sing. After the air is finished, they re-enter the box and the cover closes of itself. The snuff-boxes in which they are inclosed are decorated in all possible ways, with inlaid enamel work, Japanese designs upon silver and gold, old silver, repoussé work, inlaid work, etc. All styles are put under contribution, and especially the Louis XV. and Louis XVI. in gilt silver.

A very ingenious model is the one that we represent in the form of a pistol (Fig. 4). When aim is taken with the pistol and the trigger is pulled, the bird, which was first concealed in the barrel, makes its exit, sings its song, and then re-enters the weapon.

The first automatic singing birds had a motion of the bill only, and it was by means of a bird organ or a music box that they seemed to sing. As nothing better was to be had, these had to answer ; but they really produced no illusion. Several types of this kind, of the time of Louis XV., are in existence.

The invention of the true automatic singing birds, and the improvements afterwards introduced by Mr. Bontems, consisted in the substitution of a genuine warbling for the music box, and in giving these little singers the perfect appearance of life. A reproduction of the true song of all birds has been successfully obtained, and we have been enabled to hear all our ordinary artists, with the repertory peculiar to each of them ; the nightingale, the blackbird, the chaffinch, the canary, the lark, the goldfinch, the bullfinch, and the warbler, and, among exotics, the tanager, the chewit, etc. We shall now explain the principle of the mechanism with which it has been possible to reproduce the modulations of the song of birds, and which we may observe is the same for every song.

Fig. 5 gives a general view of the apparatus with its principal parts. The clockwork movement, consisting especially of a spring coiled in its barrel, is placed at M. It sets in motion an axle, A, that carries a star-wheel or eccentric, B, which, through the levers, D, and the rods, H H, communicates motion to the bird. These rods turn the head, open the bill, make the tail waggle and cause the wings to flap ; and the various motions do not take place at hazard during the song, but are naturally combined with the warbling that occurs at the same instant. This warbling is produced as follows : The same axle that carries along the star-wheel revolves, at the same time, two coupled wheels, C, which, irregularly toothed, cause the piston or whistle (3) to act through the rod, G, and the regulator of the bellows, F, to act through the rod, E. The longer it takes the

FIG. 3.—MECHANICAL BIRD IN A SNUFF-BOX.

This article first appeared in a French periodical, was reprinted in the *Scientific American* for 30 July 1892, and appears here from the *Picture Magazine* published in London for April 1894.

FIG. 4.—MECHANICAL BIRD MAKING ITS EXIT FROM A PISTOL.

grave or slow. It will be understood that the whistle may vary in diameter and length, and have a more or less rapid escapement of air, so that its effects may be modified.

We have said that in snuff-boxes, pistols, and other small objects in which a singing bird and its mechanism are concealed, the opening of the object causes the bird to make its exit and to begin its song. It is here a question of a curiosity, and no attempt is made to produce an illusion, but rather astonishment. In the other birds, always exposed and visible, it suffices to press a detent placed behind the box, M, to set the apparatus in motion or to stop it. Of course, this detent does not produce its effect unless the clockwork movement is wound up. The little mechanical songster, whose plumage leaves nothing to be desired, when placed either in a cage or in

teeth to pass, the longer the valve is open and the longer the bellows (2) is actuated. The motion of the teeth is communicated to the rods, G and E, behind the support, S.

It will be understood that the song of the bird may differ so long as the two wheels, C, have not made a revolution, but that the same song must then begin again at the second revolution of the wheel, the same teeth commencing again to actuate the rods, G and E. There has been an improvement introduced that consists in placing upon the same rod three pairs of wheels instead of one pair, and, when the air noted upon the first pair is finished, in bringing the following pair, by means of a snail, in front of the levers, where it replaces the one that has just been driven forward.

In order to be complete in this explanation, let us add that the intermission in the song is produced by the lever, P, which acts upon the bellows, and that the latter itself is actuated by a ratchet placed behind the box, M, of the motor. The apparatus that we have just described is same for all birds. It is larger or smaller, more or less strong, and is placed in one direction or another, according to the space left free in the mechanical piece, but the principle does not change. In each bird, and especially when it is a question of a new song to be created, the delicate point of the adjustment is the whistle, aided by the bellows and piston, that will give the true character of the song and modulate it so as to make it rapid, sharp,

FIG. 5.—MECHANISM OF A SINGING BIRD.

a spray of flowers or foliage, gives the illusion of life very accurately.

Thomas Reid of Edinburgh was a famous clockmaker who became free of the Clockmakers' Company in 1825. Besides contributing the article on horology to two editions of *The Edinburgh Encyclopaedia*, he wrote a book called *Treatise on Clock and Watchmaking* which was first published in 1826 and ran to six editions. One whole chapter of this work was devoted to cylinder-pricking for musical clocks—how to set music on a barrel. This is reproduced here from the first edition. Reid's closing comments on tuned steel teeth in musical watches make interesting reading.

CHAPTER XXIII.

On Clock Chimes and Bell Music, mode of pricking Barrels, construction of Organ Clocks, &c.

CHIME, in its general meaning, is applied to the sounding of bells, such as change-ringing by church bells, or the striking quarters of the hour by a clock on two or more bells, or to tunes played by a clock on a series of nine, twelve, or sixteen bells, tuned to their respective notes on the scale. Clocks that play tunes on bells are called musical clocks; when quarters are chimed or struck by the clock itself, for example, on six, or on eight bells in octave, it is called a quarter clock, and sometimes a chime clock; and when the quarters are struck by a string being pulled, it is called a pull quarter or a repeating clock, whether the quarters are struck on six or eight bells, or whether they are given by a double blow on the hour-bell, as in the repeating watch. A time-piece, or going part, and having no hour striking part, but having a repeating part, is by some called a silent pull.

Various ways may be adopted for pricking tunes on the music barrels of clocks. The earlier mode of doing this was by taking a piece of writing paper of such a size as to cover exactly the surface of the barrel, and in a direction perpendicular to the axis of the barrel, to draw as many lines parallel to one another as there were notes in the tune to be laid down on the barrel, the lines being equidistant, and corresponding perfectly with the hammer tails as they stood in the hammer frame. They were marked at each end with the letters or notes they were to represent in the gamut or scale of music; and, according to the number of bars in the tune, as many spaces were made by lines drawn equidistant and parallel to each other, intersecting the others at right angles. The junction of the ends of these bar paper, when applied round the barrel, represented one of these bar lines. The length or breadth of the spaces (which might be either squares or parallelograms) contained between the bar and note lines, was again divided on the note lines into as many parts or spaces as the number of crotchets in a bar, and for notes of lesser value a less space was taken. While the paper was lying on a table, the notes in the tune proposed to be laid on the barrel were marked by a black ink dot on their respective lines, and in the same order as the bars of the music lay. After this was done, the paper was pasted on the barrel: the note lines now appeared like so many circles traced round the circumference of the barrel, while the bar lines lay longitudinally on the surface of it. By this means the black ink dots were transferred and marked on the barrel by a punch or finger drill. This mode might answer very well where large barrels were used, and only one tune laid on; but in smaller work, and where several tunes were to be put on the same barrel, it is neither sufficiently neat nor accurate.

We are not acquainted with the method adopted by those workmen in London who practice the pricking of music on clock barrels; but having had occasion to construct some musical clocks above thirty years ago, and having no opportunity of getting the music pricked on the barrels by any professional person, it became necessary to contrive some methods for this purpose. One way consisted in applying the barrel concentric with the arbor of a wheel-cutting engine, whose dividing part consisted of an endless screw and wheel; and having fixed their apparatus on the engine for this purpose, different numbers of turns of the endless screw were taken for the longer or shorter notes, and the tunes were as accurately put on the barrel as could be wished. Another way consisted in placing the barrel and its train of wheel work and regulating fly in the frame. A force was applied to turn the barrel, wheel work, and fly round in the order of lifting the music hammer tails, and an apparatus was used to mark the dotes on the barrel. The fly made 360 revolutions for one turn of the barrel; or, should this be thought too quick a train, it might be made by altering the numbers of the wheel teeth to make 250 or 260 revolutions for one turn of the barrel; the train or revolutions of the fly being fixed, were made use of in the same way as the endless screw in the former way, by taking a greater or a smaller number of turns of the fly for the longer or the shorter notes. Knowing the number of bars in the tune, and the crotchets in a bar, by calculation, the number of turns of the fly was obtained (and parts of a turn if necessary) that a crotchet required, so that the tune might go round the barrel, leaving a small space for locking and running; this was all that was required to be known: quavers and semiquavers came to have their proportion according to the value of the crotchet. Although the process of putting tunes on barrels answered very well by both these methods, yet it was rather tedious, and attended with some trouble and embarrassment in the operation; and a more simple and easier method of doing this was afterwards contrived and adopted, by which we could lay on a tune with the greatest accuracy and expedition in nearly ten minutes.

Although bell music is not of a favourite kind, yet for the benefit of such clockmakers as may be disposed to construct music clocks, and have not the opportunity of getting the music pricked on the barrel by those whose profession it is to do this sort of work, we shall give a description of the tool and its apparatus, which will be found very well adapted for this purpose, and also of the manner of using it.

Having a good strong turn-bench, such as those used by clock-makers for their larger sort of work, to the standards or heads of it let there be attached supports on each side; to the supports on the side nearest the workman, let there be fixed a straight cylindrical rod A B, Plate XVII. 79, about ten or twelve inches long, and in diameter a quarter of an inch, or even three-tenths of an inch. A spring socket C D must be made for this rod to slide easily and steadily along it, somewhat like the socket which slides on the upright stalk or rod of a watchmaker's glass stand. In the thick and strong part of this socket E is fixed a steel arm E F G, bent into a curve, which lies over and above the music barrel when in the turn bench, as shown in 80, at EFG. The steel rod A B may at pleasure be placed at any distance from the barrel, about an inch or rather more, and should stand parallel to the barrel arbor MN, and nearly in the same plane with it, but rather a little above this than otherwise. On the outer end of the curved arm is fixed a flat piece of steel G, a little more than half an inch long, in breadth not quite so much, and about one-tenth of an inch thick. The lower and front edges of this flat piece of steel should be neatly and smoothly rounded off, so as to allow it to come easily and freely into the notches a, b, c, &c. which are on the edge of a thin brass scale, whose use will come afterwards to be explained. To the supports attached to the turn-bench heads, and on the opposite side to that where the round steel rod is placed, let there be fixed a slip of brass X Y, about ten or twelve inches long, an inch and a half broad, and nearly a tenth of an inch thick, the inner edge of which must be made to stand parallel with the barrel, and the flat side to stand nearly in a plane between the upper surface of the barrel and its centre, the edge being placed so as to stand clear of the tops of the teeth of a high numbered wheel W W screwed on to the end of the barrel. Near the ends of this slip of brass, slits are made,

through which screws s, s, pass, which screw it to the upper side of the supports; the slits serving to allow it to be moved a little occasionally lengthwise when required. On the upper side of the slip of brass is fixed another, but not quite so thick, the length being about that of the barrel, and breadth one inch and three quarters. On the inner edge of this are made as many notches a, b, c, &c. as there are hammers, bells, or notches to be used in the tune or tunes to be marked on the barrel. These notches are equidistant, and the middle of them should correspond to the middle or line of the hammer tails; their width being such as to admit the flat steel piece G on the end of the curved arm EFG; the depth of them cut on the edge of the brass should be about one quarter of an inch. The edge of this piece of brass, or music scale as it may be called, must also stand parallel with the barrel, and at a little distance from it, not nearer than three-tenths of an inch, so that the flat steel piece on the end of the curved arm may have room to get in a little way, and to pass through at the same time to a certain degree of depth. On the upper side of this brass slip, the letters of the scale of music or gamut are marked to those notches which correspond with the hammer tails, and hammers intended to strike on the bells the notes so marked; but in an inverted order to the usual way in which they are marked in the scales of music, the lower notes being on the right hand side, and as they rise going to the left. This is done to suit the way in which the bells are commonly, though not necessarily, placed in music clocks, see 81; it is in the power of a clockmaker, of any ingenuity, to contrive the barrel to turn any way he thinks proper, and place the bells to stand in the order of the music scale, if there is any advantage to be derived from it. In the curved arm EFG, 80, is fixed a punch f, having a very fine and sharp conical point, at the distance of four inches or so from the centre of the sliding socket, and not quite an inch from the outer end of the flat steel piece; the punch, when applied to the barrel, should stand upright, and directly over the centre of it. This apparatus being all adjusted, as we have directed, it is evident that when the curved arm is raised up a little way, the socket can then be made to slide easily along the steel rod, and by this means bring the outer end of the flat steel piece very readily into any notch required, and the point of the punch is brought at the same time with the greatest precision to the place of the note on the barrel, leaving the flat steel piece for the time in the notch. The point of the punch touching or resting on the barrel, a stroke from a very small hammer on the top of it will cause the point to make a pretty deep mark or conical hole on the surface of the barrel.

96

PLATE XVII.

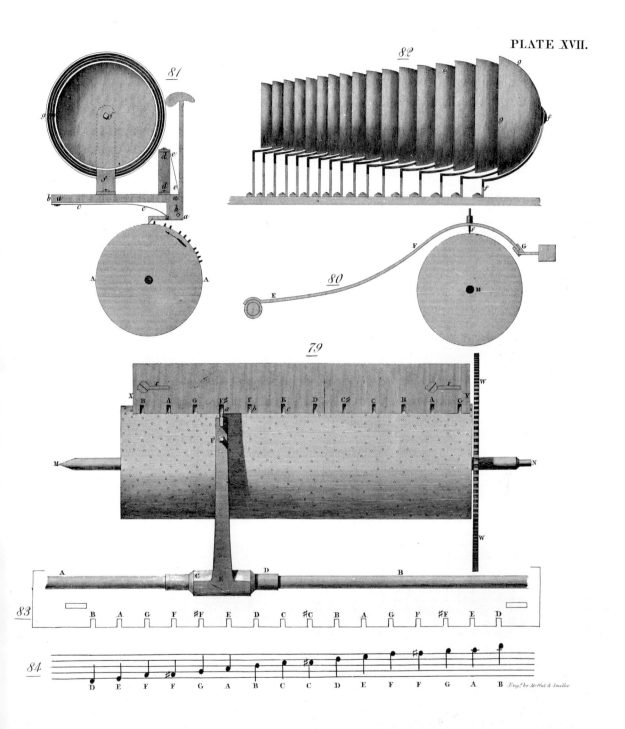

It now remains to be shown how the time or the lengths of the different notes are determined. Long or slow, short or quick notes, such as the minum and demi-semi-quaver, are not well suited to bell-music, and, of course, are seldom introduced into tunes chosen for it; the crotchet, quaver, and semiquaver, forming the greatest part of the composition: the minum and demi-semi-quaver may, however, be brought in at some parts. It may be unnecessary to state, what is pretty generally known, the proportional value of the notes to one another; suffice it to say, that a minum is equal to two crotchets, a crotchet to two quavers, a quaver to two semi-quavers, and a semi-quaver to two demi-semi-quavers. The time in which the barrel turns, after striking or lifting a hammer-tail, to strike any note on a bell, must be in the same proportion with the notes, according to their respective character. Let a wheel of 250 teeth, for example, be fixed on the end of the barrel, and let both be placed in the turn-bench, with the apparatus which has been described. To the turn-bench is now attached a steel or brass spring, having a knee or bending at one end, so that it may fall into the spaces of the wheel teeth.

The tune proposed to be laid on the barrel contains 20 bars of three crotchets each, being 60 crotchets in all: if 250, the number of the wheel teeth, is divided by 60, the number of the crotchets, we shall have four for the quotient, and ten for the remainder; showing that we may take four teeth spaces for every crotchet, ten, the remaining part of it, serving as a run for locking, and the other part for a run at unlocking for a tune to be played. Now, as a crotchet is equal to four spaces, a quaver must be equal to two, and a semi-quaver equal to one. Suppose the first note, in the tune proposed, is F. 79; the curved arm is brought to the left hand, and the flat steel piece put into that notch; the punch is then made to mark the barrel; and this being a semi-quaver, or the fourth part of a crotchet, the spring index is shifted into the next space of the wheel teeth, and the curved arm moved to the next note, which is G, on the left hand, and the flat steel piece being put into the notch corresponding to G, the punch is made to mark it on the barrel. This being a semi-quaver also, the spring is shifted into the next space, and the curved arm moved to note A on the left; the steel piece is put into the corresponding notch, and the punch marks this on the barrel. A is here equal to a quaver and a half; therefore the spring index must be moved over three, or into the third space, and the curved arm moved to the next note, being B, on the left hand; the steel piece being put into this notch, the note is marked on the barrel; and as it is a semi-quaver, one space is taken for

it, and the arm moved to G. This being marked, and as it is a quaver, two spaces are taken, and so on. When crotchets are marked, four spaces are taken after marking them. In the tune which we have used, nine bells or notes are all that are required; and three more, or a dozen, would give such a compass as to take in almost any tune that might be required. In place of the spring index, it would be better to have a single threaded endless screw to work into the wheel teeth, one turn of which would be equal to a tooth or space. The arbor of the screw being squared on one end, and a small handle for turning it being put on, there would be less danger of making mistakes with the screw than with the index. On the arbor of the screw there might also be put a hand or index to point to a circular space or dial of eight or ten divisions. This would give room to make parts of a turn, where great nicety is wanted. After one tune is laid on the barrel, either it or the music scale must be shifted a short space when the next one is to be put on. To shift the music scale is perhaps the preferable way of the two; and the spaces for shifting should be marked on the top of one of the supports, and close by one end of the long slip of brass; or they might be marked on a short line drawn longitudinally on the surface of the barrel at or towards one of the ends of it; or by taking both methods, the one would serve as a check on the other. The length of shifting depends on the distance between the hammer tails, and the number of tunes to be put upon the barrel. For example, if the distance between the hammer tails is four-tenths of an inch, and it is proposed to put eight tunes on the barrel, then if we divide four-tenths by eight, we shall have half a tenth for the length, or space to shift for each tune; and this is taking advantage of the whole space between the hammer tails, a circumstance which is frequently overlooked; for where the shifts have been confined to a less space for shifting than might have been got, so much room is lost. The distance between the hammer tails depends on their number, and on the length of the barrel. We have made the distance a quarter of an inch, where the number of hammers were eleven, and the length of barrel about three inches and a quarter, the number of tunes put on the barrel seven, the spaces for shifting were three hundred parts of an inch or thereabouts, and where the clock of itself shifted the tune. When the hammer tails are thin, a number of tunes could be made to have their shifts in a very short distance between the tails; the diameter of the lifting pins must also be taken into account, being of some consideration where the spaces for shifting are extremely limited. Although we have taken the number of the wheel teeth for dividing the notes at pins by the file must be taken off; this is done by a piece of steel wire, about six or seven inches long. The end where it is twirled about by the fore finger and thumb, should, for the length of an inch or so, be made into an octangular form, for the more readily turning it round backward and forward. On the face or point of the other end, two notches are made across each other, which may be either angular or round at bottom; the latter may be the better of the two, if rightly executed, and should be made with the round edge of a flat file, whose thickness should not be more than the diameter of the pins. The point where the notches are cut should be hardened, and the inside and bottom of the notches polished, so that a sharpness may be given to take away the burrs easily from the top of the pins.

The shape of the hammer tail is such as is represented at 81. a form which makes the hammer easy enough to be drawn, and the nib of the tail takes little or no room when falling; and should two pins or notes succeed each other rapidly, the nib or point of the hammer tail will not be interrupted by the succeeding pin. In the first musical clocks, and even in those made long afterwards, the bells were all placed on one strong iron bell stud, the opposite end of which was supported by what may be called an auxiliary stud, which occasioned a crampness that prevented the bells, when they were struck by the hammers, from vibrating, or giving out that full tone which they might have otherwise been made to produce; and the improvement made on this, as well as on the quarter bell studs afterwards, was effected by placing each bell separately on its own bell stud, which was made of well-hammered brass, having some degree of elasticity. The sweetness given to the tone of the bells by this method was truly surprising. The bells in this kind of music may be sounding at the time that a succeeding note is struck out and sounding too, which may not be so pleasant to a very nice ear. This can be prevented by having a double set of hammers, and having every tune pinned twice over on the barrel, one set of the hammers having the heads of buff leather, or having a brass head with a piece of cloth sewed over it. These, when they strike the bell, will damp the sound of the note which is last struck. The buff hammer should fall on the bell to be damped, at the same instant that the brass hammer strikes the succeeding note on its bell. This improvement, however, must greatly increase the expence on such a clock; but the effect of buff or cloth hammers is so striking, that the additional price ought not to be grudged.

In Plate XVII. 81. A A is a circle representing an end view of a clock music barrel, and a few of the lifting pins. The dart

250, yet either a greater or a less number may be assumed; all that is required is, to proportion the number of turns of the endless screw, and parts of a turn, to the number of bars in the tune, to the notes in each bar, and to have the tunes to go nearly round the barrel, so that a small part of a revolution of it, after the tune is played over, may be left, for what is called locking and running. If the dividing wheel was taken at 128 teeth, and the tune being supposed to have 20 bars, each bar having three crotchets, as in the former example, 128 teeth divided by 60, the number of crotchets, the quotient would be two, and the remainder would be eight; so that each crotchet would require two teeth or turns of the endless screw, a quaver one turn, and a semiquaver half a turn, and the remaining eight teeth would serve for locking and running. When the tunes are all marked on the barrel, each mark must be drilled to obtain holes for the lifting pins to be driven into them. Great care should to taken to have a stiff and excellent drill, so as to run no risk of breaking, which would occasion a great deal of trouble; and it should be of such a temper, and well and judiciously whetted up, so that it may drill all the holes without requiring to be once sharpened: the object here is to have all the holes of the same width, so that the lifting pins may be all of the same diameter. The holes being drilled, and the barrel polished, a number of pins should be prepared into lengths of half an inch or so each, and a very little tapered at one end. The stronger and harder the brass wire for the pins is, so much the better; some of the best kind of pins used in the female dress are very fit for this purpose. In placing the pins in the holes, if they should be found too long for knocking in by the hammer, they should be shortened by the cutting plyers before the hammer is applied, which will prevent bending, and allow the pins to have a more secure hold of the barrel rim. After all the pins are put in, they must now be shortened to an equal and proper length or height. For this purpose, prepare a hard cylindrical steel collet, having a hole in its centre sufficiently wide to allow it to be put readily on the pins; the lower end of it hollowed, the upper end rounded, and the height of the collet about one-twentieth of an inch or a little more; the height depending on the size of the barrel and the diameter of the pins. The collet being placed on a pin, the cutting plyers are applied to cut the pin just over by the rounded end; a small touch of a file takes away the burr made by cutting, and as the hardness of the collet prevents the file from taking any more away from the height of one pin than from another, they must all be of an equal height. This operation being finished, the small burrs made on the top of the being equal to the space from one tune to another. On these steps rests the kneed end of a double lever, about four inches long, whose centre of motion is in the middle, and is either upon strong pivots run into a kind of frame, or upon a stout pin, which goes through the lever and the brass stud in which the lever moves. The other end of the lever bears on the end of one of the pivots of the music barrel, which is pressed against it by means of a pretty smart steel spring, acting against the end of the opposite pivot. Concentric with the hoop-wheel, and fixed on the same arbor, is a star-wheel of a number according with the steps on the hoop-wheel, a jumper with a pretty strong spring, works into the star-wheel, by which means the barrel is kept always to its place, by the lever bearing at one place on every step. Although the Figures which have been given to represent the hammer frame, hammers, springs, and counter-springs, bell studs, and bells of music striking, are not exactly like those which are commonly made to strike quarters in clocks, yet they are equally well calculated for the purpose: only the nibs of the hammer tails need not be so far from their centre of motion, being less confined by the pins in the quarter barrel, which are fewer in number than those on a music barrel. A quarter barrel need not be much in diameter, if five quarters are only to be put on it. If ten is intended to be put on, then the diameter should be double that of the other.

After having described the method of laying down the tunes on a music clock barrel, it may be thought unnecessary to explain the method of putting on the quarters of a clock quarter or chime barrel. But, simple as it is, we conceive it will be both interesting to the general reader, and acceptable to workmen who may not be in the habit of contriving for themselves, or who may not have had an opportunity of seeing it executed by others.

Quarters are commonly struck on a set of eight bells, from G to G in octave, or they may be numbered 1, 2, 3, &c. on to 8. The quarter barrel may have eight circles, faintly turned on it, so as to correspond to the quarter hammer tails. Five, and sometimes ten quarters, are put on the barrel; we shall, however, in this instance, only lay five on the barrel. Take a wheel cut into 50 teeth not rounded off, and screwed temporarily on the end of the barrel; provide an index, and a piece of brass bent so as to apply to the barrel when in the turn bench, in the manner of a straight edge, and the index spring tight in the teeth; take a point, and make a slight trace across the circle, which corresponds to high G or No. 1, then move the index a tooth, in the direction the quarter barrel turns when moved by the wheel work; make a trace across the circle intended for the second hammer,

shows the direction in which it turns. The letters a, a, a, a, represent a section or end view of a brass piece thus shaped. The length depends on that of the barrel, and the number of hammers to be let into this brass piece, which is called the hammer frame, the length of it being sometimes three or four inches, sometimes ten or twelve. The flat part of the hammer tails fills up the thick part of the hammer frame, into which slits are made to receive the hammers. Near to the outer and lower angular part at a of the frame, a hole h is made through the whole length of it, not drilled, but ploughed, *as the workmen call it*, and this is done before any slits are made in it for the hammers. A wire is put through this hole, and through corresponding holes in the flat part of the hammer tails. This wire is their centre of motion, and the holes in them are made so as to have freedom on it, and the flat part of the hammer tails are also made to have freedom in the slits made to receive them. On the under side of the hammer frame at b, the hammer springs c, c, are screwed, one for each hammer, acting on that part of the hammer tail just where it comes out of the thick part of the hammer frame. When the pins in the barrel raise up any hammer by the nib, and carrying it away from the bell, at the instant the pin quits the nib, the spring c, c, by its returning force, makes the hammer head give a blow on the bell to elicit the sound. To prevent any jarring in the bell by the hammer head resting or touching it after having given the blow, each hammer has a counter-spring acting near the lower end of the shank, and inside of it. All the counter-springs are made to project from one slip of well-hammered brass, and screwed on the top of three kneed brass cocks, fixed to the upper side of the brass frame. d d is a view of the side of one of the cocks; and e e an edge view of one of the counter-springs. f f is a side view of one of the bell studs, which are also screwed on the upper side of the hammer frame: an edge view is seen at f f, 81. g, g, g, g, are edge views of the bells. g, g, 82, is a side view of one of them as fixed to its stud. In some musical clocks, in place of the barrel being made to shift for change of tune, the hammer frame is made to shift, carrying with it all the hammers and bells. The change or shifts of the barrel is either done by the hand or by the clock itself. The mechanism for this commonly consists of a wheel fixed on a steel arbor, on the square of which a hand is put, which points to the name or number of the tune marked on a small dial, at which the barrel for the moment stands. The diameter of this wheel is about one inch and a half, and sometimes more or less. The rim is a strong and thick hoop or contrate form, having as many steps on it as there are tunes set on the barrel, the height of the steps and so on. When the eighth circle has been marked, move the index two teeth or three spaces, and trace here for the first hammer of the succeeding quarter, and so on till the whole is completed; the barrel may then be drilled and pinned accordingly. Should the intervals between the quarters be thought too little for locking, the wheel in place of 50, may be cut 55, and this will allow three teeth in place of two for the intervals, the hammers will be then a little quicker in their succession to one another. G, A, B, C, D, E, F, G, may also be represented by the figures, 1, 2, 3, 4, 5, 6, 7, and 8. No. 1 being the high G, and 8 the low G. The changes given in the following set of chimes or quarters, will exhibit how to proceed in putting them on the barrel, after what has been already said. It will save trouble even to a good reader of music, but much more so to those who cannot read it, to have the straight edge piece of brass, numbered from the bells, 1, 2, 3, 4, 5, &c. so as to correspond with the faint traces on the quarter barrel, or with the hammer tails; let the notes of the chimes have *their number* marked as in the example given here, in the order they stand in the gamut; by this means the notes can very quickly be transferred to the barrel.

A set of Chimes for Clock Quarters; the barrel making two revolutions in the hour.

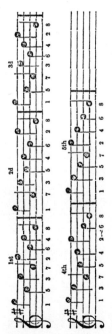

With the number of 8 bells and hammers for the quarters of a chime or quarter clock, a great variety may be produced; and where it may be preferred to have the chime or quarter barrel to make one revolution for the ten quarters which are given in the course of every hour, we shall give a specimen of a set of chimes which may be put on such a barrel. The wheel put on for this must have 100 teeth, taking the same steps as with the wheel of 50.

A set of Chimes for Clock Quarter Barrels, which make one revolution in an hour.

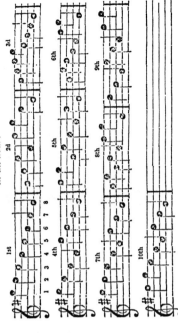

Organ Clocks.

That music which is produced by clocks with organ barrels, must be greatly preferable to that of bells, and the apparatus for marking the tunes on clock barrels is equally suited to do the same on barrels intended by machinery to work or to sound the pipes of an organ; the difference consisting in marking off on the barrel the spaces of the longer and shorter notes, as in place of pins they have staples or bridges of various lengths, according to the length of the note, or the time which the pipe should be allowed to sound it. The very short notes are by pins of different thicknesses. When an organ part is put to a clock, considerable power or force of weight or spring is required; small as the organ may be, or its wind-chest, some force is required to work the bellows, so as to keep the wind-chest full and no more. To work the bellows, that is, to move the lower board of them up and down, on the inside of which is an air valve that opens on the board being moved downwards, and on the motion upwards it shuts, and the air being then compressed, it is forced into the wind-chest by a communication between them for that purpose, and is ready to give sound to any of the organ pipes the moment when any of their valves should open. This operation with the bellows, though of a different shape, is just the same as with the common bellows when blowing up a fire. The bellows is worked by means of a short crank fixed on one end of the arbor of an endless screw, which works into a trundle of a high numbered pinion, which is on the end of the organ barrel, and nearly of the same diameter with it. On the other end of the endless screw arbor is fixed a small jagged pulley, over which is put an endless silken cord, which being continued, goes round another jagged pulley on the

Musical Springs.

Within these few years a new species of music by steel springs has been invented at Geneva. From the smallness of the machinery which plays the music, it is very surprising and curious, as it has been put into rings, seals, watches, and snuff boxes. Two ways are used to lift the ends of the springs which give the different notes : one is by a very small barrel, the other by a plate wheel. The last being more adapted to take up little room, is chiefly used in watches. The space for the springs falling, after being bent up, is short. A double set of springs for giving the same notes is made, without which the beauty of the music could not be produced. The number of springs varies, for the most part, from sixteen to twenty-four, or upwards. Those springs which are lifted by the barrel pins are straight, while those which are lifted by the pins in the plate wheel have a sort of part projecting from the end at one side ; and this side edge of the spring lying over the top of the pins is taken away so as to clear them. The projecting part at the end of each spring corresponds with its own lifting pin. As the pins are on both sides of the plate-wheel, this allows a greater variety of notes than the barrel can perhaps admit. The springs on the upper and under sides of the plate-wheel are sometimes sixteen or seventeen on each side. On the plate-wheel are traced 16 or 17 concentric circles, for the pins to meet their corresponding notes in the springs, whose ends come each to their corresponding circle both above and under the plate-wheel. An apparatus on a small scale being made like that which has been described, will serve to put or mark the places for the notes both on the barrel and the plate-wheel ; the only difference is, that the barrel will require to be marked by a curved arm sliding on a steel rod. The concentric circles on the plate-wheel must have short and faint traces across them. This is regulated by a thin straight edge laid in an oblique direction across the circles, and the intersections are afterwards marked by a point. The springs may be easily tuned to their respective notes, as the least thinning or shortening them will make a very sensible alteration on the tone. *The tongue of a steel trump, or Jew's harp, shews, in some degree, what may be done in this way by steel springs.* The train which regulates this very minute musical machinery, as may very easily be conceived, must be composed of a few very small wheels, the motive force being proportionably small. It must be a great effort of patience and ingenuity to make them play two or more tunes. However beautiful and ingenious the machinery of these small contrivances is, they can only be considered as toys for amusing children. A spiral steel spring has been lately introduced into clocks, in place of bells.

end of a pinion arbor or one of the quick running or fly wheels in the organ train. These wheels are regulated by a fly, by which the velocity of the organ barrel in turning, is brought to keep the time required for the music. The wheels, on being impelled by the moving power, which is considerable, (being greater than that used in bell music), communicate their motion by means of the endless cord, and turn the organ barrel. The pins, bridges, or staples, on the barrel turning, act on the tails of levers, nearly similar in form to the hammer tails of the bell musical clock, only they are a little longer, and equally moveable on a centre or wire. The other arms of these levers are in an opposite direction, and are about the same length as those which are lifted by the staples on the barrel when turning, and are a little broad and flattish towards the end, where the under side (on the opposite ends rising) press down on the upper ends of the slender rods, whose lower ends then by this means open the valves of the organ pipes, and the sound is prolonged according as the lift is pins or bridges. What has been described constitutes the chief machinery in an organ clock. Many ways may be contrived to set the organ barrel in motion, and at the same time while playing, and at the end of a tune, to make the clock of itself shift the barrel from one tune to another.

By experience, when making up an organ clock, we found the making of the bellows to be rather a nice piece of business ; if the leather is on the thick side, it requires a great force to work them and turn the organ barrel at the same time ; the bellows leather should be of the thinnest and finest kid, such as that of which ladies' gloves are made ; by this means the force necessary to work them will be greatly lessened, though still considerable, as it consisted of two large barrels, three inches and a half in diameter, and near to two inches broad, each containing a pretty powerful spring ; the two fusees, on one arbor, were in diameter at the base, near to two inches and a half. In the organ train of wheels, the numbers of the wheel teeth were 80, 70, 60, and 16, the pinions 16, 14, 12 and 4 threads to the endless screw, on whose upper end the wings of a fly were put, the fly wheel of 16 worked into the screw ; the wheels, barrels, and fusees were contained in a double frame, composed of three plates. It may easily be conceived, by having so great a force, that the first or great wheel would require to be thick, and to have strong teeth, the leaves of the first pinion of course to be also strong. The double frame, with the wheel work for driving the organ barrel, was fixed in the upper part of the clock-case ; the organ barrel, bellows, wind-chest, &c. were placed in the lower part. The clock, a spring one, struck the hour, and the quarters were struck by a double blow, the pendulum 15 inches in length, the whole got up in an elaborate manner, yet we trust not injudiciously so.

CHAPTER 4

Tin Discs and Music for the Masses

THE cylinder musical box, as a means for interpreting music, was at best a cumbersome device. For the number of tunes which it played it was both large and expensive. Those instruments which offered an optional change of programme through the facility of extra interchangeable cylinders were on the one hand commensurately larger and more expensive, and on the other hand infinitely more prone to sustaining damage during the changing of the programme and the storage of the spare cylinders. These were, after all, musical boxes which were meant to be used in the home with a reasonable degree of equal facility by both young and old, lady and gentleman.

So it was that the evolution of a new type of musical box—that which played changeable flat discs—was a major advance indeed. It was argued with some measure of justification that the cylinder musical box could never be equalled, let alone bettered, for range of notes and tone and certainly the exquisite tone of an 1850-vintage overture-playing cylinder box was never matched by the disc-playing instrument. Nevertheless, from its rather imprecise inception in 1886 through to the outbreak of the 1914–1918 war, both scale and range of tone of the disc-playing musical box underwent a progressive improvement both in Germany (its birthplace) and in the United States to which it was an early immigrant. Among the later Swiss makers, only Mermod produced notable improvements, both tonal and mechanical.

It was invented almost simultaneously in London by Ellis Parr and in Leipzig by Paul Lochmann. The two inventors, initially at loggerheads, saw the various merits of their respective ideas and so joined forces to produce what was to become the Symphonion. Production of practical instruments did not get under way until about 1890 but at last the time had come when the public could buy a musical machine upon which any number of different tunes could be played at the extra cost of, in many cases, a matter of a few pence.

The centre of the musical box industry shifted from Switzerland to Leipzig, eventually over-spilling into Berlin as well and this shift was entirely due to the disc machine.* It was to take some while for the Swiss to try to rally round to meet the challenge other than by reducing the quality of their cylinder musical boxes and the first Swiss disc machines were not to appear until the mid-1890s. In the same way that Augsburg is considered to have been the cradle of mechanical music in the seventeenth century, and Ste Croix the cradle of the comb-playing musical box proper, Leipzig now became the breeding ground for a vast new mechanical music industry. Within the space of but a few years, a large number of companies came into being for the purpose of manufacturing organettes, disc musical boxes and all forms of musical novelties.

The major proportion of the output of these factories was exported and the two principal

* In 1895, there were nine firms making musicwork in Leipzig and only two in Berlin.

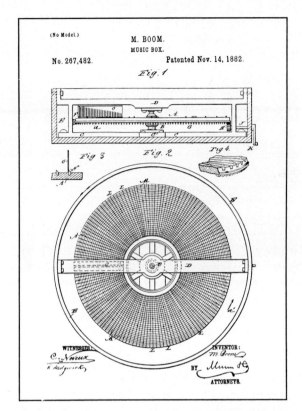

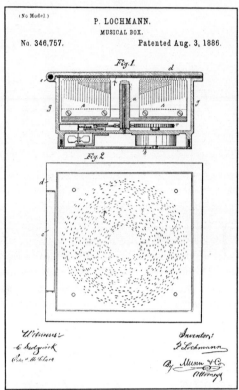

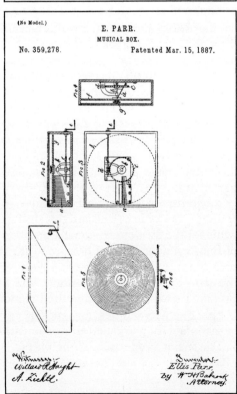

The first patent for a disc-type musical box was awarded to Miguel Boom of Port au Prince, Haiti, in November 1882. Boom's invention employed the principle of the carillon and the musical box in that he used a radially-marked disc into which movable pegs could be inserted so as to pluck the teeth of a musical box-type tuned steel comb and so play a tune. This patent marks as much as is known of the inventor and nothing further seems to have come of either invention or patentee. Paul Lochmann's patent was for a far more workable instrument based on an idea for a reed organette he had patented earlier. Here the tune was represented by a fixed and stationary sheet. Projections punched into this sheet plucked the teeth of a vertical musical box comb which was rotated beneath it by clockwork. The idea was neat but no provision was made for damping the vibrating teeth. The combs, being attached to a rotating frame, could not have produced a very loud sound since no form of sound resonance chamber was provided. The patent of Ellis Parr, a London musical instrument factor and inventor of several improvements to other instruments, was taken out in London in September 1885, just a week before Lochmann's invention was patented in England. The illustrations here are from the later American patents. Parr proposed a much more practical instrument using a fixed, vertically-mounted musical comb above which a perforated disc could be rotated by turning a handle. It was Parr's principle which was put into production by Lochmann in Leipzig as the Symphonion (see page 113) and so it could be said with some justification that the disc musical box was a British invention.

markets were Czarist Russia and Great Britain. High import tariffs imposed early on by United States Republican President William MacKinley largely precluded exports to that part of the world until after 1901 and this forced both the makers of the Polyphon and the Symphonion to set up separate companies in America. The former became the Regina Music Box Company of Rahway, New Jersey, and the latter the Symphonion Music Box Company of Asbury Park, New Jersey. Indeed, the 'protective tariff' of America caused great damage to the industries in Klingenthal and Markneukirchen which, because of it, lost way in the market.

For Europe, though, London was a major market for musical automata. Both the industry and the commerce of England were riding the boom and this was reflected in the increasing numbers of *nouveau riche*, all of whom were potential musical box owners. From the primitive world of the time of King George III to the closing years of Queen Victoria's reign, England had come a long, long way—far more, perhaps, than in any other similar period in her history. Factories were being equipped with 'the electric light' so that workers no longer needed to strain their eyes by the flickering yellow gas light (even so, many a church organist shunned the thought of playing upon an instrument with the relatively new electro-magnetic action due to the uncertainties of the power supply). The steam engines which drove the wheels of our factories now also drove electrical generators—one piano factory in North London actually installed a ten horsepower steam engine solely for the purpose of producing the electric light current—indeed an expensive luxury.

England was thus a vast market for mechanical musical instruments—and London was the point of access. Progress in Leipzig was rapid and new inventions in musical automata plus new factories in which to produce them came thick and fast. Ludwig Hupfeld, formerly J. M. Grob, opened up what was to be the largest factory in the whole of Europe for the manufacture of automatic musical instruments and here, in the centre of Leipzig, he produced a range of electro-pneumatic pianos which could be played either from the electric light current or from storage batteries.* Indeed, Hupfeld's inventions in electric pianos preceded those of American companies by a number of years.† At the almost equally vast Polyphon factory at Wahren, also in Leipzig, almost a thousand people were employed on disc musical box manufacture at the height of production at the end of the nineteenth century. Symphonion, at Gohlis, Leipzig, employed a maximum of about four hundred and Paul Ehrlich, owner of the Fabrik Leipziger Musikwerke (established as early as 1877) which made the Monopol disc machine and the Ariston organette, had something like the same number. The total employed in mechanical musicwork in Leipzig was three thousand in 1898.

Many makers and agents had a London office or warehouse address. If we take these more or less alphabetically, there was Barnett Henry Abrahams at 128 Houndsditch as the London warehouse of the Swiss B.H.A. company which made both cylinder and disc musical boxes including the Britannia and the Imperial. At 31 Aldermanbury was the warehouse of Ball, Beavon & Company—a major and long-established importer. Karl Bender & Co. had their warerooms at 2a Dysart Street, Finsbury. George Bendon & Co., who were wholesalers, could be found at 36 and 37 Ely Place, Holborn, with additional premises at 1 Charterhouse Street. Beutner & Company specialised in organettes as well as musical boxes and they had a special line of these including the Ariosa and the Phoenix at 65 and 66 Basinghall Street. Their warehouse was at 5, 6 and 7 St Georges Avenue in East London. Camerer, Kuss & Co. were also agents for Black

---

* It is worth noting here that electricity was only thought of as being usable for the production of electric light at this period and any machine which could operate from the same current was considered something of a novelty.
† Hupfeld also produced billiard tables and gaming machines.

Forest clocks and cuckoo clocks and had their offices at 56 New Oxford Street (they are still there today) and 2 Broad Street, Bloomsbury. Thomas Dawkins & Co. was at 17 Charterhouse Street with their factory down among the Italian barrel piano makers at 49 Warner Street in Clerkenwell. Holding the Royal Warrant for the manufacture of musical instruments for Queen Victoria was Imhof & Mukle at 110 New Oxford Street. Across the river Thames at 17 and 18 Railway Approach, London Bridge, was King's Universal Supply Limited who operated as retailers of a number of makes of boxes.

Another retailer was Hermann Lange at 13 and 14 Camomile Street, E.C. Antoine Lateulere sold musical boxes at 19 Clerkenwell Road where he advertised that he employed Swiss craftsmen for his repair work. Mermod Frères had their London premises at 81 Milton Street, E.C., and Mojon, Manger & Co. were at 26 and 27 Bartlett's Buildings. Alfred Müller retailed boxes at 23 Sloane Street, S.W. and Nicole Frères sold cylinder boxes as well as Polyphons and the 'two-tunes-per-disc' Sirion at 21 Ely Place. C. Paillard & Co. had showrooms at 28 Berners Street (a road full of music shops and piano showrooms) off Oxford Street having moved from 62 Holborn Viaduct in 1894. Silber & Fleming Limited could be found at 56½–62 and 71 Wood Street, E.C. and also at 2 London Wall. Jerome Thibouville-Lamy & Co. were established at 7, 9 and 10 Charterhouse Street (they moved here in 1884 and six months later the premises burned to the ground: re-established, they survived at this address until 1941 when they were bombed out. The business is now in Clerkenwell Road). The firm of John Tritschler was at 85 Oxford Street—the business moved to 40 Great Russell Street in 1898—and Wales & McCulloch who were another long-established musical box importers, sold their wares from 20 Ludgate Hill and 56 Cheapside. Another distributor was Joseph Wallis & Son at 133 and 135 Euston Road.

If musical boxes were to be sold, then they had to be backed by a repair service and repair specialists included Dawkins, Imhofs, Lateulere, Nicole Frères, Paillards, Joseph Fackler at 6 St John's Square (he could also pin new cylinders) and William Savage at 110 St John Street (he died in 1897). Manager of the repair depot at Nicole Frères was Henri Metert—on 25 June 1906, he formed a company called Metert & Co. at 21/22 Ely Place, just twenty years after he came to London.

Musical boxes abounded and the amusement side-show in Piccadilly, lit by the electric light strung from the ceiling, was just one place where one could find a 24½ inch self-changing Polyphon surrounded by people. Street music, of course, was everywhere, the Italian barrel piano makers having settled in Clerkenwell where they produced many a 'piano-organ' on a handcart. Chiappa was making street organs, barrel pianos and barrel harmoniums in Eyre Street Hill; Pasquale was producing street pianos as well as 'automatics', as they were called, for public houses. These were clockwork barrel pianos and responded musically to the insertion of a penny.

Nicole Frères, having taken over the remainder of their house in Ely Place as storerooms, stocked large numbers of Polyphons, the discs for some of which were as cheap as 5d each. They also had no fewer than a thousand cylinder musical boxes in stock. To handle the mushrooming business in Polyphons, they formed a new company at the same address which was known as the Polyphon & Regina Music Box Company which also undertook repairs to these instruments. The manager was a Mr Meitzner. American-made Reginas were imported by this enterprise.

Jacques Ullmann, partner with his brother Charles in the firm of Ch. & J. Ullmann of Paris and Ste Croix, opened up as a repairer and retailer at 9 Butler Street, Milton Street, E.C., and Alban Voigt, who stocked Symphonions, tackled all repair work at 14 Edmund Place. Voigt, incidentally, took over Paillard's interests when that firm closed its London office in 1894. This was the agency of A. Paillard of 62 Holborn Viaduct who, in 1891, became sole agent for the Berlin Musical Instruments Manufacturing Company Limited, formerly known as Charles F. Pietschmann & Son who were makers of the Herophon and Manopan organettes and the Celesta disc musical box. This last-mentioned box was not introduced until 1895 by which time this agency was held by Martin Hirsch at 9–11 Wilson Street, London E.C. This business began in that year and also factored the Symphonion.

It was around Christmas time 1895 that Henry Klein unveiled the first of the triple-disc Symphonion Eroica musical boxes to be seen in London. With its three-hundred musical comb teeth this was an expensive instrument selling at 65 guineas, but even so four were sold in a matter of weeks. Across town at Finsbury, E.C., Barnett Samuel & Sons of 32 and 34 Worship Street were the sole agents for the Orphenion, a very sweet-toned disc instrument which came in a number of sizes, the largest coin-operated models playing twice for one penny. These were made by the Orphenion Musikwerke Bruno Rückert in Leipzig.

The industry was booming. In 1898 more than three thousand people were employed in Leipzig and exports to many parts of the world showed a steady increase. Severe inroads were thus being made in the market of the Swiss industry and this was, quite naturally, of considerable concern to those who worked in that cherished cradle of the musical box—the Swiss Jura and its commerce control centre, Geneva. Several manufacturers formed themselves into a consortium. This was the Société Anonyme Fabriques Réunies founded in 1896. They set up their offices at 12 rue Bonivard in Geneva, subsequently moving to 18 Quai de St Jean. The group, which claimed to have been established in 1844, comprised the three businesses of Ami Rivenc, Langdorff Fils and the house of Billon, all Geneva-based manufacturers the oldest of whom is traceable back to 1838. A London office was opened at 3 New Union Street, Moorfields under a Mr Henry Benjamin, and they factored their own instruments—the disc-playing Gloria, table and upright models—to the British public directly, so dispensing with agents' commissions. There was also a clockwork-powered organette which sold for 12 guineas. Several years later, in 1901, they introduced another disc instrument, called after the Muse Polymnia, which was advertised as having 'indestructible discs'. This referred to the projections on the discs which, instead of being of the usual punched tab type, were in the form of dimples rather like those used on the Orphenion. Far from administering a trouncing to the Germans, most Swiss disc boxes served only to highlight the better quality of the products of Leipzig and Berlin.

Towards the end of 1896, Martin Hirsch in London became the sole agent for the Troubadour disc-playing musical box made by B. Grosz & Company of Breitkopfstrasse 9, Reudnitz, Leipzig (by 1909, the business was at Gellerstrasse 8, Leipzig III). Among the 'special features' listed as selling points for these instruments were the 'larger comb (with additional teeth) and metal discs'. A repertory of almost one hundred tunes was initially available and the masters for each disc were said to cost the manufacturers £3 each to make. Hirsch's showrooms contained several models ranging from the largest (six feet tall) to small table models. In May 1897 the same business became sole UK distributor of a remarkably lovely device, the Chordephon disc-playing zither which sold at 6 guineas and was available in two models—clockwork or hand turned.

The impetus of the musical box industry and its growth rate were not without internal problems. Early on, Paul Lochmann of Symphonion had taken Gustav Brachhausen of Polyphon to court over the right to use projections on musical box discs. Lochmann lost. Now another legal tangle was taking place in Leipzig. Paul Ehrlich, maker of the Ariston organette and Monopol disc box, in the newly-adopted name of his Company, the Leipziger Musikwerke, was claiming a monopoly in the use of star wheels for mechanical musical instruments. The case had come up in the summer of 1896 and Ehrlich had lost. He now appealed to the Court of Naumburg against the earlier decision. Considerable weight of objection to his appeal had been lodged by the house of Lochmann (which denied to the Ehrlich factory all rights to forbid anybody to use star wheels as plectra for the tongues of musical box combs), and other factories both in Leipzig and Berlin. It was, in fact, correctly claimed that other makers had been using star wheels much earlier than Ehrlich. The court subsequently dismissed the appeal, but with heavy costs against Ehrlich. In 1904, Ehrlich sold the company to Wwe Emilie Buff-Hedinger, the new name being Neue Leipziger Musikwerke A. Buff-Hedinger at Herloss-sohnstrasse 1–4, Leipzig-Gohlis. As well as making Ariston organettes, the business made player pianos, player organs, orchestrions and the Toccaphon xylophone piano. The mushrooming industry was accompanied with the inevitable trappings of prosperity—business take-overs, the speculators and the troublemakers. Then, as now, money made by far the loudest noise. But there were other problems which hinged on trade restrictions, duties and tariffs. In 1895, for instance, the Austro-Hungarian finance ministry decided that piano-orchestrions were to be taxed as 'finger-board instruments' at 20 florins per hundred kilos for the countries with whom commercial treaties existed, and double that for the others! And in America, MacKinley's attitude towards imports was more than just short-sighted. A valuable decade of European intercourse was lost.

To return to London, Alban Voigt dealt primarily with stringed instruments at his Edmund Place address. His entry into the musical box trade, however, was on a large scale and in 1898 he unquestionably held the largest stock of Symphonions in England. Fortunately his premises escaped the disastrous fire of 19 November 1896, which laid waste several busy streets in this, the Aldersgate area of the City.

Probably the best known of the musical box dealers and wholesalers was Henry Klein who advertised widely to the trade and published numerous illustrated catalogues. His main business was in Polyphons and amusement machines from his second-floor premises at 84 Oxford Street. In the summer of 1897, he extended his range of Amorette organettes with the new, enlarged models playing on 44 and 72 reeds and costing from 5 guineas upwards (see Chapter 6). The wholesale agent for this was M. H. Jesing of 76 Newman Street. His business, founded in 1889, went bankrupt in 1897. The Amorette was made in sizes from 16 to 108 reeds and was the product of the Euphonika Musikwerke of Friedrich Listrasse 11, Leipzig which made some of the most expensive of automatic instruments. This company also produced a rather attractive mechanical organ played by a perforated disc. Called the Euphonika, this played 48 reed notes, 20 organ pipes, a 10 bell glockenspiel, a drum and a cymbal.

Travelling into London, as your train slowed down into Broad Street (City) station, and provided that you were sitting with your back to the engine, you could have seen the large modern premises taken over in July of 1897 by Ball, Beavon & Company. Across the front of the factory was written 'Manufacturers & Importers of Musical Instruments. Wholesale Only'. The firm had begun forty or fifty years previously as Ihlee & Horne and had the singular distinction of having patented the first luminous paint, the invention of W. H. Balmain of University College, London. Later, the firm became Ihlee & Sankey, changing its name to Ball, Beavon & Co. in 1886 at which time the premises were in Aldermanbury. But now the move had been completed to 5 Skinner Street, Bishopsgate Street Without. On the four floors were all manner of goods and processes, one floor being devoted to stringed instruments and most of another to musical boxes. The first lift in London had probably been the famous 'ascending room' at the Colosseum in Regent's Park built for Hornor's panorama of London (see Chapter 2). Now they were becoming commonplace although that proudly advertised at B. B. & C.'s was for goods, not persons.

Another Leipzig product was the Orpheus disc musical box made by Ludwig & Co. (Ludwig & Wild). The chief sales point of these particular instruments dwelt not on portability or compactness, but on the sheer bulk and weight of the largest in the range. This behemoth stood 86 inches high, was 30 inches wide, 20 inches deep and played discs 22⅝ inches in diameter on a comb of 220 teeth.

Whereas in 1895 and 1896, trade boomed to such an unbridled extent that Polyphons declined orders and Lochmann declared a twenty per cent dividend, a formidable cloud appeared over the whole of the Leipzig industry in the summer of 1897. Not only were there endless petty squabbles and legal hagglings among the various musical box makers as they fought manufacturing problems, patent infringements, labour difficulties and the activities of disreputable companies operating outside the recently formed mechanical musical instrument makers' association, but now something quite unexpected occurred. A steep rise in the cost of steel, particularly that of tin-plate needed for the manufacture of discs, threatened to force up the prices of instruments and thereby favour the slowly rallying Swiss industry. Workers were entreated to increase their output and achieve more work per man-hour so as to help absorb the rising costs. Assisted by cheap Bohemian labour from across the nearby border, Leipzig successfully weathered that storm. Many of the jobs in musical box factories were carried out by girls, including the stamping out of the discs. These young women were paid three to four marks per week—between £1·50 and £1·95.

In November of that year, the London showrooms of the Leipzig Music Works at 57 Basinghall Street unveiled to the public yet another giant disc-player—the seven feet tall Monopol Excelsior. In the same month, Nicole Frères became a limited liability company.

Jules Heinrich Zimmermann, who had factories in Leipzig, St Petersburg and Moscow, opened a London company in the late 1890s to stock the Symphonion, establishing a showroom at 67 New Bond Street. In 1900, the Symphonion Company established itself at 28 Ely Place, Holborn (a few doors away from the rival Polyphons of Nicole Frères) and Zimmermann, inspired by the possibilities of the disc musical box business, went on to make and sell the Fortuna and, later, the Adler disc machines. Both these were made by Zimmermann in Leipzig, the latter being the product of a subsidiary company. Both were extremely fine instruments although some of the musical arrangements were a little florid for present-day ears.

It was now Polyphon's turn to be taken to court. In 1898, the firm of Henry Litolff's Edition of Brunswick sued the manager of Polyphon for the unauthorised transcription of *Marche Lorraine*, composed by the Frenchman Louis Ganne, on to tin discs. The case was a particularly interesting one for several technical reasons regarding the interpretation of the copyright law, the Bernese Convention and the involvement of a French national's work. However, it suffices to say here that the case went against Polyphon and in spite of an appeal, the court decision was . upheld that all discs, together with master plates, appliances for the production of the discs and so forth, should be confiscated, whether in the hands of Polyphon or their agents anywhere in the world. Polyphon acted accordingly, and *Marche Lorraine* was officially impounded and destroyed. However, a number of the discs had already been sold and had been available for several years; thus copies of this banned disc do exist and I have one in my own collection.

Still the musical boxes came, though, and Ernst Holzweissig opened his large warehouse in Newman Street, London, in 1898 to reveal a giant Symphonion on which he is said to have played Lohengrin's 'Wedding Song' (sic) as a demonstration piece. This vast model was mounted in a carved oak case and stood nine feet high. Its appointments included a set of bells and it sold for all of thirty guineas. He also stocked the coin-operated Kalliope which sold at about ten guineas, the Adler, a range of smaller, table models, Amorettes, musical chairs, decanters and other musical fancy goods.

But for the largest musical box to be seen anywhere in London, one had to go to the showrooms of William Gerecke at 8 and 9 Goring Street, Houndsditch. Gerecke was agent for the Komet made in Leipzig by Weissbach & Co., and one model he showed was no less than eleven feet tall, had 618 musical comb teeth, and played discs almost 33 inches across. This was advertised as 'the largest musical automaton in the World'. Gerecke's business, though, did not succeed and, having formed a limited liability company in July 1901, he absconded to South Africa, being declared bankrupt in October 1902.

Although Nicole Frères, now operated from London, and several other reputable makers of cylinder musical boxes declined to lower their standards and by that decision so gradually lost much of their share of the market to the disc makers, many others moved with the times. The factories of Paillard, Thorens and Karrer all girded their loins and took to mass production. In the late 1880s and 1890s, the chief rival to the cylinder box had been the rather brash and, to some ears, unmusical tones of the hand-turned organette, some of which sold for as cheaply as a few shillings. Although certain of the later organettes were of undoubted quality, the disc musical box had much to offer as a musical interpreter and the whittling away of the cylinder musical box market by the organette was transferred double-quick to the disc box.

It fell to the Swiss to invent the comb-playing musical box operated by a disc without projections. Mermod Frères introduced the Stella in 1896 which had perforated discs smooth on both sides. In 1903, the same manufacturer produced the Mira and the Empress (a version of the Mira made for the American market), both of which had discs with projections. The Stella discs, however, were nowhere near as delicate as those of the majority of musical box discs whose projections could become bent and jam in the playing mechanisms.

The Stella and Mira agency was first held by Alfred Gaeter of 105 St John Street Road, London, E.C. Gaeter had formerly been manager for A. Paillard whose business, as already related, was acquired by Voigt. From 1898 onwards, however, the sole agency for Mermod Frères passed to Imhof & Mukle in New Oxford Street. The Empress was sold in Chicago by Lyon & Healy, and this was the same as the Mira. During the 1914-18 war, it is significant that Gaeter, now at 339 St John Street, again advertised as distributor for both these Swiss-made disc boxes.

Today many people mis-spell and mispronounce the name of the products of the house of Lochmann in Leipzig as 'Symphonium' instead of 'Symphonion'. That this is no new foible is shown by the number of references in contemporary sales material to the instrument as 'Symphonium'. The name Symphonium was applied by Wheatstone to the first mouth-organ while the name Symphonion was first used by Kaufmann when he introduced his orchestrion of that name at the St Martin's Hall (built for John Hullah, the famed 'tonic sol-fa' singing teacher, and which burned down on 26 August 1860, later to rise again as the New Queen's Theatre) to a select gathering in 1851 (see Chapter 5).

Polyphon did not escape the misrepresentations of the public either, and the name Polyphone was not uncommon then, nor is it so now. Indeed, as pianola came to be the generic name for the player piano, polyphon(e) came to be the like term for the disc-playing musical box.

The Symphonion Company opened its London headquarters in 1900 in that stately row of mansions in Holborn built on the site of the famous palace of Ely Place. As well as stocking their own musical boxes, they sold phonographs, the Phoenix organette and also did repairs to all types of musical boxes.

It was during 1900 that Paul Lochmann moved from Leipzig to Zeulenroda (Thuringen) in Central Germany to set up the Original-Musikwerke Paul Lochmann GmbH. Here he put into production his new brainchild, the Lochmann Original series of disc musical boxes. These were very fine pieces of workmanship and, no doubt following on the accoustical teachings demonstrated by the Regina, used the entire case as a resonator (the Swiss Britannia upright machines did the same thing). He also made a disc-operated piano orchestrion called the Original Konzert Piano in 1902. Within a few years, the widsom of his move away from the centre of the mechanical music industry with its pool of workers, its facilities for supplies and the value of its industrial associations was proven unwise and so he returned to Leipzig and took premises at Querstrasse 15/17 where with his partner, Ernst Lüder, he distributed his wares which included pianos and, later, gramophones. The factory, however, remained in Zeulenroda.

Although the Lochmann Original was a fine instrument, it was too late in the development of the disc musical box to gain for itself a worthwhile share of the market already exploited so adequately by its progenitor, the Symphonion, and the Polyphon. Another instrument which did not get very far was the Sun made in Geneva by Schrämli & Tschudin. This was available in both upright and table models. Even less-known was the New Century sold (and probably manufactured) by Henry Vidoudez of Ste Croix in 1900. Q. David Bowers, however, has discovered evidence which appears to suggest that the mechanisms of both this and the Sirion were manufactured by Mermod Frères.

With all these musical boxes being made, the production of their discs and the equipment for making the discs also became big-time business and at least one firm, Julius Berthold & Co. of Klingenthal, made the special stamping presses for both discs and strip perforated music. This firm would supply not only the machinery and the blank discs, but would also undertake under contract the complete production of discs for those manufacturers too small to establish their own disc-stamping plant.

In 1902, the last great enterprise of the Symphonion company in Leipzig materialised. This was the giant 25-inch disc self-changer. Made no doubt as their answer to the similar machines being turned out by Polyphon and Regina, the cost of developing this complex instrument was probably the cause of the cessation of their musical-box production only a year or two later. The patents for this were taken out in 1901 (British Patent No. 14,249), and in 1902 British Patent No. 2583 was issued covering a horizontal self-changer disc musical box. Both were in the name of the Fabrik Lochmann'scher Musikwerke of Leipzig. No examples of either are known to survive although it seems certain that models of the 25 inch upright instrument were produced.

The decline of the cylinder musical box continued during the ten to fifteen brief years of the boom in the disc musical box, but before the new century was more than five years old, it was obvious that the musical box in all its forms was on the slippery slope. The great names closed their doors for the last time, the 'For Sale' boards went up. Dealers either shut down or took up other lines, such as the up-and-coming 'talking machine'. Even the ebullient Henry Klein was forced to diversify, first in 1903 with cycle speedometers and Pathé records, then gaming machines. Finally, in the spring of 1906, he retired full of years and his business was amalgamated with that of the New Polyphon Supply Co. who hired instruments to public places. Nicole Frères, whose talking machine trade boomed in 1902–3, turned to making records and in 1903 they opened a new factory at Great Saffron Hill, Clerkenwell, to produce the Duplex

disc. This sold at a shilling (7-inch) and half a crown (10-inch). Within a year, others were making cheaper discs and so Nicole Frères was forced into liquidation. In New Jersey, the Regina Company emulated the great Gavioli fair-organ factory in Paris and turned to making vacuum cleaners and other electrical domestic appliances (the company sold its last musical box in 1921). The 1900s were filled with their own sounds and these did not include those of the musical box. And the passing was gradual which meant that, since the new sounds generated their own excitement, nobody mourned the old. Germany shrugged its shoulders and applied all its talents to the improvement and perfection of the orchestrion organ. The 1914–18 war created an enforced break, more serious matters to concern Mankind, and retrenchment. After that was over, the musical box really was of a past age. Just as the public entertainments of the early Victorian years appear somewhat childish to us today, the musical box was discarded as old-fashioned. As a tool for the production of music, it had had its day. It belonged with the wine-cooler, the gas iron, the candle lamp and the flintlock pistol, and so the freshet of progress swept all before it.

The first disc-playing musical box to enter production was the Symphonion made in Leipzig by Paul Lochmann. Lochmann was an enterprising industrialist and inventor who manufactured, among other things, table fountains. The first instrument, however, was the joint conception of Leipzig and London. In the former, Frederich Ernst Paul Ehrlich was experimenting with automatic reed instruments having a stationary perforated tune sheet beneath which was rotated a reed box and bellows, crank operated. Ellis Parr in London was designing very similar instruments. Lochmann, no doubt inspired by Ehrlich's invention, patented a similar machine which used a tuned steel musical box-type comb under the fixed music sheet. Ellis Parr was contriving just the same thing. Both men, coincidentally, stated that an alternative interpretation of their invention could be a stationary musical comb and a rotating tune sheet in the form of a disc. The *Pall Mall Budget* for 16 February 1888 fills in the story.

MUSIC BY MECHANISM.

An Interview with the Inventor of the Symphonion.

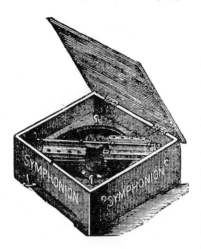

THE old notion which has been so often expressed that it has almost become a proverbial saying, namely that we are not a nation of musicians, is still widely prevalent, although the severe saying has been somewhat toned down. As we understand ourselves at present, we are, though not innate musicians, at all events endowed with a sense which makes us understand and appreciate good music almost as well as those musicians by the grace of God, the Italians and the Germans. Anything, therefore, connected with vocal and instrumental music is deemed of interest, and the latest of inventions in the kingdom of " sweet sound " is at this moment receiving considerable attention. This is the symphonion, a development of the musical box, which is now being exhibited on the premises of Messrs. Ellis Parr and Co., at 16, Long-lane, E.C. Mr. Parr, who has taken out the patent for the symphonion, called at the office a day or two ago, and furnished our representative with some interesting particulars concerning his invention.

" How is it," Mr. Parr was asked, " that in this age, when everybody plays some kind of instrument, there is still a demand for automatic musical instruments ? "

" That question is easily answered," said Mr. Parr. " People like change, and if every human being were a good pianiste the trade in musical boxes would be brisker than ever. People get tired of playing, or of hearing others play, with more or less perfection, and here they have, without any trouble, pleasant music, faultlessly performed. And not only is there a demand, but there has been an increasing demand for musical boxes ever since they were improved, as of late years they have been, to produce really good music, and a variety of it. The only drawback has always been that a box only played a limited number of tunes, of which people naturally got tired, after hearing them again and again. Dealers have often and often said to me that if we could invent some means by which any tune might be played on a box, there would be an endless demand. And this want has now been supplied by the symphonion, the mechanism of which is similar to that of the ordinary musical box, but which, instead of the fixed barrel, contains a disc which is easily and quickly adjusted. If you want another tune you substitute another disc, and as we have an infinite variety of them there can be no longer any question of monotony."

" But do not the discs make the symphonion rather an expensive instrument if you wish to have a variety of tunes ? "

" Not by any means. We have the instrument in different sizes, at prices ranging from 5s. to fifty guineas ; the very small ones are, of course, more toys than anything else ; but the discs cost at the most only about 2s., which price you have to pay at least if you buy the same piece of music at any music seller's."

"Which class of the public takes best to the symphonion ? "—"All classes alike ; those who can afford it buy large and expensive instruments, and those who cannot are satisfied with the smaller. But both in London and in the country the sale is very good indeed, and we do a good business in exporting."

"To what countries chiefly ? "—" To the Australian colonies."

"Then is your symphonion made abroad too, and is it not somewhat unfair to employ foreign labour when so many are compelled to idleness in this country ? "

"Yes, the symphonion is made at Leipsic, where my co-patentee, a German gentleman, is at the head of our factory. Of course I should employ

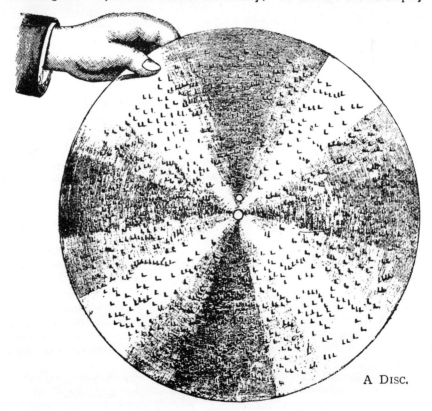

A DISC.

English labour, if such were possible, but as yet we have not the necessary skill in this country. It requires a long and thorough education before the work can be done, and workers skilled in this particular handicraft are not to be found in England. We employ about 120 hands in the factory at Leipsic, besides a number of girls who prepare the discs at their own homes, but we shall require a much larger number before long, for as it is, the demand for the symphonion is very great, and it is still increasing. I have only lately ordered four hundred to be sent to me, and I find that the order cannot be executed sooner than March. As a curiosity it may perhaps interest you to know that Mr. Lochmann, my German co-patentee, made precisely the same invention only a week after I made mine. I was on my way to Switzerland without knowing anything about him, when at the Leipsic fair I heard of his invention. At first I took action against him to prevent his interfering with the sale in England, but eventually we became partners, and are now both trying to improve our instrument in every possible way, till it shall be quite perfect.'

"I suppose you could not reproduce any longer pieces of music on the symphonion? For instance, parts of an oratorio, or a whole quadrille?"

"Not with one disc, but with a series of discs without difficulty. There are, in every musical composition, intervals of longer or shorter duration, and as the changing of the disc requires only about one quarter of a minute, no objectionable break need occur. In dance music it is even easier, as between each part of, say, a quadrille, there is necessarily a pause. As the time can also be regulated on the symphonion, there is not the slightest reason why the instrument should not be as successfully used in a ballroom as anywhere else."

"But even supposing every other difficulty could be removed, would not the music be insufficient in volume to make it suitable as an accompaniment to dancing?"

"In a large public room, yes. In a private room of 50 ft. by 25 ft. it would be perfectly sufficient, owing to its clear, carrying tone, which, like the sound of the violin, is heard above far larger and more powerful instruments."

From Parr's and Lochmann's simple beginnings, Symphonions went from strength to strength. An American subsidiary was formed and, in *McClure's Magazine* for February 1898 we see the above. In 1903, Lochmann invented a large and spectacular self-changing instrument—the Style 100. This is illustrated overleaf. None of these has been seen.

Symphonion No. 100 „Non plus ultra".

WM. F. HASSE,

Successor to T. F. KRAEMER & CO.

1894—1895.

IMPORTER OF

Symphonion and Polyphone

MUSIC BOXES.

No. 107 East 14th Street,

Adjoining Steinway Hall,

NEW YORK.

Before the establishment of the Symphonion Manufacturing Company in New York, William Hasse handled the instrument in that city, along with its rival, the Polyphon, and also the first American-made disc instrument, the Regina. This catalogue is followed by a well-illustrated catalogue published in London by Polyphon about 1905. Unfortunately some of the pages are slightly damaged.

SYMPHONION No. 28.

✳ SYMPHONION ✳

MUSIC BOXES.

The most important invention in the line of self-playing Music Boxes, by means of changeable Metallic Tune Plates, thousands of different tunes may be played on the same instrument. The Music comprises Hymns, National Airs, Operatic Airs, Dances, Songs; etc. Speed can be regulated. The instruments play from ten to thirty minutes with one winding, according to size and speed allowed.

The Tune Plates are made of steel and are indestructible. The mechanism is simple and strong, therefore not apt to get out of order easily. The tone of all these instruments is sweet and melodious.

Complete stock of tunes always on hand. New tunes are being added constantly.

Tune Lists on Application.

DISCOUNT TO THE TRADE.

NOTICE.—First Prize was awarded to the **Symphonion** Music Boxes at the World's Fair, Chicago.

No. 28. 40 STEEL TONGUES.

With Crank for turning.

Case of Imitation Rosewood, with ornamented cover.

Dimensions: 6½ x 6½ x 3½ inches.

Diameter of Tunes, 5½ inches.

PRICE, - - $6.00, incl. 1 tune.

Additional Tunes: 30 cents.

SYMPHONION No. 10.

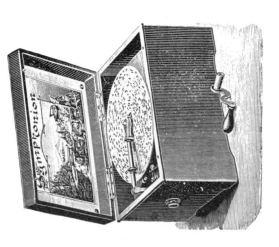

No. 10. 41 STEEL TONGUES.

Self Playing. Clock Movement. Detachable Winding Handle.

Elegant Rosewood Case, with Marquetry.

Dimensions: 10½ x 8 x 6½ inches.

Diameter of Tunes, 7½ inches.

PRICE, - - $20.00, incl. 1 tune

Additional Tunes: 40 cents.

SYMPHONION No. 28 S.

"SIMPLEX."

No. 28 S. 40 STEEL TONGUES.

Self Playing. Clock Movement.

Case in Ebony or Rosewood finish, with gilt inscription on cover.

Dimensions: 7¾ x 6¾ x 4¾ inches.

Diameter of Tunes, 5½ inches.

PRICE, - - $14.00, incl. 1 tune.

Additional Tunes: 30 cents.

WM. F. HASSE, NEW YORK.

SYMPHONION No. 4 N.

No. 4 N. 72 STEEL TONGUES.

With Clock Movement.

Fine solid Walnut Case, with fancy Veneer.

Ornamental Cover. Detachable Winding Handle.

Dimensions: 16 x 12½ x 9½ inches.

Diameter of Tunes, 9 inches.

PRICE, - - $46.00, incl. 1 tune.

Additional Tunes: 60 cents.

WM. F. HASSE, NEW YORK.

SYMPHONION No. 2 N.

No. 2 N. 60 STEEL TONGUES.

With Clock Movement.

Splendid solid Walnut Case, with lock and key; ornamental cover.

Improved Machinery; Great volume of Tone; Detachable Winding Handle.

Dimensions: 15 x 11½ x 9 inches.

Diameter of Tunes, 8 inches.

PRICE, - - $42.00, incl. 1 tune

Additional Tunes: 50 cents.

SYMPHONION No. 25 N.

SUBLIME HARMONY.

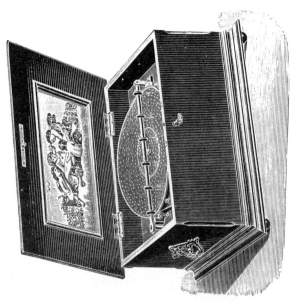

No. 25 N. 84 STEEL TONGUES.

Sublime Harmony.

Beautiful solid Walnut Case, with lock and key. Very sweet, full and melodious tone.

Dimensions: 18½ x 15 x 11 inches.

Diameter of Tunes, 11¾ inches.

PRICE, - - $36.00, incl. 1 tune.

Additional Tunes: 85 cents.

SYMPHONION No. 6 N.

No. 6 N. 84 STEEL TONGUES.

With Clock Movement.

Fine solid Walnut Case, with fancy Veneer.

Ornamental Cover; Detachable Winding Handle; Loud and Deep Tone.

Dimensions: 18 x 13½ x 10 inches.

Diameter of Tunes, 10½ inches.

PRICE, - - $52.00, incl. 1 tune.

Additional Tunes: 70 cents.

SYMPHONION No. 30 N.

SUBLIME HARMONY—PICCOLO.

No. 30 N. 100 STEEL TONGUES.

Sublime Harmony—Piccolo. Four Combs.

Powerful Tone, beautiful and clear Music. Solid Walnut Case, with lock.

Dimensions: 21 x 17 x 10½ inches.

Diameter of Tunes, 13½ inches.

PRICE, - - $96.00, incl. 1 tune.

Additional Tunes: $1.00.

SYMPHONION No. 25.

SUBLIME HARMONY.

No. 25. 84 STEEL TONGUES.

Sublime Harmony.

Very elegant Walnut Case, with fancy Veneer and Marquetry, carved columns and glass cover over the work inside. Rich and sweet tone.

Dimensions: 19¼ x 15 x 9½ inches.

Diameter of Tunes, 11¾ inches.

PRICE, - - $80.00, incl. 1 tune.

Additional Tunes: 85 cents.

HALL CLOCK.

WITH SYMPHONION—SUBLIME HARMONY—PICCOLO.

No. 30. 100 STEEL TONGUES. HALL CLOCK.

Highly elegantly finished Case in Oak or Walnut. First-class 14 day clock-work, French movement, striking and playing the full hour. The Music can be played independent of the clock. Cathedral gong.

Dimensions: 8 feet high, 24 inch. deep, 24 inch. wide. Diameter of Tunes, 13½ inch.

PRICE, - - - - - - - - - - - $250.00, incl. 1 tune.

ADDITIONAL TUNES: $1.00.

WM. F. HASSE, NEW YORK.

14

SYMPHONION No. 30 A.

SUBLIME HARMONY—PICCOLO.

No. 30 A. 100 STEEL TONGUES.

Sublime Harmony—Piccolo. Four Combs.

Rich and powerful tone. Highly finished Walnut Case, with beautifully inlaid Marquetry Cover, carved columns, and glass cover over the work inside.

Dimensions: 22 x 18 x 11 inches.

Diameter of Tunes, 13½ inches.

PRICE, - - $112.00, incl. 1 tune.

Additional Tunes: $1.00.

WM. F. HASSE, NEW YORK.

REGINA No. 13.

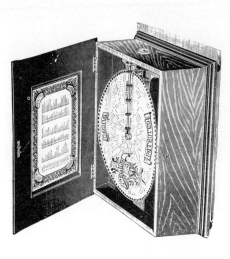

No. 13. 78 STEEL TONGUES.

The tone of this instrument is very melodious and effective.

Highly polished Cases in solid Walnut, Mahogany or Oak.

Dimensions: **21 x 18½ x 7½ inches.**

Diameter of Tunes, **15½ inches.**

PRICE, - - **$70.00, incl. 1 tune.**

Additional Tunes: **$1.00.**

WM. F. HASSE, NEW YORK.

REGINA No. 22.

WITH CLOCK MOVEMENT.

No. 22. 41 STEEL TONGUES.

Highly polished Case in solid Mahogany or Oak.

Dimensions: **9¾ x 8¾ x 7 inches.**

Diameter of Tunes, **8½ inches.**

PRICE, - - **$19.00, incl. 1 tune.**

Additional Tunes: **50 cents.**

WM. F. HASSE, NEW YORK. 22

REGINA No. 10.

DUPLEX.

No. 10. 156 STEEL TONGUES.

Two Combs.

Elegant Case, of Antique Oak, beautifully carved.

Dimensions: 22 x 20 x 12 inches.

Tune Sheets: 15½ inches Diameter.

PRICE, - - $136.00, incl. 1 tune.

Additional Tunes: $1.00.

WM. F. HASSE, NEW YORK. 21

REGINA No. 11.

DUPLEX.

OPEN VIEW.

Showing position of the Two Combs.

No. 11. 156 STEEL TONGUES.

Case with drawer for 15 tune sheets.

In Walnut, Mahogany, Cherry and Oak.

Dimensions: 22 x 20 x 11½ inches.

Tune Sheets: 15½ inches Diameter.

PRICE, - - $120.00, incl. 1 tune

Additional Tunes: $1.00.

POLYPHONE No. 45.

TWO COMBS.

No. 45. 156 STEEL TONGUES.

Sublime Harmony—Piccolo.

Full and vigorous tone; beautiful Case of fine French Walnut, with inlaid Marquetry on Cover and with Drawer to hold tunes.

Dimensions: 25 x 20 x 12½ inches.

Diameter of Tunes: 15½ inches.

PRICE, - - $136.00, incl. 1 tune

Additional Tunes: $1.00.

POLYPHONE No. 44.

No. 44. 78 STEEL TONGUES.

Beautifully ornamented Case of fine French Walnut, with inlaid Marquetry on Cover.

Dimensions: 22 x 18 x 8½ inches.

Diameter of Tune Sheets: 15½ inches.

PRICE, - - $90.00, incl. 1 tune.

Additional Tunes: $1.00.

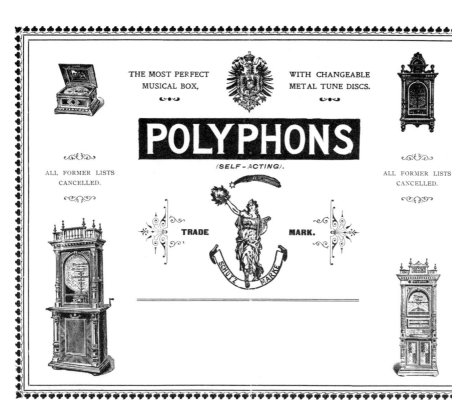

THE MOST PERFECT
MUSICAL BOX,

WITH CHANGEABLE
METAL TUNE DISCS.

POLYPHONS

(SELF-ACTING).

ALL FORMER LISTS
CANCELLED.

ALL FORMER LISTS
CANCELLED.

TRADE   MARK.

Autumn, 1899.   Printed in England by FOLSUE & ALFIERI, Ltd., 4 & 5, Gough Square, London, E.C.

THE POLYPHON

has been **imitated** by many, but none can compare with the quality of tone or the solid workmanship of the Polyphon. Considered from every point, the Polyphon is the **cheapest** and **best mechanical** instrument in the world.

🍎 🍎 🍎

REPAIRS of all kinds of Musical Boxes promptly executed at moderate charges.

🍎 🍎 🍎

LIST OF TUNES for the different sized POLYPHONS printed separately and forwarded on application. In order to avoid mistakes in ordering tunes, state diameter of tune, and **give a few extra numbers in case we are out of some.**

🍎 🍎 🍎

SPRING STUD WHEELS are supplied to all Penny-in-Slots unless specially ordered with Fixed Studs.

🍎 🍎 🍎

GOODS SENT BY RAIL should be examined on receipt, and in case of damage, *do not* return same to us, but *make your claim* at once to the Carriers or Railway Company.

🍎 🍎 🍎

CASES OR BOXES in which each instrument is packed are free and not returnable.

127

No. 28 POLYPHONS No. 28s

No. 28, Closed.

No. 28 POLYPHON, with 30 Tongues, Imitation Rosewood Case, with coloured picture top.

MANIVELLE

SIZE:
7¼-in. by 7¼-in. by 3¾-in.
Net Weight about 3¾ lbs.

PRICE:
Including 6 Tunes,
16s. 6d.

EXTRA TUNES
for Nos. 28
6⅜-in. diameter, **5d.** each.

No. 28s. Closed.

Self-Acting.

No. 28s POLYPHON Self-Acting (to replace the old No. 35-36,) in Imitation Rosewood Case.

SIZE:
8-in. by 7½-in. by 5-in.
Net weight about 5½ lbs.

PRICE:
Including 6 Tunes,
6⅜-in diam, **£1 12s.**
Extra Tunes, 6⅜-in. diameter, **5d.** each.

No. 28s. Open.

No. 28, Open.

3

No. 41 POLYPHONS No. 41b

No. 41, Closed.

Self=Acting.

No. 41 POLYPHON. Self-acting, with 41 Steel Tongues in Polished Veneered Walnut Case.

SIZE:
10-in. by 9-in. by 6-in.
Net weight about 7 lbs.

PRICE:
Including 6 Tunes, **£2 11s.**

Extra Tunes, 8¼-in. diameter, **8**d. each.

No. 41, Open.

No. 41b, Closed.

Self=Acting.

No. 41b, same as No. 41, but in Antique Shaped Case. With Lock and Key.

SIZE:
10¾-in. by 10-in. by 6-in.
Net Weight about 7½ lbs.

PRICE:
Including 6 Tunes,
£3.

Extra Tunes, 8¼-in. diameter,
8d. each.

No. 41b, Open.

4

No. 46, Closed.

No. 46, Open.

New Model.

No. 46.

POLYPHON, self-acting, in Walnut Case, new size tunes, between Nos. 41 and 42.

46 steel tongues.

———

Size :
12½-in. by 11½-in. by 7-in.
Net
Weight about 11¾ lbs.

———

Price :
Including 6 Tunes,
£4 5s.

———

Extra Tunes,
1/4 each.

5

No. 42, Open.

No 42, Closed.

No. 42.

POLYPHON, with 54 Steel Tongues in Handsome Polished Walnut Case, with Lock and Key, Self-acting, sweet and powerful tone, hundreds of tunes to select from.

———

Size :
13¾-in. by 12½-in. by 8-in.
Net weight 17½ lbs.
No. 46n in oblong case.

———

Price :
Including 6 Tunes and wooden packing case, **£5 15s.**

———

Extra Tunes, 11¼-in. diameter, **1s. 8d.** each.

No. 42b, Closed.

No. 42b, Open.

No. 42b
POLYPHON,
with
54 Steel Tongues,
in Antique Shaped Veneered Walnut Case, with the word "POLYPHON" in marqueterie on top, with lock and key.

Self-Acting.

———

Size :
14½-in. by 12¾-in. by 8-in.

———

Price :
Including 6 Tunes.
£6 6s.

———

Extra Tunes,
11¼-in. diameter,
1s. 8d. each.

No. 42d POLYPHON.

With 108 Tongues (54 double tongues) Veneered Handsome Walnut Case, Marqueterie on top.

Lock and Key.

Size - - 8½-in. by 16-in. by 14½-in.

Net weight - 19lbs.

Price, including 6 Tunes - - - **£7.**

Extra Tunes, 11½-in. diameter - **1s. 8d.** each.

No. 42d, Open.

6

No. 43b, Closed.

No. 43b, Open.

No. **43b**
POLYPHON, with 78 Steel Tongues, self-acting, grand tone, 2000 tunes to select from, in handsome Walnut Case, with beautiful marqueterie on top, and lock and key.

SIZE:
21½-in. by 18½-in. by 10½-in.
Net weight 36 lbs.

PRICE:
Including 6 Tunes,
£8 10s.

Extra Tunes, 15-in. diameter, **2/6** each.

7

No. 44, Open.

No. **44**. POLYPHON, with **100** Steel Tongues, self-acting, excelsior piccolo, in handsome Walnut Case, lock and key, splendid quality tone, with marqueterie on top. 2,000 Tunes to select from.

SIZE: 21½-in. by 19½-in. by 12-in. Net weight 38 lbs.

PRICE: including 6 Tunes, **£12.**

Extra Tunes, 16-in. diameter, **2s. 6d.** each.
No. **44d** (77 Double Tongues), 154 tongues, **£14.**
Sublime Harmony Piccolo (same as No. 45.)

No. 45, Open.

No. 47, Open.

No. **45** POLYPHON, with 154 Steel Tongues (77 Double Tongues), excelsior piccolo, celeste harmony, magnificent tone, and marvellous effect. This is one of the finest Polyphons made, and for its size cannot be surpassed. 2,000 Tunes to select from.

SIZE: 23-in. by 20¾-in. by 13¾-in. Net weight 50 lbs.

PRICE: With 6 Tunes, in Walnut or Oak, **£16 10s.**

Extra Tunes, 16-in. diameter, **2s. 6d.** each.

No. **45s**, in Blackwood Case, incised and gilt, **£17 10s.**

NEW POLYPHON FOR THE TABLE. Forte, Tremolo, 118 Tongues. The Case is in carved Walnut (similar to No. 45 Case), but the work is an exquisitely finished No. 104 (Imperial). The tone is powerful, without being too loud.
PRICE: Including 6 Tunes, 20-in. diameter, **£21. NO. 47s, in Blackwood Case, £22.**
Extra Tunes (same as No. 104), 3/6 each.
SIZE: 27-in. by 25-in. by 14-in. Net Weight, 60 lbs.

8

THIS REPRESENTS THE

TUNE CABINET

For Polyphons No. 103, 104 & 105.

Price of the **Tune Cabinet only** (without the instrument),

With compartments, for 103/II ...	**£3 18s.**
„ Ditto, ditto 104/II ...	**£4 15s.**
„ Ditto, ditto 105/II ...	**£5 15s.**
Plain Stained Open Stand, without partition	**£2 2s.**

For Prices of Instruments with or without Clocks, see other pages.

9

⏤ TIMBROS ⏤

for fixing on top of combs of Polyphons by which some very charming effects are obtained, it can be changed while playing.

Prices for Nos. 28s, 41, 46, 42, 43b, 44.
2/6 3/- 4/- 4/6 5/6 5/6

Prices for Nos. 45, 103, 47, 104, 118, 105, 159, 1.
10/- 11/6 13/- 13/- 13/- 16/- 16/- 16/-

No. 103. **POLYPHONS** No. 103u.

PENNY-IN-SLOT POLYPHON.

Plays all the popular airs of the day. Grand Tone. Visible Machinery. Metal Tunes. Penny-in-Slot. Pays its own cost in three months. The best Bar Polyphon Musical Automaton. Two Large Steel Combs. 78 Tongues on Two Combs. Powerful Tone. Plate Glass Door. Arranged to hang up or stand on table or bar. 2,000 Tunes to select from. A very fine instrument. Supplied with Starting Key for private use.

SIZE :
44-in. by 24-in. by 13-in.

Price, including 6 Tunes - - - - **£14.**
Same, with Clock in top piece (No. 103u) - **£15.**
With Spring Stud Wheels, **2**s. **6**d. extra.
Extra Tunes, 2s. 6d. each.

10

No. **103u**, and 6 Tunes - - - **£15.**
With Spring Stud Wheels, **2**s. **6**d. extra.
The same as No. 103, but with Eight Day Clock.

131

THE 'GRAND IMPERIAL'
with 118 Steel Tongues.
No. 104.

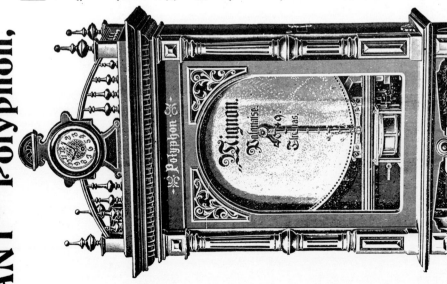

OR FOR PRIVATE USE

Arrangement to Play Twice.   Flat bottomed with deep Cash Drawer.

PENNY-IN-SLOT.

No. 104 POLYPHON. Grand Tone, splendid for Dancing, Operatic Selections, popular and high-class Songs and Pieces. Highly-finished Cabinet Work in Walnut. To stand or hang up. Tunes played complete. All the latest tunes. 52-in. high by 28-in. wide by 15½-in. deep.

Net Weight, about 1 cwt. Gross Weight, about 1 cwt. 2 quar.

Price, with 6 Tunes, showing the Working Parts under Glass Cover, £17 10s

No. 104u—Same, with Clock (8 day), £18 10s.

Extra Tunes, 20-in. diameter, 3/6 each; with spring stud wheel, 2/6 extra

ANT" Polyphon,
No. 105u.

PENNY-IN-SLOT OR PRIVATE USE.

Without Tune Case.

159 Tongues.

Magnificent Tone.

Best Value.

Largest Tunes made

25-in. diameter.

To hang up or Stand.

Plays 20 minutes with one winding.

Moderate Price.

Height, 5-ft., with Gallery.

Width, 2-ft. 8-in.

Depth, 16½-in.

PENNY-IN-SLOT, OR FOR PRIVATE USE.

Price, including Six Tunes, with Eight-Day Clock, £26 10s. 0d.

Extra Tunes, 25-in. diameter, 6/- each.

The New "B" Giant Polyphon.

No. 105s.

159 STEEL TONGUES WITH TWO COMBS.

THIS is similar to the well-known "Giant" Polyphon, it plays the same tunes and has the same combs: the difference lies in the Case and in the Spring, which is the same as in the No. 104. Plays 20 minutes with one winding.

SIZE: 86 by 32 by 19½ inches.

WEIGHT: about 220 lbs net.

PRICE: including 6 tunes, 25 in. diameter, **£35.**

Self-acting, plays twice for a penny, or once only, a lever is provided to set it at will. Tune cabinet holds about 100 tunes. Extra tunes, 25 in. diameter, 6/= each.

No. 118.

The 'Palace' Polyphon.

HANDSOME WALNUT OAK CASE.

MAKES VERY FINE PIECE OF FURNITURE.

NY-IN-THE-SLOT, OR FOR PRIVATE USE,)

Price, including 6 Tunes - - - - £28 10s. 0d.

EXTRA TUNES, 3s. 6d. EACH.

Size 7-ft. high by 29-in. wide by 17½-in. deep.

Net Weight, 150-lbs. Tunes, 20-in. diameter, **3/6** each.

During Dinners or Banquets it creates quite a sensation.

It is the Instrument for a Gentleman's House.

It will be welcomed by the visitors in Hotels.

IT WILL REPAY ITS OUTLAY IN LESS THAN THREE MONTHS.

It is the greatest attraction for Garden Parties.

It plays the Complete Tunes, not only Parts, as in many other instruments.

The scale is chromatic, and the pieces are therefore played with all the accidentals, as written by the composers.

IN WALNUT OR OAK CASE.

No. 54. (159)

THE "GIANT."

FOR GENTLEMEN'S HOUSES.

ARRANGED AS AUTOMATOMS FOR————,

Hotel Exhibitions, Banquetting Halls, &c.

PENNY-IN-THE-SLOT, OR PRIVATE USE.

The is marvellous and cannot be described, the scale is chromatic, and pieces are therefore played with all the accidentals, as originally written by the composers.

The "G" Polyphon is the most glorious and sweetest toned instrument ever produced.

DURING DINNERS OR BANQUETS IT CREATES QUITE A SENSATION.

For country it is the greatest attraction; for dancing purposes it is equal to an orchestra.

The largest instrument ever made with Changeable Tunes. The best substitute an orchestra. Each tune plays about two minutes, and the "GIANT" will play about 40 minutes with one winding.

A greature is the playing of the COMPLETE Tunes, not merely fronts as in all other instruments with changeable tunes.

Size, 90-in. by 34-in. by 20-in. Net Weight, 260 lbs.

Price including 6 Tunes, - - £50.

Extra Tunes, 25-in. Diameter, 6/- each.

POLYPHONS

GREAT NOVELTY.

16

POLYPHON-PIANO,

This is an Iron Framed, Full Trichord Piano, 7 Octaves, with brass Sconces and brass Pedals, in combination with a Giant Polyphon built into it. The Polyphon is with 159 tongues, just the same as in the Giant Polyphon, with penny-in-slot, or can be started by pulling a knob. It is tuned to the Piano, so that some charming effects can be produced by accompanying the Polyphon on the Piano, but they do not play automatically together.

As a Novelty and a handsome piece of furniture combining two excellent instruments, this is unique, and will appeal to the Artist as well as the Amateur.

No. 2459, with gallery, burr walnut, as in sketch, 4-ft. 6-in. by 5-ft. 2-in. by 2-ft. 6-in. Including 6 Tunes.

Price, carriage paid, including Walnut Case - - **£100.**

No. 2460, without gallery, 4-ft. 6-in. by 4-ft. 11-in. by 2-ft. 6-in. Including 6 Tunes. Price, carriage paid, **£90.**

Tunes for the Polyphon, 25-in. diameter, 6/- each.

6 Tunes are included with each Instrument.

KALLOSCOP Penny-in-Slot

LIVING PICTURES.

In Solid Oak Case holding 18 Photographic Slides, Nine of which are shewn for a penny.

When the penny is dropped in the slot, the slides revolve one after another on pressing a knob in front. When nine slides have passed, it stops until another coin is put in.

At night a lamp fixed at the back gives a brilliant light.

No. 102.

Size, 17½-in. high by 12-in. by 12-in.

PRICE, including 18 Slides in Colours and Candle or Oil Lamp ...

£5 10s.

With Hydraulic Time Shutters ...

£6 10s.

DIRECTIONS FOR USE OF TIME-SHUTTER KALLOSCOP.
(No. 102).

The Kalloscop is sent out with the hydraulic cylinder closed by a cork; when placed in position the cork should be pushed up half way by the piston, then the shutter will automatically fall 15 secs. after the knob is pressed.

Nine slides are shown for one penny; then the shutter will remain open until another penny is put in. When sending the Kalloscop away or tilting it, the cork should be firmly pushed in to the cylinder again, otherwise the oil will run out.

These Kalloscops are lighted with candles, for which ordinary **carriage lamp** candles are used.

Price - £6 10s., *with 18 Coloured Slides.*

SAVOYARD POLYPHON AUTOMATON

No. 100

PENNY-IN-SLOT.

With 78 extra large Steel Tongues
Size: 58-in. high by 24-in. by 30-in.

PRICE, including 6 Steel Tunes,
£26.

Extra Tunes, 16-in. diameter, **2 6**

This is one of the most striking Polyphons, drawing crowds wherever placed. The Boy is made of Terra Cotta, in seven waterproof colours, moving the arm, and turning the handle while the instrument is playing. The group of Figures move as soon as the Instrument is started.

17

POLYPHONS

TUNE CASE

For No. 1 Polyphon.   Price, £4.

18

New 5 Octave Pianette.

"BACH" MODEL.

Style 174, Black and Gold, 22 Gns.

SIZE: Height, 3-ft. 8-in. Width, 3-ft. 4-in. Depth, 1-ft. 8½-in.

Packing Case Included.

One sign of the times is the provision being made on all sides for home and for students' practice. H. PETERS & Co. (of Leipzig) have introduced an iron-framed Educational Pianino, specially suitable for small rooms and for students. Those who delight in playing the old masters, for instance, will find a neat reproduction of the old clavier in upright form of pure sympathetic tone. The instruments are handsomely got up, and sold at marvellously small prices.—*Musical News.*

These Pianinos supply a long-felt want for Schoolrooms, Libraries, Yachts, Houseboats, Dances, Garden Parties, Dining-rooms, Halls, Bedrooms (for Invalids), Studies (for composers), Public and Private Schools, for the Humble Cottage, as well as for the Mansion, where space and portability are a consideration. The price is so low as to bring it within reach of the **Million,** whilst it compares in quality with many pianos costing treble the amount ; in fact, **it is a real instrument and not a mere toy ;** the exterior is so elegant as to make it an ornament to any drawing-room. The compass is within the range of all pianoforte tutors and of most Songs, Oratorios, Hymns, Dance Music, &c.

Here is a Piano which can be easily moved about, taken to the sea side, packed in a case (which is included in the price), or carried into any room desired. It takes up little space in the breakfast-room, where the little ones can practise comfortably, instead of going into a cold room. They need only be seen and heard, and a purchase is sure to follow.

20

No. 1
POLYPHON

With 12 Inter- . . changeable Tunes.

The Greatest Invention of the Age.
TUNES CHANGE AUTOMATICALLY,

Price with 12 tunes - £75.

Extra Tunes 25in. diameter - 6s. each.

Ready Early in 1900.

Orders can now be Booked.

THE ROYAL AMORETTES

In Black and Gold Case, with Dancing Figures. Including Six Tunes.

PRICE: **£1 18s.**

SIZE: 13½-in. by 10½-in. by 7¼-in.

Extra Tunes, 9-in. diameter, 8d. each.

No. 16F.

COUNTRY INN.

Including 6 Tunes.

PRICE - - **£2 2s.**

SIZE: 14-in. by 14-in. by 11-in.

Extra tunes 9-in. diameter 8d. each.

No. 16W.

No. 16.

The New Portable Patent Organette.

When ordering Tunes, please give a few extra numbers, in case we are out of some. The numbers alone are sufficient.

THOUSANDS SOLD IN A FEW MONTHS.

A Child can Play it.

No knowledge of Music required.

SIZE: 14-in. by 10½-in. by 8-in.

NET WEIGHT: 6½-lbs.

GROSS WEIGHT: 13-lbs.

16 STEEL REEDS.

In handsome Black and Gold Case, with 16 Steel Reeds, including 6 Interchangeable Round Metal Tunes, **25s.**

The "Amorette" Organette is the sweetest toned handle instrument ever produced, the tone is full, sonorous and broad, the valves are *closed* when not in use, thus preventing the dust from choking them up, as in the old construction.

The turning goes very easily, a child will not get tired; the case is in black and gold; all the latest tunes will be made as they come out.

21

THE ROYAL AMORETTES.

No. 18.

SIZE: 17-in. by 13-in. by 8-in.

18 Steel Reeds, Metal Tunes. 10½-in. diameter.

NET WEIGHT, 8lbs. GROSS WEIGHT with case, 13lbs.

PRICE, with 6 Metal Tunes, No. 18, with 18 Steel Reeds, **£1 16s. 0d.**

No. 18d, with 18 **Double** Steel Reeds, **£2 7s. 0d.**

Extra Tunes ... ... *1/2* each.

No. 24.

NEW.

SIZE 18-in. by 15-in. by 9½-in.

NET WEIGHT, 8½-lbs. GROSS WEIGHT, 16-lbs.

24 Steel Reeds. Metal Tunes, 12-in. diameter.

PRICE, No. 24, with Six Tunes ... **£2 10s. 0d.**

„ „ 24, with **Double** Reeds (48) **£3 15s. 0d.**

Extra Tunes . . . ... *1/6* each.

22

The Royal Amorettes.

Nos. 36 and 36d.

No. **36**, with 44 Steel Reeds, including 6 Tunes · · · £5 5s. 0d.

No. **36d**, with 72 Steel Reeds, including 6 Tunes · · £6 6s. 0d.

Extra Tunes for Nos. 36 and 36d, 17½ inches diameter, 3s. each.

THE "Amorette" Organette is the sweetest toned handle instrument ever produced, the tone is full, sonorous and broad, the valves are closed when not in use, thus preventing dust getting in to choke them up.

23

THE turning goes very easily, a child will not get tired. The case is in black and gold. All the latest tunes will be made as they come out.

POLYPHON FACTORY.

Damaging a Polyphon.

AT the Marlborough Street Police Court, last month, Mr. C. F. Barham, a public house broker, of John Street, Bedford Row, was summoned before Mr. Denman for maliciously, wilfully, and unlawfully damaging a polyphon belonging to the New Polyphon Supply Co. (Lim.), of Oxford Street.

Mr. H. C. Biron, barrister, prosecuted; and Mr. Cecil A. Lumley, solicitor, appeared for the defence.

Mr. BIRON, in opening the proceedings, said that the main object of the prosecution was to show that persons would not be allowed to damage the machines of the company with impunity. The company had a number of machines in various licensed houses in the metropolis, and it would therefore be readily seen how important it was to them that their instruments should not be tampered with.

Mr. WALTER COOMBE then deposed that on October 15th last he was in the "Carpenters' Arms," Whitfield Street, Tottenham Court Road, on behalf of the official receiver. While he was in the house the defendant, who was a public house broker, and who was acting on behalf of Miss Hicks, the lessee, came in. Mr. Barnum began to take stock on behalf of Miss Hicks. The polyphon in question was in the bar, and with the piece of iron produced and a mallet he broke the drawer of it open and abstracted the money from it, remarking as he did so,—" If any inquiry is made about this give them my name and address."

Cross examined.—Mr. Barham told him he had written to the Polyphon Company. He also told him that as the company had not called he felt bound to open the polyphon.

Mr. SIDNEY H. DIXON, secretary of the New Polyphon Company, Oxford Street, said he estimated the damage done at the minimum of two pounds. The persons who rented their machines were allowed twenty per cent. of the takings.

Mr. CECIL A. LUMLEY said his client was willing to pay for the damage done, and that the case was a frivolous one.

Mr. DENMAN said that he was not sitting in the court to protect the Polyphon Company, but to decide whether there was wilful damage, and whether the defendant thought that he was acting within his rights. Perhaps the parties might put their heads together and come to some arrangement.

The legal gentlemen concerned in the case then held a discussion in private, but were unable to come to any arrangement, it being eventually decided that the magistrate should deal with the matter.

Mr. DENMAN, in giving his decision, said that the view he took of the matter was this. Mr. Barham had committed an act which he could not justify, and by a wilful act had damaged this property illegally. Though he did not intend to do it for the purpose of damaging the company, he resorted to an act which he had no business to do. It came, therefore, to a question of damage. The wood the machine was made of did not appear to be of a very valuable description, and the magistrate thought that a sovereign compensation would be sufficient, with three guineas costs.

THE HOROLOGICAL JOURNAL.

Polyphon Musical Boxes.

As you are aware we have for some years taken up the sale of the Polyphon Musical Boxes, and how very much they have been appreciated throughout the whole world will be seen by the fact that within a very short time the factory has had to be enlarged to accommodate 1000 hands. We regret to say that on the 6th June nearly the whole of the buildings were destroyed by fire : but we think we cannot give you a better report than by translating from the leading Leipzig daily paper :—

" In the night of the 6th instant the whole of the right wing of the large works of the Polyphon manufactory in Wahren was destroyed by fire. With fearful rapidity the fire got a thorough hold in the joinery and mounting shops, and the heat soon became so intense that the outer walls partly burst. Unfortunately there was a very unfavourable wind too, which soon brought the flames to the large machinery halls. But here it was possible to offer an effectual stop to a further extension of the fire. Although difficulty was experienced in getting sufficient water; as a matter of fact it was necessary in the end to get water from the distant river Elster by water-carts and other conveyances. The joinery building has been entirely destroyed, but all the workshops in the basement, where the special machines were placed, and all the machines for cutting the fine wheels and for the special mechanical parts, are saved; therefore the most valuable part of the works has really been left intact, as it will easily prove possible to erect temporary premises for housing the joinery and mounting shop and the steam engines, parts of which

began to melt through the intense heat, but these can be easily replaced. Another fortunate point was that the special buildings in which all the apparatuses for stamping and manufacturing the tunes, with all the necessary stocks of materials for the same, has been left untouched by the flames. The fire, which was favoured by the immense wood stores, partly in the joinery rooms, partly outside in large stacks, is supposed to have originated in a large stack of wood-wool, and from there the joinery at once got involved. From all surrounding villages, and from Leipzig itself, the fire brigades were in requisition, and as the fire could be seen from far and wide, help even from the military authorities soon arrived. The directorate of the works at once decided that the work should not be stopped, and that none of the 780 workmen should leave, but that provisional buildings should at once be erected, and as all the special machinery has been saved, it is hoped that no great delay, if any, will be experienced in the delivery by the many customers for these goods."

We are sure that the latter part will also be very satisfactory to our many English clients, and we can already assure them that as we have good stocks on hand, they will well carry us over the few weeks until the works are able to make us our regular deliveries again, so that all their orders will be executed with the usual promptness.

NICOLE FRERES, Ltd.,
Ely Place, Holborn Circus,
London, E.C.

Correspondence.

[JULY, 1899.

A Sentence of **THREE MONTHS HARD LABOUR** was passed upon

Frank Solomon

Watchmaker, of Norwich, at the Norfolk Quarter Sessions held at Norwich on the 18th of October, 1899, for stealing certain Monies from an Automatic Musical Instrument, known as a "POLYPHON" the Property of

THE NEW POLYPHON SUPPLY Co., Ltd., 137, Oxford Street, London, W.

THEREFORE TAKE NOTICE that the said New Polyphon Supply Co., Ltd., will henceforth prosecute with the utmost rigour of the Law any Person or Persons tampering or interfering unlawfully with any Machine whatsoever, the same being the property of the Company.

A REWARD OF TWO POUNDS

will be paid by the Company to any Person giving such information as will secure a conviction.

By Order,

THE NEW POLYPHON SUPPLY Co., Ltd.,

S. C. DIXON, Secretary.

Gas meters have for a long time been attractive to petty thieves and, in more recent times, telephone coin boxes. Once, though, it was the coin box of the public bar musical box which was deserving of the plunderer's attentions. *Musical Opinion* of 1 December 1899 carried the item (*top left*) and around the same time the New Polyphon Supply Co. Ltd., pinned the above notice into all their machines. The disaster which befell the giant Polyphon factory on the night of 6 June 1899 is recounted in the letter (*lower left*) printed in the *Horological Journal* for July 1899. One of the larger provincial agents was Guldman of Manchester. This firm stocked a wide range of automatic instruments (*see page* 151 *et seq.*) and the advertisement (*below*) comes from *Musical Opinion, c.* 1905.

GULDMAN & CO.

7, *Sugar Lane, Withy Grove,*

MANCHESTER,

WHOLESALE AND EXPORT OF

Polyphons, Concertos, German Pianos, Organs, Orchestrions,

Phonographs, Graphophones, Automatic Machines, Mechanical Novelties, &c.

Wholesale Agents for

Hupfeld's Electric Pianos

Orchestrions, Music Automatons.

HUPFELD'S ELECTRIC PIANOS are undoubtedly the best and most reliable self-playing Pianos, playing with the perfect ease, expression, and accomplishment of first class performers.

Catalogue on application.

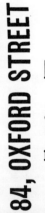

Largest dealer in automatic instruments in London in the 1890s and 1900s was Henry A. Klein. He handled Polyphons and gambling machines and his two advertisements (*left*) date from 1900 and 1901. Zimmermann (*above*) stocked the Symphonion as advertised in 1898. However, Zimmermann's Leipzig factory was hard at work building its own disc instrument—the Fortuna—launched in 1900. Later a second instrument was produced called the Adler which used the same discs and components.

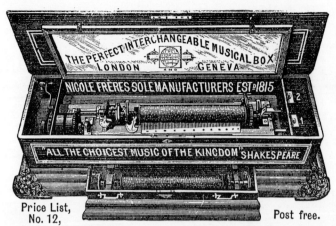

144

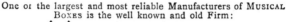

A selection of British and American advertisements. The Olympia (*top*) was a short-lived competitor for the rich U.S. market. The Gloria was one of several Swiss attempts to pluck back from the Germans the musical box trade (which was of course founded in Switzerland) by introducing a rival disc instrument. The only really successful Swiss competitor was Mermod Frères (*see next page*).

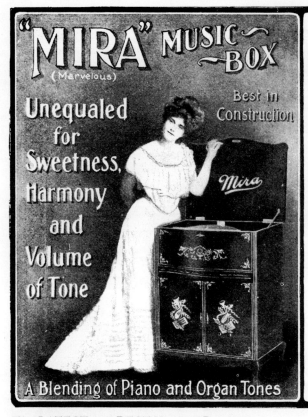

Mermod Frères of Switzerland, entered the disc musical box market with two instruments, the Mira and the Stella. Both had common features but in one important way they were different. The Mira played discs having projections in the same way as the Symphonion, Polyphon, Regina and others, whereas the discs for the Stella were smooth on both sides. The teeth of the musical combs were plucked by the usual star-shaped wheel as in other instruments, only each wheel was sprung on an eccentric centre so that one of its radial points, when presented with a hole in the disc, would rise up through it. This allowed the moving disc to turn the star wheel, so plucking the tooth, whereupon the wheel would be pushed down out of the way until the next hole came along. Mira and Stella mechanisms were shipped unboxed and fitted in locally-made cases. The Mira was sold in America by Jacot among others and the largest London distributor was Imhofs. The Mira was also called the Empress in a form made expressly for Lyon & Healy, the Chicago department store.

Jacot also handled the Stella in New York and published a catalogue of tunes (*below*). Musical 'long-case' clocks were seldom long-case and those made by Polyphon and Symphonion consisted of small bracket clocks, sometimes driven by weights, in a tall case carrying a medium-sized musical movement. The Regina hall-clock (*right*) was more like the accepted form of the long-case or so-called 'grandfather's' clock. The advertisement appeared in *Country Life in America* for October 1906. Below right is an advertisement which appeared in 1903 and shows how the rapid growth of the disc box demanded specialist disc makers and machinery.

A Chime Clock for the Front Hall

Nothing adds so much to the dignity of the hall in a country home as an old-fashioned, tall chime clock.

The chime clock of other days had the defects of the music box of other days—a limited list of tunes played over and over.

The Regina Chime clock gives you your choice from a large combination of airs— any six you like from a list of forty—and can be changed at will.

The clock part is one of the most beautiful specimens of the clock-makers' art in case, in finish and in dial.

The chime part is the famous Regina disc principle — each disc offering six airs in the beautiful chime tones. The airs are all old favorites. Any six you like may be had in combination. The best way is to buy a set of discs and change them from time to time. Thus the chime never becomes monotonous.

You cannot possibly get any idea of the beauty of these clocks or the attractiveness of their music, except by seeing and hearing them.

THE REGINA CO.

Makers of Reginapianos, Reginaphones and Regina Music Boxes

RAHWAY, N. J.

New York salesrooms Broadway & 17th St.   259 Wabash Ave, Chicago, Ill.

Alphabetical List of Tunes

for

STELLA MUSIC BOXES.

New Music in Preparation.

JACOT MUSIC BOX CO.,

39 Union Square,

New York.

Issued Sept. 1, 1902.

To begin with, Regina and Polyphon products were very similar both in style and appearance of the casework. Although the upright 19⅝ inch model never appeared in America, the 11, 12¼ and 15½ inch models were almost identical and initially components were shipped from Leipzig. Gradually, though, local woods such as oak replaced the German casework with its high proportion of German pine and lime, both carved and veneered. This advertisement from the *Youth's Companion*, 22 October 1903, shows the self-changing 15½ inch Corona and the 27 inch model plus a rare one—the library table introduced that autumn but which was short-lived. On the facing page is a description of a most unusual musical box made in New York by F. G. Otto. This played 'cuffs' which were thin metal cones with disc-type projections. Paillard was associated with its invention. Frederick Otto went on to make the Criterion and then the Olympia disc machines, but none enjoyed lasting popularity.

DIRECTIONS FOR CAPITAL SELF PLAYING MUSIC BOX.

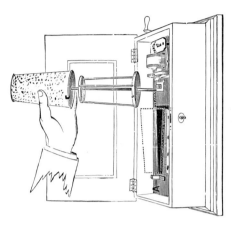

To Wind, turn the crank at right hand side of box toward you.

To Start, push the lever on the plate at right hand side from you until it cannot be pushed farther.

To Repeat, leave the lever in the position of start.

To Stop, draw the lever toward you.

To Change the Tunes, take the shaft of note holder with two fingers at A (see cut) and raise to an upright position as shown, then turn the note cylinder slightly to the left and raise it from the note holder. Take another cylinder, replace it on the holder so the bayonet lock falls over the pin on the large end of note holder, turn slightly to the right so the pin will be in the slot of the bayonet lock, then lower the note holder to a horizontal position, as shown by dotted line in cut, when it will be ready to play.

If the note Cylinders be placed carefully and ordinary care taken the Music Box will remain in good working order for many years.

To Oil, the only part that will ever need oil is the Governor or fly wheel shaft. To oil this use watch makers' oil and apply at the lower end of shaft, at the worm or screw, and at upper end of shaft. If the Music Box is received in extremely cold weather, allow it to stand in a heated room an hour before playing the same.

THE "CAPITAL" SELF=PLAYING MUSIC BOX

Patented in U. S. and Foreign Countries.

The "Capital" Music Box is constructed in the simplest manner and is very attractive, all parts being highly polished and nickel plated.

The entire mechanism is exposed to view, the action of the note projections on the star wheels, which in turn actuate the teeth of the Comb, can be seen, which makes this instrument very interesting to the eye, while the music produced is clear, and the volume of tone greater than in any Music Box manufactured. The governor used in these boxes is of the self-regulating class and insures a very steady and even speed.

The Note Cylinders are made of steel, are durable and easily placed on the holder provided for the same.

Any number of different tunes can be obtained embracing all standard and popular airs. New tunes are continually being added to the existing large variety.

PATENTED.

April 9, 1889. Nos. 401,187 and 401,188.
Dec. 17, 1889.
May 15, 1894.
June 12, 1894.
Jan. 8, 1895.

LIST OF TUNES
For Styles C, D, E and F.
"CAPITAL" MUSIC BOX.

CYLINDER, 7¾x4¼x3¼ inches.

Cut Represents Style C.

1001 Ye Merry Birds ....*Gumbert*	1025 Silver Fish, Fantasia Mazurka,
1002 Forsaken.................*Koschat*	*Ketterer*
1003 Praise the Lord.................	1026 My Queen................*Coote*
1004 Lohengrin, Bridal Chorus *Wagner*	1027 Bells of Corneville.....*Planquette*
1005 Cavalleria Rusticana, Intermezzo,	1028 Liberty Bell March........*Sousa*
Mascagni	1029 The Owl and the Pussy Cat,
1006 Don Cæsar, March......*Dellinger*	*Ingraham*
1007 Spin Spin, Song.......*Juengst*	1030 Estudiantina, Waltz.. *Waldteufel*
1008 Old Folks at Home .....*Fairbank*	1031 Potpourri, Robin Hood..*de Koven*
1009 Martha Quintette.........*Flotow*	1032 Les Sylphes, Waltz..... *Bachman*
1010 Skirt Dance.................*Lutz*	1033 Our Orioles, March,..*R. M. Stults*
1011 Last Rose of Summer, (Martha)	1034 Soldier's Glee, March.......*Holst*
Flotow	1035 Love's Spring Time, Gavotte *Holst*
1012 Morning Papers, Waltz .. *Strauss*	1036 Sweetest Story ever told, Song,
1013 Faust Waltz.... ....*Gounod*	*Stultz*
1014 Eva, Waltz.......... ....*Strauss*	1037 Lohengrin, Prelude to 3d Act,
1015 Mikado Waltz.........*Sullivan*	*Wagner*
1016 Belleville Waltz. ......*Milloecker*	1038 Somebody loves me, Song,
1017 Ak-Sar-Ben (Good Humor)	*Hattie Starr*
March ....*Arnhold*	1039 Capital March ...... *Fr. Hoschke*
1018 Zig-Zag Polka.............*Faust*	1040 Grande Valse Brillante..*Schulhoff*
1019 A Nest of Finches ....*Longey*	1041 "Athalia", Priests' March,
1020 Maggie Murphy's Home..*Braham*	*Mendelssohn*
1021 Home, Sweet Home.......*Payne*	1042 Sweet Marie, Song
1022 Star Spangled Banner............	*Raymond Moore*
1023 Old Hundred.	1043 My Pearl's a Bowery Girl, Song
1024 Artist's Life, Waltz......*Strauss*	*A. Mack*

An old and rather mutilated catalogue of the Capital instrument gives an idea of the appearance of the instrument which was produced in several styles to take different-sized 'cuffs'. Now follows the catalogue of mechanical instruments published by Guldman in 1902. Some of this repeats what has already been shown but generally the models and styles differ. This Manchester company was a major distributor throughout the Midlands and North of England.

GOLD MEDALS AT THE PARIS EXHIBITION

for Polyphons,
Graphophones, and Electric Pianos.

1902

GULDMAN and Co.,

7 SUGAR LANE, WITHY GROVE,

MANCHESTER.

• • •

Importers and Manufacturers

OF

AUTOMATIC MACHINES,

MUSICAL . . . .

INSTRUMENTS

AND

MECHANICAL NOVELTIES.

Specialities :

ELECTRIC PIANOS,

ORCHESTRIONS,

POLYPHONS, . . .

GRAPHOPHONES, &c.

The Best at Lowest Figure.

MIDWOOD, PRINTER 4 WHITE HART COURT, SUGAR LANE, MANCHESTER.-TEL. No. 3362.

No. 28s.
Self-acting, 30 notes, in rosewood case. Size 7½ × 7½ × 3½ ins. Tune 6½ ins. diameter. £1 12 0. Extra Tunes 5d. each.

No. 41.
Self-acting, 41 notes, in walnut case. Size 10¼ × 9½ × 6½ ins. Tune 8¼ ins. diameter. £2 11 0. Extra Tunes 8d. each.

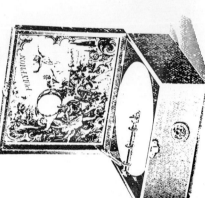

No. 28.
To turn by hand, 30 notes, in rosewood case. Size 7½ × 7¼ × 3½ ins. Tune 6½ ins. diameter. 16s. 6d. Extra Tunes 5d. each.

No. 40.
To turn by hand, 41 notes, in rosewood case. Size 9½ × 6¼ × 5 ins. Tune 8¼ ins. diameter. £1 5 0. Extra Tunes 8d. each.

The price of each Instrument includes six Tunes.

TERMS.

N order to *avoid delay in delivery* it is requested that orders (preferably on special order blank) be always made by Catalogue numbers; and in ordering tune-sheets, never by the title but by number only. (Send for a tune-sheet list).

Shipment is made at buyer's risk; it must be stated whether shipment is to be made by goods train, express, or post.

Prices are for cash, goods value £8 or above, delivered carriage paid within England and Wales; Ireland and Scotland 2½ additional, *including Packing* in original case, if not quoted for especially. Extra cases and especial packing will be at buyer's cost and will not be taken back.

Claims of any kind will receive consideration only when made immediately after receipt of the goods.

When tune-sheets are packed in cases, the packing will be at buyer's cost.

Prices and illustrations in the catalogue are not binding, and the right to make minor changes respecting style is reserved.

All transactions for both parties to be closed at Manchester.

These price-lists cancel all former price-lists at all points.

152

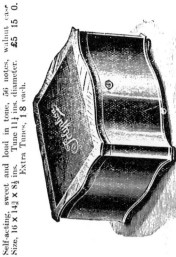

No. 42n.—Open.

Self-acting, sweet and loud in tone, 56 notes, walnut case. Size, 16 × 14¾ × 8½ ins. Tune 11¾ ins. diameter. Extra Tunes, 1 8 each. £5 15 0.

No. 42r.

Self-acting, 56 notes, walnut case. Sweet in tone. Size, 14¾ × 12¾ × 8¾ ins. Tune, 11¼ ins. diameter. Extra Tunes, 1 8 each. £6 0 0.

The price of each Instrument includes six Tunes.

No. 41r.

Self-acting, 41 notes, in walnut case. Size, 11 × 10 × 6¾ ins. Ornamental Case. Tune 8¼ ins. diameter. Sweet Tone. Extra Tunes, 8d. each. £3 0 0.

No. 46.

Self-acting, 46 notes, in walnut case. Size, 12 × 10¼ × 7¼ ins. Tune 9½ ins. diameter. Pleasant Tone. Extra Tunes, 1 4 each. £4 5 0.

The price of each Instrument includes six Tunes.

No. 44.

Self-acting, 100 notes, walnut inlaid marqueterie, piccolo, splendid tone. Size, 21 x 21 x 12 ins. Tune 15¾ ins. diameter. £12 0 0.

No. 44d.

Same case and size as No. 44, 156 notes. Tune 15¾ ins. diameter. £14 0 0. Excellent in Tone. Excelsior Piccolo.

No. 45.

Self-acting, 156 notes, walnut case, with marqueterie. Size, 22½ x 29½ x 14 ins. Tune 15¾ ins. diameter. £16 10 0.

No. 45b.

Self-acting, 156 notes, extra finished case with gold ornaments, and black polished. Size, 22½ x 29½ x 14 ins. Tune 15¾ ins. diameter. £17 10 0. Both instruments have a magnificent tone, in fact, one of the finest Polyphons made, and for their size cannot be surpassed. Large supply of Tunes. Extra Tunes for 44, 44d, 45, and 45b, 2/6 each.

The price of each Instrument included six tunes.

No. 42d.

Same case and size as No. 42d, 112 notes. £7 0 0. Extra Tunes, 1/8 each. Powerful and sweet in tone with Piccolo.

No. 43b.

Self-acting, 78 notes, handsome walnut case, inlaid marqueterie, grand tone. Size 21½ x 18½ x 10½ ins. Tune 15¾ in. diameter. £8 10 0. Extra Tunes, 2/6 each. Large supply of Tunes.

The price of each Instrument includes six Tunes.

Latest Polyphon Novelties.

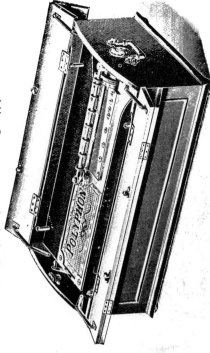

No. 49.

Self-acting, 120 notes, in rosewood case, with special constructed cover which is used for holding the plate. 16 chimes which can be switched off. Very sweet in tone and powerful. Size, 28½ × 18¾ × 10½. Tune 22 ins. diameter. £22 0 0. Extra Tunes 5/- each. Spiral spring : spring unbreakable. Large supply of Tunes.

No. 52.

Self-acting, 159 notes, in rosewood case, constructed like No. 49. Most excellent tone. Size, 28½ × 16¾ × 10½. Tune 25 ins. diameter. £22 0 0. Extra Tunes 6/- each. Large supply of Tunes. Spiral spring : spring unbreakable.

The price of each Instrument includes six Tunes.

Latest Polyphon Novelties.

No. 48.

Self-acting, 112 notes, walnut case with marqueterie, also 12 chimes which can be switched off. Very sweet in tone. Size, 20½ × 18½ × 10½. Tune 14½ ins. diameter. £12 10 0. Extra Tunes, 2/6 each. Spiral spring : spring unbreakable.

The price of each Instrument includes six Tunes.

Automatic Polyphons.

With Coin-Slot device or for private use.

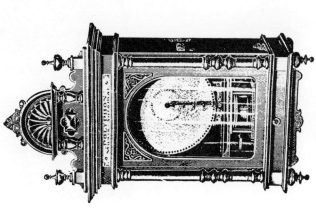

No. 103u.

Automaton, 78 notes, in walnut. Size, 45 x 24½ x 15 ins. £14 0 0. With ornamental eight-day clock on top. £15 0 0. Tunes, 15¾ ins. diameter. Extra Tunes 2 6 each. Each Automaton is arranged so as to play once or twice for One Penny.

The price of each Instrument includes six Tunes.

Latest Polyphon Novelties.

EXCEEDINGLY ORNAMENTAL CASE.

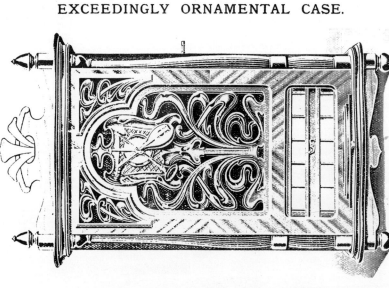

SELF-CHANGING POLYPHON.

No. 50.

With 154 Steel Accromatic notes, in handsome walnut case beautifully carved. Automatic Tune Changing Device, the base holding 10 tunes, and by moving the little indicator underneath, the tune desired will play, then goes back to its previous position. Extremely sweet in tone. Size, 50¼ X 27½ X 16½. Tune 16¾ ins. diameter. £31 0 0 including 10 Tunes. Extra Tunes, 2/6 each. Large supply of Tunes. Spiral spring; spring unbreakable.

The price of this Instrument includes ten Tunes.

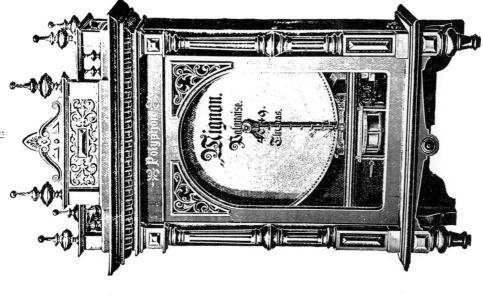

No. 104.

Automaton, 120 notes, in walnut.

Size, 32 x 28 x 16 ins.

£17 10 0.

Also with flat Cash Drawer instead of bottom feet and spring carrying wheel

£17 12 6.

Extra Tunes, 3/6 each.

Tune 19½ ins. diameter.

104u.

Automaton with ornamental **Eight-day Clock,** 120 notes, in walnut. Tune 19½ ins. diameter. £18 10 0.

Also with flat Cash Drawer instead of bottom feet and spring carrying wheel £18 12 6.

Extra Tunes 3/6 each.

Both instruments have a grand tone. All the latest Tunes played complete. To stand or hang up.

Each Automaton is arranged so as to play once or twice for **One Penny.**

The price of each Instrument includes six Tunes.

No. 105.

Automaton, 159 notes, in walnut. Size, 60 x 32 x 10½ ins. Tune 25 ins. diameter. £26 10 0. Extra Tunes 6/- each.

It is one of the most glorious and sweetest toned instruments ever made. Each tune plays for about two minutes. A special feature is the playing of the complete tune, not merely fragments. Large supply of all the latest Tunes.

Each Automaton is arranged so as to play once or twice for **One Penny.**

The price of each Instrument includes six Tunes.

P.S.—Can be supplied for private use with beautiful inlaid marqueterie front instead of glass front, at 36/- extra.

Latest Polyphon Novelties.
NO NECESSITY FOR CHANGING TUNES.

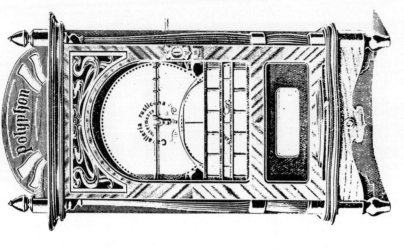

No. 51.

154 notes in beautiful walnut case, entirely new style. Automatic Tune Changing Device, the base holding 10 Tunes. The titles of the same are plainly shown in front of the instrument and by moving the indicator to the respective tune sheet, play it and then go back to its old position. Extremely sweet in tone. Size, 50½ × 27½ × 16½. £31 0 0 including 10 Tunes. Tune 15½ ins. diameter. Extra Tunes 2/6 each. Large supply of Tunes. Spiral spring; spring unbreakable. Each Automaton is arranged so as to play once or twice for **One Penny**.

The price of this instrument includes ten Tunes.

No. 6g.

Automaton, 118 notes, also 16 bells. Walnut case. Entirely new style. Size, 57½ × 32½ × 18½ ins. Price, including 6 tunes, **£23 10 0.** Tune 22 ins. diameter. Extra Tunes 5/- each.

No. 6r.— Exactly the same Instrument as 6g, but instead bells or chimes bells or chimes can be switched off. The accompaniment of bells or chimes produces a most pleasing and wonderful effect. The tone of both Instruments is extremely sweet, powerful, and attractive. Each Automaton is arranged so as to play once or twice for **One Penny**.

The price of each Instrument includes six Tunes.

No. 2.

118 notes, also 16 chimes or bells. In beautiful walnut case. This instrument has the same construction as No. 51 and No. 4 only in proportion stronger, and can be supplied in similar case as the mentioned instruments by ordering Polyphon No. 5. The musical parts are same as Polyphons 6G and 6R. Has an especially loud and sweet tone in consequence of the bells accompaniment. Size, 65½ x 36 x 20½ ins. Tune 22 ins. diameter. Spiral Spring. Spring unbreakable. The chimes can be switched off. Large supply of all the latest Tunes. The base holds 10 Tunes. Price **£45 0 0.** Extra Tunes 5/- each. Each Automaton is arranged so as to play once or twice for **One Penny.**

The price of this Instrument includes ten Tunes.

No. 4.

118 notes, in beautiful walnut case

Entirely in a style.

The mechanism is just as easily and simply constructed as No. 51.

The base holds also 10 Tunes.

The new spiral tube shaft-spring is also used by this instrument.

The tone is exactly like the instrument No. 104. Large supply of all the latest tunes.

Size, 57¼ x 32¼ x 19½ ins.

£34 0 0.

Tune 19¾ ins. diameter.

Extra Tunes 3 6 each.

Each Automaton is arranged so as to play once or twice for **One Penny.**

The price of this Instrument includes ten tunes

Zithers or Timbros.

For fixing on top of combs of Polyphons by which some very charming effects are obtained; it can be removed while playing.

No.	Price s. d.	No.	Price s. d.	No.	Price s. d.
28½	2 6	44	5 0	118	13 0
41	3 0	45	5 6	105	16 0
46	4 0	103	10 6	54	16 0
42	4 6	47	11 0		
43	5 6	104	13 0		

Table Cordephon with Clock-works.

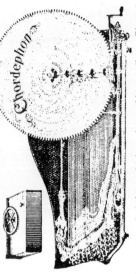

Chordephon

44 Strings, mechanical zither with interchangeable tune discs. Dimensions in case, 27½ x 18 x 6½ inch. Weight, 10 lbs. Diameter of tune disc 14 inches. Price of Table Cordephon with clock-work. £8 8 0. Tune disc. £8 4 0. Automatic and different designs supplied on application.

Walnut Automaton Stands.

With movable cupboard for tunes.

Suitable for No. 103, 104, £4 4 0.

Suitable for all the other larger Polyphon Automatons, £5 15 0

No. 1n.

Size: 95½ x 40 x 29¾

Net weight: about 390½ lbs.

159 steel tongues.

With 12 self-changing & playing musical discs.

£75 0 0

including 12 tunes

Extra tunes: **6s. each.**

This Automaton is constructed as simple as possible and its functions are everywhere accurate and perfect.

The harmony is similar to that of Polyphon No. 105 page 13, but much more powerful.

Walnut or oak, or Mahogany or Rosewood case £2 extra.

When ordering tunes for this automaton please to mention with program plates.

This automaton is a marvel of ingenuity. Can be illuminated by electricity. Estimate on application.

Amorettes.

22

Amorettes.

First-class instrument, played by crank movement, with steel tone-tongues and changeable tune-discs, made with 16 to 108 tones. The only instrument of the kind in which the durability and indestructibility is expressly guaranteed.

No. 16.

With 16 steel tone-tongues. Diameter of tune disc 9 inches. Size, 13½ x 10 x 7 inches. Weight, net 5lbs. gross 12lbs. Children's instrument, but still of greater dimensions and more elegant finish than any other instrument of its kind produced.

Price, £1 2 0. Tune-discs, 6d.

No. 18.

Size, 16½ x 12½ x 8 inches. Weight, net 8lbs. gross 15lbs. Diameter of tune-disc 10½ inches. 18 steel tone-tongues. House instrument, likewise in greater dimensions and very elegant finish.

Price, £1 14 0. Tune-discs, 1,-

No. 18d.

Size, 17 x 14 x 8½ inches. Weight, net 10lbs. gross 15lbs. Diameter of tune-disc 17½ inches. 18 double steel tone-tongues (36 tones) very loud, but pleasing music. Elegant finish.

Price, £2 4 0. Tune-discs, 1,-

No. 24.

Size, 17¾ x 14½ x 9 inches. Weight, net 10 lbs, gross 22 lbs. Diameter of tune disc, 12 inches. Price, £2 10 0. Tune disc, 1,6. 24 steel tone tongues. Loud, but pleasing music, adapted for house or restaurants, etc. Is adapted for accompanying singing and for dancing in small circles.

No. 24d.

Size, 18½ x 14½ x 10 inches. Diameter of tune disc, 12 inches. Weight, net 15 lbs, gross 25 lbs. 24 double steel tone tongues (48 tones). Price, £3 12 0. Tune disc, 1 6.

No. 36.

44 steel tone tongues, (36 tones and 8 double basses). Size, 21 x 21 x 10½ inches. Diameter of tune disc, 17 inches. Weight, net 18 lbs., gross 35 lbs. Price. No. 36, £4 14 0. No. 36d, £5 19 0. Tune disc, 2 6.

No. 36d.

72 tones (36 double tones). Size, 21 x 21 x 11½ inches. Diameter of tune disc 17 inches. Weight, net 20 lbs, gross 43 lbs. With 72 steel tone tongues and driven from the outside.

1. Very loud music well adapted through its strong tone for dance music.
2. Only indestructable steel tone tongues.
3. The tune disc is driven from the outer rim, not from the middle. By this contrivance a very even movement of the tune disc is assured, so that the music plays in exact time and a retarding or accelerating of the music is absolutely impossible.
4. A solid construction throughout, whereby a necessity for repairing can hardly ever occur.
5. Light in weight, therefore especially adapted for export.
6. Low price.

21

Hupfeld's Patent Electric Pianos.

(WORLD FAMED.)

THESE magnificent Pianos, with everlasting beauty of tone and of exceedingly smart appearance represent, in combination with the newly improved "Hupfeld Patent Electric Attachment, the highest perfection of the new branch of Piano Making—that of Self-Playing Pianos.

Every Hupfeld Electric Piano is provided with self-acting Forte and Piano Pedals, by which means the music attains that fine expression as if performed by the greatest artist.

These unparalleled instruments meet the wishes of every lover of music, be he musician or not. As the Self-Playing Attachment does not interfere in the least with playing the instrument in the ordinary way, these Pianos unite the qualities of the ordinary Piano with the capacity of rendering enjoyment with most delightful music to those who have not had time or opportunity to study the Art of Piano Playing.

These advantages place this Piano in the position to be the attraction of every society circle either in Drawing Room, Club, Concert, or Dining Hall, Hotels and other places of recreation.

All classical, sacred, operatic, popular, dance and other good modern music is arranged, of which complete lists are issued.

HUPFELD'S ELECTRIC PIANOS.

In Combination with His

MARVELLOUS ART-PLAYING APPARATUS.

UPRIGHT CONCERT GRAND. Guaranteed First-class Make. Comprises 76 notes. By means of 6 Pedal Registers the following principal variations in Tone are obtained: Pianissimo, Piano, Crescendo, Mezzo Forte, Forte, Fortissimo. These tone shades cannot only be reproduced at different times, but they may be rendered at the same time, so that for instance the Bass plays Piano and the Treble Fortissimo, or many other combinations as separate chords or single notes can be emphasized, which feature has not been attained by any of the pneumatic piano play apparatus.

The grand tone, the most elastic touch, and the surprisingly beautiful expression of the Piano, and the artistically arranged tunes characterise the HUPFELD Electric Art Play Piano as the highest technical musical achievement of the present day.

A new model. Compass of the Patent Attachment 6½ octaves till fis¹ ⁴ ⁴ ².

No. 65.—Black ebonized, or Walnut Case, with single electric sconces—

(a) Without attachment and electric sconces ... **£80**

(b) With attachment for connection with an electric light installation, continuous current up to 110 volts, including 6 endless tunes **£140**

(c) With attachment for connection with an accumulator, including 25 hours' accumulator and 6 endless tunes... ... ... **£150**

7 Octaves, 3 Pedals—Height 4 ft. 6 in. ; Width 5 ft. 1 in. Electric double Sconces **£1 10s.** extra. Marqueterie is **£1 10s. extra.**

Hupfeld's Patent Attachment (Separate)

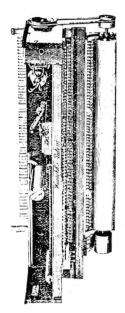

We also undertake the fitting of the Separate Attachments to any upright or horizontal Grand Pianofortes.

Pianos that are already in use may also be fitted with it. Such instruments, without sacrificing any of their pre-existing qualities, and which may have been used either a little or not at all, gain new charms through the addition of such an apparatus. Stress must again be laid on the fact that this apparatus does not act detrimentally.

It is explicitly pointed out that it is not advisable to put the apparatus in any but a **really first-class instrument**, as the superb qualities of the apparatus are fully brought to light only when the Piano possesses a good repeating mechanism; otherwise the playing is not satisfactory. For this reason, principally, proposals for putting the apparatus into inferior instruments are declined.

In ordering such apparatuses kindly state: (1) the color of the instrument: (2) the motive power for the apparatus; (3) the proportions. In order to determine the latter, take out the upper mechanism of the Piano, lay a strip of paper over the **ends** of the keys, at the **iron-frame**, and mark the middle of each note by strokes. Mark the **C** in both bass and treble with letters.

I. For Turning with Crank	...	£30 0 0
II. For connection with an existing electric light installation continuous current up to 100 volts.		£58 0 0
III. For connection with 25 hours' accumulator, including accumulator	...	£66 0 0

Prices include Fitting. For Grands, **£8** extra.

Hupfeld's "Self-Playing Electric Pianos."

Awarded with highest prizes at 14 World's and Trade Exhibitions.

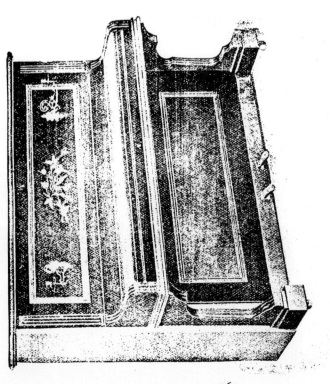

STYLE I.—OVERSTRUNG COTTAGE PIANO.

No. 60.—Black ebonized, Rosewood or Walnut and Marqueterie Case, full compass, iron frame, trichord throughout, ivory keys **£46**

(a) Without attachment and electric sconces **£96**
(b) With attachment for connection with an electric light installation, continuous current up to 110 volts, including 6 endless tunes ... **£96**
(c) With attachment for connection with an accumulator, including 25 hours accumulator and 6 endless tunes **£106**

7 Octaves—Height 4ft. 1in.; Width 4ft. 9in.
Compass of the Patent Attachment 5 Octaves, "C—c."
Endless Tunes, **7/-** each.   Long Tunes, per foot, **1/-**; per meter, **3/4.**

The motive power for the attachment is electricity. Where there is an electric light installation the Piano can be connected with the same. In case of absence of such an installation a battery or accumulator is furnished with the Pianos.

The "Hupfeld Pianos" are also supplied in cases of special design to match any style of Furniture or for Yachts. Special construction for the Tropics.

Any well-known continental piano may be supplied with Hupfeld's Piano-Play Apparatus, for which estimates will be given on application.

Hupfeld's "Self-Playing Electric Pianos."

With Art-Play Apparatus.

THE MOST EMINENT FEATURE OF THE PRESENT TIME.

For Description see next Page.

Y. A. v. E. SINGER.

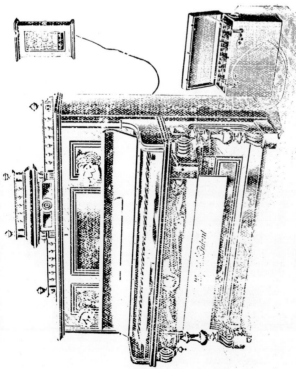

Hupfeld's "Self-Playing Electric Pianos."

Awarded with highest prizes at 14 Worlds and Trade Exhibitions.

STYLE II.—UPRIGHT GRAND.

No. 61.—Black ebonized, Rosewood or Walnut Case, full compass, iron frame, trichord throughout, ivory keys, with single electric sconces

(a) Without attachment and electric sconces £50
(b) With attachment for connection with an electric light installation, continuous current up to 110 volts, including 6 endless tunes ... £100
(c) With attachment for connection with an accumulator, including 25 hours accumulator and 6 endless tunes £112

7 Octaves—Height 4ft. 3in. ; Width 5ft.
Compass of the Patent Attachment 5 Octaves, "C—c."

No. 62.—Black ebonized, Rosewood or Walnut Case, with single electric sconces.

(a) Without attachment and electric sconces £60
(b) With attachment for connection with an electric light installation, continuous current up to 110 volts, including 6 endless tunes ... £110
(c) With attachment for connection with an accumulator, including 25 hours accumulator and 6 endless tunes £122

7 Octaves—Height 4ft. 5in. ; Width 5ft. 1in.
Compass of the Patent Attachment 5 Octaves, "C—c."

Electric double sconces £1 10 0 extra. Marquetterie £1 10 0 extra.

Orchestral Grand.

3

A semi concert grand without key board, and which by means of turning small handle and movement of lever, which acts like loud and soft pedal, everybody can render all the popular, classic, sacred, operatic music in a most brilliant manner with all the expression of a piano virtuoso. Charming Music. Admired everywhere.

Price, including 150 feet of Music, £52 10 0.

MUSIC CABINET.

For storing about 1500 feet of Music Sheets, in Walnut or Black Ebonized. £9 0 0, in Rosewood, £1 nett extra. (Figure on top not included).

More expensive Cabinets, and of special design to match any style of Furniture, are supplied to order.

MECHANICAL SINGING BIRD-CAGE,

For private use.

With 1 Bird	...	...	...	£12 12	0
" 1 " In superior cage	...	...	...	£13 13	0
" 2 "	...	...	...	£14 14	0
" 3 "	...	...	...	£16 16	0

The above can also be supplied with Coin Slot attachment costing £1 5 0 nett additional.

Electric Orchestrion.

Electric Orchestrion.

With exchangeable "long" and "endless" tune-sheets of glazed press-board.

No equal as to cheerfulness and precision of music.

Comparatively cheap considering its great advantages over other orchestrions.

Tunes up to 70 yards in length.

Most improved, durable, and reliable construction.

Very handsome case in walnut or oak.

Plays dances, marches, popular operatic, classic, and sacred music.

20 different pieces can be arranged on one roll. For coin-slot very essential.

Height. 12ft.
Width, 4ft. 4ins.
Depth, 2ft. 7ins.

Price for affixing to main current, including 10 short tunes,

£240 0 0

Price including 25 hours accumulator

£252 0 0

THE electric orchestrion constructed according to new systems has 5 registers with about 200 pipes, large and small drum, triangle, cymbal, and makes a striking impression on everybody listening to its strong powerful music and regarding the tasteful case. A principal preference of this instrument compared with all other makes of that kind is the fact, that no rollers but tough tune-sheets of pressed-board, the same kind as in the "self-playing piano" are used, viz., either "long" tune-sheets rolling up to about 60 meters, or short "endless" tune-sheets: the latter can play one or several music-pieces one after the other, as long as it is liked, and need not be rolled up. They are therefore particularly adapted for dances and concert-music. This orchestrion plays in a masterly manner marches, valses, polkas, as well as songs and whole overtures, and is, therefore, of great value not only for dance-music, but also for concert-music. The fresh, precise music, exceedingly steady in tone, of this orchestrion surpasses by far that of all similar instruments. As to the intonation of the pipes, the buyer's taste as well as the size of the room in which the instrument is to be placed will be considered, for instance, music soft and pleasant for the drawing-room, strong and full for hotels, restaurants, etc., loud and full sounding for dancing-halls. This orchestrion is a splendid substitute for 12–15 musicians; it is supplied in still larger sizes on special order. The tempo of the music can be easily changed and at will. The orchestrion is fitted with an accumulator thoroughly tested, the power of which lasts for about 25 hours of play; it is, therefore, possible to use the instrument without having electric light in the place. It is easy to charge the accumulator according to direction. The orchestrion need not be wound up, since set in motion by electric motive power, and is always ready to play, a circumstance of greatest importance for instruments provided with a **coin-slot**. The electric **coin-slot** legally protected is the simplest and best existing.

In consequence of the great simplicity and solidity of the "electric orchestrion," a guarantee for the instrument itself as well as for the tuning, the tune-sheets and the accumulator is given. The instrument is forwarded in two separate parts. It is an easy job to fix up the "electric orchestrion" its construction being so simple; only the two parts of the instrument need be put one on top of the other. For this reason, viz.— **greatest simplicity of construction** and **easy fixing up,** the "electric orchestrion" is quite particularly adapted for **export.**

Arrangement I.—Soft and delicate for drawing-rooms. Bourdon, bass and treble, æoline, vienna-flute gamba, fugara.

Arrangement II.—Strong and full for hotels, &c. Bourdon, bass and treble, viola di gamba, flute harmonique, salicional.

Arrangement III.—Loud and full sounding for dancing-halls. Bourdon with bass-flute, flute harmonique, viola di gamba, æoline, piccolo.

The Euphonika company (formerly Hermann) produced a variety of organettes. In the advertisement above (dated 1909) the word *Drehinstrumenten* is literally a hand-turned instrument. On page 145 there is an Olympia advertisement. Below is another only this time the address is 50 Sherman Avenue and Otto is issuing Webster's Dictionary as a gimmick. The Stella was first made in 1896 and Geater was the first London agent.

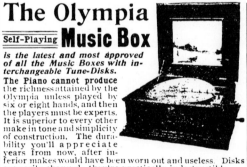

'Queen of the Musical Boxes' was the Regina designed by the inventor of the Polyphon, Gustav Brachhausen, after he went to America. It is interesting to record that both Regina (sired directly by Polyphon) and the Imperial Symphonion (another American-built offshoot from Leipzig) represented what was probably the zenith of disc musical box production. The item at the top left dates from 1900 and that above appeared in 1894. Nicole Frères, by this time a London-owned company, handled the Regina in England—this notice appeared in *The Strand Magazine* for January 1899. On the next pages is an interesting little maintenance book put out by Regina.

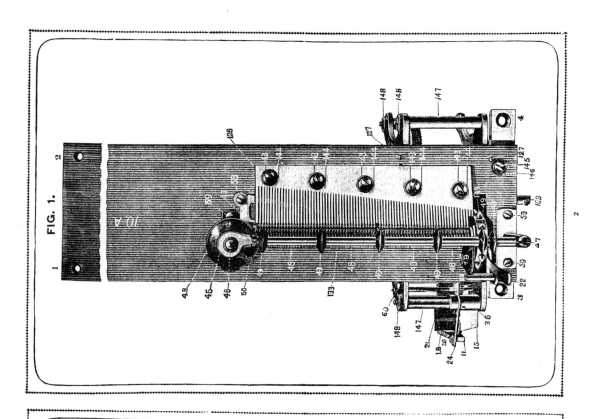

FIG. 1.

PRACTICAL INSTRUCTIONS

For Operating, Oiling and Repairing the

REGINA MUSIC BOXES

The First and Only Music Box
with Interchangeable Metallic Tune Sheets
Manufactured in the United States.

FIG. 2.

FIG. 3.

INSTRUCTIONS FOR OPERATING THE
"REGINA" MUSIC BOXES.

The Instruments are shipped with the Spring unwound or run down, and should be wound up before using. This is done by means of an accompanying crank, adapted to be connected with an arbor or keypost, situated in the large size instruments outside and in the medium and small sizes inside of the box.

If the instrument is received in cold weather, it should remain several hours in a warm room before being wound, as the sudden change of temperature may break the teeth of the comb or snap the spring.

HOW TO ADJUST THE TUNE-SHEET. Fig. I.

Press upon the catch 50, Fig. I, which secures the head of the holding-lever 45 to the centre-post 46, and turn the holding-lever back upon its hinge. Place the tune-sheet in position with its smooth side up and the centre-post 46 projecting through the hole in the centre of the tune-sheet.

Then press the tune-sheet down gently as far as it will go, care having first been taken that the word "Beginning" will be directly under the holding-lever 48 and 49.

The holding-lever is then pressed down upon the tune-sheet and locked in such position by the catch 50 engaging the centre-post, when the instrument is ready for use.

To start the instrument in operation, push forward the lever 22, and draw it back to its original position, when the music will stop at the end of the tune. If it is desired to continue the same tune, the lever 22 shall be pushed forward and allowed to remain in that position, when the tune will be repeated until the lever is again drawn back.

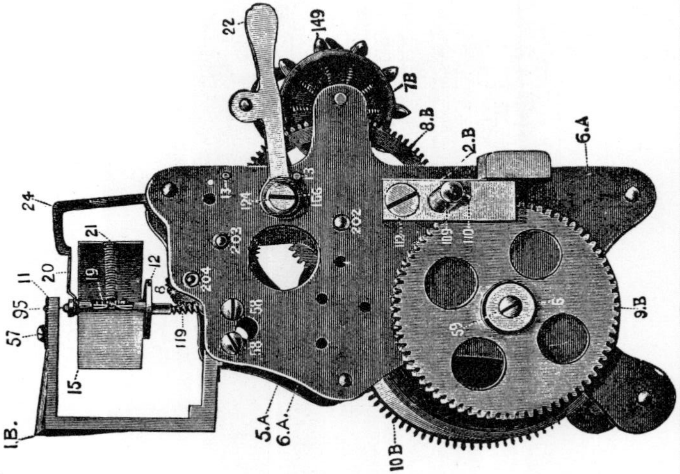

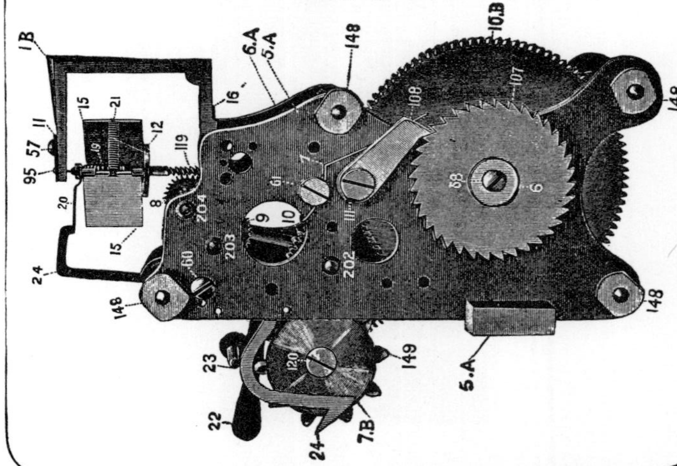

To prevent damage to the comb or the projections on the tune sheet, it is absolutely necessary that the tune sheets should not be removed before the end of a tune is reached.

When not used, the box should, for the same reason, be stopped at the end of a tune, and the cover closed, to prevent dust from settling in the movement.

HOW TO OIL THE "REGINA."

Any kind of machinery, no matter how well constructed, needs occasional oiling, and although the "Regina" requires it less frequently than other music boxes, partly because of the fact that its-movement is better protected, eventually it becomes necessary, and the necessity will be apparent when the instrument begins to run slow. In that case unscrew the board on each side of the bed plate and apply with a tooth-pick or small wire a drop of oil to the worm 119, (Fig. 2 and 3).

Should this not have the desired effect, then remove the four screws, 1, 2, 3 and 4, (Fig. 1), which fasten the instrument in place in the box.

Then take the instrument out carefully and lay it on two blocks or boxes, so as to conveniently gain access to the underside thereof, and put a drop of oil on the following parts. (See Fig. 2 and 3).

First.—The worm (119) on the shaft on which the fly or governor is mounted.

Second.—In the small oil-hole leading to the outer pivot of the fly or governor shaft. (11, Fig. 2).

Third.—To the opposite end of the governor shaft near the worm, (very important).

Fourth.—To the pivot holes or bearing of the shaft of the gear wheels on each side of the movement, 202, 203 and 204.

Fifth.—On the winding post (109, Fig 2). Should the worm 119 and wheel 8, which gears therewith need cleaning, it can be accomplished with a soft tooth-brush dipped in benzine, after which the parts should be properly lubricated, as above described.

When this is accomplished, the instrument should be replaced in the box exactly in its original position, but before fastening it with the screws, the crank should be adjusted to the winding post to prevent a deviation thereof.

As a general rule, a few drops of oil occasionally, say once every three months, would keep the instrument in good running order, and if lubricated in time, will prevent the wearing of the parts mentioned above. It is of importance that the proper kind of oil be employed. The ordinary watch and clock oil has not enough body for this purpose, and we therefore carry a specially prepared oil which can be procured by our patrons for 25 cents a bottle.

The foregoing instructions can be carried out without un-screwing any part of the instrument. We especially caution against so doing without the assistance of a skilled person.

REPAIRS.

In case any part of the movement has been damaged, a competent watchmaker or jeweler should be called upon to make the necessary repairs. If, however, no jeweler or other person competent to make the repairs be at hand, it will be preferable to express the movement (Fig. 2), or the whole instrument (Fig. 1) to our agent.

To remove the movement from the bed plate, proceed as follows:

First, unscrew lever, (22, Fig. 2).

Second, remove the screw on top at the bed-plate, (145, Fig. 1).

Third, remove the screw below the bed plate, (5 A, Fig 3).

Then disengage the bed-plate from the movement with great care, so as to leave washers which may be found between the two in their position. These washers should be well preserved and preferably tied, or otherwise attached to the holes to which they belong; since it is of the greatest importance that they be replaced in their original position again.

The movement (Fig. 2) can be packed and properly secured with paper or excelsior, in a small box, so that it will not become displaced or broken in transportation.

The whole movement (Fig.1) can be shipped in suitable case having supports inside on which to fasten it similar as it was in the music box.

5

6

Examine sprocket wheel (7 B, 149), and observe whether or not it runs easy; if not, put a drop of oil on the screw forming its shaft. An oil hole is provided for the purpose.

If a main-spring is broken, our advise is to return the drum, with the broken spring and the arbor left in it, to our agent, who will replace it at the smallest possible cost.

FIG. 4. **FIG. 5.**

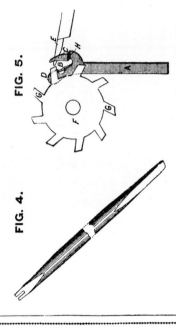

THE DAMPER.

The Damper (A) is crotch shaped (as illustrated in Fig. 5), and the broad arm (D) thereof is provided with a cam (B), which is adapted to project into the space between the spurs (G) of the star-wheel (F), which is to operate that particular damper. The tension of the spring of the body portion of the damper (A) is exerted toward the star-wheel, which is to operate it so that each spur of such star-wheel will, in its rotation, come in contact with the cam (B) of the damper and force the same to one side. Projecting from the same face of the damper as the cam (B) is the arm (C) of the crotch, which forms the damping finger proper. This finger projects up between the tooth (E) of the comb, which is to dampen and the next adjacent tooth. The damper is normally out of contact with the tooth which it is to dampen, but is forced against the side thereof and dampens it when a spur on the star-

This is especially recommended, if movements are to be shipped from a considerable distance, as it would save express charges and not expose the music-box to injury in transportation.

If the movement to be returned belongs to a No 14 Automaton, the money-shovel and lever may be removed in order to use a smaller packing case.

Before the governor or any other part of the movement is removed, ascertain whether the main-spring is down. If it is, the main-spring barrel 10 B, Fig. 3, will be found loose, if not, it will bind rigidly with the other gear wheels. Whenever proper oiling, as directed above, does not give the desired result, it is advisable to examine the governor. The governor and its mounting comprises the angle piece (1 B), the worm-shaft 119 with governor-fans mounted thereon, a jewel mounting 11-57, jewel 95, and adjustable pivot plate 16.

To dismount the governor, remove screws 58, then with handle of a screw-driver, knock carefully against the base of the angle-piece I B, until disengaged. Then loosen the adjustable pivot plate 16, and take out the worm-shaft with the governor-fan mounted thereon.

The pivot plate 16 can be adjusted in a direction transverse to the governor shaft for the purpose of bringing the worm 119 thereof into proper position with relation to its gears. If a mark does not exist showing the original position of this adjustable plate 16, it would be well to make one before removing it. Examine the jewel to discover whether or not it has been worn by the pivot of the governor shaft. If it has become worn, remove and replace it. The pivot of the governor shaft should, on its head, be round, smooth and well polished. On this condition, as well as on a perfect polished jewel, depends largely a uniform running of the movement.

In certain cases where the governor has been allowed to run a long time without oil, the gear-wheel 8, which meshes with the worm of the governor shaft, may be worn on the edges and a new one required.

wheel (F) comes in contact with the cam (B) on the damper, and just before the spur vibrates the tooth of the comb which it is to operate.

Thus, it will be seen, that a very slight movement is had on the part of the damper, and should it be observed that one or more do not dampen properly, it will be necessary to test them separately, until the defective dampers are found, when a careful observance of their action may prove that the damping-fingers (C) have been slightly bent by some accident or careless handling, and that a bending back thereof into position is all that is necessary. For this purpose it is desirable that some such tool as is illustrated in (Fig. 4) should be employed. It will be observed that one end has the form of a screw-driver, while the opposite end is provided with a groove, which should be of about the thickness of the metal of the damper. One end of this tool can be used to turn the star-wheels, while the purpose of the grooved end is to straighten the damping-finger (C), should it by any accident become bent out of its normal or vertical position.

As the slightest displacement of the damping-finger is sufficient to impair the usefulness of the damper, it will be understood that the operation of regulating it is a delicate one, and therefore that the operator should proceed with care; it being borne in mind that the damping-finger should be vertical and perfectly straight, since, if it is bowed the slightest amount, the damping will be rendered ineffective.

For this reason care should be observed that the damping-finger (C) be bent only at the curve (H) where it connects with the body portion. This can be done by gently pressing down the two tongues of the comb, between which the damping-finger protrudes. (Fig. 6 A.)

In order to know to which side the defective damping-finger (C) is to be bent, it should be tested; that is to say, the star-wheel should be rotated a tooth at a time at intervals of about two seconds.

9

If a whizzing sound is noticed, the damper is too far away from the tongue it is to dampen. If the tongue does not vibrate or has a dead sound, the damper is in too close a position to it.

The damper holder, (43 and 58, Fig. 6) star-wheel standard (74, Fig. 6), or centre-post (46 and 59, Fig. 1), should never be unscrewed or disturbed from their position unless absolutely necessary, as when these parts have to be replaced by new ones.

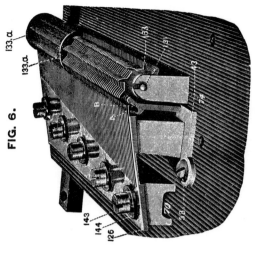

FIG. 6.

COMB AND STAR WHEELS.

If the comb needs repairing, it can be removed, but great care should be exercised in its removal.

After the screws of the comb have been carefully removed, there may still be some resistance to the removal of the comb, on account of the pins fastened to the bed-plate and fitting tightly in holes in the brass base of the comb, which are intended to assure the comb being placed in exact position intended for it.

10

Should difficulty be found in removing the music-comb after the screws have been removed, wedge a screw driver in at one end between the bed-plate and the foot of the comb, (Fig. 6, 7o), so as to slightly lift it.

In case of breakage of a tooth of the comb it is advisable that no attempt be made to repair it, because such a repair necessitates the employment of great skill. By forwarding the comb to the agent any such repair will be made at a small cost and with such satisfaction as could not be otherwise obtained.

Before replacing the comb, care should be observed that all the star-wheels are aligned, as indicated in Fig. 6, and in such a position that the cams of the dampers between the spurs of the star-wheels, as illustrated in Fig. 5, so as to bring the teeth of the comb out of contact with the dampers. Then insert the points of the comb between dampers, so that the first damper comes between the first and second tooth, (Fig. 6a), and be careful that the points of the tongues centre with the spurs of the star wheels. If the adjustment is to be made without the guiding pins mentioned before, begin by fastening the comb with two screws, so that the tongues thereof will be only slightly engaged by the spurs of the star-wheels, then advance the comb, by lightly hammering on the heel thereof, until the first base tongue of the comb can be raised by a spur of the star-wheel about one-sixteenth of an inch, before it is released and vibrated, and the last treble about one-third the distance of the base tongue.

Exceeding this proportion, the tongues are liable to break.

However, judgment must be used, and the distance given above to which to raise the tongues of the comb is merely given as a guide.

After the comb has been properly adjusted, the screws should be fastened tight.

OBSTRUCTION OF STAR-WHEELS.

Should it be noticed that the tune-sheet, instead of turning with an easy and steady motion, jerks or stops altogether, although the movement is in good running order, it may be concluded that one of the star-wheels is obstructed. The tune-

sheet should then be taken out at once to prevent damage, and the box not be allowed to play until the cause of the obstruction is removed.

First examine the instrument to discover whether or not any of the tune-sheet projections have become broken and fallen between the wheels; if so, remove them. If difficulty is still found in the operation, then every wheel should be tested separately until the obstructed wheel is discovered. This can be accomplished by turning each star-wheel until it has made a complete revolution, with any such tool as is represented in Fig. 4. If the cause of the obstruction is not visible, try a small drop of oil on the groove of the obstructed star-wheel or wheels, which will release it if the obstruction is on the shaft. If, by using reasonable force, and rotating the star-wheel in both directions, it will not yield, then it is probable that one of the spurs (133, Fig. 6) has been bent, and is thereby prevented from rotating in the groove of the standard which supports the star-wheels. If it is a single-comb instrument, the star-wheel can be turned backward by slightly raising the tongue to let the spur of the star-wheel pass, when the defective spur can be brought into such position that it can be straightened with a pair of small plyers. If it is a double-comb instrument, it would be necessary to remove the front comb, as otherwise the bent spur, after having once passed beneath the combs, could not be reached.

It sometimes occurs that a spur on one or more of the star-wheels becomes slightly bent, so that while it will pass through the groove of the standard in which it rotates, there will be frictional contact between the bent spur and the sides of the groove. This should be remedied, and the bent spur or spurs straightened, until the wheel moves easily on its supports, otherwise it may cause injury to other parts of the instrument, as well as destroy the efficiency of that particular part.

There is provided on the center-post a brass supporting disc, (4 B, Fig. 1), for supporting the tune-sheet. This disc is provided with a set screw which engages with the centre-post to allow of an adjustment of the disc, the rim of which should be on a level with the uppermost portion of the support-washers, (133 a) on the shaft of the star-wheels.

Two musical boxes which are rare in England and probably even rarer in the United States are the Libellion and the Imperator, both made in Leipzig by the industrial group of F. Ad. Richter & Co. The Imperator came in a number of sizes. Note the disc pressure bar extending across the disc as in the larger Symphonions. Only one size of the Libellion has been seen. This has the advantage of being able to play very long selections. Another scarce box, although to be found in numbers both sides of the Atlantic, is Zimmermann's Fortuna (*see page* 143). Two of the largest styles are shown overleaf. Again the original print is damaged.

"Fortuna" Automatons.

"THE MARVEL".

NEW! NEW!

118 broad steel tongues. 14 Harmonium reeds. Triangle and Drum.

No. 370. Weights: about 59 kg net, 112 kg gross — 130 lbs. net, 250 lbs. gross. Size: about 148 × 80 × 48 cm — 4′10½″ × 2′10½″ × 1′7½″

Stand for No. 375. Weight: about 33 kg net, 40 kg gross — 73 lbs. net, 89 lbs. gross. Size: about 89 × 85 × 50 cm — 3′ × 2′10″ × 1′7½″.

370

Very suitable for large Halls, Restaurants etc.

No.		£	s.	d.
370.	Beautifully designed and ornamented walnut case with or without coin-attachment for any coin, incl. **6** tunes "Z"	32	0	0
375.	The same as No. 370 with equally beautiful stand and cabinet for tunes combined, packed in 2 cases	37	16	0

Tunes "Z", diam. 26″ each € 0 7 0.

Complete list of greatest variety of tunes.

Ordinary packing cases free.

"Fortuna" Automatons.

"THE FORTUNA ORCHESTRION."

236 broad steel tongues, 14 Harmonium reeds, Triangle and Drum.

Size: about 206 × 160 × 64 cm = 7′ × 5′ 4″ × 2′ 2″

Weight: about 195 kg net, 295 kg gross = 425 lbs. net, 650 lbs. gross.

425.

Very suitable for Concerts and Dances.

No.   £   s.   d.

425.   Very well finished walnut case, with 2 cabinets for tunes, plays two tunes (one piece) at the same time, with or without coin-attachment for any coin, incl. 6 sets of tunes "Z"   70   0   0

Tunes "Z", diam. 26″, each £ 0 7 0.
Complete list of greatest variety of tunes.
Ordinary packing cases free.

Should the Regina Corona run slowly or unevenly while the spring is wound, it is an indication that the movement requires oiling.

TO GAIN COMPLETE ACCESS TO THE MOVEMENT, UNSCREW THE BACK OF THE CASE (THE PIANO SOUNDING BOARD) AND THE MOVEMENT IS OPEN TO VIEW (SEE FIGURES No. 1 & 2).

Figure 2.

The parts which require the most frequent oiling, are:

(IN FIGURE 2)

1. The worms and pivots of the two governor shafts (b and c).
2. The pivots of the trains of wheels meshing with the governor shafts.

The following parts of the movement should be oiled in addition at least twice a year:

(IN FIGURE 2)

1. The bearings of the shafting Q, and the parts connected with it.
2. The bearing of shafting Z (figure 1).
3. The bearing of part L, its roller d and part g.
4. The slides a of the rod A, and the corresponding parts on the opposite side of the case.
5. The roller on the part R.
6. The roller h running in the groove of the cam P and shafting f.
7. The shafting i connected with star wheel and lever X.

NOTE.—Care should be taken that only first-class clock oil be used, which will not gum. A can of such oil can be had on application.

If it is desired to play two consecutive tunes for one coin, remove the pin Y on the upper spring barrel C. (The pin Y is always in the position, as shown on the cut, when the mechanism is at rest.)

Figure 1.

Figure 2 shows this part of the mechanism enlarged

BACK VIEW OF MECHANISM.

UPPER SECTION OF MECHANISM ENLARGED.

NOTE.—To insure smooth running of the mechanism, it is necessary that the instrument stands on perfectly level ground, otherwise the tune sheet carriage is liable to move out of its proper position, and the carriers will not shift the sheets correctly.

The mechanism of the self-changing Regina Corona (*left*) was complex and extremely ingenious. On 1 January 1899, *Musical Opinion* carried news of a revolutionary new disc-playing instrument called the Sirion. This featured a centre spindle for the disc which could be moved a small amount in relation to the star-wheels and combs of the playing mechanism. These star-wheels were spaced far enough apart to allow for the passage between them of another set of disc projections. Each disc could thus carry two full tunes, selection being by shifting the disc and its spindle from one position to another. The mechanism of the Sirion, which appeared in both upright and table form, is thought to have been made by Mermod, an assumption lent weight by the discovery (by Q. David Bowers) that the co-patentees, Bortman and Keller, assigned their patents to that company. An early London agent for the Symphonion was Martin Hirsch who, in his *Musical Opinion* advertisement below, confuses Wheatstone's mouth-organ with Lochmann's product in calling it *Symphonium*. The 1900 notice (*right*) highlights the fact that the Leipzig distributors for the Polyphon were Peters.

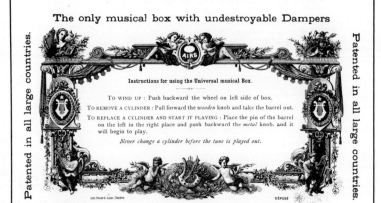
By 1900, Symphonion had formed a London company with offices a few doors from Nicole Frères in Ely Place. While Klein handled Polyphon and the Amorette organette (*see previous page*), Symphonion also handled the Atlas organette, another very well-made instrument. One of the most unusual cylinder boxes to be produced was that by Cuendet-Develay, Fils et Cie of Switzerland in 1891. Rugged and robust in intent and appearance, it was also very crude. The label above tells the story. Each cylinder played just one tune and its pins were like small nails! This was one attempt both to cheapen cylinder box production and to approach the certainly greater robustness of the disc box mechanism. Meanwhile in 1902, Mermod produced the sophisticated Electric Stella Orchestral Grand. On the next page, Campbells of Edinburgh announced, about August 1894, one of the most attractive models of table Symphonion. The carved case was, in truth, masterfully-moulded veneer, sawdust and glue!

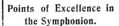

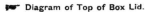

The Berliner Musikinstrumenten Fabrik, formerly Ch.F. Pietschmann & Söhne, specialised in producing organettes but in 1893 launched into production with the Celesta (*above*). Other than Campbells in Edinburgh, the lack of a major British agent stifled extensive sales. Below is a 1903 advertisement for Thorens musical boxes. Thorens's disc box, the Edelweiss, was widely sold in table models ranging from diminutive disc-playing photograph albums to medium-sized cabinets. The business was founded by Eugène Thorens who was Ernst Paillard's brother-in-law. Another popular instrument was the Kalliope, a late catalogue of which begins on the facing page.

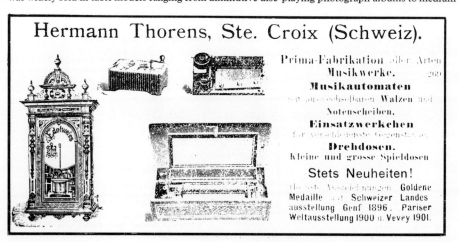

Kalliope-Spieldose Nr. 26.

Selbstspielend.

Gehäuse Nussbaum imitiert. 26 Stahlzungen, mit Bremse. Kurbel-Aufzug.

Grösse 20½ × 16½ × 13 cm

Netto-Gewicht ca. 2 Ko.   Brutto-Gewicht ca. 2¼ Ko.

Kalliope-Drehdose Nr. 25.

26 Stahlzungen.   Gehäuse Nussbaum imitiert.

— **Zum Drehen.** —

Ansicht und Grösse wie Nr. 26 also: 20½ × 16½ × 13 cm.

Netto-Gewicht ca. 1,7 Ko.   Brutto-Gewicht ca. 1,8 Ko.

Kalliope-Spieldose Nr. 26 gross.

— **Selbstspielend.** —

Sonst genau wie bei Nr. 26, ebenso 26 Stahlzungen, jedoch Grösse 26 × 23 × 17 cm.

Netto-Gewicht ca. 3¼ Ko.   Brutto-Gewicht ca. 4¼ Ko.

☞ NB. Bei Bestellung von Notenblättern für Nr. 26, 25 und 26 gross ist stets zu bemerken: für Nr. 25. Stahlnotenscheibe 14½ cm Durchmesser. Netto-Gewicht ca. 32 gr.

Kalliope

1911

Spieldosen

und deren Notenblätter

Hauptvorzug

Garantiert beste existierende Stahldämpfung Konkurrenzlose Triebwerke Glockeneinrichtung } **Patente:**

Separat-Katalogе über { Kalliope-Schallplatten / Kalliope-Sprechapparate / Kalliope-Musik-Automaten } stehen auf Wunsch zu Diensten.

Kalliope-Spieldose Nr. 40.

— 4 —

Selbstspielend. Nußbaum fourniertes Gehäuse. 36 Stahlzungen, mit Bremse. Kurbel-Aufzug.

Grösse 26 × 23 × 17 cm.

Netto-Gewicht ca. 4 Ko. Brutto-Gewicht ca. 5½ Ko.

Stahlnotenscheibe zu { Nr. 40 und 40G } 18 cm Durchmesser. { Nr. 37 und 37G }

Netto-Gewicht ca. 56 gr.

Kalliope-Spieldose Nr. 37.

— 3 —

Selbstspielend. Gehäuse Nussbaum imitiert. 36 Stahlzungen, mit Bremse. Kurbel-Aufzug.

Grösse 26 × 23 × 17 cm.

Netto-Gewicht ca. 4 Ko. Brutto-Gewicht ca. 5½ Ko.

Kalliope-Glocken-Spieldose Nr. 37 G.

— 4 Glocken. —

Selbstspielend. und Gehäuse wie Nr. 37.

36 Stahlzungen. Sonst Werk

Netto-Gewicht ca. 4½ Ko. Brutto-Gewicht ca. 6 Ko.

Stahlnotenscheibe zu 37 und 37G, 18 cm Durchmesser.

Netto-Gewicht ca. 56 gr.

184

— 6 —

Kalliope-Spieldose Nr. 50.

Selbstspielend. 49 Stahlzungen.
Gehäuse Nußbaum fourniert. Kurbel-Aufzug.

Grösse 30×27×17½ cm.

Netto-Gewicht ca. 5¼ Ko. Brutto-Gewicht ca. 8 Ko.

Bei Bestellung v. Notenblättern für obige Spieldose ist stets zu bemerken:

Für Nr. 50.

Stahlnotenscheibe: 23½ cm Durchmesser.

Netto-Gewicht ca. 100 gr.

— 5 —

Kalliope-Glocken-Spieldose
Nr. 40 G.

Ansicht des geschlossenen Gehäuses wie nebenstehende Abbildung von Nr. 40.

———— 4 Glocken. ————

Selbstspielend. Nußbaum fourniertes Gehäuse.
36 Stahlzungen, mit Bremse. Kurbel-Aufzug.

Grösse 26×23×17 cm.

Netto-Gewicht ca. 4½ Ko. Brutto-Gewicht ca. 6 Ko.

Stahlnotenscheibe zu { Nr. 40 und 40G } 18 cm Durchmesser.
{ Nr. 37 und 37G }

Netto-Gewicht ca. 56 gr.

Kalliope-Spieldose Nr. 52.

Selbstspielend. 49 Stahlzungen.

Gehäuse Nußbaum fourniert. Kurbel-Aufzug.

Grösse 34×32×18 cm

Netto-Gewicht ca. 6½ Ko.   Brutto-Gewicht ca. 9½ Ko.

Bei Bestellung v. Notenblättern für obige Spieldose ist stets zu bemerken:

Für Nr. 50.

Stahlnotenscheibe: 23½ cm Durchmesser.   Netto-Gewicht ca. 100 gr.

Kalliope-Glocken-Spieldose Nr. 50 G.

Ansicht des geschlossenen Gehäuses wie nebenstehende Abbildung von Nr. 50.

—— 6 Glocken. ——

Selbstspielend. 49 Stahlzungen.

Gehäuse Nußbaum fourniert. Kurbel-Aufzug.

Grösse 30×27×17½ cm.

Netto-Gewicht ca. 6 Ko.   Brutto-Gewicht ca. 8½ Ko.

Bei Bestellung von Notenblättern für obige Spieldose ist stets zu bemerken:

Für Nr. 50.

Stahlnotenscheibe: 23½ cm Durchmesser.   Netto-Gewicht ca. 100 gr.

Kalliope-Spieldose Nr. 60.

Selbstspielend. 61 Stahlzungen.
Gehäuse Nußbaum fourniert. Kurbel-Aufzug.

Grösse 40×38×19 cm.

Netto-Gewicht ca. 11 Ko. Brutto-Gewicht ca. 18½ Ko.

Bei Bestellung von Notenblättern
für obige **Spieldose** ist stets zu bemerken:

Für Nr. 60.

Stahlnotenscheibe: 34 cm Durchmesser. Netto-Gewicht ca. 200 gr.

Kalliope-Glocken-Spieldose Nr. 52 G.

Ansicht des geschlossenen Gehäuses wie nebenstehende Abbildung von Nr. 52.

—— 6 Glocken. ——

Selbstspielend. 49 Stahlzungen.
Gehäuse Nußbaum fourniert. Kurbel-Aufzug.

Grösse 34×32×18 cm.

Netto-Gewicht ca. 7 Ko. Brutto-Gewicht ca. 10 Ko.

Bei Bestellung von Notenblättern
für obige **Spieldose** ist stets zu bemerken:

Für Nr. 50.

Stahlnotenscheibe: 23½ cm Durchmesser. Netto-Gewicht ca. 100 gr.

Kalliope-Spieldose Nr. 62.

— 12 —

Selbstspielend. 61 Stahlzungen.

Feines Gehäuse, Nußbaum fourniert. Kurbel-Aufzug.

Grösse 47×45×24 cm.

Netto-Gewicht ca. 13 Ko. Brutto-Gewicht ca. 24 Ko.

Bei Bestellung von Notenblättern für obige **Spieldose** ist stets zu bemerken: **Für Nr. 60.**

Stahlnotenscheibe: **34 cm Durchmesser.** Netto-Gewicht ca. **200 gr.**

Kalliope-Glocken-Spieldose Nr. 60 G.

— 11 —

Ansicht des geschlossenen Gehäuses wie nebenstehende Abbildung von Nr. 60.

10 Glocken.

Selbstspielend. 61 Stahlzungen.

Gehäuse Nußbaum fourniert. Kurbel-Aufzug.

Grösse 40×38×19 cm.

Netto-Gewicht ca. 12 Ko. Brutto-Gewicht ca. 20 Ko.

Kalliope-Spieldose Nr. 60 D.

Ohne Glocken, aber mit **mit Doppelkamm.**

122 Stahlzungen. Gehäuse und Gewichte wie oben.

Bei Bestellung v. Notenblättern für obige **Spieldosen** ist stets zu bemerken: **Für Nr. 60.**

Stahlnotenscheibe: **34 cm Durchmesser.** Netto-Gewicht ca. **200 gr.**

Kalliope-Spieldose Nr. 108.

— 14 —

Selbstspielend. 82 Stahlzungen.

Feines Gehäuse, Nußbaum fourniert. Kurbel-Aufzug.

Grosse 64×58×26½ cm.

Netto-Gewicht ca. 24 Ko. Brutto-Gewicht ca. 40 Ko.

Bei Bestellung von Notenblättern für obige Spieldose ist stets zu bemerken: **Für Nr. 108.**

Stahlnotenscheibe: 45 cm Durchmesser. Netto-Gewicht ca. 375 gr.

Kalliope-Glocken-Spieldose Nr. 62 G.

— 13 —

Ansicht des geschlossenen Gehäuses wie nebenstehende Abbildung von Nr. 62.

—— 10 Glocken. ——

Selbstspielend. 61 Stahlzungen.

Feines Gehäuse, Nußbaum fourniert. Kurbel-Aufzug.

Grösse 47×45×24 cm.

Netto-Gewicht ca. 14 Ko. Brutto-Gewicht ca. 25 Ko.

Kalliope-Spieldose Nr. 62 D.

Ohne Glocken, aber **mit Doppelkamm.**

122 Stahlzungen, Gehäuse und Gewichte wie oben.

Bei Bestellung von Notenblättern für obige Spieldosen ist stets zu bemerken:

Für Nr. 60.

Stahlnotenscheibe: 34 cm Durchmesser. Netto-Gewicht ca. 200 gr.

The late John Clark received the above letter from the Polyphon Company as recently as 1929. By then, it was based in Berlin and the letterhead reveals the relationship with the Deutsche Grammophon company and the Polydor record label. With this letter were two manuscript lists of tunes, a total of seven $19\frac{5}{8}$ inch titles, and twenty-six for the $15\frac{5}{8}$ inch size. Small disc musical boxes were made both by Thorens (*see page 182*) and by Unghans. On the facing page is a selection of boxes which were still being made until very recent times.

— 15 —

Kalliope-Glocken-Spieldose Nr. 108 G.

Ansicht des geschlossenen Gehäuses wie nebenstehende Abbildung von Nr. 108.

— 10 Glocken. —

Selbstspielend. 82 Stahlzungen. Kurbel-Aufzug.

Grösse 64×58×26½ cm.

Netto-Gewicht ca. 25 Ko. Brutto-Gewicht ca. 43 Ko.

Bei Bestellung von Notenblättern
für obige **Spieldose** ist stets zu bemerken:

Für Nr. 108.

Stahlnotenscheibe: 45 cm Durchmesser.
Netto-Gewicht ca. 375 gr.

Boîtes à musique à ressort à disques interchangeables
Self acting music boxes with interchangeable discs
Musikdosen mit Federaufzug mit auswechselbaren Notenscheiben

Modèle N° 268

30 lames petit format, boîte imitation acajou, avec chromo.

30 Teeth small size, imitation Mahogany case with chromo.

30 Stimmen klein Format, Imitation Mahagoni Dose mit Bild.

Dim: 21×14 ¹/₂×9 cm.

Prix
Price | Fr. 16.50
Preis

N° 268

N° 269

30 lames petit format, boîte polie avec 2 cases pour disques.
30 Teeth, small size, polished case with 2 side places for discs.
30 Stimmen, polierte Dose mit 2 Notenbehältern.

Dim: 31×18 ¹/₂×14 ¹/₂ cm.   Prix - Price - Preis: Fr. 22.-

N° 269 B

30 lames grand format, boîte polie avec 1 case pour disques.

30 Teeth large size, polished case with 1 side place for discs.

30 Stimmen gross Format, polierte Dose mit 1 Notenbehälter.

Dim: 33×19 ¹/₂×17 ¹/₂ cm.

Prix
Price | Fr. 35.-
Preis

N° 269

Boîtes à musique à ressort à disques interchangeables
Self acting Music Boxes with interchangeable discs
Musikdosen mit Federaufzug mit auswechselbaren Notenscheiben

N° 276

Dimensions
24 x 18 x 14 cm.

Joli coffret couleur acajou poli avec chromo.   Musique 30 lames petit format
Tiroir pour disques 115 mm.   Remontoir de côté.
Nice cabinet polished mahogany colour with chromo.   Music 30 teeth small size
With disc-holder for discs 115 mm.   Side-wind.
Dose imitation Mahagoni mit Bild.   Musik 30 Stimmen klein Format.
Notenbehälter für Scheiben 115 mm.   Seiten-Aufzug.

Prix - Price - Preis : 21.— francs suisses.   Poids - Weight - Gewicht : Kg. 1.810

N° 280

Dimensions
34 x 20 x 18 cm.

Boîte couleur acajou poli avec décoration, et casier pour disques 135 mm.
Musique 30 lames grand format.
Cabinet polished Mahogany colour with decoration, à holder for discs 135 mm.
Music 30 teeth large size.
Dose imitation Mahagoni mit Verzierungen, und Behälter für Scheiben 135 mm.
Musik 30 Stimmen gross Format.

Prix - Price - Preis : 35.50 francs suisses.   Poids - Weight - Gewicht : Kg. 3.320

Boîtes à musique à ressort à disques interchangeables
Self acting Music Boxes with interchangeable discs
Musikdosen mit Federaufzug mit auswechselbaren Notenscheiben

N° 270

N°s	Lames Teeth Stimmen	Description - Ausführung	Poids Weight Gewicht	Dimensions Masse	Prix par pièce Price each Preis per Stück
			Kg.	Centimètres	Francs suisses
270	41	Riche boîte noyer avec modérateur	6,500	41×28×18	51.—
272	55	Rich Walnut Cabinet with moderator	11,300	49×37×24	103.—
274	110	Reiche Nussbaum-Schatulle mit Tabulator	12,100	49×37×24	120.—

Boîtes à musique à disques interchangeables
Music Boxes with interchangeable Discs
Musikdosen mit auswechselbaren Notenscheiben

N° 264   N° 265

Orgues pour enfants   -   Organs for children   -   Kinderorgeln

N°s	Lames Teeth Stimmen	Description - Ausführung	Prix par pièce Price each Preis per Stück
			Francs suisses
264	30	Petit format. Boîte imitation acajou avec chromo Small size. Case imitation Mahagony with chromo Klein Format. Imitation Mahagoni-Dose mit Bild Dim: 16×14 ¹/₂×8 ¹/₂ cm.	12.—
265	30	Petit format. Boîte naturelle polie avec chromo, 1 case Small size. Light coloured case with chromo, 1 case Klein Format. Hellpolierte Dose mit Bild und mit 1 Notenbehälter Dim: 21×15×14 cm.	14.50
266	30	Grand format. Boîte polie naturelle. Large size. Polished case. Gross Format. Hellpolierte Dose. Dim: 24×19×13 ¹/₂ cm.	22.—
267	41	Boîte polie en noyer . Polished Walnut Cabinet . Polierte Nussbaum-Schatulle . Dim: 27×24×17 cm.	35.—

GAMAGES OF HOLBORN.   — 155 —   BENETFINKS OF CHEAPSIDE.
SELF-ACTING MUSICAL BOXES, HAND ORGANS, and MOUTH ORGANS.

The Brass Band Clarion Mouth Har-monica, 40 reeds, 4¾ in. long   **1/4½**   Post 3d

The Piston Harmonica, 20 reeds, 5 in. long.   Price ..   **10½**   Post 2d.

A large selection of **Mouth Organs** at 4½d., 6d., **1 9, 1/10½, 2 6, 3 11, 4 6** each.

Angel's Clarion Harmonica, 40 reeds, 6¼ in. long. Price ..   **1/10½**   Postage 3d.

The Solo Harmonica, with 7 pipes .. **2 6** Post 3d. Do., with 8 pipes, **2 11** Post 3d.

Monopol Self-acting Musical Box. In polished walnut case, decorated lid, handsome coloured picture inside, detachable winding handle, and speed regulator.
No. 30.   Size 10½ by 8¾ by 6 in., has 30 steel tongues.   Price, including 6 tunes ..   **23 6**
Extra tunes, 7½ in. diameter, **6**d. each.
Ditto, with lock and key, 13 by 11 by 8 in,, has 44 steel notes, 6 tunes, **55 6**
Extra tunes, **1/1** each
Ditto, 15½ by 13½ by 8 in., with 50 steel notes, **75/-** Extra tunes, **1 4** each.
Zither attachment fixed to above. **3/-** extra.

Hand Organ in wooden case, 3 by 5 by 4½ in., with carrying sling. Plays 1 tune, **2 6** Postage 3d.

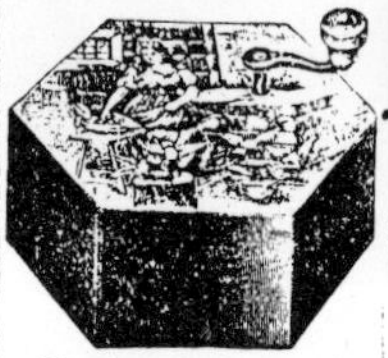

Hand Organ in metal case, as illustrated.
Plays 1 tune .. **1 6** Postage 2d.

Hand Organ, in nickelled case, as illustration.
To play 1 tune .. **1/3** Postage 2d.
Ditto, to play 2 tunes **2/-** Postage 2d.

Organ, in polished wood case, 6 by 4¾ by 3 in., with carrying sling and 3 interchangeable tunes. Price **6/6**

Organ, in polished wood case, 8¼ by 6 by 5½ in., with carrying sling and 6 interchangeable tunes **8/11**

Hand Organ in wooden case, 4 by 3½ by 2½ in.
To play 2 tunes .. **2/6** Postage 3d.
Ditto, 4½ by 3½ by 3 in.
To play 4 tunes .. **3/6** Postage 3d.

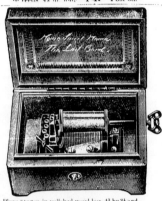

The Gaiety Organ, very loud tone, 40 reeds 4½ in. long **1/4½** Post 3d.

Plays 2 tunes, in polished wood box, 4¾ by 3¼ and 2⅜ in.   Price **3 9**   With glass cover to works, winds at side.   Ditto, plays 3 tunes, **4 6**
Selfacting Musical Boxes. Plays 4 tunes, in polished wood box, 1⅞ by 3½ by 2½ in., with glass cover to works, winds at bottom. Price **5 6**

Automatic Musical Boxes in highly finished imitation rosewood cabinets.

No. 1. Has 3½ in. barrel, plays 8 tunes, 14 by 7½ by 5 in.	**18 6**
No. 2. Has 6 in. „ „ 10 „ stop, start, change repeat levers, size 17½ by 9½ by 5½ in. ...	**2 ·'**
No. 3. Ditto, with 3 Bells	**33/-**
No. 4. Has 7 in. barrel, plays 12 tunes, 4 bells, stop, start, change and repeat levers, size 20 by 11 by 9 in. ...	**42/-**
No. 5. Has 7½ in. barrel, plays 20 tunes, stop, start, change and repeat levers, with optional mute size 22½ in. by 12 in. by 7½ in.	**52 6**

The "Empire" Organ.
Size 16 by 16 by 9½ in., polished imitation Chippendale mahogany colour case, incised and gilt. Has 24 reeds and a very powerful and sweet tone. By special patent mechanism, the levers whilst playing, shift at the end of the first revolution, thus allowing the playing of entire pieces, full songs, dances, marches, etc., and not merely the chorus or fragments of compositions, as in the ordinary disc instruments.
With 6 bright polished metal tunes, **41 6**
Extra tune **1 8**

The Midget Organ, 8 by 8 by 5½ in., has 14 reeds, strongly made and well finished, plays by turning handle. Complete with 6 tunes, **9 6**
Extra tunes, **4**d. each.

The Piccaninnies Piano.
No. 33. This is a Musical Box, with 30 steel notes, playing interchangeable tunes by turning the handle. The music is placed upon the back of the instrument. Brilliant and powerful tone. Polished rosewood case, **14 9** each. Complete with 6 tunes. Extra tunes, 7½ in. dia. **6**d. each.

A selection of musical boxes available from Gamages depart-
ment store in London from their 1908 catalogue (*facing page*).
Above are illustrations of some of the smaller Monopol musical
boxes. The toys on the right all incorporated a small musical
box which played as the toy was rolled along. Ephemera such
as these have not survived and, indeed, even the little manivelle
toy musical box which was produced in thousands is seldom
found today. The decline of the quality of the cylinder box and
its market is shown in the notice (*left*) dated January 1891.
The Demon was probably manufactured as an export model
by the well-known German makers of cheap lanterns whose
name is unknown but for the trademark E.P. It could have
been a discontinued line job lot!

193

CHAPTER 5

Orchestrion Organs and
Automatic Orchestras

THE tiny singing birds manufactured by makers such as the Jaquet-Droz, Leschot, Bruguier and Bontems were elementary mechanical organs. They used one pipe with a movable stopper to vary the pitch of the sound. This is said to have been the invention of Henri Maillardet who, for a time, worked for Jaquet-Droz. Prior to this, a somewhat unconvincing imitation of bird-song was produced by the use of a rank of small, narrow-cut, foot-voiced high-pitched organ pipes or whistles.

From the singing bird at one extreme to the giant orchestrion organ at the other, the skills and ingenuity of their makers was pre-eminent. The builder of the first orchestrion organ, so named because it could represent many of the instruments of the orchestra by the use of reed stops with variously shaped metal or wood resonators, is said to have been the work of a Petersburg clock-maker, J. G. Strasser, between the years 1789 and 1801. This played music by Haydn, Mozart and Eberl in unabridged form. Other early inventors were Jacob and Johann Blessing of Prague, Carl Heinrich and Johann Bauer, F. Blazek, and V. Hrŭbes.

The successful development of the instrument and its presentation before the eyes of the public was undoubtedly the work of the famed Kaufmann family of Dresden. They built an automaton trumpet device which could play cavalry marches, complete with drum accompaniment. This was the Belloneon. After this came the Chordaulodion organ, a larger version called the Symphonion, and then an even larger mechanical orchestra called the Orchestrion. Also in the collection was a mechanical trumpeter which was to become famous throughout Europe. These instruments are described in detail in *Barrel Organ* by the present author. On Saturday 21 June 1851, the instruments of the Kaufmann family were demonstrated at the St Martin's Hall having first been seen by the Queen and Prince Albert at Buckingham Palace. Indeed, Queen Victoria must have been mightily impressed, for she commanded a second performance a fortnight later. The description of the concerts appeared in *The Illustrated London News*. It is reproduced here with the original illustrations. If only we had had the services of that celebrated periodical, happily still with us, half a century before its first issue in 1842!

A mechanical trumpeter, maker unknown, was to be seen and heard at the Adelaide Gallery of Pictorial Science in Adelaide Street during the 1840s.

The name Panharmonicon was applied to at least three instruments, two built by the celebrated Johann Nepomucene Maelzel (born 1772; died 1838), and one by Joseph J. Gurk who was a library servant to Prince Esterhazy.

194

Gurk's Panharmonicon was shown at Wigley's Exhibition Rooms, Spring Garden, in November 1811, having first been seen in Germany in the previous year. An amusing anecdote is told of the instrument by its builder (vide *The Times*, 28 November 1811). It seems that Haydn was one of the first to see the instrument and asked Gurk what it was called. 'My child,' replied Gurk, 'has no name yet; might I presume to request the Father of Harmony to stand its godfather?' Haydn promised to think up a name and the following day sent Gurk a letter stating, 'Dear Sir,—call your instrument the PANHARMONICON; and, if any body ask you any questions about it, tell him the name proceeds from old Haydn. Your's, &c.'

Gurk returned to exhibit the instrument in London again during 1817 but after that, both Mr Gurk and his instrument fade into obscurity.

The brothers Maelzel were among the best known of the early orchestrion makers although there exists some confusion as to which one made which instruments. Leonard Maelzel was eleven years his brother's junior. Suffice it to say that Johann made his first Panharmonicon around 1792 and this was ultimately sold for 100,000 French francs to the Archduke Charles of Austria, protector of the Muses and apparently a man with a great sense of humour. It is said that he bought it for the express purpose of annoying his friends. Whether it was by courtesy of the new owner that Maelzel was allowed to continue exhibiting the instrument or whether it was the second Panharmonicon, described in a moment, is not known, but apparently the Panharmonicon was shown in Paris on the Champs de Mars for a while after this transaction. At some date after this, the Panharmonicon came into the possession of the Abbé Larroque; the subsequent deceptions offered in connection with the instrument by that gentleman are detailed in *Barrel Organ*.

His second instrument was much improved and after a celebrated period of touring (in common with other makers, it was necessary to recoup the enormous expense and time spent in building by placing it on public exhibition and, indeed, it was for this purpose that it was built), the orchestrion went to the museum in Stuttgart. Here it remained attracting, so it would seem, little attention until its total destruction during the war. It was not regarded very highly so that remarkably few illustrations exist of it and these show little of what the instrument was actually like. Happily, however, some of the barrels survive to this day, having been removed to the museum basement. From these barrels just something of the wonders of this marvellous instrument can be gleaned.

Two important names in the more recent history of the orchestrion are those of Michael Welte (born 1807; died 1880) who invented the first practical pneumatic action for orchestrion organs using a paper roll in place of the cumbersome barrel, and Imhof & Mukle. The former was based in Freiburg; the latter in Vöhrenbach in the Black Forest. The work of Davrainville in Mirecourt, France, should not be overlooked. From refined clockwork organs and with the addition of subtle-voiced reeds, resonators, percussion and paper-roll action there emerged a new generation of concert organs. On the one hand, the instrument developed into the incredibly complex reproducing pipe organ such as those made in America by Aeolian (the Duo-Art Pipe Organ) and Welte in Germany (the Welte-Philharmonic). On the other it progressed to the carousel or fairground organ. This latter division also sub-divided into showman's instruments and those built into dance-halls, skating-rings and ballrooms.

The main supplier of orchestrions in England was Imhof & Mukle whose range of instruments could be seen and heard at 110 New Oxford Street in London. Even so, this type of instrument was not as popular in this country as in France and the major output of orchestrions for export from Germany went to France and Russia.

Pneumatic action meant that conventional pipe organs as fitted in churches could be equipped with automatic roll-playing mechanisms so that the absence of the regular organist need not deprive the congregation of the services of Euterpe. The majority of organ-builders in the early part of the present century advertised their ability to make or certainly to fit player actions to organs—but this is something we will take a more detailed look at in the next Chapter. It is the mechanical orchestra which interests us here. The makers were numerous, but as with every facet of mechanical music, a handful of names constituted the top craftsmen. Manufacturers like Wellershaus, Ruth, Voigt, the Bruder family, and in France and the Low Countries, Gavioli, Limonaire, Marenghi and Mortier. Although it was to be that only the last four names reached the attention of the British public with any marked effect, all of these makers possessed various merits and of them probably the contribution made by Ignaz Bruder and the family tradition of show-organ building which he began in 1829 was the most valuable. Second is the technological advances which were to come from the Gavioli family during their period of production in France. Ludovic Gavioli, a native of Modena, established his organ factory in Paris with his two sons, Claude and Anselme, in 1845.

What did these organs look like? What of their specifications and price? A rare catalogue dated around 1895 shows the range of instruments made by Ruth & Söhne. It is in German but it is easy to translate and it is reproduced here. A catalogue of the organs produced by Wellershaus is reproduced in *Barrel Organ*.

Chiappa in London also made and factored organs and 'military band organs' suitable for skating rinks—roller skating enjoyed a brief but widespread popularity in England in the years immediately preceding the 1914–18 war.

The orchestrion makers in the early years of this century were numerous and were mostly situated in the Black Forest, Leipzig and Berlin. Some instruments were nothing more than player pianos to which was added a wind department and a few ranks of organ pipes. This type was later to become very popular in the United States where there were many makers too. Others were full-blown and massive orchestras of such prodigious dimensions that their ownership today demands a ceiling height of ballroom proportions. One may smile wryly at Welte's description of the so-called Cottage Orchestrion which stood ten feet high, and conclude that the Freiburg area must be dotted about with some very tall cottages.

Small orchestrions there were as well, however, and Leopold Mukle, whose place of business was 92 Albany Street, Regents Park with a factory in Furtwangen, Baden, manufactured a line in

In the world of the orchestrion, two names stand out—those of Welte and Imhof & Mukle. These two notices come from an 1894 copy of *Musical Opinion*, and refer to the wares of the latter.

orchestrions for use in 'yachts and steamship saloons'. At the International Music Trades Exhibition, July 1896, he introduced his Patent Pneumatic Orchestrion which, instead of being driven by weights or by the electric light current, was driven by 'compressed air' supplied by an 'atmospheric engine'. All this was an anemometer-type wind motor which drove the barrel through a worm gearing. Wind was fed to the motor 'from motive power'. Just what this was, and how the wind was fed to operate the organ was not stated.

The spectacular monster orchestrions of Lösche, Popper, Dienst, Philipps (who invented the automatic music-roll changer in 1905 so as to allow long programmes of music) and others have all but disappeared now. A tiny proportion of the many thousands made are in private collections where they demonstrate the dictum 'old musical instruments should be heard as well as seen'. A vast number have been destroyed. Some still lurk in a forgotten corner, hopefully awaiting discovery by an appreciative person before it is too late. It is a cold world to these devices today and time is running out fast. Time was indeed almost expired for one very recent discovery. A collector in the south of England happened to peer into the gaping windowless ruin of a house being demolished near London. There on the landing, waiting to be sent crashing down with the rest of the building, stood the battered remains of a once fine orchestrion. Too large to move easily and in any case unwanted, its previous owners had abandoned it to the wreckers. Happily, this one was saved with hours to spare and will soon play again with a new lease of life.

The Kaufmann family from Dresden, perfectors of the early orchestrion organ

THE ILLUSTRATED LONDON NEWS.

[JULY 5, 1851.

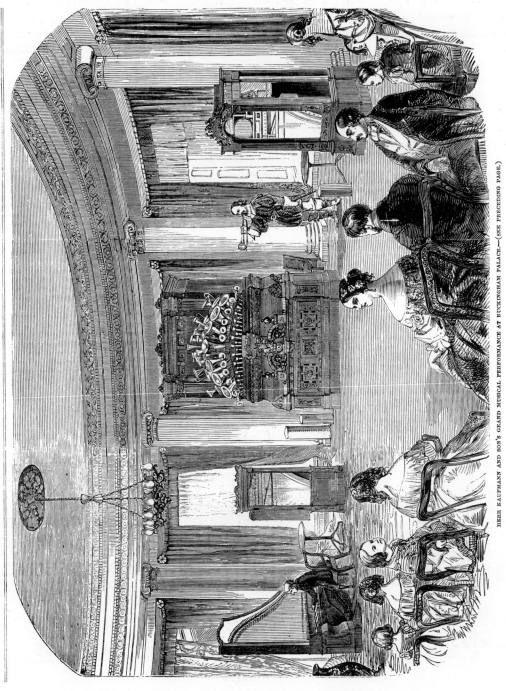

HERR KAUFMANN AND SON'S GRAND MUSICAL PERFORMANCE AT BUCKINGHAM PALACE.—(SEE PRECEDING PAGE.)

SELF-ACTING MUSICAL INSTRUMENTS.

On Saturday, the 21st ult., at St. Martin's Hall, there was a private exhibition of the following new instruments—The "Orchestrion," the "Chordaulodion," "Symphonion," and "Trumpet Automaton," four self-acting instruments. There was also exhibited the "Harmonichord," which is played upon like the organ, with manuals and the pedals. Herr Kaufmann and his son, the inventors of the above instruments, are from Dresden, and for many years have been unremittingly occupied in perfecting their novel conceptions. Our artists have illustrated the "Orchestrion;" it is the most picturesque in appearance, and most complete in its action, of the five instruments. It will be seen from the Engraving it is a combination of the brass and wood instruments; for every one of those metallic and wooden tubes has an eloquent speaking voice. The front of the lower portion of the case being opened, discovers the percussion instruments, the kettle and military drums, and triangle. The Orchestrion was invented by Herr Kaufmann, jun. It was five years before he had completed this marvellous mechanical contrivance, as a substitute for a full military orchestra—the tones of flutes, flageolets, clarionets, cornets, bugles, trumpets, bassoons, horns, oboes, trombones, drums, &c., being most successfully imitated. There can be no mistake—all the instruments depicted in our Illustration actually emit sound, and are by no means decorative. How the maker has so ingeniously contrived that the cylinders move with such mathematical exactitude, and that the supply of wind (of course, varying for each tube) should be so precisely regulated, is scarcely to be conceived even by the thoroughly initiated in matters of mechanics and acoustics. For instance, it is almost miraculous to hear the light and shade of this invisible instrumentation, to mark the just gradations of crescendo, diminuendo, and sforzando, besides the usual fortes and pianos. We never heard anything so perfectly astounding as the *finale* of the "Don Giovanni:" shutting one's eyes, it seemed as if the famed vocal and orchestral forces of Costa were exclaiming at one time, with portentous effect, "Trema!" In the dance music, the three different times going on in the *finale* were observed with unerring precision, the mechanical agents doing what the living artists will rarely accomplish—keep together. Nothing could be finer than the Coronation March from Meyerbeer's "Prophete." Godfrey's Coldstream Band must look to their playing, for the Orchestrion is a formidable rival.

Perhaps the most practical instrument for general purposes is the Harmonichord, deliciously soft and mellow in tone; it is in the form of an upright grand pianoforte, and it is stated that its action arises from the friction of a cylinder against wire strings. For small churches and chapels, and for a chamber organ, the Harmonichord is most desirable. Herr Kaufmann and Fraulein Kaufmann played on it in turn with delicacy and skill.

Furstenau's variations on themes from "Il Flauto Magico," of Mozart, on the Symphonion, was another triumph of mechanical skill, containing flutes, piccolo, clarionets, cymbals, and drums, with pianoforte accompaniment: the precision with which the chromatic scale, ascending and descending, is attained, would dismay a Richardson or a Rémusat. The Chordaulodion comprises flute and string play.

The Trumpet Automaton is a figure not unlike Mario in the "Puritani," with the instrument at its mouth. It was invented many years ago by Herr Kaufmann, and won the admiration of Carl Maria Von Weber. What is most remarkable and inconceivable in this extraordinary piece of mechanism, is, that it produces double sounds of equal strength and purity, and flourishes in octaves, tierces, quints, &c., are heard. Perhaps this acoustic curiosity may supply some key to Vivier's wondrous horn effects, certain notes accompanying particular chords. If this discovery should be established, that one instrument can do the same with equal perfection as two instruments, it may lead to something, as natural intonation may surely effect what a piece of machinery can do.

We have as yet referred specially to the execution of each instrument, but the greatest marvel was when the Harmonichord, played by Herr Kaufmann, and the four mechanical instruments, all were heard at one time in a fantasia on our national melodies. This is truly a miracle, for sometimes one instrument is heard as a solo, and the other relieves it at the exact stand; then two go together, and finally all the works are in movement, keeping exact time, and each one having its special duty to perform. The triumph of mechanical ingenuity can no further go, and the visit of Herr Kaufmann and his son to this country will no doubt be patronised largely. Their difficulties must have been enormous; first, in the just investigation of sound; and, secondly, in its application by mechanical means. To construct such instruments without models, for they are quite original, the maker must be a musician, a mechanic, a mathematician, and a philosopher.

The first public performance was on Tuesday, the 24th ult., the instruments having been exhibited on the 11th ult. at Buckingham Palace before her Majesty, Prince Albert, and the Royal family. On their way to this country, Herr Kaufmann and son gave concerts, with the greatest success, at Leipzic and Hamburg.

There was to have been a second concert at St. Martin's Hall, on the 27th ult., but her Majesty having been graciously pleased to command a second performance at Buckingham Palace, on the morning of that day, the entertainment was postponed to last Monday, a notice of which will be found under the head of "Music.",

Our artists, in addition to the Orchestrion described above, have depicted the execution of the Self-acting Instruments before the Queen and Prince Albert, the King of the Belgians, and the Royal Family, on Friday. The Royal amateurs expressed their high gratification at the quality and ingenuity of the inventions, and complimented Herr Kaufmann and Son on their success.

THE ORCHESTRION.

The Kaufmann family was widely acclaimed amongst the early orchestrion builders. Friedrich Kaufmann and his two sons, John Gottfried and Friedrich Theodore, toured Europe with their instruments, described and illustrated here by *The Illustrated London News* for 5 July 1851, and were received into every Court. Finally, the instruments were set up on permanent exhibition in what the Kaufmanns called their 'accoustic cabinet' in Dresden.

Agents for street barrel organs frequently applied their own names to the instruments, so creating some confusion when we try today to identify the actual makers. Frati's Berlin-made organs were handled in New York by Pollmann (*right*). John Arrigoni (*lower right*) was agent for Wm. Bruder & Sohn as shown in this 1894 *Musical Opinion* notice. He went bankrupt in 1896 and then worked as manager for the Berlin firm of Cocchi, Bacigalupo & Graffigni when they operated in London. A descendant of that firm, John Cocchi, was still in business as a maker and repairer in the 1920s as shown by the trade card (*below*) which was found inside an old Gavioli street organ.

Every make of show organ had its own characteristic sound and one distinctly bright tone is the Limonaire. This famed Paris maker opened up a London factory in 1889 but the enterprise was short-lived and Paris remained the sole Limonaire factory. These organs were unpopular with English showmen since they were reputed to have a typically French (!) nasal sound which did not go down well when compared with, say, the sound of a Gavioli.

The Ehrlich Brothers established the Leipzig Musikwerke in 1877 for the manufacture of mechanical musical instruments. In 1904, the business was taken over by Adolf Buff-Hedinger who, besides continuing with production of the Ariston and Empire organettes, introduced an electric piano with the awesome title *Primavolta*. This notice (*right*) comes from Paul de Wit's 1909 musical instrument trades directory, Leipzig.

POLYPHON

Orchestrions

Saiteninstrumente

Pneumatische Orchestrions

Elektrische   Klaviere

Sprechapparate   Schallplatten   Notenscheiben   Schatullen

Verlangen Sie Kataloge.

Erstklassige Fabrikate.

Polyphon-Musikwerke A.-G.

Wahren-Leipzig.

In 1909, Polyphon was making piano orchestrions playing perforated cardboard music. One model was similar to the Regina Sublima made in Rahway, New Jersey at the same period, and another employed pneumatic action. The company made a wide range some of which had additional percussion effects and a few of which were disc-playing rather than roll-playing like the one illustrated here. The Sun musical box would seem to have enjoyed but a brief life since none are known. Schrämli & Tschudin was established in 1902, advertised as makers of musical boxes in 1903 (*below*) and were still in existence at least as late as 1909. Crasselt & Rähse (*facing page*) also announced their piano orchestrion in 1903 and this bore a distinct mechanical resemblance to the Regina Sublima.

Schrämli & Tschudin

„Sun" Music Box Manufacturing Co.

Fabrique de Pièces à Musique en tous genres

2. Rue des Pâquis 2.   Genève, Suisse.

Boîtes à musique à Disques et à Cylindres interchangeables	Musical boxes with interchangeable Disks and Cylinders
Orchestrions	Orchestrions
Phonographes Suisses	Swiss-Phonographs
Cylindres régistrés et vierges	Registered and unregistered Cylinders
Panorama à musique avec Lumière éléctrique	Panoramas with Music and electric light
Articles de fantaisie	Musical Fancy Goods
Oiseaux chantants	Singing Birds
Nouveautés, etc.	Novelties, etc.
Garantie 1ère qualité.	Guaranteed 1st quality.

Vienna, Austria.

The Pneumatic Orchestrion with which you supplied me is an endless source of enjoyment and pleasure, owing to its marvelously artistic precision in its rendering of all kinds of music.

Wishing you a well deserved succes,

I am yours truly

F. Hauschka Esq.
K. K. Kommerzienrat.

H. H. THE MAHARAJAH
OF KARPURTHALA
East India.

HON. J. Mc. MILLAN
Washington D. C.

WILLIAM MACDONALD
ESQ.
Water Establishment
Pitlochry Scotland.

F. W. CHANCE ESQ.
Carlisle, England.

Mrs. GEORGE LEWIS Jr.
New York City.
and Tarrytown N. Y.

VENDOME HOTEL
Chicago, Jllinois.

No. 3
Cottage-Orchestrion

With kettle drum effect, Snare and Bass-Drum, Triangle and Cymbal.

Height 8 ft. 11 inches. — Width 6 ft. —
Depth 3 ft. 4 inches.
Price including 12 music rolls . . . $ **1800.**—
Extra music rolls, each . . . . . . $ **10.**—

The Welte company of Freiburg turned out a fine range of paper-roll-playing orchestrion organs. Emil Welte invented the pneumatic action for orchestrions in 1887. His father, Michael Welte, was apprenticed to Joseph Blessing, who built what was probably the first orchestrion organ. Welte is also known for the development of the early reproducing piano and piano player.

From the 1909 German musical trades directory come these advertisements of orchestrion makers. Dienst and Popper were both sold in the United States, the instruments of the latter being very popular. Paul Lochmann's Walzen-Orchestrion (*walzen* = musical barrel) was unusual in being a barrel instrument at a time when most makers were favouring punched cardboard.

More European orchestrion makers of the 1909 period. Of these, it is believed that only Lösche and Apollo exported to the United States. Etzold & Popitz were distributors of orchestrions made for them by F. O. Glass. On the facing page are two advertisements put out by Chiappa. He succeeded Arrigoni as Bruder agent (*see page* 200) and also handled Gavioli and Gasparini organs in London.

207

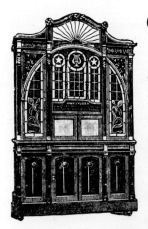

Ambrosius Weisser succeeded the old firm of Hubert Blessing (*top*). Jacob and Johannes Blessing built the first orchestrion in 1849. Schübbe's Orchester-Pianos combined pipe organ and piano and were electric. All these notices date from 1909. On the facing page starts a very rare catalogue of the fair and band organs produced by the Ruth company about the turn of the century. Ruth was one of the best of the German makers of these show instruments.

Special-Catalog für Caroussel & Schaubude-Besitzer von

GRÜNDUNG 1841

A. RUTH & SOHN

ORGEL-FABRIK

in

WALDKIRCH i. B.

Grossherzogthum Baden.

Lith-Kunstanstalt v. Jeng: Faller, Waldkirch i/B.

209

Waldkirch, Datum des Poststempels.

P. P.

Mit Gegenwärtigem gestatten wir uns, Ihnen **Illustrierte Preisliste** über unser Fabrikat in **Caroussel-, Concert- und Salon-Orgeln** zu übermitteln. In der uns sehr angenehmen Erwartung, bei Bedarf Ihre schätzbaren Aufträge uns zu überweisen, deren prompte Ausführung wir Ihnen im Voraus zusichern, bitten wir Sie, die Preislisten vorkommendenfalls auch Ihrem Bekanntenkreise zu unterbreiten.

No. 19 bis 34 welche wir als Specialität anfertigen, sind aus dem Haupt-Catalog ausgewählt und eignen sich dieselben hauptsächlich für Caroussel- und Schaubuden-Besitzer.

Hochachtungsvoll

A. Ruth & Sohn.

No. 35.

A. Ruth & Sohn, Orgelfabrik, Waldkirch, (Baden).

Orgel-Werke mit Notenblättern
mit schöner Fassade in schwarz und gold.

Nummer	Länge etm.	Höhe etm.	Tiefe etm.		M.	Pf
35	145	168	76	Carroussellorgel, immer forte spielend, mit 60 Clavis, die Instrumentierung wie No. 30 mit 50 Meter Noten vom Repertoir	2000	—
				per Meter Noten vom Repertoir	2	50
				und können solche nachgeschickt werden.		
36	185	177	95	Concertorgel, forte und piano spielend, mit 76 Clavis, die Instrumentierung wie No. 23, grosser und kleiner Trommel mit Becken in Seitenflügeln zum abnehmen, mit 50 Meter Noten vom Repertoir	3400	—
				per Meter Noten vom Repertoir	3	50
				und können solche nachgeschickt werden.		
37	225	186	105	Concertorgel, forte und piano spielend, mit 90 Clavis, die Instrumentierung wie No. 24, grosser und kleiner Trommel mit Becken in Seitenflügeln zum abnehmen, mit 50 Meter Noten vom Repertoir	5000	—
				per Meter Noten vom Repertoir	4	50
				und können solche nachgeschickt werden.		

Der Preis der Musikstücke verdoppelt sich, wenn die Stücke nicht im Repertoir verzeichnet sind Reichere bemalte Fassaden mit Figuren, drehbare Säulen etc. werden besonders berechnet.

Orgues à cartons.
Façade elegante noir et dorée.

Numéro	longueur etm.	hauteur etm.	largeur etm.		fr.	cts.
35	145	168	76	Orgue pour carroussels, jouant continuellement forte, 60 touches, même instrumentation que numéro 30. Inclus 50 mètres de musique du répertoire	2500	—
				Prix des morceaux du répertoire le mètre	3	20
36	185	177	95	Orgue-concert, jouant forte et piano, 76 touches, même instrument que numéro 23 avec tambour, grosse caisse et cymbales en 2 niches. Inclus 50 mètres de musique du répertoire	4250	—
				Prix des morceaux du répertoire le mètre	4	40
37	225	186	105	Orgue-concert, jouant forte et piano, 90 touches, même instrument que numéro 24 avec tambour, grosse caisse et cymbales en 2 niches. Inclus 50 mètres de musique du répertoire	6250	—
				Prix des morceaux du répertoire le mètre	5	60

Le prix des morceaux de nos différents modèles d'orgues est doublé lorsque ces morceaux ne figurent pas à notre répertoire. Façades colorées, laquées, statuettes, colonnes etc. sont comptés à part.

19   20 und 21

Salon-Orgeln
für Museum- und Tanzsäle-Besitzer.
Der Prospekt vergoldet. — Sämmtliche mit Schwungräder.

Nummer	Gewicht	Tiefe	Länge	Höhe	Ohne Schwungrad gehen 10 Mark ab.	Mark	Weitere Walze
	Kilo	ctm.	ctm.	ctm.			Mark
19	220	70	128	155	Orgel mit 56 Tönen, bestehend in Bass- und Begleitpfeifen, Geigenstimmen, Spitzflöten, Trompeten, Bombardon, Mixtur zum abstellen, 9 Stück spielend, Walze 64 Takt	1200	150
20	220	72	110	160	Orgel mit 59 Tönen, bestehend in Bass- und Begleitpfeifen, Clarinett mit Beistimmen, Spitz- und Zauberflöten, Trompeten, Bombardon, 8 Stück spielend, Walze 64 Takt	1500	150
21	290	78	153	175	Orgel mit 66 Tönen, bestehend in Bass- und Begleitpfeifen, Clarinett mit Beistimmen, Spitz- und Zauberflöten, Trompeten, Bombardon, 9 Stück spielend, Walze 64 Takt . . , ...	2000	200

26, 27, 28, 29, 30, 31 ohne Säulen.   32, 33, 34.

Grosse Orgel-Werke
für Caroussel-, Panorama- und Tanzsäle-Besitzer,
sämmtliche mit Schwungräder.
Der Prospekt vergoldet. — Bei Angabe der Höhe ist der Aufsatz nicht mitgerechnet.

Nummer	Gewicht Kilo	Tiefe ctm.	Länge ctm.	Höhe ctm.	Ohne Schwungrad gehen 10 Mark ab.	Mark	weitere Walze Mark
26	1C6	63	115	140	Orgel mit 50 Tönen, bestehend in 4 Registern, Pfeifen, Zauberflöten, Spitz-Flöten, Trompeten, Bombardon, 9 Stück spielend, 64 Takt . . .	760	120
27	177	66	115	145	Orgel mit 50 Tönen, bestehend in 5 Registern, Pfeifen, Zauberflöten, Spitz-Flöten, Trompeten, Bombardon, 9 Stück spielend, 64 Takt . . .	880	130
28	190	70	126	150	Orgel mit 54 Tönen, bestehend in 5 Registern, Pfeifen, Zauberflöten, Spitz-Flöten, Trompeten, Bombardon, 9 Stück spielend, 64 Takt . . .	1010	140
29	220	72	134	155	Orgel mit 59 Tönen, bestehend in 5 Registern, Pfeifen, Zauberflöten, Spitz-Flöten, Trompeten, Bombardon, 9 Stück spielend, 64 Takt . . .	1160	150
30	260	73	145	160	Orgel mit 63 Tönen, bestehend in Pfeifen, Spitz- und Zauberflöten, Trompeten, Basstrompeten, Bombardon, 9 Stück spielend, 64 Takt	1310	167
31	300	75	153	165	Orgel mit 66 Tönen, bestehend in Pfeifen, Spitz- und Zauberflöten, Trompeten, Basstrompeten, Bombardon, 9 Stück spielend 64 Takt	1440	184
32	340	77	164	170	Orgel mit 70 Tönen, bestehend in Pfeifen, Spitz- und Zauberflöten, Trompeten mit Beistimme, Basstrompeten. Bombardon, 9 Stück spielend, 64 Takt	1660	200
33	380	80	170	175	Orgel mit 75 Tönen, bestehend in Pfeifen, Spitz- und Zauberflöten, Trompeten mit Beistimme, Basstrompeten, Bombardon, 9 Stück spielend, 64 Takt	1850	220
34	420	82	189	180	Orgel mit 85 Tönen, bestehend in Pfeifen, Spitz- und Zauberflöten, Trompeten mit Beistimme, Basstrompeten, Bombardon, 9 Stück spielend, 64 Takt	2260	300

Concert-Orgeln

Nummer	Gewicht Kilo	Tiefe ctm.	Länge ctm.	Höhe ctm.	Bei Angabe der Höhe ist der Aufsatz nicht mitgerechnet.	Mark	weitere Walze Mark
20A	230	76	132	155	Orgel mit 56 Tönen, bestehend in Bass- und Begleitpfeifen, Geigenstimmen, Spitzflöten, Trompeten, Bombardon, Mixtur zum Abstellen, 9 Stück spielend, Walze 64 Takt	1300	160
21A	300	80	149	165	Orgel mit 64 Tönen, bestehend in Bass- und Begleitpfeifen, Geigenstimmen, Spitz-Flöten, Trompeten, Bombardon, Mixtur zum Abstellen, 9 Stück spielend, Walze 64 Takt	1600	190
22	385	86	176	171	Orgel-Werk mit 72 Tönen, Bass- und Begleitpfeifen, Geigenstimmen, Spitz-Flöten, Trompeten, Bombardon, eine Mixtur zum Abstellen, 10 Stück spielend, Walze 80 Takt	1850	230
23	460	87	191	177	Orgel-Werk mit 80 Tönen, Bass- und Begleitpfeifen, Geigenstimmen, Spitz-Flöten, Trompeten, Bombardon, eine Mixtur zum Abstellen, 10 Stück spielend, Walze 80 Takt	2350	300
24	530	190	214	183	Orgel-Werk mit 90 Tönen, Bass- und Begleitpfeifen, Geigenstimmen, Spitz-Flöten, Trompeten, Basstrompeten, Bombardon, mit Mixtur zum Abstellen, 10 Stück spielend, Walze 80 Takt	3100	400

Grosse Concert-Orgel
für Panorama- und Museum-Besitzer.
Diese Orgel eignet sich in Folge ihrer Construction, forte und piano, vorzugsweise für
Ouverturen, Quodlibets, überhaupt für Concertmusik.
Diese Orgel kann in einen gedeckten Eisenbahnwagen nicht verladen werden.
Der Prospekt vergoldet. — Mit Schwungrad.

Nummer	Gewicht Kilo	Tiefe ctm.	Länge ctm.	Höhe ctm.	Bei Angabe der Höhe ist der Aufsatz nicht mitgerechnet.	Mark	Weitere Walze Mark
25	750	110	261	200	Orgel-Werk mit 107 Tönen, Bass- und Begleitpfeifen, Geigenstimmen, Spitz- und Zauberflöten, Trompeten, Baridon, Bombardon, eine Mixtur zum Abstellen, 10 Stück spielend, Walze 80 Takt	4500	500

Bezugs-Bedingungen.

Jeder Besteller beliebe bei Bestellung $\frac{1}{3}$ zur Bestätigung zu entrichten, den Rest auf Nachnahme, oder gegen Einsendung in Baar vor Versandt.

Briefe und Gelder werden franko erbeten.

Kiste und Verpackung wird extra berechnet.

Für Kisten in gutem Zustand wird bei franko Retournierung $\frac{2}{3}$ des berechneten Betrags rückvergütet, welcher durch Nachnahme erhoben werden kann.

Der Versandt erfolgt auf Rechnung und Gefahr des Empfängers.

Um deutliche und genaue Adresse wird freundlichst gebeten.

Orgel No._____ kann bei sofortiger Bestellung in ungefähr_____ bis_____ Monaten geliefert werden.

Die Orgeln sollen möglichst vor direkter Sonnenhitze, sowie vor Feuchtigkeit und Nässe bewahrt werden.

No. 36.

More orchestrion announcements are on this page. Surprisingly, many makers of this period—the early twentieth century—never put their names on their instruments or, if they did, they were in the form of separate, screwed-on plates which would often be removed by the agent to ensure that any 'follow-up' business in the way of repairs, new music and suchlike should come through him. Often the agent would affix his own name to the instrument (*vide* Arrigoni and Bruder, page 200). Many of the unidentified orchestrions found today may thus come from these lesser-known firms and now defy positive recognition.

CHAPTER 6

Parlour Organettes and Self-Playing Organs

THE first pneumatic actions to be used in music were those which formed the basis of the little organette. These organettes were reed-playing instruments with anything from one-and-a-half abbreviated octaves (14 notes) up to 24 notes. Although some were advertised with 36, 48 or 72 reeds (one with 104!), all this meant was that there were several reeds to each note, implying several stops or ranks of reeds.

A number of men worked contemporarily on the organette as it came to be known both in France and in the United States but it was the work of the Americans and mainly the work of two men, McTammany and Gally, that prepared the sound foundations of a great industry.

The vogue of the organette lasted only slightly longer than that of the disc-playing musical box, namely from about 1882 to 1912. The instrument had two primary advantages over all other domestically aimed musical instruments which worked mechanically. It was extremely cheap and it was fundamentally simple to use since it had no clockwork to get out of order. Furthermore, being small and light in weight, it could be sent through the post easily. Prices ranged from about 22s 6d upwards and their popularity, particularly with the young, was both instant and immense.

The majority of the early organettes came from America but their development and sophistication was left to the German musical box industry in Berlin and Leipzig, instruments such as the Amorette, Phoenix and Ariosa playing progressively better music. The most popular organette in Europe was Ehrlich's Ariston while the three British-made organettes of any merit, Dewhurst's Orchestrone, Draper's English Organette and Maxfield's Seraphone, enjoyed only average popularity. The arrival of the Gem Roller Organ from the United States (its proportions grossly exaggerated in the illustrated advertisements to make it look bigger than it actually was) was rewarded with a measure of success. This was about 1894 and Campbell & Co. of Glasgow was the main distributor. The Gem sold for 30 shillings and extra tunes, in the shape of pinned wooden rollers (known in the United States as 'corn cobs'), cost just one shilling each.

From the little organette it was but a short step, in the hands of the competent inventor and manufacturer, to enlarge the instrument in conjunction with the American organ and produce a player reed organ capable of operation either by keyboard or by perforated paper roll.

Among the earliest of these to reach London was Story & Clark's Orpheus in 1897, followed by Wilcox & White's Symphony, first produced in the early 1890s and made by Murdoch & Murdoch. George Whight & Co., who already distributed the Victolian player organ which cost only 17 guineas, began factoring the Aeolian at their 225 Regent Street showrooms as early as 1896—

and soon became involved in an important copyright case. Boosey, the music publisher, alleged infringement of musical copyright in the selling of Aeolian music rolls. The three rolls in question were 'My Lady's Bower', 'The Better Land' and 'The Holy City'. Judgement was found for Boosey on a technical point. In September 1899 Whight's business was taken over by the Orchestrelle Company at the same address. Their manager, Mr Mason, unveiled in November that year a new model of a player organ called the Aeola (Style D) which retailed at £100 and which was described as a medium-priced instrument.

William Gerecke at 8 and 9 Goring Street, Houndsditch in London was distributing the Pneuma which was made in Germany by Kuhl & Klatt. This self-playing organ was operated either by electricity (via storage battery or the 'electric lighting current') or by a crank. One assumes this to infer a crank*handle*! Another London distributor was Robert M. Marples & Son of 57 Holborn Viaduct who had the agency for Kimball organs, introduced in 1898 at £37 13s.

So far, all the instruments listed here have been of either American or German origin, with the former having the greater share. There was only one major British maker and this was Maxfield of Liverpool Road, London. Maxfield invented one of the few British-made organettes, the Seraphone, and went on to make a manual and self-playing organ which sold for £25 in 1899.

Without any shadow of doubt the finest player organs of the reed type were those produced by the Aeolian Company and called the Orchestrelle. These came in a wide variety of styles from about 1898 onwards at prices which ranged from 21 guineas up to £1,000 for the twin-tracker-bar, two-manual-roll-playing, 116-note Model F introduced about 1910. An orchestra in your own home and at the command of your finger-tips, suggested the advertisements. There was a strong measure of truth in this, for the instrument employed a number of banks of reeds, called tone ranks, each of which featured a particular characteristic of reed and resonating chamber. The instrument, when operated in skilful hands, was capable of reproducing music from a perforated roll with remarkable colour and variety. These organs were a far cry indeed from the somewhat primitive appliances of only ten years earlier.

In the years that followed, player organs underwent development to absolute perfection. First came the famed Mustel organ from Paris fitted with roll-playing attachment. Soon every organ manufacturer was supplying and fitting player actions for organs. Makers such as Jardines, R. Spurden Rutt, Henry Poyser of Chester, Charles Lloyd of Nottingham, Hilsdon of Glasgow, and many, many others all over Europe and America advertised self-playing attachments.

Alas! None of these survive with their player actions preserved. The tuner who would recommend the owner of a player piano to 'modernise' the instrument and throw the player action out (see Chapter 7) was only doing what his opposite number in the organ world had been doing for years before him. For various reasons which are not hard to appreciate, tuners hated player actions. They were just another unnecessary complication within the organ, something else to go wrong. Indeed, one gathers the impression that as fast as a builder would place a player within an organ, the next tuner would come along and recommend its removal! With the availability of plenty of people who could play manually, the thirties and forties spelled doom for many an organ player action. Ironically, with the diminishing number of people who are learning to play a keyboard instrument today, the odds are that within a decade or two the words of Mason, Precentor of York Minster from 1763 to 1797, in his *Essays Historical and Critical on English Church Music* (1795) may take on a new significance. He wrote that he preferred '. . . the mechanical assistance of a Cylindrical or Barrel Organ to the fingers of the best parochial organist.' A case of Man's rejection of his own invention and failing to take into consideration the characteristics of another of his own inventions—the wheel which has the habit of turning the full circle . . . .

Perhaps the present opportunity will be the most convenient to speak of the AUTOPHONE, although it is more a musical than an acoustic instrument. Until lately Barbary organs and piano organs have been the only means by which poor people have been able to hear any music, and that not of a very elevated class. Besides, there is a good deal of expense connected with the possession of an organ. But the Americans, with a view to popularize music, have invented the AUTOPHONE, which is simply a mechanical accordeon, manufactured by the Autophone Company, of Ithaca, New York.

The principle of the instrument is represented in fig. 186, and is extremely simple. An upright frame carries within it on one side a bellows, and on the other a flexible air chamber, which serves as a reservoir.

The upper portion contains a set of stops like an accordeon, but the escape of the air through the small vibrating plates can only take place by the upper surface of the frame work, upon which slides a thin plate of Bristol board pierced with holes at convenient distances, and set in motion by the mechanism shown in the annexed diagram (fig. 187).

The figure represents an axle furnished with a series of "washers," which, acting upon the plate, cause it to move round. It is the bellows

Fig. 186.—The Autophone.

movement that turns the axle by the aid of two "catches," B and C, which work upon a toothed wheel fixed upon it.

The "catch" B moves the paper on which the tune is "perforated," when the bellows is empty, the other catch when it is distended; but a counter catch, D, represented by the dotted lines in the illustration, is so arranged that the paper cannot pass on except the tooth of the catch D is opposite a hole pierced upon the plate above. In the contrary case there is no movement of the paper during the dilatation of the bellows. The effect of this very ingenious arrangement is to give to the "musical" band of "board" an irregular movement, but it economises it in the case of sustained notes. The whole action of the instrument depends upon the correct working of the bellows.

The effect, from an artistic point of view, certainly leaves something to be desired, but the instrument is cheap, and not cumbersome, and the

Fig. 187.—Detail of the Autophone.

slips of paper upon which the music is "cut out" can be made by machinery, and consequently are not dear. So far, the Autophone is fitted for popular favour and use, and may supersede the barrel organ.

The first 'organette' to enter production was an unusual little instrument called the Autophone which played strips of cardboard. As shown (left) it was worked by rhythmically squeezing the bellows, so inching round the music transport roller by means of two catches. This illustrated article comes from *Popular Scientific Recreations* by Gaston Tissandier, c. 1885.

The first successful British-made organette was Draper's Orchestral Organette. This is described here (1898) and on page 233. The instrument was very cheaply made although it was of adequate design and performance. From the notice at the bottom of the page, it was obvious that the main revenue came from the sale of suitable music. This is the catch to the 'free organette' advertisement on page 234. As well as Draper, John Dewhurst made a very cheap reed instrument called the Orchestrone (*facing page*) which sold for just 1s. 6d. A far more practical device was the American Orguinette introduced into England in 1880 by Metzler (*right*). The Herophon was made in Berlin by C. F. Pietschmann & Söhne who made a number of other organettes, some very similar to Ehrlich's Ariston. The Herophon, however, had a square tune 'disc' which remained stationary while the mechanism rotated beneath.

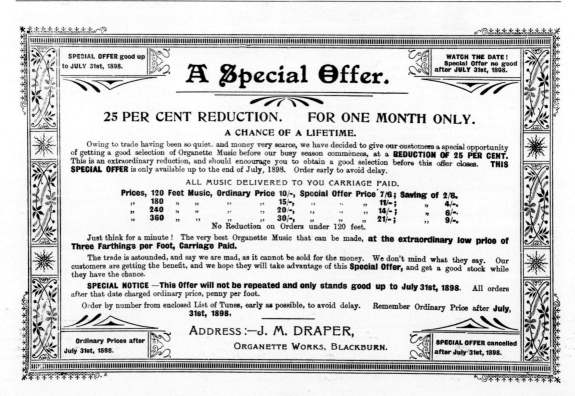

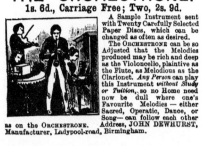
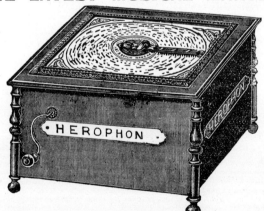

From Campbell's 1898 catalogue come these pages advertising the Gem roller organ produced in several styles by the Autophone Company of New York which manufactured the instrument shown on page 221. The style seen here was the cheapest.

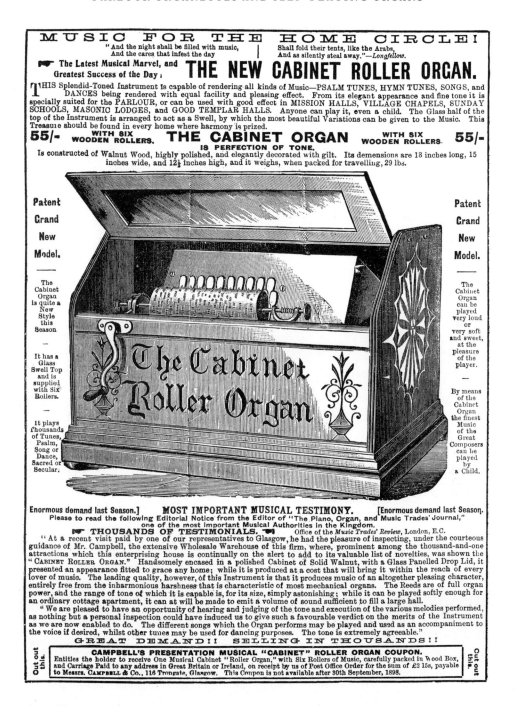
From the basic Gem came the Cabinet Roller Organ, the mechanism of which was the same. A flap at the back of the case could be used as a 'swell'. The small wooden barrel, studded with pins, played spirally making three revolutions per tune.

In the manner common at the time, testimonials were solicited (or perhaps offered in the knowledge that they might be published?) from notable personages. The Rev. David Alfred Doudney was one such person with the difference that he died before publication in 1894.

From this page one would justifiably expect the Gem to be of fairly considerable proportions. Alas! it was much smaller in size, unless it was posed here with pygmies. Of passing interest here is the table fountain playing centre right at the back.

The Latest and Best Automatic Musical Instrument of the Day,
THAT PLAYS MUSIC WITH METAL ROLLS, IS THE
MUSICAL DOLCINE

THE construction of this excellent little instrument, as will be seen from the drawing below, is quite a new departure from the old style of Instruments that produce Music with PAPER SHEETS or ROLLS. The Music of the DOLCINE will be found much superior to all other Instruments of this class at the price, and our well-known reputation for supplying only Instruments of Real Musical Merit is a guarantee that the DOLCINE will give satisfaction to the purchaser. Although it has only been in the market a short time, the sale has been very large on the Continent and America. We will send the DOLCINE carefully packed in Wood Box, with Six Tunes, carriage paid, at the merely nominal price of 25s., with following Coupon.

The New Patent Automatic
DOLCINE
Produces Music with Metal Bands.

The DOLCINE has a nicely-polished Case with fine mouldings on top; It has Broad Reeds, and music is produced by Endless Metal Bands.

The Dolcine, for rapid Music, Waltzes, Quadrilles, Polkas, and all other similar compositions, has no superior.

We have prepared for an enormous demand.

Extra Tunes, Metal, 9d each.

2,000 TUNES NOW READY.

A CHILD CAN PLAY IT.

"DOLCINE" TESTIMONIALS

8 Compasses Row, Broomfield Rd., Chelmsford, 1894.
Dear Sir—I received the "Dolcine" quite safe, and I am very well pleased with it. The tone is charming. It makes a beautiful present, which I have made of it to a friend.
Yours truly, W. HEARD.

Farm Hall Mill, Kumirley, near Oswestry, 1894.
Dear Sirs,—I received the two "Dolcines" quite safe, and they have given me the greatest satisfaction. They are beautifully-finished instruments, and have a splendid tone. All my friends are delighted with them, and hope to send you up a few orders shortly.
Yours truly, THOMAS JOSEPHS.

18 John St., Barrowford, 1894.
Dear Sirs,—The "Dolcine" came duly to hand. I am greatly pleased with it, and consider it a charming instrument, the tone being pure and sweet.—Yours truly,
WILLIAM ROBERTS.

| Cut this Out | £1 5s. | CAMPBELL'S MUSICAL "DOLCINE" COUPON. | £1 5s. Entitles the holder to receive one Musical Dolcine, with Six Rolls of Music, carefully packed in Wood Box, and Carriage Paid to any address in Great Britain or Ireland, on receipt by us of Post Office Order for the sum of £1 5s., payable to Mr. JOHN CAMPBELL, at the General Post Office, Glasgow. This Coupon is not available after 30th September, 1895. | Cut this Out |

Beware of spurious and worthless imitations. The DOLCINE can only be bought from us or our Agents specially appointed. Every Instrument will bear our Name and Address—without which none are genuine.

Campbell's Superior Musical Boxes
Have a World-Wide Reputation for High-Class Workmanship and Durability.

MUSICAL BOXES in Handsome Carved Wood and Inlaid Cases, playing Superior Music, and fitted with Finest Clockwork Mechanism. LARGE MUSICAL BOX, as per drawing, plays 8 Popular Tunes, price only 50s.

Largest Stock in the Kingdom.
SPLENDID VALUE.

Musical Boxes, playing 2 Tunes,	..	13s.
Musical Boxes, playing 3 Tunes,	..	18s.
Musical Boxes, playing 4 Tunes,	..	21s.

Just Out—New Style Musical Box,
38s. | THE "WONDER." | 38s.
Special] Playing 12 Popular Tunes. [Coupon

Fitted with a 3½ in. Nickel-Plated Cylinder, New Tune Indicator, and plays 2 Tunes with each revolution of the cylinder. This Wonderful Box should sell in thousands at the price. Sent carefully packed and Carriage Paid for £1 18s. *Cut out this Coupon.*

Largest Stock in the Kingdom.
SPLENDID VALUE.
Newest Styles in Presentation Musical Albums, Quarto, playing 2 Tunes, 21s. free.

Musical Albums, Large Quarto, playing 2 Tunes, 28s. free.

Musical Albums, Large Quarto, playing 3 Tunes, 38s. free.

Special Price List of Larger Boxes, Fitted on Tables, on application.

EXTRA LARGE SIZE
MUSICAL BOXES
⬥ NOTHING FINER OR BETTER MADE. ⬥
EXTRA LARGE SIZE.

These Boxes have Patent Lever Winders, and all the latest improvements, the various working parts being strongly made and finely finished.

Just Out—New Style Musical Box,
£3 10s. | THE "MARVEL." | £3 10s.
Special] Playing 12 Popular Tunes. [Coupon.
With NEW CRANK WINDER.

Fitted with a 7½ inch Nickel-Plated Cylinder, New Tune Indicator, and Charming Zither Accompaniment. This Marvellous Box we send carefully packed and Carriage Paid for £3 10s. At this give-away price this beautiful Box should find its way into every Music-loving home in the land. *Cut out this Coupon when ordering.*

No. 4.—Splendid Musical Box, extra large size, plays 12 Popular Tunes, and has 5 beautifully engraved Bells. This is a handsome Box, beautifully inlaid with various coloured woods, powerful yet sweet tone. A very fine box indeed. Price reduced to only £7 7s.
No. 6.—QUITE NEW STYLE—The Cabinet Musical Box, opens with two doors in front. This is a very handsome Box, plays 8 Tunes, has the Charming Zither Accompaniment, and finest quality of music. Very fine inlaid case, extra large size. Price £10 10s.
No. 7.—QUITE NEW STYLE—The Cabinet Musical Box, opens with two doors in front. This is a very handsome Box, plays 10 Tunes, and has visible Drum, 5 visible Bells, and visible Castignet accompaniment. Very fine inlaid case, extra large size. Finest Box made. Price £12 12s.

One of the products of the Leipzig Musikwerke Euphonika was the Dolcine organette, also handled by Campbell of Glasgow. The tune strips here were made of metal. Notice the range of cheap cylinder musical boxes which are also listed.

PARLOUR ORGANETTES AND SELF-PLAYING ORGANS

The Victorian young man's activities were nothing if not industrious and he was encouraged to follow all manner of practical pursuits. One of the useful ways in which our grandfathers could pass their boyhood hours was by making tunes for organettes. The *Boys' Own Paper* for Saturday 6 July 1895 provided full details of how to do this, along with a fair amount of moralising. The article remains, nevertheless, essentially practical and its instructions are just as valid today as then.

HOW TO CUT OUT TUNES FOR AUTOMATIC MUSICAL INSTRUMENTS.

By Reginald A. R. Bennett, M.A. (Oxon.),

Author of " How to make a Stereoscope," " How to make a Half-plate Camera," etc., etc.

On this occasion we enter quite a new field of research; this is not going to be a photographic, or an electrical paper. But for one boy who goes in for photography or electricity there must be hundreds who are the possessors of what are commonly known by the above title of "Automatic Musical Instruments," so that I feel quite justified in addressing a new audience on the subject of their hobby. Moreover, these instruments are bought by the very boys to whom this paper is likely to be of use, for those who buy them are not usually those who can turn off a sonata of Beethoven's or a fugue of Bach's by the instrumentality of their own fingers. It is those who are unable to do this, either from want of learning or practice, that become purchasers of the machines which will (theoretically) play any tune by merely turning a handle.

I should think there can be but few articles of merchandise which have undergone such a profusion of changes and so many developments as the one before us. I can call to mind, not so very many years ago, the time when what was practically the first of these instruments was sold, and in those days no one thought that anything very wonderful was likely to come of it. "What!" said the admirer of Haydn's "Symphonies" and Mendelssohn's "Songs without Words," who had toiled for years to give their due meed of expression to the works of the greatest masters, "shall we indeed live to behold a time when the toil of our early days will be supplanted by the use of paper bands, with no attempt made to render the expression of the original music?" and the unfortunate "automatics" were condemned as being a "soulless" people, devoid of all capabilities of comprehending the mysteries of the Harmonic Muse. These instruments were—some of them—retailed at the not very considerable price of 16s., so perhaps there was reason for the remarks of the critics, since under such circumstances one can imagine that even the "Hallelujah Chorus" or the "Wedding March" would lose much of its charm.

But "the old order changeth, yielding place to new," or, as it is beautifully expressed in your French phrase-book, "Nous avons changé tout cela." I have before me at the present moment a book of 207 pages, containing a list of music published for the "Æolian Organ," an instrument lately brought out by Messrs. G. Whight & Co., 225 Regent Street, w., which contains pieces by Handel, Mendelssohn, Bach, Liszt, Sullivan—every imaginable author, and a vast lot of whom I never in my life heard before! To buy the most expensive of this instrument you have to put down your cheque or banknotes to the *tune* (this is not a joke) of 104*l*. sterling! This is a double manual (excuse the expression) organ, some part of which is played by an operator, but the larger part is done entirely by automatic paper bands. When both are playing together the effect is obtained of two players,

so you can easily imagine that some very grand results can be attained. Those who have testified to the musical qualities of this instrument include Messrs. Sarasate, Dan Godfrey, Jean de Reszke, Madame Berthe Marx, and Mrs. Kendal; I have only chosen those you are likely to know.

When I have made my fortune I quite intend to get one of these instruments; at present we will consider those of a somewhat humbler class. However, I may remark that, if you can afford to buy one of them, you can cut out music for it by the rules which are to come, if you have a sufficiency of brain power to enable you to alter the keys and the number of notes to suit the larger instrument.

Those who can afford to buy the more expensive organ can, however, usually afford to buy the music, but my object is to teach those who have the humbler sort to cut out simple tunes for themselves. After all, I daresay they will get as much fun by cutting out "Daisy Bell" or "'E dunno where 'e are" as the "gilded" owner of the other machine will by his success in rendering Chopin's Concerto in E minor, Op. 11, Allegro Maestoso.

The one grand difficulty with which the manufacturers had to contend in developing this class of organ was that the notes produced by the passage of the wind through the holes of the paper were liable to be *slurred* by the too gradual admission of the air, which in the case of the first thing of the kind (which was manufactured in 1848, and exhibited by the Society of Arts in 1851) was too awful to be endured by the educated ear. In this case, however, ordinary organ pipes were used, and it isn't very wonderful that they did not produce a very satisfactory effect.

The next thing to be done (I am sorry I have to go into details, but it is really an interesting history, and you ought to understand the construction of your own grinder if you are to work properly) was to use reeds instead of pipes. However, the result was still far from pleasing, and success was regarded as impossible until some brilliant genius hit on the plan that the alterations ought to be made in the method of admitting the wind, instead of in the reeds themselves. Observe at this point how fortunes are made by the direction of your intellect in a different course to other people, for by striking out a fresh line that individual brought it to pass that millions of instruments have been sold of a sort which would have otherwise been involved in the romantic interest of a bygone age! So great a success has been accorded to the efforts of succeeding experimenters in this line that it is perfectly impossible to tell, in the case of superior instruments of this class, that they are not being played by a most experienced and skilful musician! Some leading-musical man is popularly reported to have said that the day of manual practice was over, and that the people of the future would play by

means of paper bands! This does appear to me to be going a little far in the other direction; I rather fancy that my fellow mortals will not abandon the use of their fingers as instrumentalists in my time!

To pass over the further improvements made at different times, you will find, if you look carefully at your own instrument, that it will belong to one of two classes—either the reeds are actuated by means of wind passing down channels cut in the wood bar over which the paper passes—which in the case of some machines are rather large, as the "Orguinette," and in that of others very small, as in the "Celestina"—or the air is admitted to the passages by the paper lifting little levers as it passes along, as in the case of the "Organina." The latter class gives the best musical effect, but is open to the objection that the paper has to stand a good deal more wear and tear, as the levers wear it out. On the other hand, those of the "Celestina" class can use extremely thin paper, as there is hardly any wear on it.

By far the commonest of its class is the "American Orguinette," which presents itself in a variety of forms to the purchaser. We will first think of the method of cutting out tunes for these, as they are the most often met with, and the same system can be carried out, by making the required alterations, in the case of any other instrument.

The paper used for the Orguinette is $7\frac{1}{4}$ inches wide, and of a peculiar whity-brown colour. You can buy it from the makers, or—if they are disagreeable—from McArthur & Co., Dalsholme Mills, Glassford Street, Glasgow. In experimenting with short tunes you can use ordinary cartridge paper. If glued together at the end of each strip, and the hole cut across the join, it will not affect the tune.

It is quite easy to cut out music for the Orguinette, and no knowledge of music whatever is required except the names of the notes, and the relative values of quavers, crotchets, etc. Before you attempt to transpose a tune you must find out what is the scale of notes on your instrument. The ordinary Orguinette is set in the scale of A, and the notes are A, B, C sharp, D, E, F sharp, G, G sharp, A, B, C sharp, D, E, F sharp. Those notes are selected which will give the largest range of tunes without alteration. In this scale it will be seen that we have all the notes in the ascending scale of A, with G natural introduced; this is often wanted, in fact it would be frequently impossible to play a tune without it.

In all large shops where these instruments are sold and the music manufactured there is a man retained expressly to transpose the tunes—*i.e.* to change them from their original scale into the one in which the instrument plays, so that they will sound all right on it. The number of tunes which they get into it is simply marvellous in the case of the Orguinette. Imagine Handel's feelings if he had been told that the "Hallelujah Chorus" would in future years come to be ground out by a mechanical instrument having only fourteen notes! Yet this and the "Dead March in Saul" are mentioned on every list.

The following rough-and-ready way will enable you to cut out your tune without any musical knowledge. Simply sit down to the piano and play the tune through, only allowing yourself the fourteen notes on the instrument. You will find that, in one way or another, you can get it all in. Then mark the notes on your strip of paper, as I shall direct presently. Having got in the treble, you have now to get in the bass, chords, etc., using the lower notes on your scale, and thus rig out the complete tune. Try a simple tune first; for if you attempt a too elaborate one you will produce an effect more interesting than beautiful.

Now for cutting out the music. I will tell you how you can cut out some for the Orguinette, Celestina, or similar instrument, as I don't think many of you will have the 63l. or 104l. "Æolian" with its five octaves, and, if you had, you could most likely buy the music as easily as you could make it, as there is hardly any tune that cannot be obtained for these instruments.

We do not want anything but the paper, a sharp knife, and a piece of glass to cut on, but we have first to construct a scale of notes. Taking the Orguinette as my first example, I give an illustration of the required scale. It is simply made of a piece of thick cardboard, the width of the music—viz. 7¾ inches—and about 4 inches long. This scale being cut out of cardboard, and the exact width of the paper, with the notes marked on it in their proper places, all you have to do is to place the scale on the top of the band and mark out the positions of the notes with a pencil. But the scale only gives the breadth of the notes and their position: how are you to judge of their length? To do this you must mark off some measures on the side of the gauge, taking some small note as a unit. The most convenient note for this is probably the crotchet, and I find that in ordinary music for the American Orguinette a crotchet is represented by a hole about ⅛ inch in length. All the other notes have now to be based on this standard, so that their relative values may be kept up. For example, the semibreves will be four times as long, and a minim between the two—twice a crotchet and half a semibreve. You must not have a smaller note than this, as too small an opening does not admit the air properly; so that if a shorter note than this occurs in the piece you must take this as the standard instead of the crotchet (e.g. a semiquaver), and the crotchet must be a multiple of that.

In actual working you can save yourself much time in measuring by the marks on the side of the gauge, which are made as shown in the illustration (fig. 1). You have then only to run your pencil down the side of the cardboard to mark the required length, join top and bottom, and the note is then marked out.

In order to show the appearance of the tune-band when cut out, and the relative sizes of the notes, I give a picture of the first few notes of one (fig. 2).

The standard in this case would have to be the semiquaver. I have given the treble

only, in order not to confuse you with too many notes, as both bass and treble are so close together. The holes can be cut out with a sharp penknife, on a piece of glass, taking care that it cuts clean, and does not

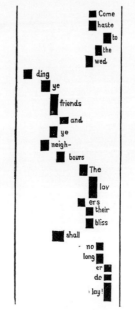

FIG. 2.—FIRST LINES OF TUNE FOR ORGUINETTE.

jag the edges. It saves time to cut all the strokes one way first, and then, turning the band round, to cut all the other way, thus completing the holes.

The Orguinette, taken at its best, is not a *very* musical instrument, though no one would believe who hadn't tried it what a number of tunes can be got into such a small compass of notes. The "Organina," "Celestina," and other instruments of that class, are productive of vastly superior effects, the "voice" being prompter, and they have another advantage (those of the latter class, e.g. the Celestina), that the paper, by the special pneumatic construction of the wind channels, is subjected to very considerably less strain, which enables much thinner paper to be used, and it therefore takes very much less room on the roller.

The width of the "Celestina" music is 5¾ inches, and in this compass we have to get sixteen notes. The notes on one that I have, and I believe they are the same on all of them, are—G sharp, C sharp, D sharp, F sharp, G sharp, A sharp, C, C sharp, D, D sharp, E, F, F sharp, G, G sharp, A sharp, C, C sharp, D sharp, F. This is a curious kind of mixture, but in practice it seems to give very satisfactory results, and enables almost any tune to be played with fair accuracy. There is no occasion for me to draw another gauge, for it is exactly the same for

this music, except that, of course, the width has to be that of the paper, and the position of the notes correspond. The shortest note on this scale must be about $\frac{3}{16}$ inch.

The channels for the air in this instrument, by an ingenious piece of mechanism, open out in a fan shape as they get nearer the notes which are at the bottom, so that at the upper end we have the whole compass of the reeds gathered up into the smallest possible space at the top, where the paper passes over the entrances, thus enabling us to use very much narrower paper.

The method of cutting out the music is, of course, the same as with the Orguinette, using the other scale. In playing your tune first you will get into a mess if you try to remember the notes on the piano, so you had better mark them temporarily with a little piece of paper, and then only use the marked ones. A person with musical knowledge could, of course, transpose the tune straight off, without necessarily playing it first.

Having cut out our music, we have to consider the best way to keep it in order for future use. In the case of the "Celestina" music this is usually wound on rollers, which form part of the machine and can be turned backwards when it is desired to wind the tune back on to them. But in the case of the Orguinette, and other similar machines, the music has to be kept separately. The best method of doing this is, perhaps, in the case of rather long tunes, to crease them purposely at given intervals, say about a foot, which causes the music to fold itself up as it emerges from the machine, a much more desirable plan than leaving it to twist about on the floor and get torn. Rolls of music should have labels attached to them (on which is the name of the piece) at the end of the roll at which the piece begins, on the side that is uppermost when placed in the instrument: this enables them to be placed in the right position at once. Otherwise you may put it in backwards, which, I assure you, produces a most singular effect, not always harmonious.

Elastic bands should be placed round the rolls when not in use to prevent them from becoming unfolded and possibly torn.

Fractures in the music can best be mended by tracing the notes spoilt on another piece of paper, including a few chords above and below, cutting the paper clean through, so as to remove the torn piece, and joining on the new one in its place. The joins are best made in the centre of a chord, as, the wind escaping through the notes at that point, there is less probability of a note sounding in the wrong place owing to inequality in the paper at the join.

This is, I think, all that is required to enable anyone to cut out tunes for himself; and I can assure you that on a cold winter's evening, with the snow falling and the wind howling, it is a very nice little amusement, especially as, if one can play the piano well oneself, and is so independent of turning handles, there are often plenty of juveniles to whom the operation is a great pleasure.

In this article I have supposed that you are only in possession of a small musical instrument of this class; but if there are sufficient readers who have the larger ones—"Æolians" and such like, who would like to be told how to cut out music for them, I shall be pleased to tell them how to make a special instrument for cutting out music of a larger kind (as, if you have to cut out notes for five octaves, it becomes rather a more elaborate undertaking) if they will write to the editor and ask for an article on that.

There are several instruments on the market that require circular music, the tunes for which can be cut out in the same way, only you must have a gauge of such a shape that it forms a section of the circular disc, and the notes have to be cut out in the direction of the circle, which makes it rather harder to manage. These have the advantage, however, that the circle can usually be got pretty easily into a not very large piece of thin cardboard.

The Aurephone was one of many organettes turned out by the Massachusetts Organ Co. of Boston. This advertisement dates from 1883. The Atlas (*left*) was a very well engineered and fine-toned French organette. Another British-made instrument was the Seraphone invented by Maxfield (*see page* 235). Paul Ehrlich's Ariston and other organettes were distributed in England by Gilbert & Co. as shown in the notice below from an 1897 issue of *Musical Opinion*.

THE CELESTINA.

✳ PERFECTION ✦ AT ✦ LAST. ✳

Price

£6 : 6s.

With One

Roll of Music.

| Length, 16 inches. | Width, 14 inches. | Height, 14 inches. | Weight-Boxed, 32 pounds. |

 HE above Illustration represents an ENTIRELY NEW **AUTOMATIC MUSICAL INSTRUMENT,** which far surpasses anything of the kind ever placed before the Public for either

✳ SACRED ∵ OR ∵ SECULAR ∵ MUSIC. ✳

It has three very important advantages, which place it in a position far above other Mechanical Musical Instruments, viz:—

FIRST.—The Music Rolls are **so small and compact** that they can be carried in the pocket without inconvenience.

SECOND.—The price of this Music is **less than one-third that of any other Instrument,** having the same capacity, we have ever put on the market. Dealers and consumers will at once see the advantage of this great saving. One of the most serious objections buyers have made heretofore to our Instruments has been the expensive music.

THIRD.—The **TONE** of the **CELESTINA** enchants every one who hears it. The reeds are situated the same as in a Reed Organ, the valves being opened by a very novel and ingenious device, not liable to get out of order, causing a rich, round, mellow tone—full and powerful—equal, if not superior, to any Reed Organ in the market.

This Instrument can be used either in the Parlor, Church, Hall, or Dancing Academy, and can be played by a child as well as a grown person, without any knowledge of Music.

EVERY INSTRUMENT FULLY WARRANTED.

JOHN G. MURDOCH & CO., Ltd.,

London:

91 & 93, Farringdon Road, E.C.

Melbourne:

23, Lonsdale Street East.

The Celestina had a very similar mechanism to the Seraphone and, in spite of its very high price, it sold well. Whereas Draper, on the facing page, produced a low-price instrument with costly music, the Celestina was an expensive instrument with very cheap but properly-spooled music rolls or endless music bands.

Amorette

ORGANETTE.

The only reliable Organette in the market. Fitted with *Steel Reeds* and *Metal* Rollers. Each Instrument and Reeds guar'n'd. Interchangeable discs
No. 36 with 36 Steel Reeds.
No. 24 with 24 Steel Reeds.
No. 18 with 18 Steel Reeds.
No. 16 with 16 Steel Reeds.
Superior tone. All latest Tunes published and added daily. Lists post free.
Wholesale Agent: **M. JESING,**
76, Newman St., Oxford St.

JEROME THIBOUVILLE-LAMY & Co., 10, CHARTERHOUSE STREET, LONDON, E.C.

THE CŒLOPHONE ORCHESTRE.

37 NOTES.

New Automatic Musical Instrument worked by compressed air and by means of perforated paper.

Patented S. G. D. G. in all countries.

Dance Music.

Valses, Polkas,
Mazurkas,
Galops, Marches,
Quadrilles,
etc.

Various Selections from
Operas,
Comic Operas,
Operettas,
Songs,
Religious Airs,
Psalms, Masses,
etc., etc.

Length 26ins.; height 17ins.; width 14ins.

The **Cœlophone**, invented by the celebrated Claude Gavioli, improved and made at our Grenelle factory, is an instrument of a special nature on an entirely new system. It produces an original sound, which, by its remarkable harmonious effects, raises it far above other organs with handles.

Nothing is more charming than this new instrument which unites so many qualities. Its shape and the case are very elegant in appearance. The sound produced is powerful enough for 60 to 80 persons to dance to.

By the disposal of the scale and the original nature of the tone, it produces the same effect as an orchestra. The tone of the high notes combining with that of the saxophones and basses, give to the pieces executed a variety of vibrations and shades and an orchestration hitherto unknown in instruments of this class.

By a new system of expression, for which we have recently taken out a patent, the tone can be quickly changed from Forte to Pianissimo.

Numbers.							£	s.	d.
968	Cœlophone Orchestre, black wood, varnished, gilt incised panel	...	...	...	...	each	15	0	0
	Music for Cœlophone orchestre	...	...	...	...	per yard	0	1	8
	Endless music for ,,	,,	...	...	...	per piece	0	5	0

The Cœlophone (*left*) was invented by Claude Gavioli and, with its brazen carrying handles, was quite large for an organette. The Amorette (*above*) was a good, low-cost instrument with zinc discs. It came in a number of sizes and gave a powerful sound. By June 1901 Draper was offering to give organettes away (*below*). The snag was that you had to buy a certain quantity of music in order to qualify—and the music, as we have already seen, was not cheap.

PARLOUR ORGANETTES AND SELF-PLAYING ORGANS

NEW INVENTIONS & DESIGNS.

The Orpheus Self-playing Organ.

THE first delivery of "The Orpheus" arrived at Messrs. Story & Clark's a month ago; and ere the first one was unpacked, Mr. Charles Wagener was "booted and spurred," and soon on the war path with a sample instrument. Fourteen were disposed of in a week after their arrival, all of Story & Clark's agents having the "first refusal." One energetic dealer took forcible possession of the sample, and Messrs. Methven, Simpson secured the Dundee territory. Ere these lines see the light, seven additional instruments will have arrived; but

they are all sold. About the first day of this month, Mr. Wagener will take another sample round the Midlands. "The Orpheus" is a handsome American organ played by means of perforated slips, and pedalled in the usual manner. At present there are a hundred tunes available, but shortly there will be on sale twelve times that number. It was a pleasure the other day for us to hear the overture to "Semiramide" rolled off. But a musician may discard the perforated rolls if he likes, and play by the manual. The organ has three and a half full sets; and all reeds sound, whichever way they be utilized. The retail prices are from £75 upwards. Mr. Clark (the patentee) worked upon the invention for six years.

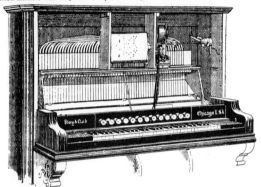

Self-playing organs were first produced by Wilcox & White in Connecticut in 1888 and soon, as with the later piano player, everyone else in the business was making them. Story & Clark's Orpheus (*left*) reached London in 1898. Soon the demand was so great that instruments were shipped over in part form and assembled in London. However, so superior was the tonal appointment of the American organ that a customer resentment was built up against British-made reed organs. And when it became known that Story & Clark were assembling organs here, the rumour got around that the Orpheus was an inferior British copy! The manufacturers had to assure their customers that it was indeed American-made and not British. Soon, though, the profitability of a London assembly line became marginal and the factory was closed, all subsequent instruments being shipped over complete. The few British-designed and built American organs such as the Maxfield (*below*) did not prove popular.

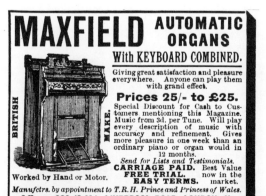

George Whight imported the Victolian in the late 1890s followed by the Aeoline and then the Aeolian. Other American-made instruments were the Kimball, distributed by Robert Marples, and the Phoneon, made by Malcolm & Company. But it was the Aeolian which was to gain the greatest popularity in England as well as elsewhere in the world. George Whight found himself involved in a history-making copyright case concerning royalties and the music roll. Whight's business prospered and in September 1899 became the Orchestrelle Company of London. As the Aeolian Grand and Orchestrelle models attained popularity, so finally the business became the Aeolian Company of London, with Bond Street showrooms. On the facing page are two contemporary advertisements followed by a composite catalogue of Aeolian organs. So many case styles and variants were made, though, that this cannot be taken as a complete listing.

The Aeolian Orchestrelle

HITHERTO lack of opportunity to command repetition has been the greatest obstacle on the road to musical appreciation or understanding. In all other arts there is the element of permanency. That quality is inherent in a book, for example. You can stand in front of a painting or a statue as long as you wish, but a musical work of art is no sooner sounded than it disappears. To recall it in its entirety or to study a detail that is obscure—that has been the problem heretofore. And it is precisely this essential that the Aeolian Orchestrelle supplies.

The main object of the Aeolian Orchestrelle is to allow anyone to reproduce Orchestral Music. But *all* music, whether written for the orchestra or for a single-toned instrument, can be played on the Aeolian Orchestrelle. At the same time its greatest musical value lies in its orchestral capabilities, and these have won for it the well-deserved name of the "Home Orchestra." There is no gainsaying the fact that orchestral music is the finest and noblest of all music. When writing for the orchestra the composer can give the fullest play to his inspirations—he is not confined to the limits of a single-toned instrument. It is such music that one hears only on the rarest occasions, and in all probability one never hears many great works at all. Many people are forced to go through life with never an opportunity of listening

to the greatest masterpieces, for even when an orchestra is available they cannot select their own programme, and when a fine symphony or oratorio is heard the effect is fleeting—it has passed before the listener has had time to study or understand it. In short, he cannot command repetition.

The Aeolian Orchestrelle not only allows everyone to have whatever music they wish, and as often as they wish, but it allows them to play it themselves with full orchestral effects. The erstwhile occasional listener becomes the actual performer, playing even the most difficult and complicated of orchestral scores in a way that can only be equalled by a complete orchestra of skilled musicians. He becomes more than the conductor of an orchestra, for unlike the conductor he can vary his tones at will. He can call on brass or flute, wood-wind or strings. He has direct personal control over the music he is producing. He can vary the volume of tone just as readily as he varies the tones themselves. He has the utmost possible control over the music he is producing. The part of the Aeolian Orchestrelle is to sound the correct notes for him. To play the Aeolian Orchestrelle requires no practical knowledge of music. All that is necessary is the desire to play. The music of Beethoven, Brahms, Haydn, Mozart, Wagner, Strauss, etc., etc., becomes immediately familiar to all owners of this wonderful instrument, who, through being able to produce the works of the masters for themselves, gain an insight into and appreciation of masterpieces which they could never acquire by any other means.

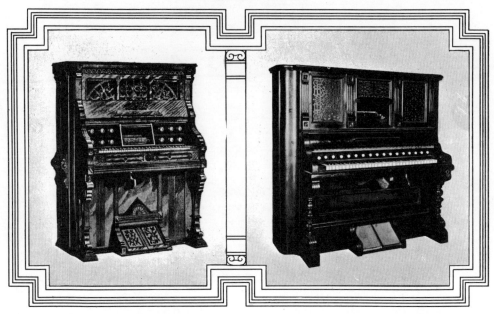

AEOLIAN ORGAN, STYLE 1050

A roll-playing instrument as applied to the ornate parlor organs of the period, which imparted a touch of elegance to the homes of that time.

AEOLIAN ORGAN, STYLE 1500

This instrument marked a definite forward step in the development of Aeolian instruments. Playing a 46-note roll, it was handsomely finished in beautiful case woods and polished like a piano.

AEOLIAN GRAND

This was the first Aeolian instrument to play the expanded 58-note roll. In artistic appearance it compared favorably with present-day standards.

AEOLIAN ORCHESTRELLE

The highest musical development of the reed organ. Its rich tone gives the Orchestrelle virtually the effect of a small pipe-organ.

The Aeolian Orchestrelle

STOPS

TREBLE

Muted Strings
Violin
Orchestral Flute
Piccolo
Clarionet
Trumpet

BASS

Muted Strings
Viola
Orchestral Flute
Flute
Bass Clarionet
Trombone

PEDAL STOPS

Contra Bass. Double Bass

ACCESSORIES

Tempo. Re-roll. Tremulant. Pneumatic to Manual.

DIMENSIONS

Height 4 ft. 11 in.   Width 5 ft. 6 in.   Depth 2 ft. 6 in.

PRICE £110

Model A

Model A

The Aeolian Orchestrelle

STOPS

BASS
Muted Strings
Aeolian Harp
Viola
French Horn
Orchestral Flute
Flute
Oboe
Trombone

TREBLE
Muted Strings
Aeolian Harp
Violin
French Horn
Orchestral Flute
Piccolo
Oboe
Trumpet

PEDAL STOPS
Contra Bass. Double Bass

ACCESSORIES
Tempo Indicator. Re-roll and Tremulant.

DIMENSIONS
Height 5 ft. 9 in.   Width 6 ft. 7½ in.   Depth 2 ft. 6 in.

PRICE £400

In Mahogany, Walnut, or Oak Case

Model Francis the 1st

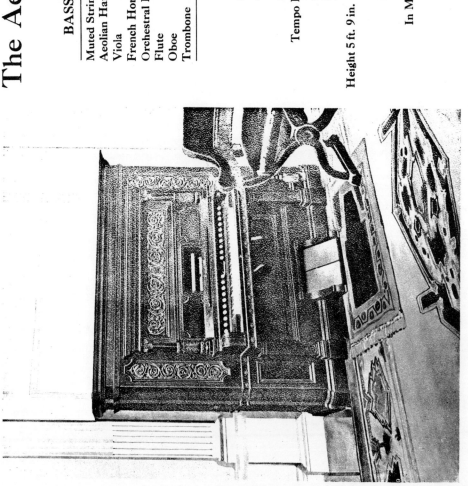

Model Francis the 1st

The Aeolian Orchestrelle

STOPS

BASS

Muted Strings
Viola
Flute
Melodia
Trombone
Tremulant

TREBLE

Muted Strings
Aeolian Harp
Violin
Piccolo
Melodia
Trumpet

PEDAL STOP

Contra Bass

ACCESSORY

Re-roll and Manual

DIMENSIONS

Height 5 ft. 4½ in.　Width 6 ft. ½ in.　Depth 2 ft. 6 in.

PRICE £175

Model S

Model S

243

THE SOLO ORCHESTRELLE

STYLE F

NAMES OF STOPS

SWELL ORGAN	GREAT ORGAN
Oboe, 8 ft.	Open Diapason, 8 ft.
Clarionet, 8 ft.	Melodia, 8 ft.
French Horn, 8 ft.	Dulciana, 8 ft.
Salicional, 8 ft.	Flute d'Amour, 4 ft.
Stop d Diapason, 8 ft.	Trumpet, 8 ft.

PEDAL	AEOLIAN ACCESSORIES
Bourdon, 16 ft.	Tempo Re-roll

ACCESSORIES	COMBINATION PEDALS
Swell to Great	Swell Piano
,, ,, ,, Octaves	,, Forte
Swell to Pedal	Great Piano
Great to Pedal	,, Forte
Tremulant	Great to Pedal
Balanced Crescendo Pedal	Full Organ
,, Swell ,,	

Price - £1,000

The AEOLIAN ORCHESTRELLE

STOPS

BASS

Muted Strings
Aeolian Harp
Viola
French Horn
Flute
Oboe
Trombone

TREBLE

Muted Strings
Aeolian Harp
Violin
French Horn
Piccolo
Oboe
Trumpet

PEDAL STOPS

Contra Bass. Double Bass.

ACCESSORIES

Tempo. Re-roll. Vox Humana. Pneumatic to Manual

DIMENSIONS

Height 5 ft. 5½ in. Width 6 ft. 3 in. Depth 2 ft. 5½ in.

PRICE £350

In Walnut, Mahogany, or Oak Case

MODEL V

MODEL V

The Aeolian Orchestrelle

STOPS

BASS

Muted Strings
Aeolian Harp
Viola
French Horn
Orchestral Flute
Flute
Oboe
Trombone

TREBLE

Muted Strings
Aeolian Harp
Violin
French Horn
Orchestral Flute
Piccolo
Oboe
Trumpet

PEDAL STOPS

Contra Bass. Double Bass

ACCESSORIES

Tempo. Re-roll. Vox Humana. Pneumatic to Manual

DIMENSIONS

Height 5 ft. 9 in.   Length 6 ft. 5¼ in.   Depth 2 ft. 5½ in.

PRICE £400

In Walnut, Mahogany, or Oak Case

Model W

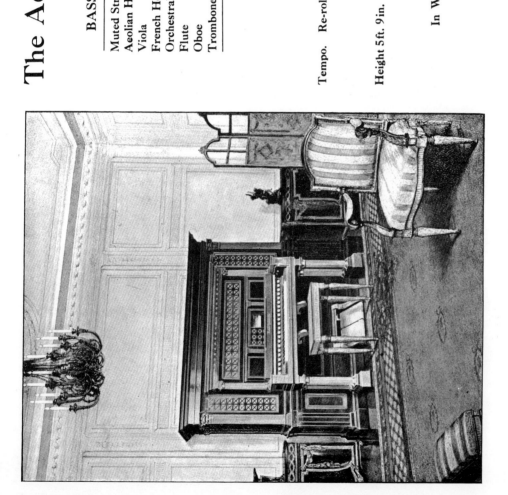

Model W

The Aeolian Orchestrelle

STOPS

BASS

Salicional
Dolce
Muted Strings
French Horn
Flute d'Amour
Melodia
Piccolo
Stopped Diapason
Clarionet
Bassoon
Cornopean

TREBLE

Salicional
Dulcissimo
Muted Strings
Gemshorn
Flute d'Amour
Clarabella
Piccolo
Doppel Flute
Clarionet
Oboe
Trumpet

PEDAL STOPS

Contra Bass. Double Bass

ACCESSORIES

Tempo. Re-roll. Vox Humana. Pneumatic to Manual

DIMENSIONS

Height 8 ft. 4 in.   Width 6 ft. 4 in.   Depth 3 ft. 3 in.

PRICE £600 NETT

In Walnut, Mahogany, or Oak Case

Model Y

Model Y

THE ORCHESTRELLE

NAMES OF STOPS

MANUAL I.

BASS
Muted Strings
Æolian Harp
Melodia
Bass Clarinet
Flute

TREBLE
Muted Strings
Æolian Harp
Melodia
Clarinet
Piccolo

MANUAL II.

BASS
Dolce Viola
Viola
French Horn
Orchestral Flute
Oboe
Trombone

TREBLE
Dolce Violin
Violin
French Horn
Orchestral Flute
Oboe
Trumpet

PEDAL STOP

Contra Bass
Double Bass

ACCESSORIES

Vox Humana
Re-roll and Manual
Couplers { Grand
Normal
Reverse }
Right Expression Swell
Left Crescendo Swell

DIMENSIONS AND WEIGHT

Length, 8 ft.   Height, 8 ft.   Depth, 3 ft. 6 ins.

Net Weight, 1,370 pounds

Price £1,000 net

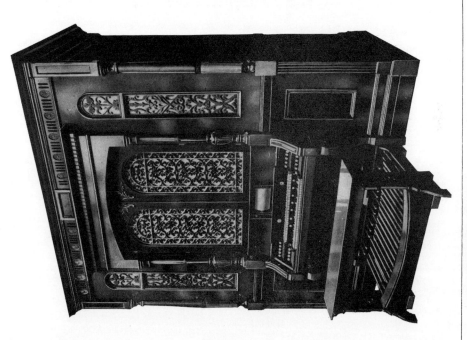

TWO MANUAL AND PEDAL

249

The Aeolian Pipe Organ

A RECENT INSTALLATION

by

The Aeolian Company Ltd.

AEOLIAN HALL
131-137 New Bond Street
LONDON W.1.

Specification

MANUAL 1

Swell Box No. 1

1. Principale Grande.................8′
2. Violin Primo.......................8′
3. Viol Sordino.......................8′
4. Voce Celestes......................8′
5. Flauto Lontano.....................8′
6. Flauto Minore......................4′
7. Corno di Bassetto..................8′
8. Oboe...............................8′
9. Vox Humana.........................8′
10. Tromba............................8′
    Tremolo.

Swell Box No. 2

11. Horn Diapason.....................8′
12. Viola Pomposa.....................8′
13. Viol d'Amore......................8′
14. Flauto Primo......................8′
15. Flauto Traverso...................8′
16. Violetta..........................4′
    Tremolo.

MANUAL 2

Swell Box No. 1

17. Principale Grande.................8′
18. Violin Primo......................8′
19. Viol Sordino......................8′
20. Voce Celestes.....................8′
21. Flauto Lontano....................8′
22. Flauto Minore.....................4′
23. Corno di Bassetto.................8′
24. Oboe..............................8′
25. Vox Humana........................8′
26. Tromba............................8′
    Tremolo.

Swell Box No. 2

27. Horn Diapason.....................8′
28. Viola Pomposa.....................8′
29. Viol d'Amore......................8′
30. Flauto Primo......................8′
31. Flauto Traverso...................8′
32. Violetta..........................4′
    Tremolo.

PEDALE

33. Contra Basso.....................16′
34. Violone..........................16′

Couplers

35. Manual 2 to Manual 1.
36. Manual 2 to Manual 1 8ve.
37. Manual 2 8ve.
38. Manual 2 sub 8ve.
39. Manual 2 Unison Release.
40. Manual 2 to Pedal.
41. Manual 1 8ve.
42. Manual 1 sub 8ve.
43. Manual 1 Unison Release.
44. Manual 1 to Pedal.

Aeolienne Control

Normal.   Unison.   Reverse.

Accessories

4 Combination pistons to Manual 1.
4 Combination pistons to Manual 2.

Pedal Movements

Balanced Swell Pedal to Box No. 1.
Balanced Swell Pedal to Box No. 2.
Balanced Crescendo Pedal (Operating Stops).

Percussion

Harp and Chimes.

DETACHED CONSOLE.
"DISCUS" BLOWER.

The Organ is built in two swell boxes which are immediately behind the screen in the right of the photograph. The console may be seen in the left-hand corner of the picture.

What some of the greatest musicians have said of the Aeolian Orchestrelle

To give to a musical work an absolute and exact interpretation ; to make clear the composer's most intimate thoughts ; to bring into play a wealth of execution which only the orchestra can give ; in a word, to translate all the shades of colouring intended by the composer—this is the achievement of the Aeolian Orchestrelle.

MASSENET.

I am delighted to add my testimony in favour of a very remarkable invention, which astonished and pleased me at the same time. It has so many points in its favour that success is sure to attend it in the future.

Sir A. C. MACKENZIE.

In the production of the Aeolian Orchestrelle you have achieved a grand success. It is a musical instrument which embodies features that will interest everybody, and its use will improve the taste for music, inasmuch as the finest music may be heard, correctly played, at all times and without the aid of accomplished musicians.

I recognise it as one of the greatest inventions of the present century.

LUIGI ARDITI.

I have listened to and examined your remarkable instrument, and was surprised and pleased by it.

The Aeolian Orchestrelle places the best music at the doors of all, and affords a simple means of enjoying and studying the conceptions of the masters of music, ancient and modern.

The Aeolian Orchestrelle is so cleverly constructed that if the performer can grasp the inspiration of the composer the instrument affords him every facility for interpreting the music with feeling.

I take pleasure in wishing you every success.

JEAN DE RESZKE.

I am amazed at what I have just heard. Your Aeolian Orchestrelle, it seems to me, is destined to revolutionize the music world, and it is my sincere belief that it will achieve a universal success.

ED. COLONNE.

I shall be glad to have you add my name to the notable list of musicians and critics who have commended your admirable instrument.

I believe that the Aeolian Orchestrelle is destined to become a most potent factor in the cultivation of the musical taste of the people of the world.

Please accept my hearty wishes for its well-merited success.

EMIL PAUR.

I am of the same opinion as our great French organist, Guilmant. I have been charmed with the Aeolian Orchestrelle. It is a masterpiece which the whole world will admire.

POL PLANCON.

With an Aeolian Orchestrelle all who do not know a note of music, but who are gifted with a refined musical taste, can readily become familiar with what is most elevating in the musical art. The Aeolian Orchestrelle, however, is to music what a vast encyclopedia is to science.

G. PUCCINI.

The WIRSCHING ORGAN CO., Salem, Ohio

Music-Room Organ of Modern Design

ORGAN MUSIC IN THE HOME

Detached Console with Wirsching Self Player

Player pipe organs were made by a number of companies. One American maker to offer such an instrument was Wirsching and this advertisement dates from 1909.

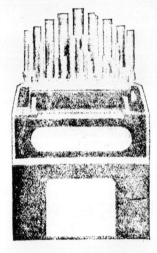
The true steam organ was the Calliope which consisted of a steam boiler, a keyboard and a set of steam whistles of chromatic pitch. Feature of fêtes, parades, the Mississippi sternwheelers and other pleasure boats of the twenties and thirties, musical steam instruments of the kind shown above were essentially an American invention and can be traced to Joshua C. Stoddard from Worcester, Massachusetts. A beekeeper by vocation, he once heard the sound of a locomotive whistle and immediately had visions of a vast musical instrument whose tonal resources were locomotive whistles. His financial backer, Arthur S. Denny, ousted Stoddard, assumed the invention as his own and finally brought the Calliope to England, where it was demonstrated to a singularly unappreciative British public at the Crystal Palace in 1859 (*see page* 300).

CHAPTER 7

Player Pianos and
a Maestro in Every Home

FROM the invention of the organette and the player organ came the understanding of pneumatic action and how air at a pressure different from that of the atmosphere, either marginally above or marginally below it, could be made to perform functions. These functions, as the inventors of the organette proved, could result in the production of musical notes when a suitable system, such as that of the advanced organette and player organ, was devised.

There will always be controversy over who made the first pneumatic action piano player, for it was the piano player which preceded the player piano. Generally it is believed that the first man to make such an instrument was an American, E. S. Votey. Melville Clark, a fellow American, also contributed much and is generally thought to have been the second. Credit for pushing the instrument ahead and making a saleable item out of it and then actually putting it on the market must go to William Barnes Tremaine and his son, Henry B. Tremaine.

Self-playing pianos, it must be said, existed long before the pneumatic action and cardboard-playing pianos of the closing years of the nineteenth century. The early ones, like the street pianos and barrel organs, were played from a pinned barrel. Some were operated by a handle, others by clockwork—Clementi made a clockwork piano which would play for more than half an hour. Debain's planchette-playing Antiphonel piano was seen at the Great Exhibition in 1851.

The detailed history of the instrument, along with full details how to repair and overhaul it, is contained in my book *Player Piano* and will not be repeated here. Sufficient to say that over the years from 1900 to the late thirties, player pianos were very big business throughout not just the United States, but also the United Kingdom and Europe.

The styles of advertisement adopted, as seen from the contemporary ones reproduced on the next few pages, were subtle. In the same way that, in more recent years, cigarette advertising dwelt on the implication that possession of a cigarette was the key to successful relationships with the opposite sex, so player piano advertising often showed the young man serenading his lady-love by music-roll. And the winsome young thing delicately footing her way through some romantic ballad was assured, again by implication, of the requiting of whatever had hitherto apparently been unrequited. It possibly sounds a bit corny today, but only because the mass standards have been lowered and customs and manners impoverished. Croquet on the lawn with the sounds of an electric piano coming through the open French windows probably produces an iconoclastic belly-laugh, yet this did used to happen. I can remember it when I was a small boy—and I'm not that old today!

Mention should be made of Soblick's Patent Piano Player, a device for which Henry Klein of musical boxes fame secured the sole agency from H. Peters & Co., the Leipzig manufacturers. First seen in the summer of 1894, this looked like the lid of an elongated typewriter. Holes in this lid, numbered from one upwards on the left side, and lettered from *a* upwards on the right, were provided for knobs which the 'player' could insert into the case. To play a tune, all one had to do was to follow a primitive 'score' and strike the appropriate knobs. It was not, as one may deduce, a mechanical device in the proper sense of the word. The selling price, though, was all of 50 shillings.

The player piano, in the form of the piano player, first came to London in the early 1890s and within the space of a few years, instruments were in wide demand. Consequently, makers became prolific both in numbers and individual output of instruments. In 1898, the Orchestrelle Company showrooms at the old George Whight premises, 225 Oxford Street, were doing a brisk trade in an instrument called the Pianola. This was an appliance which was pushed up against an ordinary piano and was provided with pneumatically-operated fingers to operate the piano keys. This was the first of many such piano players, commonly termed 'push-ups', and the Pianola became the precursor of a long line of players which traded on the apparently magical suffix 'ola'. The first Pianola played just 65 of the piano's complement of keys and cost £65. Hardman & Goetze of New York appointed Kaps of 92–94 Newman Street, Oxford Street, as agents for the Hardman player in the same year. Prices for this push-up ranged from £29 to £39 and it was one of the earliest to use a brass tracker bar in place of the usual wooden one. The increase in business which the player created necessitated the rapid expansion of many businesses. Thus the years 1888–1905 saw a massive reorganisation of the piano trade in London, a shuffle which was in no way specific to London alone but one which was reflected in every other major town and city.

Chase & Baker, another New York company, started selling their push-ups in London from a warehouse in Covent Garden in 1886. Within eighteen months expanding business forced them to move to newly-erected, larger premises at 45 and 47 Wigmore Street. The first piano fitted with an 'attached player' to be seen in London was the Angelus made by Wilcox & White of Meriden, Connecticut. Stocked at the new Berners Street showrooms of Gerald H. Murphy in 1897, this had the roll-playing attachment fitted under the keyboard with the entire pneumatic action hidden out of sight within the piano case. The bellows protruded only 9 inches out of the back of the piano case and the music roll could be watched as it unrolled in a small housing to the right of and just below the piano keyboard. Edward H. White's first piano player, a box about 15 inches long and fitted under the right side of the keyboard, appeared in 1895. The box had a mirror in the front so the player could read the expression instructions printed on the roll.

Other pianos were available in England at this time. These were the electric ones which were primarily the product of the houses of Kuhl & Klatt, Dienst and Hupfeld in Germany. Initially, the first two used the superior Hupfeld actions. These could be had with their own power supply so that they were independent of the 'electric light current'. The power supply came from a wet-cell rechargable accumulator probably made by the Berlin firm of Pfluger Accumulatoren-Werke, Akt.-Ges. which was one of several companies manufacturing batteries suitable for mechanical musicwork.

Earlier, mention was made of Kenry Klein. This man also had the agency for the Piano Melodico made by Racca in Italy, and produced in two forms—either hand-turned or worked by a spirit lamp and hot-air engine. For the latter, made in Germany, the music was sold by the yard and one operatic selection was forty yards long! The cardboard music could be joined end to end to form a continuous programme and, once filled, primed, lit and warmed up, these ingenious pianos would play for ten hours without attention.

The player piano was commonplace. Everybody knew what one was, many people owned one and certainly within your particular circle of friends there would be at least one instrument. It depended on the social circles in which you mixed whether it was a cheap, pedal-pumped upright or a sumptuous electric reproducing piano bearing a 'gilt-edged' name on the fallboard. The ·depression of the late twenties and thirties killed off the player piano, the war effectively erased the instrument from the memory of most. In the interim, television had been perfected and there were great strides in wireless entertainment which was a medium the war years had done much to foster. Certainly it was the mass entertainer since people did not go out much during the war, least of all in the evenings.

When peace was restored, and with it the great white hope of a new and better world, we may forgive ourselves (or our parents) for casting out all the trappings of what were then believed to be 'the bad old days'. Player pianos were thrown out, discarded, destroyed.

But there was another reason for disposing of not just player pianos but other instruments of mechanical music. Many of these were robust devices made to last indefinitely. However, they needed attention. Nobody likes something which does not work properly or give of its best and the war years had deprived us of many craftsman-repairers. The cost of labour was slowly rising as well. Here, then, was another incentive to discard the old. The piano tuner would decry the player piano because he found it fiddley to work with (probably because he didn't really understand it) and they were time-consuming. He would advocate throwing the player part away and 'converting' the instrument (some actually called it 'modernising') to just manual use. Another remarkable ploy was the story that the presence of a player action in a piano actually had a deleterious effect on the sound given out by the instrument. For the owner who still remained unswayed and pressed for an estimate to restore the player action, the tuner would sometimes be tempted to cover himself against both eventualities and his own dislike at working on them and put in a heavy quotation. Times being difficult (have they ever been otherwise?), this sometimes proved the last straw for the owner who then agreed to 'modernising' or who paid to have the instrument taken away (there was virtually no second-hand market for pianos in those years immediately after the war).

The player piano possessed one quality at least which was rare. It permitted a degree of inter-relationship between itself and its player-owner which was rivalled only by the less popular player organ. The piano, always associated with skill, sensitivity and achievement, could perform at the will of its operator whatever music he chose—and he didn't need to be able to read so much as a note of it! Far, far more people spent far, far longer hours seated at their player pianos throughout the land than any other person spent with any other type of musical instrument. The degree of personal involvement depended entirely on the operator who, by skilful use of the controls provided, might render each performance of the same roll quite different. It has been argued and, I feel, with a strong measure of certitude, that a good player piano operated by a talented player-pianist might produce music as good as, if not better than, that played by a top pianist. The reason and judgement behind this sweeping statement is that the player-pianist, having all the mechanics of 'aiming' and striking his notes done for him, could concentrate all his faculties into the subtle nuances of phrasing, *tempi* and accentuation attainable from his controls. 'Ah!' says the concert pianist. 'Rubbish! I feel the music in the very moment of contact between my finger and the piano key and the sound which that hammer produces when it strikes the string is regulated before I even depress the key.' True, quite true. But give the sensitive player-pianist a roll and let him play it through thirty, forty times or more until he gets to know it (*never* expect to play a roll properly until you have *learned* it thoroughly), and then notice how he, too, can 'feel' his individual notes, not with his fingers, but with his toes on the piano's treadles before the notes actually sound.

One thing remains certain. In its day, the player piano did much to spread interest in music among the ordinary public. That surely must count for a great deal.

The Electric Self-Playing Piano Company of 333 W. 36th Street, New York produced this unusual player piano in 1895. It was described in *Scientific American* for 28 December in that year.

Melography, the recording on to paper of musical sounds as they are played, was a subject which taxed the inventive abilities of many men during the burgeoning days of mechanical music. As long as there has been music and musical intelligence, Man has striven to perpetuate the fleeting melody so that, like the spoken word which is then written down, it may be heard again. For those who could use musical notation and interpret quickly, the task was easier, but still there could be no immediate preservation of an extempore performance. When the invention of pneumatic actions and, later, electro-magnetic actions, allowed instantaneous punching of the holes representing musical sounds into paper, melography became a thing of the past. Today, when we speak of melography, we think automatically of the Frenchman, Carpentier, who made an instrument called the Melograph and a player called the Melotrope. But there were others who contributed to the successful melograph. One was Creed, who later went on to perfect the teletyper. Others were John Frederic Unger and Hohlfeld. The following article deals with another inventor and his work and appeared originally in *Das Neue Universum* published by W. Spemann of Stuttgart in 1883. It is here rendered into English.

THE MELOGRAPH
A Machine for Recording Music on Paper

IT HAS NOW become debatable whether it may be desirable to possess an apparatus which permits the recording of the improvised performance of a pianist, so that an expert can translate the written result into notation just as the telegraphist converts the dots and dashes on the paper roll of his apparatus into ordinary script. For us it is not a question of the suitability or usefulness of such an apparatus but the means by which this aim could be attained – indeed has been attained.

As long ago as 1856, Du Moncel carried out experiments aimed at this but without obtaining a satisfactory result. At a time when electric batteries were still very imperfect, this had to wait. However at the Vienna International Exhibition of 1873, an apparatus designed expressly for the purpose was exhibited by the engineer Roncalli and, although it did not meet all the requirements, it is through it that the first steps in the solution of the problem were taken and it is interesting to follow the means employed.

At the outset it is essential to have paper which is soaked in a mixture of equal parts of a solution of yellow alkaline salt (calcium iron cyanide) and saltpetre ammoniac (ammonium nitrate). If one allows a steel stylus to glide over writing paper which is thus prepared; glazed and slightly moistened, it will produce hardly any variation. If, however, an electric current passes from the stylus through the paper to a metal surface beneath, there is produced a ferric oxide salt which, in the presence of potassium iron cyanide, gives a blue precipitate which appears on the whole line which the pin or stylus traces on the paper. This immediately ceases when the current is interrupted. If, instead of a steel stylus, one of copper or

copper-alloy is used, the line becomes red; cobalt produces a brown line; that from a stylus of bismuth becomes visible only after the paper strip has been placed in clean water when it shows up as a bright yellow line. Nickel and chromium produce green lines and silver an invisible trace which turns brown after exposure to light.

It is clear that by these means a particular notation can be obtained. Roncalli's Melograph (Melody-writer) makes use of these chemical phenomena. In the musical instrument shown in Figure 1, there is situated on the right the writing apparatus which is connected by copper wires to the individual keys. At the left is a clockwork motor by which means the paper strip, upon which the writing will be made, is rolled. Between both components is an ordinary metronome or time-counter.

Now let us consider this ingeniously-constructed note-writer more closely. It is depicted to a larger scale in Figure 2. The metal roller A is connected with the negative terminal of an electric battery. B is a comb-like metal strip comprising as many closely-spaced teeth as the piano has keys (which are tape recorded). The teeth representing the semi-tones are of a different metal from those which are connected with the keys for the whole notes. The insulated wires E lead to the block D from which they are connected through wires G with the individual keys. By means of the lever N, the comb can be pressed in contact with the cylinder A or drawn clear of it. Between comb and roller A is the prepared paper strip which is wound on the barrel M and finally passes between the two rollers F and C. The former is set in motion by the clockwork (Figure 1) via a small driving belt.

To nine forks on roller L there correspond nine toothed rings which are pressed against F by a spring.

Below the keys of the piano, harmonium or whatever instrument the Melograph is connected with, there lies a brass strip which is connected to the positive terminal of the battery. If a key is depressed, a spring establishes contact with the corresponding wire G of the key. The circuit is closed and the current passes through the paper whereupon the corresponding tooth of the comb lies. Immediately, the chemical reaction takes place and produces a coloured line on the moving paper so long as the key is depressed.

As, however, the paper continuously unrolls, a line must be traced on another part of it when the same or another key is subsequently depressed. Precisely as this is with one key, so it is with all the keys (which are so connected): as soon as they are depressed, they must react on the paper and produce a sign there. It is, how-ever, understandable that the writing apparatus makes no difference between c♯ and d♭, and that is subsequently the business of the transcriber to write in the correct notes.

In the case of more complete instruments with five and more octaves, the writing apparatus with its many teeth would be very broad and prove deficient. The paper strip would also have to be of considerable width. Roncalli has therefore hit upon a device in his Melograph so that the outermost octaves are connected with the preceding ones. Thus the first writes in the path of the second, the fifth in the path of the fourth. So that they may be distinguished from one another, the writing teeth are of different metal and consequently the lines are coloured differently.

The speed remains a very strange defect in the whole of this simple and ingenious device. The metronome marks the time in a set way and the performer must accommodate himself to it. If, however, he exceeds this speed, it is not discernible in the longer and shorter lines on the written paper. One can, with the help of the pedals which can be connected electrically with a special tooth of the comb, produce a particular sign on the paper. This is to say that whilst there may be a difference in the speed, which performer, when improvising, pays regard to such detail?

Chemical telegraphy with a writing stylus on prepared paper, despite the long time it has been known, has not been widely adopted. The principal reason may perhaps be that the metal baseplate, like the stylus, tarnishes in use and, for this reason, makes a difficult and meticulous cleaning frequently necessary. This inherent defect must stand in the way of Roncalli's Melograph, but the development of the principle is already of special interest while only such short accounts of it are found in textbooks specially devoted to telegraphy that they are insufficient to enable an exact understanding of the apparatus.

The Pneuma piano player (*below*) was made in Berlin by Kuhl & Klatt and sold in London in 1899 through the warerooms of William Gerecke.

Appliances for the automatic playing of pianos were initially contrived as separate instruments. Some played cardboard discs and others cardboard rolls such as are seen in the top advertisement of 1903 vintage. These were mechanically operated devices. J. M. Grob was founded in 1872 and was acquired by Ludwig Hupfeld in 1892. The American-made Pianola and Cecilian, on the other hand, were pneumatic in operation. These piano players were known colloquially as 'push-ups' because they were pushed up in front of the piano's keyboard.

Frankfurter Musikwerke-Fabrik J. D. Philipps & Söhne
Frankfurt a. M.
Gegründet 1877.

Spezialfabrik pneumatischer Orchestrions
in höchster Vollendung mit selbsttätigem Notenwechsel
für elektrischen Antrieb und mit Gewichtsaufzug.

Letzte Neuheit!

Kunstspiel-Klaviere
„Cäcilia" und
„Corona"

in verschiedenen Ausführungen

mit effektvollem modulations-reichem Spiel und prachtvollen Nüancierungen.

Künstlerisch arrangierte Noten.

Elektrische Pianos

mit Geigen, Mandoline, Xylophon und Schlagzeug

Musterlager in der Fabrik

Patente
in fast allen Kulturstaaten

Prämiiert mit vielen goldenen Medaillen und Ehrenpreisen

Export nach allen Weltteilen

Besondere Bauart für alle Klimate.

Metzler Piano Player

DAILY RECITALS at 42, GREAT MARLBOROUGH STREET, LONDON, W.

A1 Model:

with Patent Transposing Device.

Loud and Soft Pedals.

ONLY

£35 net.

Library Subscription: Four Guineas per Annum. 24 Rolls per Month.

COME AND SEE IT AT ONCE.

A2 Model:

with Patent Transposing Device,

£28 net.

Loud Pedal only.

A3 Model:

without Transposer.

£25 net.

Library Subscription: Four Guineas per Annum. 24 Rolls per Month.

METZLER & CO., Great Marlborough St., London, W.

These two advertisements make an interesting comparison. Both are *c.* 1903. The pneumatically played piano, albeit a piano-orchestrion, was already well developed and with it the technique of putting player actions inside pianos. However, both England and America were still producing push-ups in their thousands—the Pianola was still being advertised in 1912 (*see page 277*). One explanation was that nearly every home already had a piano and sales of a replacement instrument fitted with player action would never be as profitable as sales of an appliance to play a standard existing piano.

Electric pianos and piano-
orchestrions were well established early in the 1900s.
Giovanni Racca's Piano
Melodico made in Italy was
available in two variants. The
hand-turned miniature grand
piano came in sizes from four
to six octaves. The upright
Verdi was operated by a hot-
air engine and could play for
ten hours non-stop. *Facing
page*: the Cecilian as advertised in May 1807, and the
Angelus in November 1903.

IT COSTS YOU NOTHING

to investigate the merits of these marvellous instruments. They are absolutely pre-eminent among Players. Just think of it! You are able to at ONCE render the finest music WITHOUT practice or musical knowledge. Surely it is because you have not realised the immense enjoyment to be obtained from so modest an expenditure that has prevented you from being a possessor of one.

CECILIAN PIANO PLAYERS from 40 guineas.
CECILIAN PLAYER PIANOS from 90 guineas.

EASY PAYMENTS MAY BE ARRANGED. If unable to call, write TO-DAY for free descriptive booklet.

THE FARRAND COMPANY, 44, Great Marlborough Street, London, W.

THE REASONS WHY THE WORLD-FAMED

"Angelus"
PIANO-PLAYER

HAS BEEN PURCHASED BY

ROYALTY

AND THE WORLD'S GREATEST

MUSICIANS

IT IS THE MOST PERFECT, ARTISTIC, AND HUMAN-LIKE IN TECHNIQUE, CONTROL OF TEMPO, AND EXPRESSION

THE "ANGELUS" IMMEDIATELY ENABLES EVERYONE TO PLAY

all the classical and popular music of the world like an accomplished pianist with all the gratifying sense of power and interest which the player loves.

TESTIMONIAL from
Mdme. CLARA BUTT.

"*I think the 'ANGELUS' splendid! Apart from the pleasure it gives one, I am sure it is instructive in every sense of the word. I have heard all the other inventions of this kind, but the 'ANGELUS' is far and away the best.*"

THE "ANGELUS" IS THE ONLY PIANO-PLAYER WITH ORCHESTRAL ORGAN COMBINATION, or may be obtained as a PIANO-PLAYER ONLY. Discount for Cash. **ON EASY TERMS.**

ALL LOVERS OF TRULY ARTISTIC MUSIC should write for Catalogue No. 39, giving full particulars, which is sent free.

J. HERBERT MARSHALL,
Dept. 39, REGENT HOUSE,
233, REGENT STREET, LONDON, W.

The Melville Clark Apollo came out in 1899 as a 58-note player. An unusual feature was a clockwork motor, wound by the foot treadles, which drove the music roll independently of the foot action, and stored enough power for rewinding the roll at the end. The above notice comes from *Chambers Journal*, May 1901, and that below from *The Connoisseur* for December 1905. Elias Parkman Needham invented the upright action used in reed organs which formed the basis of the organette and player organ. His patents were sold to the Mechanical Orguinette Company, the nucleus of the later Aeolian Company of New York. The Paragon piano player was invented by Needham but did not sell well in England. The advertisement, right, appeared in *The London Magazine* for November 1903.

266

Daimonion (Δαιμόνιον).

Das neueste und epochemachende Erzeugniß auf dem Gebiete der mechanischen Musikwerke ist unstreitig das

Daimonion
(Δαιμόνιον).

Dasselbe stellt Alles, was bisher auf dem Gebiete der Drehpianos geleistet wurde, vollständig in den Schatten. Die Ausstattung des Instrumentes ist eine hochelegante, die Mechanik so sauber und solid gearbeitet, wie bei dem theuersten Salonflügel. Das Instrument hat

vollständigen Eisenrahmen und widersteht jedem Witterungswechsel.

Reparaturen sind fast gänzlich ausgeschlossen.

Die Tonfülle ist geradezu großartig und befriedigt auch den verwöhntesten Musikliebhaber. Es ersetzt vollkommen ein Klavier mit Streichinstrumenten-Begleitung. Zum Spielen werden die uns patentirten kreisförmigen Notenscheiben benutzt. Das Repertoir ist außerordentlich reichhaltig und wird täglich vermehrt. Bestellungen bitten wir möglichst frühzeitig zu machen, damit die Lieferung rechtzeitig geschehen kann.

Orchestrionettes,
mit endlosen, bandförmigen Noten zu spielen.

Non plus ultra,
mit und ohne Deckel, in verbesserter Construction.

Außerdem empfehlen wir:

Klavier-Automaten
in vorzüglich sauberer Arbeit.

Aristonettes,
19tönig.

Preis-Verzeichnisse u. Noten-Cataloge stehen zu Diensten.

Fabrik Leipziger Musikwerke
vorm. Paul Ehrlich & Co. zu Gohlis bei Leipzig.

Keyboardless mechanical pianos were very popular in the United States but few appear to have been made in Europe. When Emil Welte manufactured his keyless 'red Welte' reproducing piano, it did not sell well because it could not be played upon manually if required. Paul Ehrlich's Daimonion, seen here in a 1903 advertisement, was obviously aimed at public places, restaurants and hotels. No actual instruments are known. The lower part of the advertisement illustrates a large, cardboard band-playing 'orchestrionette' (large organette) and a disc-type mechanical piano player similar to that shown on page 262. Overleaf is shown the Kastner Autopiano player piano invented by Maximilian Macarius Kastner (born 1876; died 1924). The advertisement is from *The London Magazine*, January 1907.

BOYD

Boyd Pianos

are well and favourably known to the music-loving public, and to-day the name of BOYD on a Piano is accepted as standing for all-round excellence.

BOYD PIANOS are produced under expert supervision by craftsmen of great skill and experience at the new Boyd Works at Harringay, the most up-to-date Pianoforte factory in the Kingdom.

BOYD L.T.D.

Wholesale Department:

32 Worship St., London, E.C.

BOYD PIANOS in conjunction with the

Pistonola

the new All-Metal interior player, form an ideal combination.

BOYD PIANOS, although on an artistic level with the most costly instruments made, are moderate in price and within the reach of all.

"THE BOOK OF THE BOYD PIANOFORTE," Edition de Luxe, 1914, contains a full description of each Boyd Model, and all interested in the progress of British pianoforte construction are cordially invited to write for a copy

PIANOS

Boyd's Pistonola was a most unusual instrument. The player action was based entirely on cylinder and piston action which was intended to provide a very prompt response and require the shifting of considerably less air than a normal action. The all-metal player with compacted graphite pistons was difficult to repair and regulate in service. The Artempo music roll for pianos came in the usual cardboard box but the interesting point was the label stuck to the box top (*shown right*) which was an artist's impression of a roll-perforating machine.

HAND PLAYED ROLL

269

Hupfeld (*right*) made a fine range of pianos, player pianos and reproducing pianos under the Phonola title as well as the Phonoliszt-Violina piano with violins, and a range of orchestrions. Welte, early makers of orchestrions, also built the Welte-Mignon reproducing piano of which Professor Arthur Nickisch wrote, 'In my opinion the Welte Mignon reproducing apparatus is an epoch-making invention. The artist's performance recorded in the apparatus is right in every respect, not only concerning the pure technical virtuosity but also the musical poetical element. It is so frankly natural that one really thinks the artist is there in person and that one hears him play. The value of this invention is not only in the teaching influence on one learning, but also in a quite marvellous way for those who wish to sit down comfortably to an hour of artistical enjoyment and only wish to listen to an accomplished artist.'

THE PIANOLA

You have heard the name, but—
Have you heard the instrument?

THE PIANOLA IN USE WITH UPRIGHT PIANO. PRICE £65.

THE PIANOLA is a piano-player, or rather it does that part of the playing which the fingers do in ordinary hand-playing—it strikes the notes, while the musical taste of the player (in either case) is responsible for the expression. Both "touch" and "tempo" are regulated by him, thereby portraying his musical personality in the result.

It is this human effect which has astounded the musical world, and which is not fully understood, except by those that have heard it.

As shown in the block, the Pianola looks like a small cabinet. When you wish to play the piano by hand, the Pianola may be rolled to another part of the room. When you desire to play a selection outside of your repertory, you roll it into position again, so that its felt-covered fingers rest upon the keys of the piano, and insert the roll of music to be played.

By the use of the expression-levers you render the selection according to your own interpretation of the composer's meaning, or to suit your particular mood.

The operation of the Pianola is simple, requires no musical knowledge on the part of the player, and yet there are no limitations to the artistic effects obtainable.

Price £65. Can be purchased on the hire system if desired.

Visitors always welcome. Our instruments are gladly shown to the merely curious as well as to intending purchasers. If unable to call at our warerooms, write for Catalogue 32, giving full description.

The Orchestrelle Co., 225 Regent St., London, w.

(THE PIANOLA IS SOLD AT NO OTHER ADDRESS IN LONDON.)
And HENRY M. BIRGE, Sydney, Australia.

Liverpool, J. Smith & Son, Ltd.   Birmingham, Stockley & Sabin.   Manchester, Hime & Addison.
Bristol, Milsom & Son.   Glasgow, Marr, Wood & Co.   Dublin, Cramer, Wood & Co.

Most famous among the names of player pianos and piano players was that of the Pianola made by Aeolian. Indeed, although a registered trade name, it became to many people a generic term for the instrument. This early push-up played only sixty-five of the normal piano's eighty-eight full-compass notes. On the next page is a series of notices about the Metrostyle Pianola push-up from *The Strand Magazine*, and, facing that, two 1905 notices from *The Connoisseur*.

·The· METROSTYLE· ·PIANOLA·

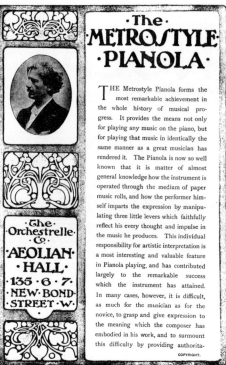

The Orchestrelle Co. AEOLIAN· HALL· 135·6·7· NEW·BOND· STREET·W·

THE Metrostyle Pianola forms the most remarkable achievement in the whole history of musical progress. It provides the means not only for playing any music on the piano, but for playing that music in identically the same manner as a great musician has rendered it. The Pianola is now so well known that it is matter of almost general knowledge how the instrument is operated through the medium of paper music rolls, and how the performer himself imparts the expression by manipulating three little levers which faithfully reflect his every thought and impulse in the music he produces. This individual responsibility for artistic interpretation is a most interesting and valuable feature in Pianola playing, and has contributed largely to the remarkable success which the instrument has attained. In many cases, however, it is difficult, as much for the musician as for the novice, to grasp and give expression to the meaning which the composer has embodied in his work, and to surmount this difficulty by providing authorita-

---

The ~ ~ METROSTYLE· ·PIANOLA·Cont'd

Music Roll for the Metrostyle Pianola showing Interpretation specially marked by I. J. PADEREWSKI

tive interpretations is the mission of the Metrostyle Pianola.

The Metrostyle Pianola does two things. It enables an artiste to record on the music roll by means of a pen affixed to the tempo lever (one of the expression devices) a red line which shows how he considers any given selection should be rendered. Secondly, the substitution of a metal index or pointer in place of the pen permits any other person to guide his playing by following such marking, and thereby reproduce the virtuoso's performance in its entirety.

Music rolls for the Metrostyle Pianola have been marked by PADEREWSKI, by HOFMANN, by BAUER, by MOSZKOWSKI, by CHAMINADE, to mention only a few well-known names. In every case the highest authority has been chosen, and where possible the composer himself has been selected, thereby ensuring interpretations which are artistic, musical, interesting, and absolutely beyond question. As a further guarantee, a facsimile of the artiste's holographic authorisation is

---

The ~ ~ METROSTYLE· ·PIANOLA·Cont'd

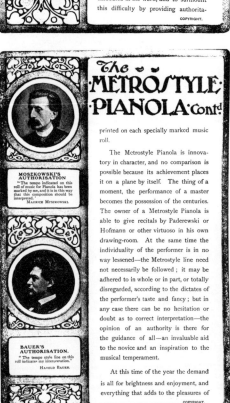

printed on each specially marked music roll.

The Metrostyle Pianola is innovatory in character, and no comparison is possible because its achievement places it on a plane by itself. The thing of a moment, the performance of a master becomes the possession of the centuries. The owner of a Metrostyle Pianola is able to give recitals by Paderewski or Hofmann or other virtuoso in his own drawing-room. At the same time the individuality of the performer is in no way lessened—the Metrostyle line need not necessarily be followed; it may be adhered to in whole or in part, or totally disregarded, according to the dictates of the performer's taste and fancy; but in any case there can be no hesitation or doubt as to correct interpretation—the opinion of an authority is there for the guidance of all—an invaluable aid to the novice and an inspiration to the musical temperament.

At this time of the year the demand is all for brightness and enjoyment, and everything that adds to the pleasures of

---

The ~ ~ METROSTYLE· ·PIANOLA·Cont'd

home life is eagerly sought after. The claims of music in this particular direction are acknowledged by everyone, and in music at the present moment the most potent factor is the Metrostyle Pianola.

The Metrostyle Pianola is on view at our Showrooms, and may be seen by anyone who favours us with a call. A descriptive illustrated catalogue will be sent to anyone who writes asking for Catalogue F.

The Orchestrelle Co. AEOLIAN HALL 135·6·7· NEW BOND S! · LONDON · W ·

ACHIEVEMENT!

THOSE who are fond of music but cannot play a note on an ordinary piano, can achieve their desire and indulge their musical inclinations to the full with a Triumph Autopiano.

The latest numbers from Musical Comedies, up-to-date Dance Music, or the Masterpieces of the great composers can be played with perfect expression and time.

To those who are fond of singing, the Triumph Autopiano gives endless pleasure. With the Triumph Song Rolls the words are easily read whilst playing, and the latest transposing device enables one to sing in the Key to suit the voice. The time and expression levers are so simple to operate that anyone can be a perfect accompanist.

Why not exchange your silent piano for a

Triumph Autopiano

which anyone can play?

Visit our Showrooms for a demonstration and inspect the large selection of Upright and Baby Grand Triumph Autopianos always on view, or if unable to call, write for Catalogue " T."

Payments by monthly instalments can be arranged and any ordinary piano taken in part exchange.	*There is a Circulating Library Service of over 20,000 Music and Song Rolls to choose from.*

TRIUMPHAUTO, LTD.,
TRIUMPH HOUSE (*Opposite Galeries Lafayette*)
187-191, REGENT STREET, LONDON, W.1.

By 1929, the Kastner Autopiano had been renamed Triumph with the Kastonome action. Murdoch's Minerva did not reach the market in quantity but the Angelus, seen below in a 1912 advertisement, was popular. On the facing page is an article on the Pianotist which was made in Leipzig and in New York by Klaber.

EVOLUTION OF THE PIANO PLAYER.

THE PIANO OF THE FUTURE.

EXTENSIVE advertising and intrinsic musical merit have rendered us familiar with the fact that years of study and hard work are now not essential to becoming a skilled and accomplished piano player. One has only to pick up any magazine or newspaper to learn that such artists as Paderewski, Rosenthal, Calvé, and De Reske, candidly and frankly admit that these weird instruments, yclept "piano players," clumsy and unsightly though they be, provide the means of producing music from any ordinary piano that few professionals can equal and none excel.

PIANOTIST IN USE WITH UPRIGHT PIANO.

The main objection that can be urged against these "players"—and there are not less than a dozen or so of them—is the fact that the piano to which they are fitted is for the time being placed *hors de combat*, and that an unsightly and clumsy addition is made to the piano, in a room often too crowded as it is. That the player has to be removed every time it is desired to use the piano in the ordinary manner is also a great nuisance. Their inordinately high price (£65) and the fact that operating under air pressure the pumping is laborious, are points that were bound sooner or later to be overcome. Apart from these conditions, these contrivances operate faultlessly, and give their owners a full return for the amount invested.

Hardly are the words uttered in praise and endorsement

of these instruments before a veritable genius arises and condenses the whole operative mechanism into such small space that it can be fitted into *any piano, out of sight*, thus not interfering at any time with the use of the piano in the ordinary manner. Not content with this unquestionable advantage, the inventor of this instrument has provided what he is pleased to call "melody stops," whereby "the otherwise fatal accuracy and equal dynamic force" of all the fingers of a mechanical player may be varied at the will of the performer. The bass notes of a composition may be subdued, and the melody in the treble accentuated, or if desired a melody brought out in the bass, while the treble provides merely a whispered accompaniment. This is a great achievement hitherto unknown in mechanical piano players, and, in the opinion of those best qualified to judge, it places this instrument far ahead of any other instrument of its kind. A simple frictional device has been substituted for pneumatics, with a consequent result that only 2lbs.

PIANOTIST IN USE WITH GRAND PIANO.

pressure is required as against 14lbs necessary to operate the cabinet form of piano players.

In the opinion of some of the greatest artists and musicians who have seen this invention, it is considered artistically superior to anything of its kind, and such artists and musicians as Adelina Patti (Baroness Cäderstrom), Mark Hambourg (the great pianist), Henry J. Wood (conductor Queen's Hall orchestra), Wilhelm Ganz, Tito Mattei, Landon Ronald and many others, have not hesitated to put

such opinions to paper over their own signatures. From the fact that the Pianotist (this is the name of this remarkable instrument) when fitted to a piano in no way interferes with its use, or injures it in any way, it may be reasonably prophesied that the piano of the future will be capable of performing the dual rôle of "an old century piano" and a "new century piano player." Such manufacturers as Erards, Steinways, Pleyels, &c., &c., are eulogistic in praise of the Pianotist, and all those contemplating the purchase of a piano player would do well to call at the showrooms of the Pianotist Co., Ltd., 56, Regent-street (near Piccadilly

MARK HAMBOURG.

Circus), and see and hear this latest invention before finally making their choice.

A strong Company has been formed for the manufacture and sale of the Pianotist, and as indicative of the success of this instrument it may be stated that a number of prominent people have already availed themselves of an offer made by the Pianotist Company to change their old style instrument for the Pianotist, the Company making a fair allowance in exchange therefor.

Whether a purchase be contemplated or not, the time expended in paying a visit to the Pianotist rooms is well repaid, as the lucid and courteous manner in which the Pianotist is shown and explained leaves one with a most pleasurable memory of the visit.

KUHL & KLATT

Fabrik pneumatisch selbstspielender Musikinstrumente.

Wusterhausener Str. 17.   **BERLIN NO.**   Runge-Strasse 18.

Nähe der Jannowitzbrücke.

Musterlager:
Wien,
Wallfischgasse 4.

Pneuma, elektrisches Piano **Pneuma,**

Patentirt
in allen
Kulturstaaten.

Pneumatist

Patentirt
in allen
Kulturstaaten.

Vorsteller, Klavierspiel-Apparat.

Ludwig Hupfeld, Leipzig,

am Berliner Bahnhof   ✳   **Apelstrasse No. 4.**   ✳   am Berliner Bahnhof

Erste und älteste Fabrik
selbstspielender Pianos
und Flügel.

Elektrische Kunstspiel-Pianos

76 Töne und
6 Nuancirungszüge = 82 Clavis.

Mit oder ohne Geldeinwurf.

PHONOLA

Letzte Neuheit!

Pneumatischer Klavierspiel-
apparat mit Papiernoten
umfasst 72 Töne, hat
getheilte Scala und kann
von Jederman ohne jede
Notenkenntniss wahrhaft
künstlerisch bethätigt
werden. Der Apparat ist
zum Treten und an jedes
Klavier mit Leichtigkeit

Letzte Neuheit!

anzustellen.
Grösstes Notenrepertoir.

Phonolamusik ist nach
dem Urtheil erster
Künstler sowohl hinsicht-
lich des Anschlages
wie des Ausdruckes dem
persönlichen Spiel gleich-
zustellen.

Orchester-Musikwerke mit Streichmusik

mit Gewichtsaufzug oder Motor- bezw. elektrischem Betrieb
in allen Grossen und Preislagen.

Filialen unter eigener Firma:

Berlin W.,   ✳   **Wien VI,**
Leipziger Strasse 106.   Mariahilferstrasse 9.

◆◆◆◆◆◆◆◆◆◆◆◆◆◆

Jul. Berthold & Co.

Maschinenfabrik

Klingenthal in Sachsen.

Maschinen für
Holz- u. Metallbearbeitung
für die gesamte Musikindustrie.

Langjährige Spezialität:

Notenperforier-Maschinen.

◆◆◆◆◆◆◆◆◆◆◆◆◆◆

Electric pianos were made by Hupfeld and Kuhl & Klatt who also included a xylophone register. These were all quality machines built with typical German precision. The vast pneumatic player industry encouraged machine-makers Julius Berthold & Co. to produce roll-perforators as well as musical box disc-punchers (*see page* 147).

An artistic triumph for the Pianola

Played at Queen's Hall with the London Symphony Orchestra, conducted by Herr Arthur Nikisch,

the Pianola recently vindicated once and for all the unique position which it holds in the artistic world. On this occasion the Pianola was used to play the well-known Greig Concerto in A Minor and the Liszt Hungarian Fantasie. The Pianola was also used to accompany the celebrated vocalist, Miss Elena Gerhardt, in songs by Strauss and Wolf. Immense enthusiasm was aroused amongst the public and press by this concert, but none greater than that of Herr Arthur Nikisch himself, who wrote after the performance: " Save for the fact that the instrument supplies the performer with absolutely perfect technique, the Pianola should never again be referred to as a mechanical instrument."

Call at Æolian Hall and play the Pianola Piano, or write for Catalogue "AA."

THE ORCHESTRELLE Co. Ltd.
—— ÆOLIAN HALL ——
135-6-7, New Bond Street, London, W.

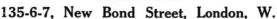

Typical advertising of the period—*The Connoisseur* for April 1912 carried this announcement about the Pianola push-up. The piano player was by this time well on the way out having been ousted by the player piano. Within a few short years, though, the end of the player era loomed in sight. On the next page we find the Aeolian Company leaving its fine Aeolian Hall in Bond Street. This half-page advertisement appeared in *The Daily Express* for 15 May 1930. The boom was over.

277

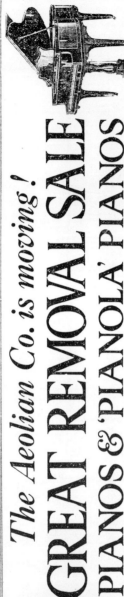

278

CHAPTER 8

The Gramophone

I‍T IS generally accepted that the end of the era of the musical box was heralded by the arrival on the market of the gramophone or phonograph as it was originally called. While there is little doubt that it did precipitate the end of the age by bringing into the home that sound which captivated Man's imagination—his own voice—the assumption that had the gramophone not been invented, the mechanical musical instrument would have survived indefinitely is not justified.

Times were changing and the rush to manufacture and sell 'talking machines' throughout the world did, it is true, make the musical box a thing of the past. However, standards were changing, people were changing and the catalyst of war was at hand. At the end of the Great War, the ability to make noise in a multitude of ways was upon us and the voice of the musical box was swamped by that of the player piano, the dance organ and the nickelodeon. In its own right, the gramophone and, later, wireless, were part and parcel of the twentieth century.

But the gramophone was clockwork music after a fashion, although its main claim to success was the fact that it was a clockwork *voice*. It very nearly did not amount to anything more than a toy, for it was thus that Edison first saw his invention.

There exists some confusion as to whom it was that first made a device for reproducing sound. One Professor Luca de Samuele Cagnazzi who taught at the University of Naples during the early years of the last century is said to have exhibited an ingenious apparatus for the reproduction of sound before a science congress held in Florence in 1844. Be that as it may, Sir David Brewster, F.R.S. (born 1781; died 1861) wrote in his *Letters on Natural Magic* that in his opinion a singing and talking machine would be numbered among the conquests of science before the end of that century. He was discussing the apparatus contrived by Baron Wolfgang Kempelen, the Hungarian mechanician (born 1734; died 1804) and the more recent researches of Felix Savart, the French student of the theory of sound (who was born in 1791 and died in 1841), upon the mechanism of the human voice.

As Henry Seymour points out in his work *The Reproduction of Sound*, it was not difficult for a man of scientific insight to hazard so certain a prediction, because the large array of scientific knowledge already at hand only needed some sort of ordered classification and synthetic deduction to render such a proposition more than mere hypothetical conjecture.

We have already looked into the question of talking statues and the more than likely explanation that these were cleverly-engineered hoaxes. There is, however, an interesting account of a 'pre-history' device related by the Irish government official, Sir Robert Hart (born 1835; died 1911) who spent many years in China. He stated that Chinese books cover almost every conceivable subject and that nearly half a century before the first phonograph reached Pekin, the

279

Governor, Kwang Tung, personally told him that an ancient book dating back two thousand years before related how, one thousand years earlier still, a certain Chinese prince sent messages to a brother prince by speaking them into a curiously shaped box. The recipient, on opening the box, heard with his own ears the actual words and the voice of the sender.

The Imperial Academy of Sciences at St Petersburg offered a prize to anybody who could analyse the nature of vowel sounds and this inspired the Germany physicist, Christian Gottlieb Kratzenstein (born 1723; died 1795) to devise a machine by the operation of which it was demonstrated that the vowel sounds could be properly pronounced by mechanical agencies when air was passed through a reed into cavities or resonating chambers of various specific forms and sizes. This invention was superseded by that of Kempelen who applied the principle of the vibrating reed to a single cavity made to represent the human mouth. By the use of his hand, he was able to manipulate the shape of the artificial mouth so as to utter the vowel sounds successively. He was later to develop this into a mechanism comprising levers, tubes and bellows so as to enable a complete sentence to be articulated distinctly.

In 1843, Herr Faber devised an even more remarkable device which he called the Euphonia and was an elaborate instrument whose vocal abilities were produced by means of air in tubes, flexible rubber lips and tongue. These were operated by an ingenious mechanism concealed in the trunk and controlled by a keyboard. Demonstrated at the Egyptian Hall in London before a completely non-appreciative public three years later, the model produced its vowels and consonants with considerable accuracy, while a vibrating ivory reed was mounted in the throat to simulate vocal chords. The size and shape of the oral cavity could be modified instantly by a lever device. To produce the rolling of the letter r, a tiny windmill was fitted into the throat while the rubber tongue and lips expressed the other consonants. Faber, a native of Freiburg, had followed astronomy at Vienna until failing eyesight forced him to retire and allowed him to pursue studies in anatomy and mechanics.

These speaking devices were contrivances designed to produce speech and as such were possessed of the same powers of original sound as the musical box, only they had no pre-recorded programme to utter. A newer school of experimentalists now turned to the more profitable and commercially attractive proposition of sound reproduction. What had to be learned here was not how to shape a sound with rubber lips to produce a perfect vowel, but to analyse the sound and see just what processes were involved in its production.

The father of modern acoustics was the German physicist, Ernst Floreus Friedrich Chladni (born 1756; died 1827). Earlier, Georg Christoph Lichtenberg (born 1742; died 1799) experimented with scattering electrified iron powder over an electrified resin cake, the arrangement of the powder revealing the electric condition of the surface. This inspired Chladni with the idea of rendering sonorous vibrations visible by means of sand scattered on to the surface of a vibrating steel plate. By the latter part of the eighteenth century, he had discovered the principle of motion which govern sounds of the harmonious series, rendering visible their nodal signs.

The next significant step was the invention of the Phonautograph by M. Leon Scott in 1856. This was probably the first attempt in recent times to record speech through the action of a vibrating diaphragm. Scott used a roller affixed to a spindle, one end of which was extended and equipped with a screw thread. As the roller was turned by a small handle, the screw (which passed through one of the supporting standards) caused it to be moved laterally. The surface of the roller was covered with a sheet of paper which was prepared with a coating of lamp-black. A Plaster of Paris sound-focussing chamber terminated in a parchment diaphragm to which was fixed by sealing wax a short hog's bristle. This was maintained in contact with the surface of the revolving drum, removing particles of lamp-black and so leaving a distinct mark. As a means of permanently recording the effects of sound, Scott's machine succeeded. But it offered no system whereby the prepared and recorded roller could be processed back into sound.

A Mr Fenby took out the first patent for an instrument which he called a phonograph in 1863 and which recorded sound electrically and was capable of subsequent reproduction. Edison's invention, also called the Phonograph but operating on an entirely different system, was patented in 1878. A controversy as to whether Edison or the Frenchman, Charles Cros, was the true inventor of the instrument later arose. Cros deposited a description of his instrument with the French Academy of Sciences in April 1877, earlier than Edison's earliest patent. However, the matter has never been adequately cleared up.

Edison stumbled upon his invention by accident. He was experimenting with a machine intended to repeat Morse characters recorded on paper by indentations which transferred their messages to another circuit automatically, when he detected a humming noise of a musically rhythmic character which followed the rapid movement of the impressed paper. He had come back to the elementary teachings of Robert Hooke (born 1635; died 1703) who, in 1681, demonstrated the making of musical sounds with the help of teeth in brass wheels—equal-sized teeth made musical sounds while unequal teeth made vocal sounds. Savart and many others were later to exhibit the same principle in various ways.

Edison's Phonograph was very similar in many ways to Scott's Phonautograph except that Edison's roller was spirally grooved and covered with tin foil. A steel point was attached to the centre of the diaphragm and the whole was adjusted so that when the drum was evenly revolved by means of the crank provided, it shifted laterally. The recording, when made, became an inherent part of the machine since the tinfoil, pressed into the spiral groove of the drum, was now impressed with a series of minute indentations on the 'hill-and-dale' principle. When once more the steel point was placed at the start of the groove and the drum rotated, the point imparted rapid motion via the indentations to the diaphragm, so re-converting them into the original sounds.

Edison was unable to see any commercial possibilities in his instrument and so for some years it remained purely as a scientific novelty. Then two other inventors, Graham Bell (born 1847; died 1922) and Tainter, devised a method of recording using a cylindrical wax blank which could be removed from the machine after recording. This was cut using a sapphire stylus and produced superior results. In 1887, Emile Berliner (born 1851; died 1929) took out patents for his instrument which recorded on flat discs, initially of prepared zinc, instead of bulky cylinders. The talking machine was born.

Pathé Frères in Paris perfected the method of pressing records in a shellac composition. As with the mass-produced musical boxes of a few decades earlier, the talking machine had to be part of everyone's home and they were made in all shapes and sizes at prices ranging from a few shillings to many pounds.

Just as musical boxes had appeared in novelties, so did the talking machine. As early as 1893, Lioret of Paris devised mechanical dolls which contained a small phonograph with reproducer. The recording was pressed in celluloid from a steel pattern and was cylindrical in form. Talking novelties were popular in the years to come and I well remember a dreadful blue-painted cigarette box which my father had. When the catch for the lid was slid back, the top would open slowly accompanied by the grinding whirr of machinery and an obsequious voice would be heard saying 'Would you care for a cigarette?'—no doubt to the consternation of the visitor hell-bent on surreptitiously filling his cigarette case at my father's expense. Lamentably, over the years, the 2-inch record within wore out. Thoughtfully provided with an identical track on the opposite side, reversal of the disc only staved off the inevitable, and soon that track, too, was needled into nothing but a noise. Not, I might add, because my family were heavy smokers, but because to my youthful satisfaction and appreciation it was considered highly amusing and thus had to be heard at every opportunity. The cigarettes within yellowed with age after repeated exposure to sunlight. Ultimately, my requests were granted and I was allowed to dismantle it. At this point in time, the disc was entreating the box-opener 'Aaahjjouaaakkkmmenn?', so one could say that its useful life had expired. It certainly never worked again after my attentions (I was about seven years old) although to this day I have most of the pieces.

Significantly, the early instruments were known as talking machines (*sprechmaschine* in German; *machine parlante* in French). Their ability as reproducers of music, admittedly very inferior, was in no way seen to be as important as their ability to reproduce that most elusive sound of all—that of the human voice. To hear the voice of a great statesman, famous entertainer or beloved artiste and to be able to preserve their individual sounds was the one characteristic of the phonograph which appealed to the imagination and which instantly placed it in a class of its own.

It has been said that selling phonographs was the first big deal the early American advertising agents ever had. That they succeeded there is no doubt; that nobody needed the musical box is fact.

This chapter was to have been much shorter. As written in my original notes, it went: Chapter 8. The Gramophone. 'The gramophone came in and the musical box went out.'

Pathés Phonograph

Nº 4

DUPLEX

£ 8-10-0

Includes. — The Phonograph and polished Case.
One Mandrel for Ordinary size Cylinders.
One Mandrel for Salon size Cylinders.
One Mandrel for Grand Concert Cylinders.
One " Pathé " or " Rex " Reproducing Diaphragm.
One Large Flower Horn, nº 5o5 (Diameter 16 inch).

Fitted with independent crank winder

Important Notice. — Unless specified, we reserve ourselves the right of substituting an Aluminium Horn for the Flower Horn.

A Pathé phonograph of about 1903 equipped to take three different sizes of cylinder.

New Columbia Graphophone.

A GENUINE COLUMBIA GRAPHOPHONE FOR 15/-

Plays the "**X.P.**" or any small cylinder Records with remarkable clearness and brilliancy. Not a cheap toy, but a well-made musical instrument, that will afford unending entertainment in the home.

HAS
FEED SCREW
LEATHER
BELT
SPEED
REGULATOR

PRICE,
15/-

Columbia
"X.P."
Records,
now 1/3 each.

GRAND
PRIX,
PARIS,
1900.

Write for Price Book **X** *to*

Don't send stamp if you mention this Advertisement.

COLUMBIA PHONOGRAPH Co., Genl.,
89, GREAT EASTERN STREET, LONDON, E.C.

NEW YORK, PARIS, BERLIN, CHICAGO.

The Columbia Graphophone advertisement appeared in *The London Magazine* for November 1903. Imhof & Mukle were still advertising musical boxes with Berliner's disc gramophone in *Harmsworths Magazine*, May 1901 (*below*) but three years later in *The London Magazine*, only orchestrions and player pianos were mentioned along with HMV gramophones (*right*).

THE **GRAMOPHONE.**

**THE WONDER
OF THE
TWENTIETH
CENTURY.**

(Berliner's Patent.)
Loudest and most distinct sound - producing machine yet invented. Goes by clockwork. Record-discs practically indestructible. Loud enough to fill a hall holding 500 people.
A Customer writes : "Your Gramophone exceeds all our expectations. We find it magnificent in the open air."
Hundreds of Records to choose from. Records sent on approval if postage paid.

GRADUAL PAYMENTS.
Length of Trumpet, 16 inches.
Imhof's Patent ORCHESTRIONS without Barrels.
Patent ELECTRIC PIANOS.
Patent REGINA MUSICAL BOX, changing its tunes automatically.
Patent STELLA MUSICAL BOX, discs without projections.
POLYPHON MUSICAL BOXES in all Sizes.
TEN GOLD MEDALS.
BY APPOINTMENT TO HER LATE MAJESTY THE QUEEN.
Send for Illustrated List (Free).
IMHOF & MUKLE, 110a, New Oxford St., London, W.

**Price £5 10s.
Records 2/6 each.**

GRAMOPHONES

FROM 3 GUINEAS TO £20.
The New No. 3, in Oak Case, **£3 3s.** wonderfully clear and natural in tone. Records on approval if remittance sent with order for quantity required. Prices—**2/6, 5/-** and **10/-** each.

"HIS MASTER'S VOICE"

Thousands of Records: by Madame Calvé, Caruso, Kubelik, Mde. Kirkby Lunn, Sarah Bernhardt, Ben Davies, Grenadier Guards, Haydn Quartette, Dan Leno, Geo. Robey, &c.
Illustrated List (FREE.) Gradual Payments.
Makers of Electric Orchestrions, Pianos and Piano-Players, &c. *By appointment to the late Queen Victoria.*—IMHOF & MUKLE, **110, New Oxford Street, London, W.**

283

Thomas Alva Edison and Alexander Graham Bell, phonograph inventors, gave their names to the Edison-Bell as announced (*above*) in the *Strand Magazine* for December 1899. Nicole Frères, according to *Harmsworths Magazine,* May 1901, were selling Edison's Phonograph, the Gramophone made by Berliner and the Zonophone made in U.S.A. In the same year, a Wolverhampton dealer described his Edison wares in glowing terms . . .

284

From *The Pictorial Magazine* of 13 December 1902 comes this notice (*above*) for the 'Santa Claus', a German-made phonograph. The Saxon Trading Company had the same address as Henry Klein (*see page* 142). The idea of teaching languages by recorded example was being published as early as the days of the cylinder phonograph. Funk & Wagnalls Co (*below*) advertised to this effect in *The London Magazine* of February 1904.

The *London Magazine* for January 1907, carried this full-page announcement by the National Phonograph Co., Ltd. The style and wording is reminiscent of the Aeolian Orchestrelle advertisements. What a boon the phonograph must have been to the family in the days before wireless! Comparable in effect to the panoramas of the early nineteenth century, it served to take people out of their own diminutive surroundings into what was for them another world. Today, when appliances in our homes can give us music, news and sport from around the world, when we can see transmissions live from distant space, or from the bottom of the ocean, and the other side of the world is physically only hours away, we may smile at the gramophone being described as 'the wonder of the nineteenth century' in *The Strand Magazine* for December 1899. It must, though, have seemed just that.

Make Merry this Yuletide

—there is an endless source of amusement and enjoyment in a Genuine Edison Phonograph. As you sit by your cheerful fireside, you can hear the music you like so well—listen to the songs that endeared themselves to you in years gone by—to the latest pantomime successes or the old-time Christmas carols.

Genuine Edison
Gold = Moulded Records

provide an infinite variety of selections : favourite old songs ; instrumental solos ; sacred and classical music ; a waltz by Strauss or Berger ; stirring marches by Dan Godfrey or Sousa ; grand or comic opera— you can hear them all, rendered with "feeling," expression and wonderful clearness.

Can you think of a Christmas gift that will give more pleasure and enjoyment to every member of the family than an Edison Phonograph with a selection of Genuine Edison Gold-moulded Records.

But remember that only with *Genuine* Edison Gold-moulded Records can you secure those full, clear, musical reproduc-

tions of the best singers and music. These records are made by a patented process that retains every shade of expression and tone, making the reproduction so perfect that you can easily imagine you are actually listening to the singer or the orchestra as the case may be.

Call on your dealer, hear the Edison Phonograph and ask for a list of the latest Edison Records. In case of difficulty, write us, and we will send you the address of the nearest agent, and also our special Christmas Supplement. Address Dept. 13.

Genuine Edison Phonographs from £2 2s.
Genuine Edison Gold-moulded Records, 1/6 each.
Genuine Edison Grand Opera Records, 3/- each.
To protect you we put this signature on every *Genuine* Edison Record and Phonograph.

TRADE
Thomas A. Edison
MARK

National Phonograph Co., Ltd.,
25, Clerkenwell Road, E.C.

CHAPTER 9

Miscellany

THE gramophone went through the musical instrument industry like a virulent blight. Everybody wanted talking machines and the outcome was immediate. Manufacturers of phonographs sprang up everywhere and inventors were clamouring to patent all manner of weird devices each of which was claimed to provide superior reproducing qualities. Something I normally prefer to forget was the existence many years ago of such an inventor within my own family who produced what would by today's standards be called a 'sound system' and which bore a name that was a cruel pun upon that of the family. This device, which happily passed with rapidity into contemporary oblivion, was known as the Audio-Humanovox.

The demand for talking machines and the threat which it presented to the musical box industry was appreciated by many musical box manufacturers. Some, like Polyphon, Regina and Mermod, rapidly produced dual machines like the Gramo-Polyphon, (the German name for this was Polygraphon), the Reginaphone and the Carillon-Mira of 1905, which could with equal facility render music from a perforated disc or reproduce via soundbox and steel needle a popular song sung by a favourite artist. Those manufacturers who had entered the musical box trade late in its life, or who had recently introduced a new line, were hardest hit and were in many cases forced out of business. Others, more financially secure, cut their losses and went straight into the new occupation of producing talking machines. Polyphon produced the Polyphon gramophone and suitable records under both the house name and the Corona label. B.H.A. in Switzerland threw away the musical box interiors for their $9\frac{1}{8}$ inch disc size upright model Britannia and fitted a phonograph into the cabinet along with pigeon-holes for the cylindrical records.

Polyphon diversified still further: in 1908 the company was also making the Polygraph typewriter and the Polymobil motor car having earlier produced the Oldsmobile under licence. In about 1917, Polyphon bought out the now-famous Deutsche Grammophon company and the Polyphon record label first appeared in 1920. Mermod, Paillard and Manger all made gramophones. The musical box agents and importers switched to these goods as well, the contacts and the system being already established. Messrs J. Sinton Limited of 37 Dean Street, Soho were, by 1903, sole agents for Paillard (which manufacturer seemed to have a high turnover of 'sole agents') selling their musical boxes and the Echophone gramophone.

Immediately after the 1914–18 war, the industry and the market needed a break and for several years there was nothing new. As much as anything else, the English market for German goods had undergone a dramatic change as a result of the war and many surviving German-made musical instruments were thrown out just because they were of German origin.

The centre of the mechanical musical instrument industry, partly due to the interregnum created by the war and partly due to the continued development in the United States, was now on the other side of the Atlantic and Germany's place as a world leader in mechanical music had really gone forever.

For many years to come, Germany still produced fine instruments such as the orchestrion organs, the show organs and the quality reproducing pianos, but the best times had passed. The industry was on the decline if only due to loss of favour and consequent dwindling of the vital export market. Polyphon came up with the Triola mechanical zither in 1919, Höhner with the Music Organa accordion which featured pneumatic action and could accompany itself on drum and cymbals attached by umbilical pneumatic lines. This was in 1925.

The emphasis had shifted from pinned barrel, through perforated disc to punched cardboard and the perforated paper roll. The giant concert organs performed intricate music and selected their own stops with such deftness that no doubt even John Flight Jnr might have released an appreciative gasp had he heard them, for it was he who so expertly pinned the barrels of Flight & Robson's finest organs, including the Apollonicon. The public was getting accustomed to mechanical music. The stylish restaurants with their orchestrion organs, Phonoliszt-Violinas and reproducing pianos caused no raised eyebrows. The fairground carousel or roundabout with its blaring organ was accepted. The thin voice of wireless and the gramophone, however, began slowly to make more sense. Why bother with a large and expensive instrument with a selected but rather inflexible repertoire when, for less money, music can be had in a more compact and certainly more varied form?

The order of the boot was being administered! The fashionable restaurants reverted to a troupe of live musicians, the fairground found a gramophone and an amplifier easier to transport around and set up, and the noise it produced was rather louder. And on a Sunday, *paterfamilias* could switch on the wireless and listen to real music with his family.

Clockwork music as part of the everyday world was finished.

ROLL-MONICA

This unique Musical Instrument is very popular, being instantly playable by young and old. Simply insert Music Roll, breathe in mouthpiece in a natural manner and turn playing handle.
Metal body, highly nickel-plated with fitted Harmonica, two Music Rolls, in fancy tartan box with full instructions
Each   **11**   **8**

The Roll-Monica was a late-comer in the world of mechanical instruments. Patented by Joseph Le Roy Banks of Baltimore in November 1925, two sizes were made, one with 12 notes and one with 16. It was played rather like the Phonographic Cornet on page 307 and one blew into the mouthpiece whilst turning the handle. The illustration comes from a London wholesaler's 1935 catalogue.

In the Bibliothèque Royale in Brussels is a fifteenth century manuscript breviary containing a miniature of the Jesse Tree. The reclining figure of Jesus Christ is seen and from His body there sprouts a tree bearing His ancestors who are represented as playing musical instruments and forming a celestial concert. The figure right of centre is playing a semi-automatic instrument shaped like a primitive *vielle* or hurdy-gurdy consisting of strings which are played with one hand while a drone is sounded by turning the handle. A somewhat similar instrument is in the collection of Messrs W. E. Hill in London. This has a small wooden cylinder from the inside of which project long wire plectra. As this is rotated by the handle, the strings are sequentially plucked.

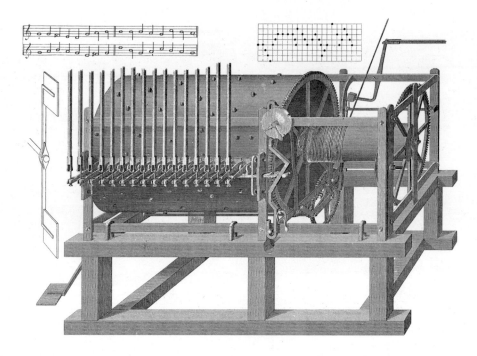

These two plates from a nineteenth century encyclopedia depict an early application of the pinned cylinder or drum used to sound a chime of bells. The clockwork-driven mechanism shown is of the type built into the musical clock. At the top is shown a plan of the pinning to play the tune of the Old Hundredth Psalm.

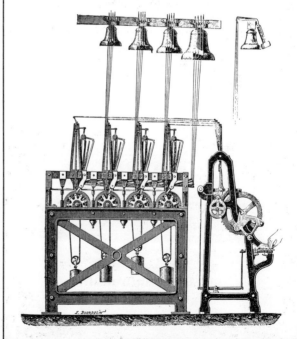

Automatic carillons have been a feature of the Low Countries for centuries and belfries such as that at Bruges (*top right*) are provided with automatic bell-playing mechanisms. Above is shown a device entitled 'Messrs J Warner & Son's Patent Chiming Machine by which a Lad entirely Unaccustomed to Music may Correctly Chime a Whole Peal'. Right is a diagram of Collins' chiming apparatus as built into the carillon of Saint Germain in Paris between 1863 and 1878. It will be seen that this barrel and finger mechanism has provision for each bell to have its own potential-energy motor and key pressure purely releases a light detent to allow the hammer to strike the bell. Imhof later used just this principle to sound large percussion instruments from the tiny leverage afforded by a barrel orchestrion key.

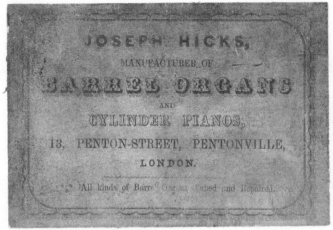

The portable street piano, illustrated above from Mrs O. F. Walton's book *Christie's Old Organ*, is thought to have been made first by Joseph Hicks, who worked in Bristol between 1816 and 1847. Distin was his apprentice and continued the Bristol business. The Joseph who came to London was probably a son. John Baylis was in business between 1854 and 1864. These little instruments cost between £8 and £10 each according to *Chambers Edinburgh Journal*, 1834. The street pianos which caught on later, of course were the larger ones on carts like that below (*Scientific American*, 18 May 1895).

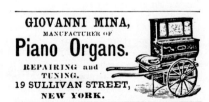

In Yorkshire, they called them 'tingalarys'; the Italian makers called them 'piano-organs'; the recipient public loathed them as 'barrel organs'; the Americans chose to call them 'hurdy-gurdies'; the scholar today calls them 'street pianos' or 'barrel pianos'. Whatever the appellation by which they were known, the handle-piano trade was a large one. The first of these instruments is said to have been made in Torino and the Italian makers of the cylinder piano (the original name for the street piano) travelled from their native country to all parts of Europe and even to America to set up industries. 'Music by the handle' was not always synonymous with poverty, and this rather exhausting work could bring in big money. In 1885, for example, it was revealed that the proprietor of one South London hiring establishment could afford to take weekly trips to the seaside to dine out. Not so one G. Marini of Whitechapel Road whose hiring business failed in the same year. And what of the men who took the piano-organs out? One, arrested in Manchester for failing to desist from playing to the public annoyance, had £37 in his pockets! The full story of these instruments is contained in *Player Piano*. Here, though, from *The New Penny Magazine* of 12 January 1901, is an article describing a visit to Pesaresi's piano factory in Clerkenwell. The quality of the pictures—then a very new process in magazines—is extremely poor, but a few things can be learned from them, such as the special barrel-pricking piano on this page which has one string only to each note, a tapered right side and a music desk. On the next page we see a piano laid on its back for stringing. Surviving pianos today are either in the hands of collectors and museums or are used to raise funds for charity. One such piano, rebuilt by the Author, earned £600 in just three days over Christmas 1971. But let's go back seventy years, to 30 Warner Street.

ALL ABOUT PIANO ORGANS.

A VERY great deal has been said and written about street organs, their proprietors and "players"—mostly in the nature of "fairy tales." There are those people

Of course, most of those who profess to know all about these things have no basis of fact for their statements, and are speaking for the most part purely at random.

MARKING CYLINDERS READY FOR PEGS TO BE DRIVEN IN.
(*Photo: Cassell & Co., Ltd.*)

rabidly anti-organic, so to speak, who have made wild statements about the number of instruments on the streets, and the fabulous fortunes made by the proprietors out of those who "turn the handle." Then there are the super-subtle and over-optimistic folk, who, with an elaborate wink, vaguely aver that "those organ-grinding chaps make a pretty penny, I can tell you," frequently adding that many of those of "Southern blood" return to their native land with an independence ground out of an organ.

Piano organs have again and again been voted an uncompromising public nuisance, and many worthy citizens, had they the power, would unhesitatingly consign instruments and all concerned to instant and permanent oblivion. There is, in fact, a Bill now under consideration to prohibit this wholesale trafficking in melody.

Personally, I have no violent antipathy to a piano organ, provided it is tuneful, that the selection of airs is not too antiquated, and that I am not deep in Euclid or the philosophy of the ancients. The time has gone by when "Tommy Make Room for Your Uncle" had any charms for me, but I do not mind "The

DRIVING PEGS IN CYLINDER.
(Photo : Cassell & Co., Ltd.)

Absent-minded Beggar," and for the sake of peace I will even endure "She bumps." But, at the same time, I sympathise with those who have no "music al ear," and I am not surprised at their "going to lengths" over the matter.

Messrs. Pesaresi and Son, of Clerkenwell (the heart of the piano organ industry), are makers of piano organs on a large scale, and Mr. Pesaresi was recently good enough, in response to an eloquent appeal from me, to show me over his premises, and to explain a good many interesting things in connection with his business.

In passing, let me say there appears to be quite a remarkable amount of reticence with the Italians in this business, and it seems to require the services of "all the king's horses and all the king's men" to induce them to talk of their trade.

The man who can construct a handle piano organ knows something of the points of an Erard or a Broadwood. The former might be taken as a very early stage of either of the latter.

All the wood used in the construction of a piano organ must be thoroughly seasoned—kept in stock five or six years before it is any good. If this were not done it would warp after a few weeks in the street, and render the instrument useless. After each process, too, a period must be allowed for drying before proceeding, so that it takes some weeks to complete one of these little organs. The whole thing could, however, be put together in one week if taken right through without stopping, but that would not do.

The barrel is made of wood, being first put together in sections, and afterwards smooth-planed. The surface is then covered with a layer of thick paper, ready to receive the "music." This, perhaps, is the most skilful operation of all, for it requires the services of a musician with mechanical knowledge. The frame having been placed in the outer case on much

FITTING WIRES.
(Photo : Cassell & Co., Ltd.)

294

the same system as that adopted with an ordinary piano, the barrel is introduced into the front of the instrument. At the base of every hammer is a metal tongue with a sharp point, situated close to the barrel. A piece of sheet music is placed in front ; the operator sits down, and practically plays the tune over on the hammers. Every time he presses one of the latter, which represents a note, the point

frame ; the worker takes up a pin point down in a pair of pliers, and holds it over one of the holes in the barrel. A slight pressure of the foot causes the cross-piece to come down sharply on the pliers, and drives the pin home. There are thousands of pins in one barrel, and all are practically put in by hand.

When all the pins are thus fixed the barrel is returned to the instrument, which is then,

REMOVING OLD PEGS FROM CYLINDER AND PREPARING FOR NEW TUNES.
(*Photo : Cassell & Co., Ltd.*)

of the metal tongue at the bottom presses into the barrel, and leaves a clear indentation.

One revolution of the barrel represents a tune. Say the instrument is fitted with twelve. To change a tune a twist of the index outside will cause the barrel to move a certain distance horizontally ; another twist will send it further still, and so on up to six. The seventh twist will bring the barrel back a pace, and it will continue to return by stages till twelve is reached, when it arrives at zero, and begins at No. 1 again.

Well, when all the tunes are pricked into the barrel, as I have indicated, it is taken out of the instrument and handed over to a man who proceeds to insert a small pin in each hole by a special process. The barrel is placed in position under the horizontal cross-piece of a

with the exception of a little overhauling, ready for use. The turning of the handle sets the barrel revolving, and the pins coming in contact with the metal tongues set the hammers working on the wires in much the same way that the pressure of the keys of an ordinary piano will produce the same result, or a similar.

I asked Mr. Pesaresi how he managed about the copyright of the music he used. Said he :

"There is no infringement ; therefore we are not liable. If I *printed* the music on paper there would, of course, be a distinct infringement, or if a monetary consideration were taken for the privilege of hearing the tunes on the organs. But this is not so ; people please themselves about giving the men money or not. They can stand and listen to the organ as long as they choose, and then walk away without subscribing a farthing.

"To show you how nice the law is on the point, there was an action brought some time ago by a firm of music publishers against the makers of some small hand organs, where the music is contained on lengths of perforated paper. The latter had conveyed a copyright melody to one of their instruments, but in defence they argued that they had not infringed any right, as they had not actually *copied* the music. This defence would have succeeded had it not been for the fact that they had really copied a single word from the sheet music— the word 'copyright.' That one word broke down their defence."

"Do you ever receive complaints on the score of copyright?"

"Sometimes, but there is no reasonable ground for them. As a rule, music publishers are desirous of getting certain of their melo-

four hours, and is done with remarkable speed. All the holes are then filled up with a solution of glue, a new layer of paper fitted on, and the pins stuck in as in the case of a new barrel.

A barrel will stand many of these operations before it becomes useless. The periods for renewal differ with the different instruments, say from a year to eighteen months. Tunes are changed every six or eight months, and

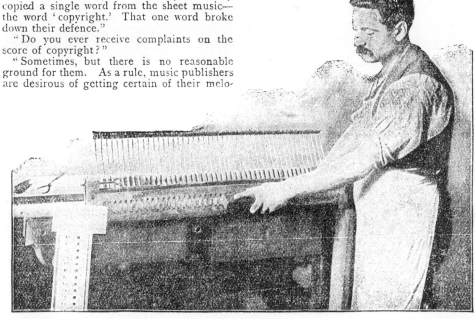

MAKING KEYS.
(Photo: Cassell & Co., Ltd.)

dies placed upon our organs, for it helps the sale of copies by popularising the tunes. In proof of this I may tell you that we are constantly receiving new music from publishers 'with compliments.' Here are several pieces so inscribed just to hand."

There was a huge pile of music of every conceivable description in the room—waltz, galop, march, quadrilles, pathetic melody, comic ditties, martial measures, etc., all having passed through the hands of the "master musician" of the establishment.

Periodically it becomes necessary to supply a fresh set of pins to a barrel, the old ones becoming worn and practically useless. The barrel is removed from the instrument, and a worker armed with a special pair of pliers draws out all the pins, and the paper is removed. This operation takes about three or

a thorough oiling must be indulged in three times a week. An instrument will last for six or eight years, when it begins to exhibit signs of decay, and calls aloud for remedial treatment. A process of patching up will fit it for a further span of active years, when another visit to the hospital will probably be necessary to enable it to eke out its "latter days." When at the age of a score years its musical and bread-winning mission will be over, and, sans stability, sans music, sans everything useful and attractive, it will subside into lumber. The only realisable portion of its wreck are the steel pegs round which the wires are twisted. These go to make pegs for boys' tops. Its chords of life are worse than useless; they are cumbersome, and of its frame is firewood made.

Alas, poor Orpheus!

When I first entered Messrs. Pesaresi's premises I thought I had somehow stumbled into a native workshop. On all hands were sons and daughters of Italian soil, the latter picturesquely attired in multi-coloured draperies. One smiled so sweetly on me that had she had a "little tambourine" I should have been forced to drop a coin in it. These were probably the "West Enders," denizens of the fashionable quarters, and aristocrats of the calling. More alluring ways are necessary for Mayfair than St. Giles'. With the

Some of the men were discharging liabilities with the cashier, a ceremony in which both gold and silver figured.

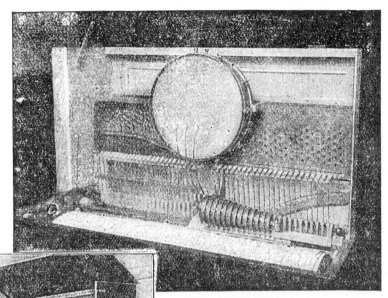

AN UP-TO-DATE PIANO ORGAN.
(Photo: Cassell & Co. Ltd.)

The charge for the hire of an organ is 1s. 8d. per day, which is reduced during bad times to 1s. 6d. and 1s. 4d. The average earnings of the hirers is 5s. to 6s. a day. The prices of organs vary, of course, say, from £18 to £25 and £30.

It has been stated that there are several thousands of organs on the London streets. This, says Mr. Pesaresi, is a gross exaggeration. Altogether, there are not more than 500, 50 per cent. of which are taken round by Englishmen. A great many Italians give up organs for the proprietorship of ice-cream barrows, baked potato ovens, and roasted chestnut grills. Very few can afford to become proprietors of organs, as the maintenance would be too expensive. There would be 1s. a week for stabling, 2s. 6d. for tuning, £5 for a new set of tunes, 6d. for a new bass wire, 1d. for others, and so on.

In Kennington there is a piano organ depôt, where they let out instruments to Englishmen only.

At one time Viscount Hinton hired an instrument from Messrs. Pesaresi. The latter send organs to all parts of the world; not, of course, to Italy, for that would be like sending coals to Newcastle. So we do not hold a monopoly of street organ music.

TUNING.
(Photo: Cassell & Co., Ltd.)

former it is a case of music plus grace, with the latter it is often mere unrestrained gaiety.

Luck enters largely into the occupation of organ-grinding, although the "old hands" know the ground pretty well, and have certain "customers" who patronise them. They also get to know what tunes are most welcome in certain quarters, and how to make the most of their time. Novices often waste time by working on "barren ground," through ignorance of the locality.

Much money is made from the poorer classes, Saturdays, of course, being a good day. Both Wednesdays and Thursdays are bad days, but Boxing Day is the best in all the year.

In the case of Englishmen who "follow the organ," it is generally through physical inability to take up any ordinary occupation.

One thing is certain—and this is a consoling reflection to me—should I fail with the pen there is always an organ.

Before Sir Joseph Renals, at the Mansion House Police Court, on Saturday, Giuseppe Federico, 50, an Italian organ grinder, was charged with being drunk while in charge of a piano organ in Gracechurch Street.

Police-Constable Melton saw the prisoner the previous evening wheeling his organ from one side of the street to the other, and, finding that he was drunk, arrested him.

An interpreter had to be engaged to interpret the evidence, the fee being 7/6d. and in addition to this the prisoner had incurred 1/6d. Green-Yard fees for the housing of his organ for the night.

The Alderman (to prisoner): "I shall fine you 2/6d. and you must pay costs. I do not see why the city should have to pay for drunken foreign organ-grinders. This is the class of alien we want to get out of the country; it is quite clear that they are of no use in their own. They only come here, I suppose, because their own country will not keep them".

Prisoner then proceeded to pay the fine, which he did wholly in coppers, producing handfuls of halfpennies and pennies from numerous pockets.

While the process of discovering the necessary coppers to make up the fine and costs was proceeding, and Gaoler Bradford was carefully arranging the coins in little piles, each representing a shilling, the Alderman remarked, "Its quite an education. Organ grinding must be a very profitable business. It would be interesting to know how many more pockets he has and where he keeps his gold". (Laughter)

Mr. Douglas (Chief Clerk): "I have never in my experience known a prisoner to pay his fine in coppers."

Inspector Goldsmith: "The prisoner has been many years in England, and likes British beer very much". (Laughter)

The Alderman: "Yes, and British money also." (Laughter)

The above news item is copied from *The Leicester Daily Mercury* for 1 May 1905. The story (*right*) comes from *Leisure Hour* for 1882. The 'Galignani' was a contemporary Parisian publisher.

Automaton Violin-Player.

The well-known "Galignani" gave, in 1840, the following account of this wonderful piece of mechanism, on the authority of M. Bruyere, who was present at its performance. The work was constructed by a Monsieur Mareppe, and exhibited before the Royal Conservatory of Paris. "On entering the salon," says M. Bruyere, "I saw a well-dressed, handsome figure of a man, about forty or forty-five, standing with a violin in his hand, as if contemplating a piece of music that lay on a desk before him ; and had I not gone to see an automaton, I should have believed the object before me to have been a living figure, so easy were the attitude and expression of its countenance. I had but little time for observation ere the orchestra was filled with musicians ; and on the leader taking his seat, the figure instantly raised itself erect, bowed with much elegance two or three times, and then turning to the leader nodded as if to say he was ready, and placed the violin to his shoulder. At the given signal he raised his bow, and applying it to his instrument, produced, à la Paganini, one of the most thrilling and extraordinary flourishes I ever heard, in which scarcely a semitone within the compass of the instrument was omitted, and was executed with a degree of rapidity and clearness perfectly astonishing. The orchestra then played a short symphony, in which the figure occasionally joined in beautiful style ; he then played a fantasia in E, with accompaniments, with an *allegro molto* on the fourth string solo, which was perfectly indescribable. The tones produced were anything but like those of the violin, and expressive beyond expression. I felt as if lifted from my seat, and burst into tears, in which predicament I saw many persons in the room. Suddenly he struck into a cadenza, in which the harmonics, double and single, arpeggios on the four strings, and saltos, for which Paganini was so celebrated, were introduced with the greatest effect ; and after a close shake of eight bars, commenced the coda, a prestissimo movement, played in three parts throughout ; this part of the performance was perfecly magical. I have heard the great Italian, and still greater Norwegian, Ole Bull ; I have heard the best of music, but never heard such sounds as then saluted my ear. It began pianissimo, rising by a gradual crescendo to a pitch beyond belief, and then died away, leaving the audience absolutely enchanted. Monsieur Mareppe, who is a player of no mean order, then came forward amidst the most deafening acclamations, and stated that, emulated by the example of Vaucanson's flute-player, he had conceived the project of constructing this figure, which had cost him many years of study and labour before he could bring it to completion. He then showed the company the interior of the figure, which was completely filled with small cranks, by which the motions are given to the several parts of the automaton at the will of the conductor, who has the whole machine so perfectly under control that M. Mareppe proposed that it should perform any piece of music which may be laid before him within a fortnight. He also showed that, to a certain extent, the figure was self-acting, as, on winding up the strings, several of the most beautiful airs were played, amongst which were 'Nel cor piu,' 'Partant pour la Syrie,' 'Weber's Last Waltz,' and 'La ci darem la mano,' all with brilliant embellishments. But the *chef d'œuvre* is the manner in which the figure is made to obey the direction of the conductor, whereby it is endowed with a sort of *semi-reason*."

On page 297 was shown a street piano fitted with drum and bells. These were also made as 'automatics' which were clockwork-driven barrel pianos for use in public places. Two such instruments are shown in the 1909 advertisement above. The tall case of the left one accommodates the percussion effects. Of the same vintage is the announcement (*below*) regarding organettes playing 'metal tunes' made by Schmidt under the name Phoenix. This was another very good and fine-toned model.

THE CALLIOPE, OR STEAM-ORGAN.

THE CALLIOPE.

A MUSICAL instrument known by the above name has been lately brought over from America by the inventor, Mr. Arthur S. Denny, and is now being exhibited for the first time in England in the central transept of the Crystal Palace. It may be characterised as a steam-organ, and consists of a framework of iron supporting two cylinders, upon which are arranged a series of brass tubes, answering to the open diapasons of an organ, but bearing a strong resemblance to the ordinary steam-locomotive whistle. From a boiler situated beneath the flooring the steam is conveyed into the cylinders, and from them admitted to the pipes, which produce the notes, through double-balance valves, opened by levers in connection with wires acted upon by ordinary pianoforte keys, or by pegs on a set cylinder similar to that of a barrel-organ. The instrument at the Crystal Palace is the softest-toned ever made, and is played upon at a pressure of 5lb. to the square inch—the maximum pressure employed in the church organ being but five ounces. The peculiarity of the invention consists in the fact that instruments are constructed in which the force of steam may be increased to the extent of a hundred and fifty pounds to the square inch, producing musical sounds thirty times as powerful as those of the calliope now exhibiting ; and such is the volume of sound given forth at this high pressure that the instrument is asserted to have been distinctly heard at a distance of twelve miles. The compass of sound is almost unlimited, from the soft tones of a musical-box to a power sufficient to afford music to a whole city.

On account of the quantity of steam given off during the performance the instrument has not been hitherto available for indoor exhibition ; but if, in place of steam, it be used with condensed air better music is produced and an equally powerful effect.

Various are the uses to which it is suggested the power of the calliope may be applied, amongst others as a means of conveying the orders of a General on the field of battle by signals to be heard by the whole army ; it is also capable of being used as a substitute for a chime of bells, and in St. Louis and New Orleans it has often been employed in this manner. A lighthouse belonging to the English Government, and situated on the coast of Nova Scotia, is provided with a calliope for making signal ; the Pacha of Egypt has one fixed on board his private steamer as a musical instrument ; and in this way they are frequently used in the United States.

Although the harmonies are, from the employment of steam, not always perfect, still the effect of a melody is decidedly pleasing to the ear ; and, as a musical novelty, the calliope must be considered to possess many claims on the attention of the public.

The first Calliope was mentioned on page 254. Here it is depicted in *The Illustrated London News* for 3 December 1859—a true barrel-and-finger steam-organ.

Professor Wauters was an early inventor who attempted to mechanise the violin in a practical manner. This story was printed in *The Scientific American* on 28 December 1907.

Scientific American

DECEMBER 28, 1907.

Front View of the Automatic Violin Player.

AN AUTOMATIC VIOLIN PLAYER.
BY GEORGE GILBERT.

In view of the present popularity of the piano player, and the marvelous perfection this instrument has attained in reproducing the work of the best musicians, it is very evident that it will be only a question of time before other musical instruments must similarly surrender to mechanical control. The latest development along this line is a machine which will play violins and kindred instruments. As may well be imagined, the violin offers difficulties which are peculiar to itself, and we are not surprised to learn that the violin player illustrated herewith is the culmination of seven years of continuous labor and experiment.

The instrument requires no alteration in the violin itself, and any violin may be placed in the player and removed without injury. The parts are pneumatically controlled in a manner similar to that of the ordinary piano player. A perforated music sheet selects the notes which are to be sounded. This sheet travels over a "tracker board," provided with the usual ducts in which an exhaust is maintained. There are two ducts for each note, and as these are uncovered by perforations in the music sheet, the air rushing into one of the ducts acts through the medium of the usual valves and pneumatics to press a finger down on one of the violin strings at the proper point on the finger board, while the air in the other duct puts into operation the bowing mechanism of this string. The bowing is done by means of four crystal disks, one for each string. In the accompanying drawing the details of the bowing mechanism are shown. Fig. 1 illustrates a section taken through the body of the violin *A*. The strings are indicated at *B*. The disks *C*, with which the bowing is done, are an inch in diameter and ⅛ of an inch in thickness. They are mounted in the ends of levers *D*, which are connected to the pneumatics *E*. When one of the bow ducts is uncovered, it operates a valve, which connects its respective pneumatic *E* with the exhaust chamber of the machine. The pneumatic is thus deflated, swinging the lever *D* to which it is connected, and bringing the disk *C* on this lever into contact with the selected string *B*. The disk *C* is rotated at high speed by means of a belt, which is guided along the lever *D*, as best shown in Fig. 2, and runs over a pulley *F* at the opposite end of the lever. When the lever *D* is swung into operative position by the pneumatic *E*, the pulley *F* is brought

into contact with a driving pulley *G*, and is set in motion by a frictional contact therewith. This motion is communicated to the disk *C*, which operates on the violin string. The speed of revolution may run up as high as 2,000 revolutions per minute. The rate at which the disks revolve determines the loudness of the tones. A device is provided for applying rosin to the disks. This consists of a small cup attached to a spring arm and containing rosin, which bears against the revolving disks.

The fingers of the violin player are sixty-five in number, although more can be added if desired, to reach the extreme high range of the *A* and *E* strings. There is a finger for each note. The model shown employs fingers reaching the seventh position. In front of each string is stretched a rubber band, upon which the ends of the fingers strike, thus producing a touch like that of the human finger, and making it possible to imitate the "slide." The tremolo is produced by a set of four hammers, which are actuated by electric vibrators of the type used in call bells. When a hammer vibrates against a string, next to the bridge, the tremolo effect is produced on that string. All the strings may have this effect, or one, as the character of the music demands.

Directly over the violin are four small pitch pipes, which are blown, on pressing a button, by causing air to pass through the pipes, each of which gives the tone of one of the strings, G, D, A, or E. The operator then tunes the violin in unison with the pitch pipes.

Violinists know that it is hard to keep a violin in tune. But few appreciate that this is due to the sweat of the player's fingers, which makes the strings stretch. Strings on instruments placed in the violin player do not need much tuning. Silk E strings have been found to last two months, and have stayed in tune two weeks without attention.

The tempo is varied by means of a friction pinion which is moved radially on the face of a large driving wheel. This device for varying the tempo enables the simulation of rubato passages when it is operated by a skilled musician.

Instruments of the violin family have four strings, each with a range of two octaves. The violin player enables each string to be treated, at will, as a separate violin, as each bow is controlled by a separate mechanism. In the model shown, the higher portions of the G and D strings are not utilized, but they can be by supplying extra fingers. Notes on a violin are found sometimes on each of the four strings. For instance, the G above the treble staff may be struck on all the strings; so that if a trill were being performed on that note on one string, an arpeggio passage containing the

Side View of the Player Casing Opened to Show Ducts.

AN AUTOMATIC VIOLIN PLAYER.

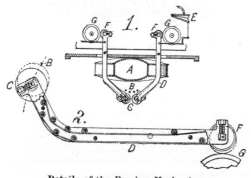

Details of the Bowing Mechanism.

same note could be produced on the other strings. Of course, no human player could do that. It is possible for the player to render a solo part, with a cello accompaniment on the bass strings, or a solo with two accompanying violin parts, all on one violin. The possibilities for combinations of orchestral effect, therefore, are seen to be many.

Harmonics are produced by the application of just enough pressure to a finger to make it rest lightly in the string sounded, thus imitating the action of the human finger. Trills are produced with striking clearness by providing a series of small perforations in the music roll. The same principle applied to the bow pneumatics produces springing bow and flying staccato.

In making the first music rolls for the player, the inventor, Prof. Wauters, of Binghamton, N. Y., had many technical details to solve. Instruments having fixed strings or tones are played on the tempered scale. But violins play on the untempered chromatic scale, and therefore it was necessary for Prof. Wauters to lay the groundwork for producing music rolls for instruments of that character.

Gramo=Polyphon
No. 105 G.P.

As related on page 287, the challenge presented by the introduction of the phonograph, particularly Berliner's disc-playing gramophone, was initially met fairly and squarely by the musical box industry. It foresaw a market for both instruments and so combined them into a joint machine such as the Polygraphon, described in the 1902 English catalogue as the Gramo-Polyphon and seen here. Regina, Mermod and others made similar dual devices but all were destined for a short life in the face of the rapid strides of the gramophone.

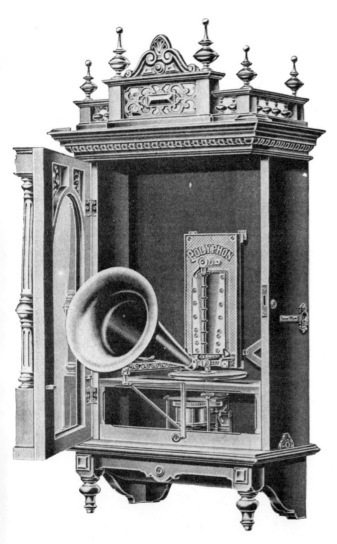

No. 105 **G.P.**—Size 60 × 32 × 16½ ins. : 159 Notes, in walnut. Tunes. 25 ins diameter.

Price including 6 Tunes - - **£31 10 0**

Extra Tunes - - - - - - -	6/- each.
Records 7 in - - - - - -	2/- ,,
Records, 9 in. or 10 in. - - - - -	4/- ,,

Latest Novelty in Automatons. For " Flat Box " Style see page 7.

Gramo=Polyphon.

No. 43. G. P.

Including 6 Polyphon tunes, 15¾ in. dia. - £15 0 0

Extra Tunes - - - - - -	2/6 each
Records, 7 in. - - - - - -	2/- ,,
,, 9 in. or 10 in. - - - - -	4/- ,,

There is no need to say anything with reference to the quality and perfection of the Polyphon Musical Boxes, same being now well introduced all the world over; and as to working of the Disc Talking Machine in connection with the Polyphon we can only say that the idea of combining the two is carried out very well indeed, and the reproduction of sound is **clear, loud, and distinct.**

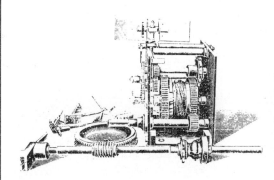
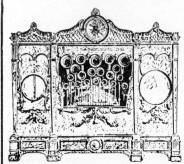
Hydraulic power was used to drive the ancient organs (*see Chapter 1*). In 1894, Bolgiano's No. 2 Water Motor was advertised as suitable for Church Organs (*Scientific American*, 12 May 1894). Specialists capable of making standard parts for orchestrions at the beginning of this century included Karl Ganter (*above*). Among the many American band organ makers, North Tonawanda (*left*) was established in 1893 and produced instruments such as the Tonophone barrel piano for Wurlitzer.

THE WURLITZER PIANORCHESTRA

Provides Musical Entertainment of the Cabaret Variety
at a Fraction of the Cost

Wurlitzer handled the products of a number of makers, not just in America. The PianOrchestra (*left*) was made by Philipps in Frankfurt and was one of a large number of orchestrions made by this company which Wurlitzer listed in his catalogue *c.* 1910. The Geneva-based Langdorff company is best known for its good quality cylinder musical boxes. What is less well known is that like another Swiss musical box maker, Heller of Berne, they also made orchestrions (*below*).

On page 135 is an illustration of a Polyphon mechanism in a piano. The Symphonion company produced a similar device (*left*). The musical mechanism was in no way mechanically connected to the piano and the mechanisms were thus independent. Note also, in this 1909 announcement, the Symphoniola gramophone. *The Windsor Magazine* for December 1905, carried the notice (*below*) concerning Nicole Frères' entry into the gramophone record business.

SYMPHONION

Schatullen.   Automaten.

Musikwerke

mit auswechselbaren Stahlnotenscheiben.

Sprechapparate

25 verschiedene Modelle
in jeder beliebigen Ausstattung vom
Einfachsten bis zum Elegantesten.

Gleichmäßig und ruhig laufende **Werke**
bester Konstruktion.

Geschmackvolle **Gehäuse** in jeder Holz-
und Stilart.

In wirkungsvollen Farbenzusammen-
stellungen lackierte **Blumentrichter.**

Schalldosen unübertroffen an Tonfülle
und Klangschönheit.

Symphonion-Doppelnadel-Schalldosen
für Saphir- und Stahlnadeln eingerichtet,
daher ohne weiteres für beide Platten-
arten verwendbar.

SYMPHONION-PIANO Nr. 83 — elektrisch-pneumatisch spielbar.

:: Symphonion- ::
Standautomat Nr. VI E
mit Gloria - Waldhorn - Trichter.

Orchestrions

für **Gewichtsaufzug** oder **elektr. Antrieb**
mit Mandolinen-, Xylophon- und Schlagzeug-Begleitung.

Verschiedenartige wirkungsvolle Lichteffekte

Elektrisch - pneumatisch spielbare Klaviere

Selbsttätige Modulation und ausdrucksvolle Nuancierung.

—— Überaus reicher natürlicher Anschlag. ——

- Symphoniola -

Tretklavier mit eingebautem Spielapparat.

Weitere hochwichtige Neuheiten befinden sich ständig in Ausarbeitung.
Wegen Katalogen und Prospekten usw. wende man sich an die

Symphonionfabrik Aktiengesellschaft,
Leipzig-Gohlis.

SAMPLE FREE

NICOLE DUPLEX·RECORDS

A REVOLUTION IN RECORDS.

Every disc talking-machine user should send at once for a FREE SAMPLE of the splendid Nicole Duplex Record. In writing send Three Stamps for cost of postage, packing, &c. Nicole Duplex Records are 3/6 each, 10-in. Records, and 1/6 each, 7-in. Records. But there is a Superb Record on each side, which makes them nearly half as cheap again as other Records—two Records for the price of one.

Write for Free Sample to NICOLE FRÈRES, Ltd. (Dept. 2), 21, Ely Place, Holborn, E.C.

We return to the piano player for this interesting and glowing description of another instrument which enjoyed but brief popularity. The Massachusetts Organ Company of Boston, as well as making organettes of the usual kind, made mouth-blown, paper-roll-playing reed instruments as well. One was called the Phonographic Cornet.

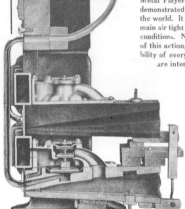

Few player piano manufacturers actually made their own player actions. One popular type fitted in many pianos was the Higel made in Toronto, Canada. Malcolm provided complete instruments or just the actions. Largest makers of piano rolls in England were the Perforated Music Co. All was not well in the industry in 1915 as seen left. The story of this company and the fire which put it out of business is told in *Player Piano*.

Moses of Ste-Croix

MANY PEOPLE wonder how it was possible that precision industries—especially watch-making—became established in a region so far off the beaten track as the Swiss Jura. The people of Ste-Croix themselves are the first to be surprised at the growth of these industries.

Financial backing and the proper technical equipment are not enough to explain the very high standard of precision attained. What was, and still is required is perseverence, a long tradition and continuity in ideas—in other words, hard-headed realists.

The traveller who arrives in Ste-Croix (not an easy place to get to) is usually surprised at the number of factories he finds there. These factories are, though, the logical extension of the artisan tradition that had its beginning two hundred years ago, when Ste-Croix lived in a way altogether different from today. Two of the most important of the former industries of Ste-Croix were the iron workings and lace-manufacture. The reputation of products manufactured from the ore of the mines around Ste-Croix, was already widespread as far back as the 16th century.

The decline of the lace industry began with the introduction of the machine, and the progress in the watch-making industry: the invention and development of music boxes finished it off.

Musical boxes

Moses Paillard presided at that time over the destiny of a tiny family music-box concern. He was succeeded by a line of other, equally active and enterprising managers —such as Ernest Paillard and his brother-in-law Eugene Thorens—who played a very important part in the life of the village which at this time numbered about 3,500 people. Orders for music-boxes began to flood in: foreign countries were particularly interested in them. The most important outlets were England, the United States, Germany, France and Austria.

Increasing demand brought about increased production and, accordingly, a gradual change in the manufacturing methods: as the family workshops were no longer in step with the industry's needs, Paillard opened the doors of their first real factory in 1875—while this could certainly not be compared to a modern factory, it was then a revolution in the music-box industry. When the small family enterprises disappeared and the effects of division of labour made themselves felt, there was greater and greater recourse to the machine. Methods and equipment evolved with the need for greater production, for it was necessary to find new bases from which to fight ever growing competition.

Through all those changes, however, the foundations of this ever-growing, modern firm remain the same: manual skill, precision, and the good team work which so characterises the Jurassians.

As in other industries, progress came to that of music-box manufacturing. Quite early on, the House of Paillard was making large music-boxes called "cartels" that could play from 3 to 72 tunes. The music-box in general was progressively modified, and in 1878 interchangeable cylinders were developed, which considerably increased sales. Everyone could afford a music-box in those days; they could be bought at any price from 85 centimes (about 10 shillings of today's money) to 10,000—Swiss francs about £2,850 now)—and up.

Gramophone

But already then, farseeing managers had understood the advantages local industry could find in new devices, for their manufacture could be carried on concurrently with that of music-boxes. One of them—Ernest Paillard—began at once methodically to make studies and enquiries in that direction. In 1898 our firm brought out the Echophone, a small gramophone with different size cylinders able to record or reproduce all kinds of songs, musical pieces and even monologues.

Having been prudent in all their projects, the members of the large Paillard family fully intended to make sure of the future of their enterprise by the wise introduction of new products whenever the market should indicate it.

Foreseeing the future in amateur cinematography, Paillard concentrated its efforts in research into that line. At the beginning of the 30's Paillard put on the market simultaneously a 16-mm. projector and camera. A few years later, in 1936, the Paillard-Bolex H16 camera, made its appearance on the market. Paillard can claim, not without pride, that they created a first-class instrument, which allows the amateur to exploit almost all the possibilities offered by the 16 mm. size film.

The first factory to produce musical boxes was built by Paillard and, though the company has changed direction several times, its name is preserved to this day and is renowned in cinematography. The manuscript for this book is being typed on a Paillard typewriter. In 1968, one of the Paillard-Bolex house magazines looked back at the company's past achievements in musical boxes. Overleaf is a detailed breakdown of the components for the 24½ inch Polyphon, and facing that is an article on the unsatisfactory state of music roll libraries in 1919.

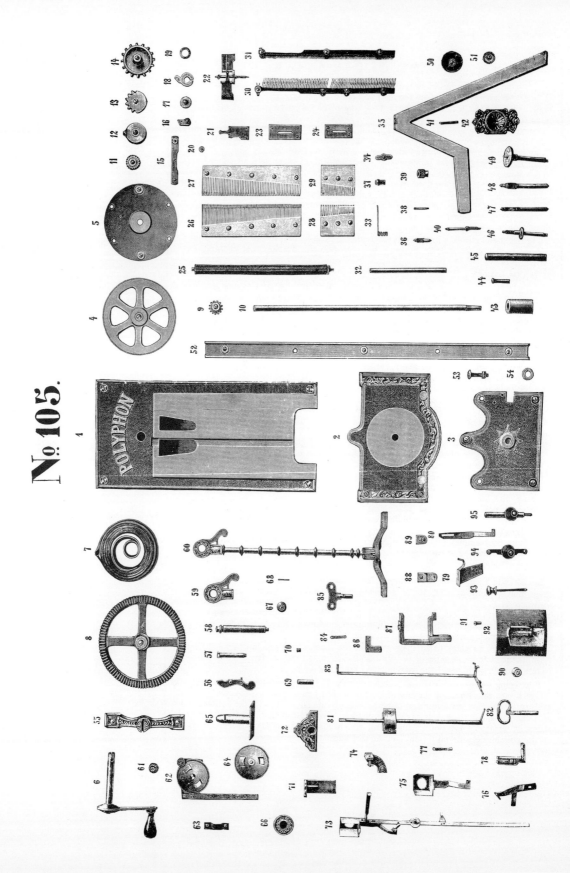

No. 105.

Music Rolls Libraries.

FOR sheer ineptitude, unnecessary expenses, inefficiency, waste, extravagance, general muddle and universal dissatisfaction, there is probably nothing to compare, in any section of the pianoforte trade, with the present rotten methods employed in the running of the music rolls libraries. A couple of decades ago this vital point, in connection with the development of the player and player-piano, loomed darkly in the future ; to-day the whole question is nothing less than a gross scandal and, in important respects, a fraud on the public. Take any town, even the largest, a town of enormous potentialities for the player-piano industry, like, say, Birmingham ; what do we find? A dozen firms of repute, of whom perhaps eight are in the front rank. Each professes to run its own library—or rather *dual* library, for both 65 *and* 88 note rolls have to be stocked. Thus we get at least eight firms running, and running most atrociously, sixteen libraries.

This means, in sequence, sixteen assistants at least : sixteen rooms for storage, sixteen ledgers, and so to do ; problems, every day and everywhere, innumerable as to collection and delivery of rolls. Changes innumerable from one library to another by dissatisfied customers, who find out in turn each library a ghastly failure. No responsible management, incompetent buying, apologies galore without any improved service, often 40 per cent. of rolls delivered faulty. The proprietors, in turn, find the library business an unmitigated nuisance, an expense, and *inter alia,* owing to want of centralisation, music dealers can rarely get an assistant to remain long in the library department. Chances of promotion and increased pay being practically negligible.

Now, the key to the problem is, undoubtedly, centralisation. Turn all the libraries, for example, in Birmingham, into one ; take ample premises—capable of expansion that is—in some central position, not by any means necessarily in a main street. Secure a staff sufficiently large to deal with the rolls on a good, well planned system. Run on a sufficiently comprehensive scale, it should be possible to finance a good first-class man as manager at, say, £400 per annum ; assistants under him in charge of the receiving room, to test all rolls returned as they come in, and before being re-placed on the racks ; a staff to advise customers, a checking hand, with other details considered on their merits.

Take buying : dozens of libraries are actually being run to-day by girl assistants, whose sympathies are either entirely musical comedy or ragtime. It is simply an insult to ask any cultured musician to join such libraries, classics being really unobtainable. On the other hand, dealers have everywhere sold very expensive player-pianos, well-knowing that their own library is a delusion and a snare ; thousands of rolls their own customers would care for (and ask for) possibly lying idle on the shelves of a competitor. Another dealer will take a remarkably good profit on a sale, and leave his *unsuccessful* competitor (the irony of it !) to incur the risk *and loss* in connection with running the library.

One can to-day assert, with confidence, that the player-piano industry stinks in the nostrils of large numbers of wealthy people in all directions ; very largely through avoidable mismanagement of the library question. In no town is delivery guaranteed : whereas, given centralisation a suitable collecting and distributing van would serve each district in turn, the fact and dates would be advertised, and the stigma removed from dealers of bungling this important detail in connection with the advance of their business.

A certain firm may advertise 25,000 rolls in its library ; but half are 65 note, which leaves 12,500. Of these about 10 per cent. at least are faulty (some libraries have as much as 25 per cent. faulty rolls) and two-thirds of the residue are out on loan, and even this is a favourable estimate. And, those joining, have to either fetch rolls themselves or *wait weeks* until the piano van is going "somewhere near " (ye gods!). By parcel post carriages become a serious item.

To sum up : so long as dealers in *every* town regard the library question, individually and collectively, as a d——d nuisance (this is their attitude) no improvement is likely to be made.

On the other hand, subscribers, with scarcely an exception, would willingly double their rates of pay *if only* a first-class library were at their disposal, with guaranteed free and prompt collection in their respective districts. The present writer has for years discussed this part, of finance, with large numbers of grievously dissatisfied customers, and can speak with some authority.

Of course, centralisation still leaves difficulties to be surmounted. Take the public book free libraries : with only *one* book returned weekly, perhaps. The indexes, cross indexes, dockets, cards, etc. ; how much more complicated things are in the music rolls library, with very often 36 rolls returned at a time, and reasonable precautions required not to send, in return, perhaps a dozen rolls the customer sent back a few weeks ago !

It would have to be made clear that no touting or canvassing (for exchanging player-pianos) was a stipulation on the part of the staff. With this fact staring subscribers in the face, both in the prospectus, and *via* framed notices on the walls, no dealer would have any fear of unfair dealing, and would automatically recommend each and every purchaser of a player-piano to the library. In fact, there should be no other library but this one to send customers to. Run on a big scale, with a big catalogue, competent management, well organised, success would never be in doubt. Towns at least fifty miles round Birmingham, for example, could and would be served, and probably further a-field as well.　　　　　P. P.

TIPPOO'S TIGER.

The engraving at the end of this article is an accurate representation of a strange toy or plaything, supposed to have been constructed for the amusement of Tippoo Sultan, sovereign of the Mysore, by some European artist at his court. It was found in the palace at Seringapatam after Tippoo's defeat and death, in 1799, in an apartment appropriated to the reception of musical instruments, and was presented to the museum of the East India Company by the army. It represents a tiger in the act of tearing to pieces a prostrate soldier,—intended for an Englishman. The tusks of the animal have just penetrated the collar-bone of the soldier, who is lying on his back, stiff as a Dutch doll, with the tiger standing upon him; the fore-paws resting on his chest, and the hind-paws on his thighs. The representation is altogether of the most primitive description, as the engraving will testify. The attitude of the tiger is perhaps not so bad, but that of the man is very ludicrous: the left hand is placed on his mouth,—the right arm, in soldierly attitude, straight down by his side;—the legs are stiff, and the feet, with well-blacked shoes and painted-yellow buckles, are turned out as though upon drill. The dress of this figure is equally droll with his attitude. He has a round black hat, with a low crown, and broad brim. His coat is scarlet, adorned with large roses, and two gilded epaulettes;—his breeches are green, and his stockings yellow.

But the great object for which this group was constructed, and the part which is said to have given the greatest delight to its royal owner, was the machinery which it contained. This, though not of nice workmanship, is simple and ingenious in contrivance. The handle seen on the animal's shoulder turns a spindle and crank within the body; to this crank is fastened a wire, which rises and falls by turning the crank: the wire passes down from the tiger between his fore-paws into the man's chest, where it works a pair of bellows, which forces the air through a pipe with a sort of whistle, terminating in the man's mouth. The pipe is covered by the man's hand; but at the moment when, by the action of the crank, the air is forced through the pipe, a string leading from the bellows pulls a small lever connected with the arm, which works on a hinge at the elbow; the arm rises in a manner which the artist intended to show supplication; the hand is lifted from the mouth, and a cry is heard. The cry is repeated as often as the handle is turned; and while this process is going on, an endless screw on the shaft turns a worm-wheel slowly round, which is furnished with four levers or wipers; each of these levers alternately lifts up another and larger pair of bellows in the head of the tiger. When by the action of one of these four levers the bellows are lifted up to their full height, the lever, in continuing to turn, passes by the bellows, and the upper board being loaded with a large piece of lead, falls down on a sudden and forces the air violently through two loud-toned pipes, terminating in the animal's mouth, and differing by the interval of a fifth. This produces a harsh growl. The man in the meantime continues his screaming or whistling, and, after a dozen cries, the growl is repeated. Such is the delectable nature of the music which pleased Tippoo so much, that he is said to have passed hours in his music-room with an attendant turning the handle of the machine. The situation of the parties was typical of the subjection of England to the Khodadad[*], and the representation consoled him with a show of power whenever his arms were unsuccessful.

But we will charitably hope that this was not the sole amusement derived by Tippoo from this instrument. On opening a door in the side of the tiger, a row of keys may be seen just withinside; although awkwardly placed, and not very easily come at, they may be played upon in a clumsy way, and may be made to produce music. There are eighteen of these keys, each differing from the next by the interval of a semitone: the part touched by the finger is made of ivory; it is not flat as the keys of a pianoforte, but rounded like a stud or button. They are arranged with the bass to the left and the treble to the right, as in our instruments; but the semitones are all in one even line, which renders it awkward in the hands of one of our performers. Behind the keys are two rows of copper pipes, in unison with each other, two unisons being played by each key: either or both rows of pipes may be made silent by drawing out one or two stops placed by the tiger's tail, contrary in this respect to our organs, which are made silent by pushing the stops in. Behind the pipes, on the further side of the tiger, are placed the large bellows which supply this part of the instrument with wind. These are larger than either pair before mentioned;—they are blown by means of a piece of string coming out of the animal's shoulder, near the handle, and may be worked by an assistant.

This part of the machinery appears to be quite unconnected with the growling and screaming portion of the instrument, and would seem to be intended merely to fill up a vacant space in the tiger's body, without reference to the original destination of the machine, as a symbol of abhorrence to Europeans. The bellows cannot be worked by turning the handle; nor, if that were possible, could the instrument be played upon while they were so worked, for the door through which the hand is admitted to touch the keys must be kept shut or the handle will not turn round. The string coming out of the shoulder, though it appears at first to be a mere temporary substitute for some other and more mechanical means of doing the work, is in fact a part of the original contrivance, as will appear on a close inspection. By pulling this string pretty briskly, so as to keep the bellows distended, a tune may be played in a clumsy way, even now, although the machine is somewhat out of order. The pipes are not

[*] **Gift of God; the name by which Tippoo designated his dominions.**

ill made, and they are tolerably in tune; but their tone is loud and harsh, not unlike the principal stop of the organ. It has been stated that the instrument was originally played like a street-organ; but, except the above-mentioned growling and screaming, this is not the case. There is no barrel, nor any means by which a barrel could let air into the pipes if there were one. The mistake undoubtedly arose from the look of the handle and pipes, which bear a considerable resemblance to those of a barrel-organ. The case for this curious piece of music is the tiger's body, which is constructed of thin hard wood, well adapted for giving effect to the harsh tones produced. The body of the tiger is perforated in several places to let out the sound, and the whole of the upper part may be taken away by removing a few screws. The man is formed all of wood, like the tiger, but, being the base of the group, it is not of so light a structure; it is put together in a clumsy way, such as a common carpenter would not like to acknowledge. The tiger is merely put upon it, and secured by common screws, with their heads sticking out of the animal's paws. So rude is the construction of the whole machine, that it has been thought to be much older than the age of Tippoo, and that in fact it was made in the seventeenth century for some sovereign of the southern part of the peninsula when the Dutch were making inroads upon them. The appearance of the soldier is certainly much more like that of a Dutchman of the seventeenth century than of an Englishman at the end of the eighteenth. In this case Tippoo would only have the credit of adopting the invention ready made, instead of that of originating the barbarous idea: at all events it appears certain that he was in the habit of enjoying the working of the machine.

Whether made for Tippoo himself or for some other Indian potentate a century and a half earlier, it would be difficult to convey a more lively impression of the mingled ferocity and childish want of taste so characteristic of the majority of Asiatic princes than will be communicated at once by an inspection of this truly barbarous piece of music.

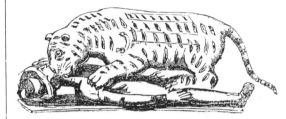

[Tippoo's Tiger.]

This article appeared in *The Penny Magazine* for 15 August 1835. It is sufficiently detailed to leave little doubt that it was written by somebody who had carried out a fairly detailed technical examination of the Tiger. This interesting relic, depicted below in its old situation in East India House (visible on table at left), is now in London's Victoria and Albert Museum where, in 1971, the present author was called in to advise on its restoration. The mechanism of the Tiger today

is markedly different from that detailed above and during a recorded rebuild in 1888 by Henry Willis, it appears that the growl mechanism, the man's scream and the blowing of the main bellows were all united to the turning of the handle. There are other components of the organ which are now not original and there is no precise manner in which the original can be visualised. Nevertheless, the instrument is now once more in working order and can be heard as it was in Seringapatam before 1799. (Picture, left, from *London Pictorially Illustrated* by Chas. Knight, 1851).

A Suitable Motor Van for Dealers.

We are indebted to Mr. G. S. Whiting, North-ampton, for the particulars relative to the delivery-van illustrated on this page, and also for the photo-graphs.—EDITOR.

To anyone requiring a useful car for ordinary deliveries we recommend a van built on the lines as shown by this car.

In our opinion it is better to do two journeys occasionally, when necessary, rather than carry the

READY TO LOAD.

extra weight about that would be necessary in a car large enough to carry two pianos at the same time, while only required in the great majority of journeys to carry one piano only.

We consider the two chief advantages of a car built on the lines of this are the Sliding Shutters instead of doors, and the loading and unloading at the side instead of at the back. The rolling

LOADING.

shutters are easily raised and lowered : never out of their place, and both quick and convenient to manipulate. Loading up from the side also gives other advantages, viz. :—You get the advantage usually of the height of the kerbstone in lifting your piano into the van after placing it on your

skeleton frame. You also are enabled in dirty or snowy conditions to avoid working in the road-way by being able to lower your instrument

" ALL RIGHT."

directly on to the pathway and so avoid the often very unsatisfactory condition of the roads.

Use pneumatic wheels—do not fail to carry a spare—have your jack, pump, and other necessary tools also with you, in a most convenient and

" RIGHT AWAY."

accessible place. Learn to know your car and study its requirements and you will find this means of transit very easy and comparatively inexpensive from a business point of view.

———

Selling a piano was one thing; delivering it another! The time-proven horse and cart was being superseded by the motor carriage and the pages of *The Pianomaker* for 1919 were reflecting experiences of various dealers with this new form of transport.

APPENDIX

Names of Instruments
and their Makers

VERY often, one will find a mechanical musical instrument bearing a trade name, with no other indication as to its manufacturer or approximate date. This Appendix sets out to list those names which have been applied over the years to different types of instrument, and states the manufacturer of that instrument. Only the barest information is provided here in order that the inquirer shall be able to find out who made his particular piece. For more details of the specific manufacturer, he is advised to consult the other works in this series which deal specifically with musical boxes, player pianos and mechanical organs. Where a date is provided, the *floruit* is that of the specific instrument and not necessarily either that of the manufacturer or implying that the established dates of the maker remain unknown. For example, Polyphonmusikwerke was established in 1886 and remained in business until the late 1920s. That company's Rossini piano-orchestrion was introduced somewhere about 1909, so the entry for the name Rossini bears a *floruit* date of 1909. A word shown in capital letters indicates that a further reference is to be found under that word elsewhere in this listing.

This is the first time that a listing of this type has ever been attempted. Like all retrospective listings, it cannot hope to be comprehensive. It lists, for example, only some of the more popular player pianos. Nevertheless it does provide much sought-after information on the wide variety of instruments which the collector may be fortunate enough to find today.

ACKOTIST. Player piano mechanism fitted in Pianora player pianos by the Pianora Company, 133 West 24th Street, New York, USA, fl. 1909.

ADLER. Disc-playing musical box made in 1900 by J. H. Zimmermann of Leipzig.

ADMIRAL. Orchestrion made by Imhof & Mukle, Vöhrenbach.

AEOLIAN. Player pianos and organs by the Aeolian Corporation, New York, London, etc.

AEOLIAN. Player reed organ marketed in London by Geo. Whight and made in USA by the Aeolian Co., fl. 1898.

AEOLION MUSIK AUTOMAT. A 'flute orchestrion' made by Hupfeld in Leipzig producing 'deep sonorous organ like tone' (sic) from 100 pipes played by perforated paper music.

AIDA. Orchestrion organ by Holzweissig Nachfolger in Leipzig, fl. 1909.

AIDA. Mechanical piano orchestrion made by Popper, Leipzig.

AIR-CALIO. Calliope made by Artizan in the United States.

AIRMATIC. Player piano apparatus made in London by the Simplex Piano Player Co.

AMABILE. Large disc-playing reed organ made in Gera by Armin Liebmann, fl. 1909.

AMERICAN ORGUINETTE, THE. Organette made by Mechanical Orguinette Co. of New York.

AMOBEAN. Cylinder musical box made by Paillard, Ste Croix, Switzerland.

AMORETTE. Disc-playing organette made in Leipzig by Leipziger Musikwerke Euphonika.

AMPHION. Player piano made in Elbridge, USA, by the Amphion Piano Player Co.

AMPICO. Reproducing piano made by the American Piano Corporation of New York.

ANGELUS. Player piano made by Wilcox & White Co., Meriden, USA and Sir Herbert Marshall in London.

ANGELUS. Reproducing piano made by Hallett & Davis Piano Co., New York.

ANIMOCHORD. Piano orchestrion made by Popper in Leipzig, fl. 1908.

ANTIPHONEL. A keyboard player made by Alexander Debain of Paris for pianos, harmoniums and organs; fl. 1862 and operated by wooden planchettes. Also produced as a complete piano with finger action and separate mechanical action.

APOLLINO. A concert organ built c. 1819 by a Mr Job Plimpton of Medway, Mass., USA. No further details.

APOLLO, APOLLO-GRAND, APOLOETTE. Names of player pianos made in the USA by Melville Clark Piano Co.

APOLLO. Piano-orchestrion made by the Apollo Musikwerke Max Espenhain & Co.

APOLLO. Orchestrion made in Prague by Fuchs, fl. 1909.

APOLLONICON. Famous concert organ made in 1817 by Flight & Robson in London. Could be played manually by five performers at once, or could perform mechanically from three pinned barrels. Dismantled. Also organ made by Bevington for the Colosseum in Regents Park, 1848, of the same name. Fate unknown.

APOLLONION. A concert organ made by an instrument-maker named Roeller of Hesse-Darmstadt which had 'two rows of keys which might be played as a pianoforte and as a chamber organ, combined at the same time with a musical automaton'. Early nineteenth century.

ARBURO. Roll-playing café organs made currently by Arthur Bursens & F. de Groof in Antwerp, Belgium.

ARCOPHON. Orchestrion made in Leipzig by Popper, fl. 1909.

ARIEL. English-made 20 note organette playing 5½ inch paper music. Same as SERAPHONE.

ARIOPHON. Orchestrion made in Leipzig by Dienst, fl. 1909.

ARIOSA. Metal ring-playing organette made in Leipzig by Musikwerke Phoenix in three sizes—16-note Intona; 18- or 36-note Ariosa and the 18-note Sonora-Ariosa. Sold in Prague by Samal Frères.

ARISTON. Organette made initially by the Ehrlich Brothers and later (1904) by their successors, Neue Leipziger Musikwerke Buff-Hedinger. Several sizes ranging from 16 notes (8⅜ inch disc) upwards. Discs of card and some in zinc. Most common size 24 note 13 inch card discs.

ARISTONETTE, ARISTON. Organettes made by Leipziger Musikwerke Paul Ehrlich, fl. 1900.

ARISTOS. Player piano made in England by Bansell & Sons, London.

ARMINIA. Musical automatons made in Gera (Reuss-Gera), Germany, by Armin Liebmann, fl. 1908.

ARNO. Small comb-playing musical box played from strips of perforated card and made by Arno and Paillard.

ARTIST. Player piano made by Bell Piano & Organ Co. of Guelph (USA) and London.

ATLAS. Disc-playing organette by Lecompte & Co., Paris (later Ch. & Jacques Ullmann). Discs are interchangeable with those of AMORETTE (q.v.).

ATLANTIC. Barrel orchestrions made in Leipzig by Hupfeld.

AUREPHONE. Organette made c. 1890 by the Massachusetts Organ Co.

AUROMATIC ORGAN. Same as DULCIPHONE (q.v.).

AURORA. Orchestrions made in Leipzig by Popper.

AUSTRIA. Piano orchestrion made in Leipzig by Popper.

AUTO-ACCORDEON. Organette playing metal musicsheets and made in Gera by Armin Liebmann, fl. 1903.

AUTO-MANUAL. Player piano made by the Bacon Piano Co. of New York, fl. 1909.

AUTO-ORCHESTRA. Pneumatic piano orchestrion, coin-operated and electrically driven, made by Berry-Wood Piano Player Co. of Kansas, c. 1910.

AUTO-ORGAN. London-made player reed organ made in 1900 by Auto-Organ Co. London agents: Wallis Ltd.

AUTOFORDE. Player piano made in New York by Hardman, Peck & Co.

AUTOGRAND. Player piano made by Kastner in London.

AUTOHARMONICON. Self-acting pianoforte shown at the Great Room, Spring Garden, London, early nineteenth century.

AUTOLECTRA. Electrically-operated player piano made in New York by the Auto-Electric Piano Co., fl. 1909.

AUTOLIAN. London-made player piano sold by Munt Brothers Limited, fl. 1909.

AUTOLYON. Player piano made c. 1910 by L. G. Lyon, 116 Camberwell Road, London, S.E.

AUTOMATIC CABINET ORGAN. Large organette made c. 1890 by Massachusetts Organ Co.

AUTOMATIC VIRTUOSO. Early version of VIOLANO-VIRTUOSO (q.v.) without piano.

AUTOPHONE. 22-note organette made by the Autophone Co. of Ithaca, New York, c. 1885.

AUTOPHONE. Instrument invented by Claude Felix Seytre of Lyons, France, in 1842 operated by Jacquard-system cardboard music.

AUTOPIANO. Player piano made in New York by the Autopiano Co. and in London by Kastner.

AUTOPIANISTE. Mechanical pianos made by Thièble at Ruyaulcourt, France, fl. 1909.

AUTOTONE. Player piano made by Hardman, Peck & Co. of New York, fl. 1909.

BADENIA. Orchestrions made in Vöhrenbach by Imhof & Mukle, fl. 1909.

BAJAZZO. Musical automata made in Leipzig by Popper, fl. 1909. Name also used by Holzweissig.

BANJO. Self-playing banjo made by Eastern Specialty Co., Cambridgeport, USA, fl. 1903.

BANJORCHESTRA. Electric, coin-freed orchestrion made in New York by Engelhardt Piano Co.

BASKANION. Organette made in Leipziger Musikwerke Paul Ehrlich which played discs and was similar to Ariston.

BAUERN. Musical automaton made in Leipzig by Ehrlich, fl. 1909.

BELLISORE. Orchestrions made in Altona-Ottensen (Hamburg) by Lüneburg & Co.

BELLOLIAN. Player attachment for reed organs made in 1901 by Bell Organ & Piano Company, London (subsidiary of US company).

BELLONEON. Automatic trumpeter made for the King of Prussia by Freidrich Kaufmann in 1805.

BELLS IN VUE or BELLS IN SIGHT. Legend found on tune sheets of Paillard cylinder musical boxes fitted with bells, often in conjunction with names COLUMBIA and EXCELSIOR.

BETHLEHEM CRIB. Beautiful automaton with organ made between 1589 and 1602 by Hans Schlottheim, Augsburg.

BIANCA. Orchestrions made in Leipzig by Popper, fl. 1909.

BIJOU. Musical automata made in Ste Croix by Thorens, fl. 1909.

BIJOU ORCHESTRONE. Organette produced by Merritt Gally in Worcester, Massachusetts, in 1886. Later became Munroe Organ Reed Co.

BOHEMIAN HARMONICON. Orchestrion made in Bohemia and sold by Harris, Heeley & Co. of High Holborn (London) and Birmingham, mid-nineteenth century.

BOUTEILLOPHONE. A percussion attachment fitted to street and other show organs which comprises sixteen glass bottles filled to pitch with, supposedly, alcohol and struck by pneumatically-operated hammers. Made by A. Gasparini of Paris.

BRABO. Piano orchestrion made by Webe, Waldkirch.

BRAUMULLER. Player pianos made c. 1909 by the Braumuller Piano Co. of New York.

BRAVISSIMO. Orchestrions made by Popper in Leipzig, fl. 1909.

BRISGOVIA. Piano orchestrion made by Welte of Freiburg, fl. 1909.

BRITANNIA. Disc-playing musical box made in Ste Croix by B. H. Abrahams.

CABINETTO. Organette made by Massachusetts Organ Co. Same mechanism as TOURNAPHONE (q.v.)

CAHILL. Automatic musical instruments made in Holyoke, USA by the Cahill Electric Music Co., fl. 1909.

CALAME. Player piano made by Robert V. Calame of Salto Oriental, Uruguay, fl. 1909.

CALLIAPHONE. Calliope made by Tangley of Iowa in the United States and worked by compressed air, fl. 1925.

CALLIOPE. Disc-playing musical box same as KALLIOPE but made for French market.

CAPELLA. Orchestrions made in Leipzig by Dienst, fl. 1909.

CAPITAL. 'Cuff'-playing musical box made by F. G. Otto & Sons of Jersey City.

CAPITOL JAZZ CONCERT ORCHESTRA. Same as MANDO-ORCHESTRA (q.v.).

CAPITOL SYMPHONY ORCHESTRA. Coin-freed piano-orchestrion made by the North Tonawanda Musical Instrument Works, New York.

CARILLON MIRA. Combined table model disc musical box and gramophone made 1905. See MIRA.

CARMEN. Mandolin orchestrions made in Leipzig by Popper, fl. 1909.

CARMINA. Piano orchestrion made by Popper, Leipzig.

CARTONIUM. Mechanical free-reed instrument patented 1861 by J. A. Teste of Nantes, France and played by perforated cardboard.

CECILIAN. Player pianos made in USA by the Farrand Organ Co. of Detroit.

CELESTA. Disc-playing musical box made in Berlin by Berliner Musikinstrumenten Fabrik, formerly Ch. F. Pietschmann & Söhne. Sole British agents Martin Hirsch, fl. 1885–1900.

CELESTE. Disc-playing musical box made by Heinrich Hermann of Bernau, Berlin, fl. 1903.

CELESTINA. Paper-roll-playing organette made by the American Orguinette Co. Same mechanism as the English SERAPHONE (q.v.). Rolls are 5½ inches wide and also play on MANDOLINA (q.v.).

CELESTINO. Automatic zither made in Altona, (Hamburg) by Lüneburg, fl. 1909.

CHOPIN. Orchestrions made in Freiburg by Welte & Söhne, fl. 1909.

CHORALION. Player piano made in Berlin by Goetze.

CHORDAULODION. Orchestrion built by Kaufmann in Dresden, 1815.

CHORDEPHON. Mechanical zither played by disc made in Leipzig by Fabrik Mech. Zithern 'Cordephon', fl. 1909. About 1910, this company was acquired by Weissbach, makers of the KOMET (q.v.).

CIRCE. Orchestrion made in Leipzig by Popper, fl. 1909.

CITOPLEX. Quick-change roll mechanism for Hupfeld electric player pianos.

CLARABELLA. Piano orchestrion made by Popper, Leipzig.

CLARENDON. Player pianos made by Haddorff Piano Co. of Rockford, Illinois.

CLARIONA. See REED PIPE CLARIONA.

CLARIOPHONE. Unusual organette made by Wm. Spaethe of Gera. Played from zinc tunesheets stamped with raised note projections and laid round a fixed barrel in the instrument.

CLAVIMONIUM. Combined piano and reed organ played by perforated rolls made for early cinema use by Hupfeld, Leipzig.

CLAVIOLA. New York-made player pianos by the Claviola Co. sold in London under Klinker & Co., fl. 1909. Also with same name is player piano by Stichel of Leipzig and Zwenkau.

CLEMENTI. Musical automatic instruments made in Hamburg by Gotz & Co., fl. 1909.

COELOPHONE. Organette playing book music invented by Claude Gavioli and made *c.* 1890 by Thibouville-Lamy of Paris.

COINOLA. Coin-freed electric pianos made by the Operators' Piano Company, Chicago.

COLONIA. Player piano by Colonia Player Piano Co. of London, 1909.

COLUMBIA. Cylinder music box made by Paillard, Ste Croix, fl. 1900.

COMMANDANT. Piano orchestra made by Imhof & Mukle, Vöhrenbach.

COMPONIUM. Pipe organ operated by two barrels and constructed in 1821 by Winkel in Amsterdam. Organ could extemporise and 'compose' music from a given theme.

CON AMORE. Piano-orchestrions made in Leipzig by Popper, fl. 1909.

CONCERT ROLLER ORGAN. Organette made by The Autophone Co., Ithaca, New York.

CONCERTAL MUSTEL. Range of large reed organs costing from 240 to 400 guineas. Made by Mustel of Paris and capable of manual or paper-roll playing.

CONCERTO. Very large disc-playing musical box made by Polyphon and Regina.

CONNOISSEUR. Player pianos, player reed organs and player pipe organs made in USA and distributed in UK by Murdoch, Murdoch & Co., London.

CONTINENTAL. Orchestrions made by Hofmann & Czerny of Vienna and sold by Peters of Leipzig, fl. 1909.

CORONA. An expression piano (semi-reproducing) made by Frankfurter Musikwerke-Fabrik, fl. 1909. Also mechanical musical instruments made by Sachs Musikinstrumente-Manufactur Schuster & Co. of Markneukirchen, fl. 1909.

CORONA. Self-changing disc-playing musical boxes made by Regina in New Jersey.

CORRECTOR. Piano orchestrion made by Imhof & Mukle, Vöhrenbach.

COTTAGE ORCHESTRION. Welte & Söhne of Freiburg, fl. 1909.

CREMONA. Early American electric piano made in Chicago by Marquette Piano Co.

CRITERION. Disc-playing musical box made in Jersey City by F. G. Otto & Sons. Name also used by deKleist in North Tonawander, USA.

CYLINDRICHORD. A mechanical instrument, believed to be stringed, made before 1852 by the organ builder John Courcell of London.

CYMBALOPHON. Automatic musical instrument made in Leipzig by Wilhelm Dietrich, fl. 1909.

DAIMONION. Clockwork piano made *c.* 1903 by Fabrik Leipziger Musikwerke (Ehrlich).

DANUBIA. Orchestrion made by Popper of Leipzig, fl. 1909.

DEA. Player piano made by Hupfeld.

DELILA. Piano orchestrion made by Popper, Leipzig.

DELPHIN. Piano-orchestrion made in Trautenau, Austria, by Albert Melnik, fl. 1909.

DIADEM. Orchestrions made in Leipzig by Popper, fl. 1909.

DIANA. 14-note organette made in Leipzig by Musikwerke Phoenix Schmidt, fl. 1909.

DIAPHON. Self-playing reed organ, probably by Kimball of USA, sold by Felvus Henn in Glasgow, fl. 1899.

DINORAH. Orchestrion made in Vöhrenbach by Imhof & Mukle, fl. 1909.

DIVA. Orchestrion made in Leipzig by Popper, fl. 1909.

DOLCINE. See DOLZINE.

DOLZINE. Organette made by Leipziger Musikwerke Euphonika in Leipzig, fl. 1909. See under MUSICAL DOLCINE.

DONAR. Military band orchestrion made by Welte, Freiburg.

DUCA. Expression player piano made in Frankfurt by Frankfurter Musikwerke J. D. Philipps & Söhne, fl. 1909.

DULCET. Trade mark of Barnett Samuel (London) musical boxes (large importers).

DULCIPHONE. Organette made for sewing-machine by Massachusetts Organ Co., *c.* 1890. See also REED PIPE CLARIONA.

DUO-ART. Reproducing piano made by The Aeolian Co., New York.

DUOPHONOLA. Pedal-electric reproducing piano made by Hupfeld in Leipzig.

DUPLEX. Musical automata produced *c.* 1902 by Metall-Industrie Schönebeck A.-G., Schönebeck, Saxony, Germany.

EDELWEISS. Musical boxes made in Ste Croix by Herman Thorens, early twentieth century.

ELDORADO. Barrel piano-orchestrions made in Leipzig by Sächsische Orchestrion-Fabrik F.O. Glass and distributed by Etzold & Popitz, fl. 1909.

ELECTRELLE. Player piano made in London by J. & J. Hopkinson.

ELECTRELLE. Electric player piano made by American Piano Co. In 1909, UK manufacture of the player action began in Manchester.

ELECTROVA. Electrically-operated, coin-freed pianos made by Jacob Doll & Sons of New York, fl. 1905–20.

ELITE. Orchestrion made by Gebruder Weber, Waldkirch.

EMPIRE. Automatic musical instruments including organette of this name made in Leipzig by the Neue Leipziger Musikwerke, fl. 1909.

EMPIRE ARISTON. See both EMPIRE and ARISTON.

EMPIRE. Orchestrion made by Dienst of Leipzig, fl. 1909.

EMPRESS. Disc-playing musical box made by Mermod Frères, Ste Croix. Same as MIRA (q.v.) but for Lyon & Healy, USA.

ENGLISH ORGANETTE. Made in Blackburn, Lancashire, by J. M. Draper.

ERATO. Orchestrions made by Gebr. Weber of Waldkirch, fl. 1909.

ERICA. Organette made in Gera by Ernst Erich Liebmann, fl. 1903.

ERIKA. Keyless piano playing endless music rolls made *c.* 1927 by Weber of Berlin.

EROICA. Orchestrions made in Leipzig by Popper, fl. 1909.

EROICA. Disc-playing musical box playing three discs and made in Leipzig by Symphonion.

EUPHONIA. Mechanical harmonica made *c.* 1909 by Leipziger Musikwerke 'Euphonika'.

EUPHONIKA. A large disc-playing orchestrion playing 48 reeds, 20 pipes and a 10-bell glockenspiel made by Euphonika Musikwerke, Leipzig, *c.* 1903.

EUPHONION. Disc musical box made in Leipzig by Leipziger Musikwerke Euphonika. 11 inch disc-size interchangeable with Polyphon.

EUTERPEON. Self-performing barrel organ playing two cylinders at once and made for the Great Exhibition of 1851 by Imhof & Mukle. Later exhibited in London by J. Kleyser at the Gothic Hall. Now in Birmingham Museum.

EXCELSIOR. Cylinder musical boxes made early twentieth century by Paillard, Ste Croix.

EXCELSIOR. Cylinder musical boxes made by Charles Ullmann, L'Auberson, Switzerland.

EXCELSIOR. The largest in the range of MONOPOL disc-playing musical boxes made by Paul Ehrlich & Co., in Leipzig. First made 1897.

EXCELSIOR. Piano-orchestrion made in Zittau, Germany, by A. E. Haupt, fl. 1903.

EXCELSIOR ORCHESTRION. Barrel piano made by Peters, Leipzig. Hand-cranked.

FAVORIT. Mechanical musical instruments including organette made by Heinrich Hermann of Bernau, near Berlin, fl. 1903.

FAVOURITE. Piano-orchestrion by Popper, Leipzig, hand-cranked, fl. 1909.

FELIX. Orchestrion by Popper, Leipzig, fl. 1909.

FIDELIO. Disc-playing musical boxes made in Berlin by Fidelio Musikwerke, fl. 1909.

FLEXOTONE-ELECTRELLE. See ELECTRELLE.

FORTE-PIANO. Type of cylinder musical box, usually having 2 combs, arranged to play loud and soft. Among best makers was Nicole Frères.

FORTUNA. Disc-playing musical boxes made by Jul. Heinr. Zimmermann of Leipzig.

FORTUNIO. Musical boxes made by Lentz in Leipzig (Mockau), fl. 1909.

FOTOPLAYER. Early cinema music player made in 1920s by American Photo Player Company of New York.

FRATIHYMNIA. Piano-orchestrion made in Berlin by Frati. In 1923, company was bought by J. D. Philipps & Söhne but continued business under Frati name.

FRATINOLA. Orchestion organ made in Berlin by Frati, fl. 1902.

FREDERICK. Player piano made by Frederick Piano Co. of New York, fl. 1909.

FRIBURGIA. Piano-orchestrion made in Freiburg by Welte & Söhne, fl. 1909.

GAMBRINUS. Musical automaton playing disc musical box made by Symphonion, fl. 1909.

GASONELLA. Automatic piano made by Fuchs of Prague, fl. 1909.

GATELY. Organette playing $8\frac{1}{16}$ inch wide paper rolls and made in USA by Gately Mfg. Co.

GAZELLE. Mechanical musical instruments made in Leipzig by Holzweissig Nachfolger, fl. 1909.

GEM. Roller organette made by Autophone Co., Ithaca, New York.

GEM ORGANETTA. Organette made by the Massachusetts Organ Co., *c.* 1885.

GERMANIA. Piano-orchestrion made by Weisser of Unterkirnach, fl. 1909.

GLADIATOR. Orchestrions made by Popper of Leipzig, fl. 1909.

GLADIATOR, LE. Book-playing mandolin sostenuto piano similar to PIANO MELODICO (q.v.) made in Paris by Ch. & J. Ullman.

GLORIA. Musical boxes made by Paillard in Ste Croix, early twentieth century.

GLORIA. Musical automata made by Wilhelm Spaethe of Gera, (Reuss-Gera), Germany, fl. 1909.

GLORIA. Disc musical boxes made by the Société Anonyme of Geneva, *c.* 1902. Name also used by Paillard & Cie for cylinder musical boxes.

GLORIOSA. Musical automata made by J. C. Eckhardt of Wirtemberg, Germany, fl. 1903.

GNOMEN. Musical automat made in Leipzig by Ehrlich, fl. 1903.

GOLIATH. Piano orchestrion made by Popper, Leipzig.

GRAMO-POLYPHON. See POLYGRAPHON.

GRAND ROLLER ORGAN. Larger version of CONCERT ROLLER ORGAN (q.v.).

GRAND THEATRE OF THE MUSES. Automaton clock made before 1729 by Christopher Pinchbeck in London.

GRANDEZZA. Piano orchestrion made by Weber, Waldkirch.

GRAZIELLA. Orchestrion made by Gebr. Weber, Waldkirch, fl. 1909.

GREEN'S PATENT ORCHESTROPHONE. See ORCHESTROPHONE.

GREGORIAN. Player piano marketed in London by the Orchestrelle Co., fl. 1909.

GUITHARMONY. Mechanical guitar operated by pinned barrel made by Gavioli, *c.* 1900.

HAN-DEE TRUE TONE CALLIOPE. Made by Haney-Deem Mfg. Co. of Kansas City, fl. 1926.

HAPECO. Expression piano made by Peters & Co. of Leipzig, fl. 1909.

HARMONIA. Disc-playing musical box made by Harmonia A.-G., Ste Croix. Known also as Société Anonyme Harmonia. Founded 1896.

HARALD. Piano-orchestrion made by the Waldkircher Orchestionfabrik, fl. 1909.

HARMONETTE. Organette playing perforated paper strip and made by the Massachusetts Organ Co., Boston, USA, fl. 1882.

HARPE-EOLIENNE. Type of cylinder musical box having 2 combs almost like the FORTE-PIANO (q.v.). Makers included F. Conchon and PVF.

HELENE. Mechanical pipe organs made in Vienna by Hofmann & Czerny, fl. 1909.

HELIKON. Organette made by Leipzig Music Works, formerly Paul Ehrlich, fl. 1900. Sole UK agents Gilbert & Co., 57 Basinghall Street, London, E.C.

HELIOS, HELIOS-PEPITA. Orchestrions made by Hupfeld in Leipzig, fl. 1909.

HELVETIA. Swiss-made disc musical box.

HERMANN, THE. Organette made in Berlin by Heinrich Hermann and very similar to the Ariston.

HEROLD. Orchestrions made by Imhof & Mukle in Vöhrenbach, fl. 1909.

HEROPHON, HEROPHONETTE. Organettes made in Leipzig by Berliner Musikinstrumenten-Fabrik, formerly Ch. F. Pietschmann & Söhne, fl. 1896–1909.

HIAWATHA. Self-playing xylophone made by Automatic Musical Company, New York.

HIGEL. Player piano actions made in Toronto by Higel Co.

HOHNER BAND. Pneumatic bass drum, side drum and tympani made by Matth. Höhner of Trossingen for attachment to an accordion, fl. 1910.

HOLZWEISSIG. Musical automata made in Leipzig by Ernst Holzweissig Nachfolger, fl. 1909.

HOTTENTOTS, DANCE OF THE. Automaton organ clock made c. 1687 for Princess Magdalena Sybille by Matthews Rungell of Augsburg.

HUMOR. Orchestrions made by Popper of Leipzig, fl. 1909.

IDEAL. Early American cinema music player made by North Tonawanda Musical Instrument Works, New York.

IDEAL. The Ideal Musical Box was made by Jacot in USA.

IDEAL. Cylinder musical box made by Mermod Frères, Ste Croix. Had interchangeable cylinders, fl. 1900.

IDEAL-MIGNON. Small player piano action made to sell at 45–50 guineas by Copplestone & Co., Ltd, 94 Regent Street, London, W, c. 1910.

IDUNA. Orchestrion by Popper of Leipzig, fl. 1909.

ILLUSIONS AUTOMAT. Made by Max Martin in Berlin, fl. 1909, this was a cylinder musical movement offered with interchangeable cylinders, a moving ballet, changing coloured electric lights and the effects of a complete theatre in microcosm.

IMPERATOR. Disc-playing musical boxes made by Richter & Co. of Rudolstadt, fl. 1909.

IMPERIAL. Disc-playing musical box same as BRITANNIA (q.v.).

IMPERIAL SYMPHONION. Disc musical boxes broadly similar to Leipzig-built Symphonion but made by the Symphonion Music Box Co. of Asbury Park, New Jersey, USA.

IMPROVED ROLLER ORGAN. 20-note organette playing metal rollers similar to the wooden rollers of the GEM (q.v.) made by Bates & Co. of Boston, Mass, in about 1895.

INTONA. 16-note organette made by Musikwerke Phoenix Schmidt in Leipzig, fl. 1909. See ARIOSA.

IRENE. Orchestrion made in Vienna by Hofmann & Czerny, fl. 1909.

IRIS. Organette made in Berlin by Heinrich Hermann.

IRMGARD. Orchestrion made in Vienna by Hofmann & Czerny, fl. 1909.

ISOLA. Orchestrion made in Waldkirch by Gebruder Weber, fl. 1909.

JUNO. Orchestrion made by Fuchs of Prague, fl. 1909.

KALLIOPE. Disc-playing musical boxes made in Leipzig by Kalliope Musikwerke A.-G. Established in 1898 and fl. 1909. See also CALLIOPE. Sole UK agent: Martin Hirsch.

KALLISTON. Reed-playing organette with drum or bells played by zinc tune band made by Ernst Erich Liebmann of Gera, fl. 1903.

KALOPHON. Organette made in Gera by Ernst Erich Liebmann, fl. 1903.

KINO-PAN. Keyboardless electric piano for theatre use made in Leipzig by Hupfeld.

KINO-VIOLINA. Similar to PHONOLISZT-V. (q.v.) but with the violins in a separate case for use in theatres.

KLARA. Orchestrion made in Vienna by Hofmann & Czerny, fl. 1909.

KLAVIER-AUTOMATEN. Piano player made by Fabrik Leipziger Musikwerke and operated by a cardboard disc, fl. 1903.

KOMET. Disc-playing musical box made in Leipzig by Weissbach & Co. who, c. 1910, acquired CHORDEPHON (q.v.). Sole UK agent: William Gerecke.

KOSMOS. Player piano made by Lehmann & Co. of Berlin, fl. 1909.

KRONE. Coin-operated automaton made by Berliner Musik-Industrie A. Pietschmann & Co., fl. 1903.

LARRIKIN. Musical automaton made in Klingenthal by Carl Essbach, fl. 1903.

LA TONOTECHNIC. An automatic instrument invented in 1775 by the Rev. Father Engramelle.

LIBELLE. Organette made in Leipzig by Leipziger Musikwerke Euphonika, formerly Heinrich Hermann, fl. 1909.

LIBELLION. Musical box played by perforated cardboard music made by F. Ad. Richter & Co. of Rudolstadt, fl. 1909.

LILIPUT. Piano orchestrions and other mechanical instruments made by Ernst Holzweissig Nachfolger, Leipzig, fl. 1909.

LITTLE DOT. 16-note organette playing 5¾ inch wide paper rolls. Made c. 1880 by the Mechanical Orguinette Co. of New York.

LOCHMANN ORIGINAL. Disc-playing musical boxes and piano orchestrions made by Original-Musikwerke Paul Lochmann, Zeulenroda and Leipzig, fl. 1909.

LOHENGRIN. Orchestrion made by Imhof & Mukle, Vöhrenbach.

LOLA. Piano orchestrion made by Popper, Leipzig.

LOLA. Mechanical musical instrument made by Ernst Holzweissig Nachfolger, Leipzig, fl. 1909.

LORD. Piano orchestrion made by Imhof & Mukle, Vöhrenbach.

LORELEY. Orchestrion made by Popper of Leipzig, fl. 1909.

LUCIA. Organette made by Musikwerke Phoenix, Leipzig, fl. 1909.

LUCIA. Piano orchestrion made by Imhof & Mukle, Vöhrenbach, fl. 1909.

LUCRETIA. Orchestrion organ made by Imhof & Mukle, Vöhrenbach, fl. 1909.

LUNA. Orchestrion made by Popper of Leipzig, early twentieth century.

LUSITANIA. Orchestrion organ made by Dienst of Leipzig, early twentieth century.

LUX. Organette made in Berlin by Heinrich Hermann.

LUX. Organette made by Leipziger Musikwerke Euphonika, formerly Heinrich Hermann, fl. 1909.

LUX. Orchestrion made by Ernst Holzweissig Nachfolger, Leipzig, fl. 1909.

LYRIST. Expression piano made in Berlin by Klingmann & Co., fl. 1909.

MAESTO. Piano orchestrion made by Weber, Waldkirch.

MAESTRO-PIANOFORTE. Keyless reproducing piano, same as Welte-Mignon, made in Paris to Welte patents by Mustel and sold in London by Metzler & Co., Ltd, 40–43 Gt. Marlborough Street, fl. 1906.

MAGIC ORGANA. Accordion playing 44-note music rolls through pneumatic action ($4\frac{1}{2}$ inch wide paper) made by Höhner of Trossingen, c. 1925. Also made model with external drum and cymbals controlled from music roll in instrument. Both models required external vacuum supply.

MANDO PIANO ORCHESTRINA. Coin-operated piano made early twentieth century by North Tonawanda Musical Instrument Works, New York.

MANDO-ORCHESTRA. Coin-freed piano orchestrion made by North Tonawanda Musical Instrument Works, New York.

MANDOLIN ORCHESTRION. Same as REGINA SUBLIMA (q.v.).

MANDOLIN QUARTETTE/SEXTETTE. Piano orchestrions made by Wurlitzer, New York.

MANDOLINA. Organette produced in New York by Merritt Gally, c. 1886. Plays $5\frac{1}{2}$ inch wide paper rolls same as CELESTINA (q.v.).

MANDOLINA. Electric orchestrions made by Hupfeld in Leipzig, fl. 1909.

MANDOLINATA. Orchestrion made by Sächsische Orchestrion-Fabrik F. O. Glass and distributed from Leipzig by Etzold & Popitz, fl. 1909.

MANOPAN(E). Organettes made by Berliner Musikinstrumenten-Fabrik, formerly Charles F. Pietschmann & Söhne, fl. 1896–1909.

MARS. Mandolin orchestrion distributed in Leipzig by Holzweissig Nachfolger, fl. 1909.

MASCOTTE. Organette made in Boston, Mass. by the Gately Manufacturing Co., c. 1888.

MATADOR. Piano orchestrion made by Popper, Leipzig.

MAURETANIA. Orchestrion made by Dienst of Leipzig, fl. 1909.

MECHANICAL ORGANETTE (also known as ROYAL). Made c. 1885 by Massachusetts Organ Co.

MELODANT. Player piano made by Marshall in London.

MELODETTE. Similar to PIANO-ETTE (q.v.) and by same maker.

MELODIA. A 14-note paper-roll-playing ($7\frac{7}{8}$ inches wide) organette made by American Mercantile Co. Rolls interchangeable with MUSICAL CASKET (q.v.).

MELODION. Musical box made in Vienna by de Ponti, fl. 1909.

MELODIONS. Musical box made by Ernst Erich Liebmann of Gera (Reuss-Gera), Germany, fl. 1909.

MELOGRAPH. Music recording machine for automatic instruments made by J. Carpentier of Paris also a similar device with the same name by Baron Pilar von Pilchau, Petersburg. Both fl. 1909.

MELOPEAN. Organette made in USA by McTammany and described as fitted with 'reed pipes'.

MELOTON. Organette made by Heinrich Hermann, Bernau, Berlin, fl. 1903.

MELOTROPE. Instrument for fitting to a keyboard and playing music prepared on the MELOGRAPH (q.v.) made by J. Carpentier, Paris, fl. 1909.

MICROCOSM OR THE WORLD IN MINIATURE, THE. Famous mechanical and musical clock constructed by Henry Bridges of Essex.

MIGNON. Organette made in Berlin by Helbig & Co., fl. 1903.

MIGNON. Reproducing piano made in New York by Welte of Freiburg, Germany, fl. 1909.

MIGNONETTE. See ORGANINA.

MIKADO. Mechanical musical instrument made by Richter & Cie of Rudolstadt, fl. 1909.

MILITAROGRAPH. 82-key band organ patented in 1908 by North Tonawanda Musical Instrument Works, NY, in two variants: one played by a barrel and the other by perforated paper.

MIMOSA. Orchestrion made in Leipzig by Popper, fl. 1909.

MIRA. Disc-playing musical box made in Ste Croix by Mermod Frères, fl. 1905–09. See EMPRESS.

MIRANDA-PIANISTA. Early name for Pianista (q.v.).

MIRAPHONE. Combined gramophone and MIRA musical box.

MONARCH. Disc-playing musical box made by the American Music Box Company, New York.

MONOPOL. Disc-playing musical box made in Leipzig by Paul Ehrlich & Co., later known as the Leipzig Music Works.

MULTIPHONE. A very small interchangeable cylinder musical box patented by John Manger in London in 1886 and made by Charles Ullmann.

MUSETTA. Player piano made by Neue Leipziger Musikwerke, fl. 1909.

MUSETTE. 16-note organette playing paper rolls $3\frac{9}{16}$ inches wide and made by the Autophone Co., Ithaca, New York (formerly Merritt Gally).

MUSICAL CASKET. Organette made by the Mechanical Orguinette Co., New York. See also MELODIA.

MUSICAL DOLCINE. Organette played by endless metal bands and sold by Campbell & Co. of Glasgow, fl. 1894. Made in Leipzig by Musikwerke Euphonika (see DOLZINE).

NATIONAL. Cylinder musical box made by Rivenc and marketed by National Musical Box Co., London. Same as PEERLESS (q.v.).

NATIONAL. Calliope made by National Calliope Corporation (see NEW TONE AIR CALLIOPE).

NERO. Orchestrion made in Leipzig by Popper, fl. 1909.

NEW CENTURY. Disc-playing musical box, probably made by Henry Vidoudez of Ste Croix, 1900. (Q. David Bowers believes the mechanism to have been made by Mermod Frères).

NEW TONE AIR CALLIOPE. Made by E. A. Harrington, Kansas City c. 1926, later renamed NATIONAL (q.v.).

NEWA. Orchestrion made in Leipzig by Popper, fl. 1909.

NON PLUS EXTRA. Organette playing endless card bands and made by Fabrik Leipziger Musikwerke Paul Ehrlich, c. 1903.

NORDSTERN. Mechanical musical instrument made in Aurich, East Friesland, Germany, by Kittel, fl. 1909.

NORMA. Orchestrion made in Leipzig (Gohlis) by Dienst, fl. 1909.

OBERON. Orchestrion made in Leipzig by Popper, fl. 1909.

OHIO. Piano-orchestrion made by Popper, Leipzig.

OLYMPIA. Musical box manufactured by Olympia Musical Automaton Co., Jersey City, USA, fl. 1909.

OLYMPIA. Disc-playing musical box made in Jersey City, USA, by F. G. Otto & Sons.

OLYMPIO. Self-playing organ made c. 1909 by Farrand Organ Company in USA.

ORCHESTRAL AUTOMATON. Mechanical musical instrument made by Leipziger Musikwerke Phoenix (Schmidt & Co.).

ORCHESTRAL ORGANETTE. An organette playing perforated paper music made by Draper of Blackburn who later formed a company known as the British Organette & Music Manufacturing Co., fl. 1898.

ORCHESTRAL REGINA. Large disc-playing musical box made by Regina of New Jersey.

ORCHESTRELLE. Player reed organ made by the Aeolian Company of New York.

ORCHESTRINA. Coin-freed piano orchestrion made by North Tonawanda Musical Instrument Works, New York.

ORCHESTRION. Instrument built in Dresden by Kaufmann in 1851.

ORCHESTRION HARMONETTE. 16-reed organette made c. 1885 by Massachusetts Organ Co.

ORCHESTRIONETTE. Large organette playing perforated cardboard bands made by Fabrik Leipziger Musikwerke, c. 1903.

ORCHESTRONE. Organette made in Birmingham by John Dewhurst in 1889.

ORCHESTROPHONE. Self-playing organ (reed) known as Green's Patent Orchestrophone sold in London by Cullum & Best.

ORCHESTROPHONE. Show or fair organs made by Limonaire in Paris.

ORCUS. Musical automaton made in Leipzig by Ernst Berger.

ORGANAUTO. Self-playing organ attachments made by R. Spurden Rutt, London.

ORGANETTE. Organette made in Blackburn, England by Draper. Also name used by McTammany for his first reed instruments made in USA in 1880s.

ORGANETTE, ORGANETTE-HARMONETTE. Organettes made by Höhner in Trossingen. Also made self-playing accordian playing perforated paper, fl. 1909.

ORGANINA, ORGANINA CABINET. Organettes made c. 1890 by the Massachusetts Organ Co.

ORGANINA. 16-note organette ($5\frac{3}{4}$ inch wide paper rolls) made c. 1882 by the Automatic Organ Co. of Boston, Mass., (formerly known as the American Automatic Organ Co.) and called 'The Musical Marvel'.

ORGANISTA. Keyboard-player attachment made by Thibouville-Lamy of Paris, fl. 1909.

ORGANITA. Organette made c. 1882 by the Automatic Organ Co. of Boston, Mass.

ORGANOCLEIDE. Type of cylinder musical box with low-pitched, resonant tone and often equipped in such a way as to produce a 'mandolin-like' repetition of the *lower* notes to imitate the sustained tones of an organ. Produced by a number of manufacturers including Bremond, Allard & Sandoz, Paillard, etc.

ORGANOLA. Self-playing attachment for pipe organs made by Walcker of Ludwigsburg, Germany, fl. 1909.

ORGANOPHONE. Self-playing reed organ made by Thibouville-Lamy of Paris, fl. 1909.

ORGANOPHONE EXPRESSIF. Organette playing Gavioli-patented book music and made by Thibouville-Lamy in Paris in 1890.

ORGUINETTE. Organette made by Mechanical Orguinette Co. of New York which was formerly the Autophone Co. and later the Aeolian Co.

ORIGINAL. Disc-playing musical boxes and piano-orchestrions made by Original-Musikwerke Paul Lochmann in Leipzig, fl. 1909.

ORIGINAL KONZERT-PIANO. Disc-playing piano orchestrion made by Original-Musikwerke Paul Lochmann, Zeulenroda and Leipzig, fl. 1909.

ORPHENION. Disc-playing musical box made in Leipzig in 1893 by Bruno Rückert, Orphenion Musikwerke Fabrik. Sole UK agents Barnet Samuel & Sons, London, fl. 1896.

ORPHEUS. Self-playing organ made by Story & Clark and F. Kaim & Söhne, fl. 1900. Later called ORPHIC.

ORPHEUS. Small piano played by perforated card discs made by Ehrlich in Leipzig.

ORPHEUS. Disc-playing musical box made in Leipzig-Neuschönefeld by Ludwig & Wild. Introduced 1897, and factored through Breitkopf & Härtel of Leipzig the following year.

ORPHEUSHARMONICON. Orchestrion built in 1814 by Leonard Maelzel.

ORPHIC. See ORPHEUS (self-playing organ).

ORPHOBELLA. Keyboard playing attachment made in Leipzig by Ehrlich's Musikwerke, fl. 1909.

OTERO. Feurich piano plus orchestrion made by Weber, Waldkirch.

OTHELLO. Piano-orchestrion made by Popper, Leipzig.

PAGANINI. Piano-orchestrion made by Philipps of Leipzig.

PAN. Orchestrion made by Hupfeld in Leipzig.

PANHARMONICON. Two instruments of this name built between 1792 and 1813 by Johann Nepomucene Maelzel.

PANHARMONICON. A mechanical orchestra invented in the early nineteenth century by J. J. Gurk of Vienna and exhibited for a time at Spring Garden, London.

PARAGON. Player pianos and player organs made c. 1909 by Needham Piano & Organ Co., USA.

PATRIARCH. Orchestrion made by Imhof & Mukle, Vöhrenbach.

PEDALEON. Very small player piano made in 1913 by Barratt & Robinson.

PEERLESS. Cylinder musical box sold by Thomas Dawkins, London. Made in Geneva by Ami Rivenc.

PENNYANO. Coin-freed barrel piano made by Keith Prowse Ltd, London, c. 1895–1910.

PERFECTA. Player piano made in London by Morton & Co.

PERFECTION. Disc-playing musical box made by the Perfection Music Box Co. in Jersey City (1898–99) and then in Newark (1900–01).

PERPLEX. Mechanical musical instruments made in Strasburg by Strasburger Musikwerke Cromer & Schrack, fl. 1909.

PETROPHON. Automatic musical instrument made in Leipzig by Peters & Co., fl. 1909.

PHÄDRA. Orchestrion made by Holzweissig Nachfolger of Leipzig, fl. 1909. Name also used by Popper.

PHILHARMONIC AUTOGRAPH ORGAN. Reproducing pipe organ made by Welte of Freiburg.

PHOENIX. Organettes and street organs made in Leipzig by Leipziger Musikwerke Phoenix, fl. 1909. London agent; Alban Voigt & Co., appointed January 1898.

PHOENIX. 72-note reed orchestrion made by Phoenix, Berliner Musikautomaten-Fabrik, Ernst Ponarth and playing from discs, c. 1909. Sole agent: Polland & Co., 5 St Nicholas Buildings, Newcastle-upon-Tyne.

PHONEON. 61-note pneumatic-action player reed organ made in 1898 by Malcolm & Co., 91 Farringdon Road, London, E.C., and selling for 36 guineas.

PHONOBELLA. Player piano made in Leipzig by Hupfeld.

PHONOGRAPHIC CORNET. Mouth-blown instrument playing perforated paper roll and made c. 1895 by the Massachusetts Organ Co.

PHONOLA. Player piano made in Leipzig by Hupfeld.

PHONOLETT. Orchestrion made in Leipzig by Hupfeld.

PHONOLISZT. Player piano made in Leipzig by Hupfeld. Also PHONOLISZT-VIOLINA piano combined with three violins all pneumatically-operated.

PIALO. Player piano made by Singer Piano Co. of Chicago, fl. 1909.

PIANELLA. Piano-orchestrion made in Frankfurt by Frankfurter Musikwerke, fl. 1909.

PIANELLA. Piano-orchestrions made by Philipps, Leipzig.

PIANETTA. Player piano made in 1910 by the London Piano & Organ Co., 14 Holmes Road, Kentish Town.

PIANETTE. Same as REGINA SUBLIMA (q.v.). Name used by Lyon & Healy, Chicago.

PIANINO. Mechanical piano made in USA by Wurlitzer, fl. 1909.

PIANIST. Piano player made in Gera by Spaethe, fl. 1909.

PIANISTA. A piano player operated by perforated rolled cardboard $10\frac{1}{4}$ inches wide and made in Paris by Thibouville-Lamy, fl. 1909.

PIANO MELODICO. Mechanical piano operated by perforated cardboard music made by Racca of Bologna and also by Spaethe in Gera, fl. 1909. See also GLADIATOR, LE.

PIANO-ACCORDION-JAZZ. Mid-twentieth century café instrument made by Seybold of Strasburg-Meinau.

PIANO-ETTE. Perforated-paper-playing instrument using small steel bars and made c. 1890 by Massachusetts Organ Co., USA. See MELODETTE.

PIANOLIN. Coin-operated musical automaton made by North Tonawanda Musical Instrument Co., New York, fl. 1900.

PIANON. Player piano made by Welte of Freiburg, fl. 1909.

PIANOPHON. Player piano made by Asmus of Berlin, fl. 1909.

PIANOPHONE. Orchestrion organ made in Berlin by Cocchi, Bacigalupo & Graffigna, fl. 1902.

PIANOTIST. Piano player attachment made by Pianotist Co. in Leipzig, fl. 1909, and by Klaber in New York.

PICCOLO. Mechanical piano orchestrion made by Popper, Leipzig.

PLAY-A-SAX. Toy saxophone played by paper roll, mouth-blown. Early twentieth century, made in USA.

PLAYOLA. Expression piano made in Chicago by Playola Piano Co., fl. 1909.

PNEUMA, PNEUMATIST. Player organs and player pianos made by Kuhl & Klatt in Berlin, fl. 1909.

PNEUMA. Self-playing attachment operated electrically for pianos marketed by Wm. Gerecke in London, fl. 1900. In 1895, Hampton & Sons of Pall Mall advertised the Pneuma as 'the simplest automatically-played piano yet invented'.

POLYGRAPHON. Polyphon (q.v.) combined with gramophone, produced in Leipzig c. 1902 by Polyphonmusikwerke.

POLYHYMNIA. Musical automata made c. 1903 by Metall-Industrie Schönebeck A.-G., Saxony, Germany.

POLYMNIA. Disc-playing musical box made in Geneva by Société Anonyme in 1900.

POLYPHON. Disc-playing musical boxes, piano orchestrions made by Polyphon musikwerke, Leipzig. Est. in 1886.

POLYTYPE ZITHER. Rare type of 2-comb cylinder musical box made by PVF and combining Sublime Harmonie, Piccolo Zither and Tremolo Zither arrangements.

POMMERSCHEN KUNSTSCHRANK (POMERANIAN CABINET). Early self-acting organ made in 1617 by the Augsburg mechanican Achilles Langenbucher.

POSAUTO. Self-playing single-manual pipe organs made c. 1910 by the original Positive Organ Co. of London.

PRECIOSA. Musical automata made in Leipzig by Holzweissig Nachfolger, fl. 1909.

PREMIER. Player piano made c. 1909 by Neue Leipziger Musikwerke A. Buff-Hedinger.

PROTECTOR. Orchestrion made in Leipzig by Popper, fl. 1909.

PROTOS. Orchestrion made in Leipzig by Popper, fl. 1909.

PSYCHO. A large 'electric orchestra' made in 1874 by Neville Maskeline with the collaboration of the American, J. A. Clarke, and used at the Egyptian Hall during Maskeline's magic displays. The instrument was not truly mechanical, being controlled by an operator from a keyboard.

PUCK. Orchestrion made in Leipzig by Popper, fl. 1909.

QUALITÉ EXCELSIOR. Musical boxes made in Paris and Ste Croix by Ullmann, fl. 1909.

QUATUOR. Cylinder musical box of the Sublime Harmonie type with four combs. Several makers, said to have been invented by David Cadet, c. 1840.

RECITAL. Player for organs made in Épinal (Vosges), France by Didier & Cie, fl. 1909.

RECLAME. Piano-orchestrion made in Vöhrenbach by Imhof & Mukle.

REED PIPE CLARIONA. Organette playing $8\frac{1}{16}$ inch wide paper rolls made c. 1890 by Massachusetts Organ Co. Rolls same as DULCIPHONE (q.v.).

REGENT. Orchestrion made in Leipzig by Popper, fl. 1909.

REGINA. Piano-orchestrion made in Leipzig by Popper & Co., fl. 1909.

REGINA. Disc-playing musical boxes made in New Jersey by Regina Co.

REGINA SUBLIMA. Mandolin-action perforated card roll-playing piano made by Regina Music Box Co. of New Jersey, USA.

REGINAPHONE. Combined gramophone and disc-playing musical box made by Regina of New Jersey.

REGINAPIANO. Electric piano made by Regina Music Box Co., New Jersey, USA.

REPRODUCO. Pipe organ photoplayer made by Operators Piano Co., Chicago.

RESOTONE GRAND. Pneumatically played glockenspiel comprising 46 flat metal bars struck by felt-covered hammers. Plays $9\frac{3}{4}$ inch wide endless paper rolls. Made c. 1900–1910 by Resotone Grand Co. of New York.

REX. Piano-orchestrion made in Leipzig by Popper, fl. 1909.

ROLAND. Mandolin-orchestrion made in Leipzig by Popper, fl. 1909.

ROLMONICA. Paper roll-playing mouth organ patented 2 November 1925 and 5 June 1928 by the Rolmonica Music Co. of Baltimore, Maryland. Advertised as 'a player piano in your pocket'.

ROSSINI. Piano-orchestrion played by perforated cardboard and made by Polyphon, fl. 1909.

ROYAL ORGANETTE (also known as MECHANICAL). Made c. 1885 by Massachusetts Organ Co.

SALPINGION. Automatic trumpet chorus which played Hallelujah Chorus from Messiah and was made early nineteenth century by Freidrich Kaufmann.

SAXONIA. Musical automaton made by Leipziger Musikwerke Phoenix Schmidt & Co.

SAXONIA. Disc-playing musical box made in Leipzig by J. Riedl, 1897.

SELECTA. Orchestrion made c. 1920 by Lösche in Berlin.

SERAPHINE. Organette playing 19 reeds from endless paper bands made by Heinrich Hermann, c. 1903.

SERAPHONE. Paper-roll playing organette made by Maxfield c. 1885 in England. Also known as English Automatic Seraphone. See also CELESTINA.

SERENATA. Pneumatic-action orchestrion distributed by Etzold & Popitz of Leipzig, fl. 1909.

SEXTROLA. Coin-freed electric piano orchestrion made by North Tonawanda Musical Instrument Works, New York.

SI-LA-FA. Orchestrion made in Leipzig by Popper, fl. 1909.

SILVA-NIGRA. Musical clocks made by Ver. Uhrenfabriken, Schramberg, Wurttemberg, Germany, fl. 1908.

SIMONOLA. Paper-roll playing concertina-type instrument, trade-mark TÄNZBAR (q.v.) made in Hildburghausen (Saxe-Meiningen), Germany, by Simon & Co., c. 1909.

SIMSON. Orchestrion made by Popper of Leipzig, fl. 1909.

SIRION. Disc-playing musical box made in Dresden in 1896 by Gustav Bortmann and Alfred Keller. Sold in London through Nicole Frères. Believed to have been manufactured by Mermod Frères, according to Q. David Bowers.

SLAVIA. Piano-orchestrion made in Prague by Fuchs, fl. 1909.

SOLEA. Orchestrion made in Waldkirch by Gebruder Weber, fl. 1909.

SOLEIL. Orchestrion organ made in Berlin by Cocchi, Bacigalupo & Graffigna, fl. 1902.

SOLOPHONOLA. Player piano made by Hupfeld in Leipzig.

SOLOTIST. Musical automaton made in Berlin and sold by Choralion Co., fl. 1909.

SONORA. Orchestrion made by Dienst of Leipzig, fl. 1909.

SONORA-ARIOSA. See ARIOSA.

STELLA. Disc-playing musical box made in Ste Croix by Mermod Frères.

STELLA. Orchestrion made in Leipzig by Popper, fl. 1909.

STELLAMONT. Orchestrion made in Leipzig by Dienst, fl. 1909.

STEMS. Player piano made by Direct Pneumatic Action Co. Ltd, 3, 4, 5 Kendrick Place, 8a Dorset Street, Baker Street, London, W.

STEPHANIE. Orchestrion made in Brünn, Austria, by Czech, fl. 1909.

STRAUSS. Orchestrion made in Waldkirch by the Waldkircher Orchestrionfabrik, fl. 1909.

STYRIA. Piano-orchestrion made by Weber, Waldkirch.

SUBLIMA. See REGINA SUBLIMA.

SUN. Disc-playing musical box made by Schrämli & Tschudin of Geneva, fl. 1903.

SUPEREXTRA. Trade mark of Charles Ullmann for his small cylinder musical boxes.

SYMPHONIOLA. Player piano produced in Leipzig-Gohlis by Symphonionfabrik A.-G., fl. 1909.

SYMPHONION. Disc-playing musical boxes and piano orchestrions made in Leipzig by Symphonionfabrik A.-G. and in Asbury Park, New Jersey, USA.

SYMPHONION. Larger version of Kaufmann's CHORDAULODION (q.v.) built in 1838.

SYMPHONISTA. Electric piano also known as the Corona Xylophone. Seven models available from £125 to £215. Probably made by Popper; sold in London by New Polyphon Supply Co., 2 Newman Street, in 1908.

SYMPHONY. Self-playing reed organ made by Wilcox & White of Meriden, Conn., USA.

SYMPLETTA. Simple piano player made in England by Simplex c. 1910.

TÄNZBAR. Paper-roll-operated 28-note accordion patented by A. Zuleger and manufactured in Hildburghausen by Simon & Co. c. 1909. Played $4\frac{1}{4}$ inch wide rolls via mechanical action. Another size played 20 notes from rolls $2\frac{9}{16}$ inch wide. See under SIMONOLA.

TARANTELLA. Mechanical musical instruments made by Ernst Holzweissig Nachfolger of Leipzig, fl. 1909.

TELL. Violin-piano-orchestrion made by Imhof & Mukle, Vöhrenbach.

TITANIA. Mandolin-orchestrion made in Leipzig by Popper, fl. 1909. Name also used by Lösche.

TOCCAPHON. Xylophone piano made c. 1909 by Neue Leipziger Musikwerke A. Buff-Hedinger.

TONIKA. Orchestrion made in Leipzig by Popper, fl. 1909.

TONOGRAPH. Mechanical music recorder invented in 1899 by Robert A. Galley, son of the US organette inventor.

TONOPHONE. Electrical barrel piano with pneumatic action made early twentieth century for Wurlitzer by North Tonawanda Musical Instrument Works, New York.

TONSYRENO. Roll-playing American reed organ factored in 1889 by Geo. Whight in London.

TORPEDOPFEIFEN. Mechanical pipe organ made c. 1903 by Berliner Musik-Industrie A. Pietschmann & Co.

TOURNAPHONE. 25-note organette made by the Massachusetts Organ Co., c. 1890. See CABINETTO.

TOWER OF BABYLON. Beautiful automaton with organ made between 1589 and 1602 by Hans Schlottheim, Augsburg.

TRAVIATA. Orchestrion by Dienst of Leipzig, fl. 1909.

TREMOLO. Orchestrion made in Leipzig by Symphonion-Fabrik, A.-G. fl. 1909.

TRIBUT. Orchestrion made in Vöhrenbach by Imhof & Mukle, fl. 1909.

TRIOLA. Mechanical zither played by perforated paper roll. Made by Polyphonmusikwerke in Leipzig, fl. 1919.

TRIPHONOLA. Reproducing piano made by Hupfeld in Leipzig.

TRIUMPH. Piano-orchestrion made by Popper, Leipzig.

TRIUMPH. Disc-playing musical box made by the American Music Box Company, New Jersey.

TRIUMPHATOR. Orchestrion made in Leipzig by Popper, fl. 1909.

TRIUMPHOLA. Player piano made by Rachals & Co. in Hamburg, also Kastner in London, fl. 1909.

TRIUMPHWAGEN. Early mechanical automaton incorporating self-acting organ made c. 1617 by the Augsburg mechanician Achilles Langenbucher.

TROMPETER VON SÄCKINGEN. Piano-orchestrion made by Imhof & Mukle in Vöhrenbach, fl. 1909.

TROUBADOUR. Disc-playing musical box made by Troubadour Musikwerke B. Grosz & Co. of Leipzig, fl. 1909.

TRUMPETO. Paper-roll playing, mouth-blown toy trumpet made in USA, c. 1900.

TUYAUPHONE. Cylinder musical box fitted with tubular bells made by Baker-Troll of Geneva.

TZIGANA. Mechanical musical instrument made by Ernst Holzweissig Nachfolger, Leipzig, fl. 1909.

UNIKA. Piano-orchestrion made by Weber, Waldkirch.

UNIKON. Small comb-type musical box played by strips of perforated card and made by Emile Cuendot and Andre Junod.

UNIVERSAL. Orchestrion made by Hupfeld in Leipzig, fl. 1909.

UNIVERSAL PIANO PLAYER. Player made in England by Bansell & Sons, London.

UNIVERSUM. Polyphon musical box incorporating automaton picture gallery. First seen in London July 1896.

UNIVERSUM. Mechanical musical instruments made in Frankfurt by Seip, fl. 1909.

VALSONORA. Orchestrions made by Sächsische Orchestrion-Fabrik F. O. Glass.

VENEZIA. Piano-orchestrion made by Weber, Waldkirch.

VENUS. Mechanical organ made by Imhof & Mukle, Vöhrenbach, fl. 1909.

VERDI. Large version of the Manopan organette made by Heinrich Hermann in Berlin.

VERDI. Automatic book-playing piano made by Racca of Bologna, fl. 1909.

VERDI. Orchestrion made in Leipzig by Popper, fl. 1909.

VEROPHON. Mechanical musical instrument made by Richter & Cie of Rudolstadt, fl. 1909.

VICTOLIAN. Self-playing reed organ distributed by Geo. Whight in London and probably of US origin, fl. 1900.

VICTORIA. Musical boxes made by B. H. Abrahams in Switzerland.

VICTORIA. Organette available in three sizes (24 single, 24 double or 36 double reed size) from bands or strips of perforated music. Made in Leipzig. Also name of organette made in USA by McTammany.

VIOLANO. Piano-orchestrion made by Weber, Waldkirch.

VIOLANO-VIRTUOSO. Self-playing violin with piano made by Mills Novelty Company, Chicago, in 1908.

VIOLETTA. Orchestrion made by Popper of Leipzig, fl. 1909.

VIOLIN ORCHESTRA. Piano-orchestrion made by Philipps of Leipzig.

VIOLINA-PHONOLISZT. Combined player piano and violins made in Leipzig by Hupfeld, fl. 1909.

VIOLINISTE. A pneumatic violin-player combined with piano made by Emile Aubry and Gabriel Boreau in Paris in 1926.

VISION. Orchestrion made in Leipzig by Popper, fl. 1909.

VIRTUOS. 73-note expression piano made in Berlin by K. Heilbrunn Söhne, fl. 1909.

VOCALION. Player piano made by the Aeolian Co. in New York, fl. 1909.

VOCALION. Self-playing organ made by the Vocalion Organ Co., Worcester, Mass., USA, fl. 1909.

VOLKSLAVIER. A mechanical zither-type instrument made c. 1890 in Germany.

VORSETZER. A 'push-up' piano player made by Welte. Fully electric and reproducing from special music rolls.

WALKÜRE. Orchestrion made by Imhof & Mukle, Vöhrenbach, fl. 1909.

WALLHALL. Military band orchestrion made by Welte, Freiburg.

WEIDMANNSHEIL. Mechanical musical instrument made in Leipzig by Polyphon Musikwerke, A.-G., fl. 1909.

WEINER SCHRAMMEL. Orchestrion made in Leipzig by Popper, fl. 1909.

WELT-PIANO-STELLA. Orchestrion made in Leipzig by Popper, fl. 1909.

WELTE. Player pianos made by Welte & Söhne, Freiburg.

WELTE-MIGNON. Reproducing piano made in Freiburg and New York.

WOTAN. Brass band orchestrion made by Welte, Freiburg.

XILONELLA. Orchestrion made in Vienna by Fuchs, fl. 1909.

XYLOPHON. Piano-orchestrion made in Frankfurt by Frankfurter Musikwerke, fl. 1909.

ZAMBA. Orchestrion made in Leipzig by Dienst, fl. 1909.

INDEX

This is a fully cross-referenced Index to the contents of the Chapters one to nine inclusive. The names of instruments, where they appear in this text, are naturally included, but the reader is advised that the Index does not cover the comprehensive listing of names contained in the Appendix which is itself intended to stand as a form of self-indexing reference. Illustrations are not indexed separately and only in a few instances are old advertisements specifically indicated as such in this Index. The sources of reproduced material are indicated in the relevent caption or introduction to the particular item, where these are known.